PRAISE FOR

POLICE PROCEDURE
& INVESTIGATION

Police Procedure & Investigation is an invaluable tool for writers of mystery fiction.

— **J.A. JANCE,** *New York Times* best-selling author

This book belongs in the library of every crime writer! More than merely a reference book for writers, *Police Procedure & Investigation* is also lively and entertaining, a fascinating inside look at law enforcement, told by a police professional with a writer's eye for detail.

—**TESS GERRITSEN,** author of *The Mephisto Club*

Lots of cops know a thing or two about police procedure, but I haven't found anyone else who explains the things writers need to know with Lee Lofland's economy and humor. This is one reference book you'll use!

—**S.J. ROZAN,** award-winning author of *In This Rain*

Lee Lofland's *Police Procedure & Investigation* reads like a thriller. It's every crime writer's indispensable reference—packed with the kind of information and insider knowledge that make the police procedure in crime fiction feel authentic.

—**HALLIE EPHRON,** Edgar-nominated novelist and author of *Writing and Selling Your Mystery Novel: How to Knock 'Em Dead With Style*

Lee Lofland has written the ultimate insider's guide to police procedure, an invaluable cheat-sheet for crime novelists who want their fiction to feel as real as possible. Now every writer has a friend on The Force he can turn to for accurate information on how cops do what they do.

> —**LEE GOLDBERG,** Edgar-nominated writer for the TV series *Diagnosis Murder*, *Psych*, *Missing*, and *Monk*

This is THE comprehensive guide to American police procedure that should be on every mystery writer's bookshelf. Lee Lofland really knows his stuff.

> —**RHYS BOWEN,** award-winning author of *In Dublin's Fair City: A Molly Murphy Mystery*

Forget making endless phone calls and begging for a moment of a police officer's time for help with research for a book. Start here—Lee Lofland has done the work for you. Knowledgeable answers to many of your questions about law enforcement and investigations can be found on the pages of *Police Procedure & Investigation*. This is an essential reference work for any writer of crime fiction.

> —**JAN BURKE**, Best-selling author of *Bloodlines*, *Bones*, and *Kidnapped*, and the founder of the Crime Lab Project

POLICE PROCEDURE
& INVESTIGATION

POLICE PROCEDURE & INVESTIGATION

A GUIDE FOR WRITERS

LEE LOFLAND

FOREWORD BY STUART KAMINSKY

WRITER'S DIGEST BOOKS

www.writersdigest.com
Cincinnati, Ohio

Visit our Web sites at www.writersdigest.com and www.wdeditors.com for information on more resources for writers.

To receive a free weekly e-mail newsletter delivering tips and updates about writing and about Writer's Digest products, register directly at our Web site at http://newsletters. fwpublications.com.

11   10   09   08   07   5   4   3   2   1

Distributed in Canada by Fraser Direct, 100 Armstrong Avenue

Georgetown, ON, Canada L7G 5S4, Tel: (905) 877-4411; Distributed in the U.K. and Europe by David & Charles, Brunel House, Newton Abbot, Devon, TQ12 4PU, England, Tel: (+44) 1626 323200, Fax: (+44) 1626 323319, E-mail: postmaster@davidandcharles.co.uk; Distributed in Australia by Capricorn Link, P.O. Box 704, Windsor, NSW 2756 Australia, Tel: (02) 4577-3555

Library of Congress Cataloging in Publication Data

Lofland, Lee.

  Police procedure & investigation : a writer's guide / by Lee Lofland ; foreword by Stuart Kaminsky. -- 1st ed.

      p. cm. -- (Writer's Digest Books)

  Includes index.

  ISBN-13: 978-1-58297-455-2 (pbk. : alk. paper)

  1. Police--Handbooks, manuals, etc. 2. Criminal investigation--Handbooks, manuals, etc. I. Title. II. Title: Police procedure and investigation.

  HV7921.L64 2007

  363.2'3--dc22   2007017940

Edited by Kelly Nickell
Designed by Claudean Wheeler
Production coordinated by Mark Griffin

DEDICATION

For the men and women who gave
their lives to keep us safe.

ACKNOWLEDGMENTS

I wish I could take all the credit for writing this book, but I can't. Each page was a partnership of thoughts, memories, training, talents, and the combined experience of many law enforcement professionals, writers, medical experts, manufacturers of police equipment, and friends and family from all across the United States and Great Britain.

This cover-to-cover journey took me inside police departments, morgues, jails, prisons, police cars, SWAT vehicles, police academies, courtrooms, judges' chambers, prosecutors' offices, and sheriffs' offices. I had the wonderful opportunity to reunite with old friends and make new ones. The journey brought back a flood of memories—some good, some not so good.

It took more than two years to gather and distill this information to print. Without the help of the people I've listed below, I couldn't have accomplished such a monumental task. It would take a lifetime to repay all your kindness and hard work. I thank you all from the bottom of my heart.

There are certain people who have gone way above and beyond what I've asked of them. To those people I offer these words:

To my wife, Denene, I thank you for standing by me and allowing my dreams to come to fruition. It's because of you that I look forward to each and every day.

To Ellen, I thank you for growing into a fine young woman despite having had a cop for a father during what should've been your happiest, most carefree years. I know you had to do a lot of growing up on your own. You were a good kid and you've grown into a fine young woman. Thank you, too, for giving me a wonderful grandson, Tyler (my best buddy), and a talented son-in-law, John.

To Chris, I thank you for sharing your expertise in the martial arts and for giving us an amazing and ambitious daughter-in-law, Stephani.

To Bobbie Massey, my mother-in-law and first reader, I thank you for your support and confidence.

To Francis Thorne, I thank you for all you've done for Denene and me. I've never known a finer person.

To Brian, my brother, I thank you for many years of memories. I also thank you for riding with me on those nights while I was on patrol. You said you were interested in my work, but I know you really just wanted to make sure I was safe.

Crime Prevention Specialist Officer Dave Crawford took it upon himself to provide the majority of the photographs in this book. Dave also provided timely and detailed answers to my questions, no matter how trivial they might have been. Dave, I thank you for your tireless efforts.

To Sergeant Ed Buns, I thank you for introducing me to one of the finest police departments in the world, the Hamilton, Ohio, Police Department.

Ken Metz of the Yellow Springs, Ohio, Police Department also provided many of the photographs for the book. Ken went out of his way to provide current police information for the early stages of this book. Ken, your assistance was priceless.

I can't say enough good things about the staff at Writer's Digest Books. Jane Friedman has been absolutely wonderful; Claudean Wheeler is a brilliant artist; and Kelly Nickell is absolutely one of the finest editors in the business. Working with Kelly on this project has been a joy. I'm proud to be a part of the Writer's Digest Books family.

I also can't say enough about my dear friend, editor, teacher, and fellow writer Becky Levine. Becky has provided me with guidance and encouragement, and her superb editing skills have made this book much more interesting than I could have ever made it. I'm forever grateful to her. Then there's Becky's family, David and Ian. David makes the best gumbo on earth and never fails to feed me when I'm on the West Coast. Ian, well, he's just Ian, one of the best kids I've ever met.

I'm honored and thrilled to have this book introduced by the words of the 2006 Grand Master of the Mystery Writers of America and one of the greatest writers of our time, Stuart Kaminsky. Thank you, Stuart, for writing the foreword.

I could write something special about each and every person who helped with this project, but space won't allow me to do so, so I've attempted to list everyone below. If I've forgotten anyone, I wholeheartedly apologize. There are just so many people to thank, and age no longer walks hand-in-hand with my memory.

The list of contributors (in alphabetical order by last name):

AUTHORS

Megan Abbott, Rhys Bowen, Leslie Budewitz, Jan Burke, Jeffery Deaver, Hazel Dixon-Cooper, Hallie Ephron, Margaret Falk, Kate Flora, Tess Gerritsen, Lee Goldberg, G. Miki Hayden, Bonnie Hearn Hill, J.A. Jance, Stuart Kaminsky, Shirley Kennett, Lori L. Lake, Sheila Lowe, D.P. Lyle, M.D., Melissa Morse, Beth Proudfoot, Gabriele Rico, S.J. Rozan, Hank Phillipi Ryan, Theresa Schwegel, Sheila L. Stephens, and Penny Warner.

I thank each of you for your advice and for giving me a helping hand and encouragement.

LAW ENFORCEMENT

Sally Aiken, M.D., chief medical examiner, Spokane, Washington; Detective Kristine Allison; Donna Beyer; Coroner Richard Burkhardt, M.D., and his staff, Butler County, Ohio; Kay Callahan, Greensville County, Virginia, Circuit Court; Detective David Collins; Judge Matthew J. Crehan; Chief Phil Earle and the entire South Charleston, Ohio, Police Department; Chief Neil Ferdelman and the entire Hamilton, Ohio, Police Department; James Gilman; Chief John Grote and the entire Yellow Springs, Ohio, Police Department; Sheriff Gene A. Kelly and the entire Clark County, Ohio, Sheriff's Office; Ken Metz; Honorable Pat Moeller; Chief Stephen P. Moody and the entire Springfield, Ohio, Police Department; Detective Josh Moulin; Chief Bernard Richardson; Connie Spisak; Lieutenant Dave Swords; Toni Winters; and Chief Jon D. Zeliff and the entire Central Point, Oregon, Police Department.

A special thanks to all the undercover officers who provided information for this project. I couldn't have done it without you.

SCIENTISTS AND OTHER EXPERTS

Dr. Scott Baird, Wright State University—molecular genetics; Lois Gibson, forensic artist; Dr. Dan Krane and Jason Gilder, Forensic Bioinformatics; Dr. Denene Lofland, senior director of microbiology, TetraPhase Pharmaceuticals; John and Amy Mack, Reptiles by Mack; Gloria Louise Nusse, forensic facial and skull reconstruction expert; and Dr. Stephanie Smith, Wright State University—bacterial genetics.

CITY AND COUNTY OFFICIALS

Cindy Carpenter, clerk of courts, and her staff, Butler County, Ohio; Honorable Mary C. Graves, mayor of Bellbrook, Ohio; Dave Hamilton, city manager of Bellbrook, Ohio; Honorable Kenneth Larson, mayor of South Charleston, Ohio; and Phil Messina, city administrator of Central Point, Oregon.

MARTIAL ARTS/DEFENSIVE TACTICS

Jesse Allen and Chris Fowler.

THE TWINS

Elizabeth and Jennifer Kramer.

PHOTOGRAPHY

Dave Crawford, Stephani Fowler, Sunday Kaminsky, and Ken Metz.

POLICE EQUIPMENT AND SUPPLY

Peter Bennett, E-FIT composite system; David Edelman and Steve Kovac, Fobus Holsters; Tom Mandy and Bruce Pyatt, Mancom Manufacturing Incorporated; and Don O'Neil and Jim Gocke, Sirchie Finger Print Laboratories, Inc.

Much of the information contained within the pages of this book comes from my recollections and experiences while working in law enforcement. Any portion of the book and its information found to be incorrect is due to my ever-failing memory, not a deliberate misquote from any source.

OTHER CREDITS

The Bureau of Alcohol, Tobacco, and Firearms, the Centers for Disease Control and Prevention; the Edgar Allan Poe House and Museum, Baltimore, Maryland; Ken-Yon Hardy, police reporter, *Hamilton Journal-News*; *The Lancet*; Mystery Writers of America; *National Geographic News*; the National Institutes of Health; Sisters in Crime; *Slate* magazine; Katherine Smith, owner and designer, Byte Size Media; *The Toronto Sun*; the U.S. Department of Justice—the Federal Bureau of Investigation, the Drug Enforcement Administration, the Federal Bureau of Prisons, U.S. Immigration and Customs Enforcement, the Bureau of Justice Statistics, and the U.S. Marshals Service; *U.S. News & World Report*; Virginia State Police; Webmaster, U.S. Department of Justice, Drug Enforcement Administration; and *The Yelp*, the newspaper of Yosemite, California.

FRIENDS AND FAMILY

Deanne Devine, Debra and Lewis Grizzard, Danielle Hughes, Laura Humphries, Cathleen Hyles, Rachael Kramer, Patricia Lopez-Harris, and Victoria Ryan.

Your hard work helped make this project come together.

MY PARENTS

I miss you dearly and wish you were here to read this book.

THE MILFORD BARD

I'd like to take a moment to acknowledge my relative, Dr. John Lofland, The Milford Bard, who was a great friend of Edgar Allan Poe. I'd like to think some part of his extraordinary talent might someday find its way into my writings.

TABLE OF
CONTENTS

AUTHOR'S NOTE

The laws of our country and its states, counties, cities, towns, and villages vary greatly, with each police department in the country operating under a different set of rules and regulations. To include each of those laws and regulations in a book would be an impossible task. The material contained within the pages of this book is, for the most part, standard. For information about the laws and rules in your individual areas, please contact your local courts or police departments.

The names and places used in the legal documents and within the anecdotal portions of this book are fictional, a product of my imagination. In no way are they intended to portray any person, living or dead. The events, however, are real.

FOREWORD

I recall exchanging "helloes" with Lee Lofland at several conferences for mystery writers and fans over the years, but I didn't contact him for help that he had offered till I started writing my CSI:NY novels. I wish I had contacted him earlier. Details of police procedure in my novels would have been more accurate. More important, however, is that those details would have contributed significantly to bringing my work more fully to life.

Chicago was covered. I have a friend, a homicide detective, in the Chicago Police Department who provides me on a regular basis about what is going on in the world of crime in Chicago, and much is always going on, usually bizarre and fascinating.

When I had a question about police procedure in Bremen, Germany, I met with the Chief of Police of Bremen, had my fingerprints taken and a photo of me is now on file in Germany.

When I have questions about police procedure or forensic investigation in Sarasota where I live and write about, I call a detective or the Crime Scene Unit in the Sarasota County Sheriff's Office.

However, when I started writing the CSI:NY novels, I kept coming up with problems, both procedural and forensic beyond the scope of my then current human resources. I was stuck at one point about what the very latest in DNA equipment might be. Adjunct questions about DNA abounded. I remembered Lee's offer and got in touch with him. His answer came with clarity and detail down to the name and manufacturer of equipment that the police might use.

More recently, I had the police in a book investigating a murder scene on top of a roof in Manhattan. The problem was that they had to do it in the middle of the worst storm in New York City history. I thought the answer might be simple. I know that in other novels I could write around any difficulty I might encounter. However, I could not do this with a CSI novel. Again, Lee's response was dead-on perfect. I used what he gave me verbatim. There were other things in that and subsequent CSI and other novels that Lee provided for me, always within a day of my asking any question I had.

The book you are about to read contains many things I already knew, but far more things I did not know or that I have gotten wrong in the past. I read it from prologue to epilogue taking notes and planning to incorporate Lee's information about everything from police department uniforms to fingerprint equipment in my next book. I read it because it is so damned fascinating. I read it because I want to get it right. I owe it to law enforcement agencies and I owe it to my readers.

There are many books in my garage that purport to be what a mystery writer like me needs. Most of those books, now withering under the Florida heat and humidity, were either woefully inadequate or simply wrong. This book, even before it has come out, is now my bible for writing anything about law enforcement. It will rest next to my computer in easy reach.

One of my nephews is a police officer in Aurora, Illinois, and has been for many years. As soon as the book is published, I'm sending him a copy. Who knows? The information in it may land him a promotion.

— Stuart M. Kaminsky is an Edgar Award-winning author of more than seventy mystery novels and a Grandmaster of the Mystery Writers of America. He also has screenplay credits for six produced films, including *Once Upon A Time in America*, and was a writer on the *Nero Wolfe Mysteries* television series.

PREFACE

My twenty-year career in law enforcement was rewarding at times. One of
the more gratifying moments was when I received a card in the mail from a
woman and a small child with a picture of the two tucked inside. The little girl
appeared to be eight or nine years old. A message had been scrawled on the
inside flap of the card in thick green crayon. The writing was crude and obviously written by the child, but the message was very clear. She wrote, "Thank
you for saving me and my mommy."

Apparently, I had done something in the course of one of my shifts that
had seemed so important to her she felt compelled to write me. I did my best
to remember what I could have possibly done for them, but nothing stood out
in my mind. It could have been any one of a number of things, but that's a
cop's job. That's what we do.

There are many of those messages out there for police officers—some written and some left unsaid. I always wanted to leave the business as a role model for young people, like other officers were to me when I was a child. Things didn't work out that way, however. I'd come far in achieving my goal, and it all ended with a volley of gunfire and the death of a bank robber. He died almost instantly, but I've suffered for years.

I've lived that day over and over in my mind. I can still hear the gunshots and sirens, and if I close my eyes and concentrate, I can still smell burnt gunpowder and gun oil. I remember the moment when the flashing red lights of the ambulance went still. That's the precise moment when I knew in my heart that I had just killed someone.

I suppose I'll always wonder if I could have done something differently to spare the young man's life. I think of his family—his parents mainly. I've never met them, but I've grieved with them in my thoughts. Sometimes I feel like calling them to tell them their son lives in my memories, but I know I never will.

It's been tough, but I've finally come to terms with the fact that I shot and killed another man. I've also accepted the fact that I can never be alone again. The young robber accompanies me wherever I go. He has since that day and probably always will.

It's this kind of gut-wrenching emotion that must pour onto your pages as you write of your heroes saving a community from a serial killer or rescuing a loved one from the path of danger.

I was a cop for many years, and, for the majority of that time, I worked as a detective charged with solving major crimes. I, like most police officers, had become complacent with my daily routine: I worked my cases and went through the mundane ritual of processing criminals and shoving them through the revolving doors of the courts and jails.

Not every day was dull, but days that would be deemed exciting by the average person were boring to me at best. Drug dealers and dead bodies, sometimes one and the same, began to look alike after a while. Of course, there had been times throughout my career when I'd been scared. If you get right down to it, there were many times when I'd been scared. I've seen the wrong end of a gun a time or two, and I know what the pointed end of a knife looks like. It's my belief that all cops have been frightened at one time or another, but they suck it up and worry about the fear after the situations are over.

A crime scene can be an eye-opening event even for the most seasoned police officer, especially the scene of a violent homicide or a particularly gruesome suicide. It takes a special kind of person to deal with the violent end of human life, day in and day out, and to deal with the killers who choose to end those lives. In *Police Procedure & Investigation*, I'll guide you through the lives of the police officers whose duty it is to solve crimes and to deal with the criminals who commit them. We'll delve into police officer training, their daily routines, and their way of thinking. I'll guide you, the writer, through crime scenes so you see them through my eyes, as I did as a police detective.

A good detective gathers evidence—a great detective gathers evidence and looks for things that are *not* at the scene. The things that are missing are sometimes more important than the things left behind. But more importantly, a great detective will listen to what the dead have to say. Amid the blood and viscera, a body can speak loudly if someone takes the time to listen.

As a writer, you're charged with the task of leading your readers behind the scenes and into the macabre workings of murder. You must excite the senses of your audience, and, to do so, you must enter the minds of your characters. You must bear witness to death through the eyes of a killer and peer into the pale, milky eyes of the dead. A mystery author knows the scent of burnt gunpowder and the stickiness of spilled human blood. The writer senses the eerie stillness enveloping the homicide scene and fills the written page with anticipation and trepidation. The author's ink flows until it reaches the last page, just as the victim's blood spills until his last heartbeat.

Police Procedure & Investigation is designed specifically for the storyteller. The pages are filled with data, statistics, and things you must know to tell your story.

It's time for you, the writer, to leave the comfort of a warm house on a blustery winter night and enter a neighborhood you'd normally ride through in broad daylight with your car doors locked. It's time to touch the ice-cold skin of a bloodless human body and to witness the frenzied carnage of a schizophrenic armed with his weapon of choice—perhaps a knife, or a shotgun at close range.

For me, it's time to go to work and to sign 10-8, ready for duty. Please join me as I share a small portion of my life with you.

CHAPTER 1

LAW ENFORCEMENT
IN AMERICA

The crust that oftentimes develops around the men and women of law enforcement is the result of years of seeing the worst in the worst of people—and the worst in the best of people. Still, they remain ever ready to stand in the gap between all people and those who would do them harm. Moreover, beneath that crust, flashes of tenderness can often be seen—tears pooled in the hardest eyes, comfort whispered in the ears of victims—especially when children are involved. Essentially, while flawed, most are remarkable men and women who run toward danger when others run away.

—SHEILA L. STEPHENS, WRITER, SPEAKER, CONSULTANT, AND FORMER ATF SPECIAL AGENT

Today in America, there are many law enforcement agencies, but they all fall under the control of a local, state, or federal governing body. It's important for police officers to know that it often becomes necessary for more than one police department to join forces while investigating a crime. In order for police officers to effectively work with other police departments, they must first understand how each of those departments operates.

The first days of a police officer's career are spent in a classroom, learning about local government and how police departments were established. They learn the differences between federal law enforcement agencies, state police, county sheriffs' offices, and city, town, and village police departments. New recruits are taught that each department operates independently, with none having authority over the other.

To better understand how police departments and sheriffs' offices function, officers must first learn how individual states, counties, cities, towns, and villages are structured.

CITY, TOWN, AND VILLAGE POLICE

Not every municipality has a population large enough to be considered a city. Depending on the area or state, smaller urban areas are usually labeled towns or villages. In the United States, cities are specific areas that have separate governing bodies and power apart from the state where they're located. Most cites operate under a charter—a locally written constitution.

Cities operating without a charter are known as statutory forms of government and are organized and authorized by state laws. City mayors and council members are elected by the citizens of that city, and the laws and ordinances of the city are approved by the voters living within its geographical boundaries, or jurisdiction.

Towns and villages are generally smaller than cities, both in land area and population. That size difference reduces the amount of funds available for community services such as water, sewer, waste removal, and police, fire and rescue operations.

Towns and villages normally have the option of operating their own police departments. Sometimes a department consists of a single officer. Maintaining a police department isn't cheap—in 2003, the average nationwide cost (salary, uniforms, and benefits) for a municipality to employ a single police officer was $93,300, or approximately $200 per U.S. resident. Towns and villages that can't afford to maintain the costs associated with a police department rely on the county sheriff's office and the state police to enforce the laws of their area.

SHERIFFS' OFFICES VS. POLICE DEPARTMENTS

The difference between a sheriff's office and a police department can be confusing. While we'll go over each in great detail throughout this chapter, keep this caveat in mind: Every city, town, or village must have a sheriff's office. A police department, however, is *not* a must-have department. Because of this, it's actually possible for cities and counties to have both sheriffs' offices and police departments. It all comes down to the laws of the individual areas.

A police chief is appointed by city, town, or village officials and is responsible for maintaining the peace and enforcing the law within his jurisdiction.

On the other hand, a sheriff is elected to office by popular vote and is the chief executive and administrative officer of a county—she has supreme authority in all jurisdictions within her county. A sheriff's principal duties involve aiding all criminal and civil courts within the county, serving civil process (delivering civil papers such as subpoenas and eviction notices), maintaining the jail, and serving jury summonses. A sheriff is the chief conservator of the peace in the county where she serves; therefore, she may also be responsible for the enforcement of all laws. Sheriffs have the authority to appoint deputy sheriffs to assist them in carrying out their duties.

Normally, a police chief doesn't have the authority to serve legal documents, such as civil warrants. In some areas the local government may have sworn in their police chief as a sheriff so she may have the authority to do the work of a sheriff. In fact, many cities have a city sheriff in addition to a county sheriff who also has jurisdiction within the city in addition to a police chief. (Clear as mud, right?) It just depends on what local law dictates. For example, in the state of Virginia, no police officer has any power or any authority in civil matters. That's a function of the sheriff's office.

Now, let's take a closer look at each type of law enforcement agency.

POLICE DEPARTMENTS

Modern police departments in the United States function much like our nation's military. Due to the increased intelligence, organization, and education of modern criminals, police departments have become more military-like than ever before—so much so that they're often referred to as paramilitary organizations. To keep up with the advanced techniques used by today's criminals,

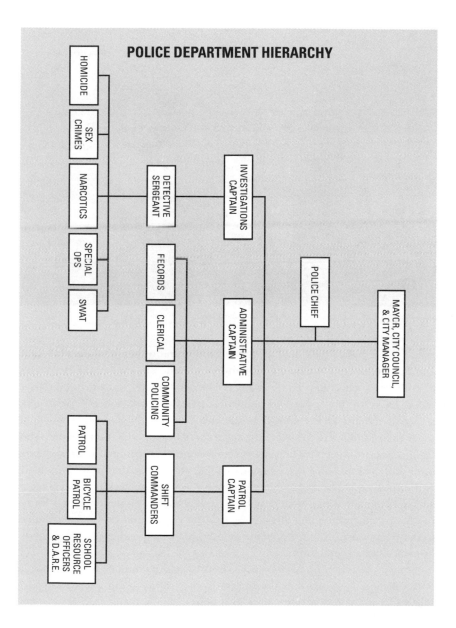

POLICE DEPARTMENT HIERARCHY

MAYOR, CITY COUNCIL, & CITY MANAGER
→ POLICE CHIEF
→ INVESTIGATIONS CAPTAIN → DETECTIVE SERGEANT → HOMICIDE, SEX CRIMES, NARCOTICS, SPECIAL OPS, SWAT
→ ADMINISTRATIVE CAPTAIN → RECORDS, CLERICAL, COMMUNITY POLICING
→ PATROL CAPTAIN → SHIFT COMMANDERS → PATROL, BICYCLE PATROL, SCHOOL RESOURCE OFFICERS & D.A.R.E.

Chief Jon D. Zoliff of the Central Point, Oregon, Police Department, wears two stars on his uniform to indicate his rank as chief of police.

police departments have had to step up the training they give their officers, and they've had to increase their weaponry to match or exceed the firepower of outlaws. To effectively battle crime, police departments must maintain strict order. To assure that rules and regulations are followed, police departments adhere to military-style chains of command.

A police chief heads up a city, town, or village police department. The chief is responsible for all law enforcement operations within the jurisdictions under his control. Since there's no actual line painted on the ground to identify the city's perimeter, the law in most areas gives a chief and his officers legal authority to exceed that boundary by a predetermined distance when preserving the peace and making a lawful arrest. The three-hundred-yard allowance in the Commonwealth of Virginia is an example of a jurisdiction that extends beyond a city's actual limits.

Police chiefs are hired and supervised by a city council, a city manager, and a mayor. They work at the behest of this ruling body and can be dismissed by them at any time. Most of a police chief's major decisions, especially the purchases of costly or nonbudgeted items, must be approved by his superiors. In addition, the council controls the budget of the city, town, and village police departments, which limits a chief's power and authority. Police Chief Bernard Richardson of Virginia sums up his department's financial woes this way:

> Funding is the worst problem I have facing me. Our budget is the largest departmental budget of the city, so it's the first to give up something. Police vehicles are thought to be an area where there could be cuts without any problems.

Police officers wear pins or insignias on their collars to identify their individual rank within the department. Police chiefs wear the gold stars of a general or a gold colonel's eagle on their lapels, which signifies they are their department's top ranking officers. The individual police chief normally chooses which style uniform and which rank insignia to wear and normally prefers to be addressed as either "chief" or "colonel."

Chief Neil Ferdelman of the Hamilton, Ohio, Police Department describes how he came to choose the colonel's insignia:

> Ego, or more kindly, the size of the organization, dictates the rank. Most major cities use a star or a number of stars because they have more ranks. Midsize to smaller jurisdiction chiefs usually use the colonel insignia, although I've seen village police chiefs with stars. Our chief's rank is set by policy. When I'm in uniform, I wear the colonel's insignia, which has been worn by chiefs here for all my thirty years in this organization.

The second-in-command of a police department is either a major or a captain. This distinction usually depends on the size of the particular department—larger agencies sometimes employ one or more majors. This officer is usually in charge of administrative duties such as payroll and personnel issues and directly supervises all lower-level heads of the various divisions. A major is identified by a gold maple leaf on each lapel.

Directly below majors in the chain of command are captains, who display double, parallel gold bars—nicknamed "railroad tracks"—on their collars. A captain is responsible for overseeing the day-to-day operations of the police department, such as shift assignments and training schedules. A captain manages shift supervisors—lieutenants or sergeants—who in turn directly supervise the remaining workforce, such as the detective divisions, patrol divisions, K-9 units, bicycle patrols, and special operations like undercover teams and special weapons and tactics (SWAT) units.

Lieutenants wear a single bar on their collars; sergeants display three stripes on their sleeves and collars; corporals sport two stripes. Officers who wear a single stripe on their collars and sleeves have a ranking equal to a private in the military. These officers are referred to as officers or line officers. Line officers respond to 911 calls and criminal complaints made by citizens. They also conduct routine patrols of neighborhoods and business districts to proactively thwart crime.

An officer without any rank insignia is usually a rookie, someone who's recently graduated from the police academy and is working toward completing a four-hundred-hour field training program. These rookie officers ride with a field training officer for the duration of that program.

Patrol supervisor's vehicle.

Other pins, medals, and ribbons worn by police officers can denote an officer's number of years of service, good conduct, marksmanship, medals of valor, and special awards deemed appropriate by the department.

Supervisors and detectives wear gold badges. Rank-and-file officers wear silver badges. A white uniform shirt normally indicates that an officer has supervisor status. Some departments letter the side of patrol vehicle doors with the words *sergeant*, *lieutenant*, or *captain* to indicate to the public that the driver is a shift supervisor. Since nearly all patrol cars within a department look the same, these reflective letters are excellent indicators to the night-shift patrol officers that their boss is approaching. This allows the officers ample time to appear busy with last-minute paperwork instead of reading their favorite crime novels while waiting for the next speeder.

POLICE DEPARTMENT HIRING PROCESS

Today's police officer candidates must be in excellent health; have near-perfect corrected or noncorrected vision; and have no physical disabilities that would hinder the performance of their duties. They must have at least a high school diploma or equivalent, and they must be a minimum of twenty-one years of age but not over the age of thirty-five. Some departments will waive the upper age limit if the candidate is highly qualified or is already a police officer from another agency. A large number of police departments lean toward hiring college graduates, and some municipalities offer monetary incentives to officers who complete their college educations while employed with the police department.

Candidates must undergo a thorough background investigation, which is normally conducted by investigators from the detective division or detectives within the internal affairs department. The investigators visit and question the candidate's neighbors, friends, family members, pastors, and former employers and teachers. Conversations with people who are close to the potential officer can offer great insight into the candidate's character and abilities.

Candidates with felony records can't become police officers. Most departments won't hire anyone with a criminal record of any kind, including misdemeanors. Investigators check Federal Bureau of Investigation (FBI) and local computer files for any documentation of criminal activity by the candidate. Detectives also obtain a copy of the candidate's credit report, because a person with a poor credit history is thought to have organizational troubles and not be the type of person who'll make a good police officer. The investigators print a copy of the candidate's driver record. They examine this record for any signs of problematic or habitual behavior, such as excessive speeding and reckless driving.

The investigating officers place the documentation of the three reports—the criminal history, the credit report, and the driver record—into what is now a rapidly growing file. Some departments also require the candidate to undergo a polygraph examination, or lie-detector test.

At this stage of the hiring process, it's not unusual for investigating detectives to discover that a candidate is wanted by the police in another jurisdiction, is a spouse or child abuser, is a drug addict, is delinquent in child support or taxes, or is a convicted felon. The foolhardy candidate with an outstanding arrest warrant is promptly taken into custody. She's then held in jail until appropriate authorities arrive to transport her to the jurisdiction in which she's wanted.

A candidate who successfully passes the background examination must undergo a battery of testing. He must pass a lengthy, written aptitude exam that requires knowledge of basic math, science, language skills, and excellent reasoning and memory skills.

If the candidate successfully passes the aptitude test, he takes a psychological test to determine whether he's mentally and morally suitable for the job. The psychological tests are designed to weed out candidates who exhibit even the slightest signs of socially deviant behavior. Test-takers are also required to respond to questions regarding lying, cheating, and stealing. The tests leave little room for error. I recall one question that asked candidates if they'd ever taken as much as a paper clip from a former place of employment.

Dr. Laurence Miller, a clinical, forensic, and police psychologist and the author of *Practical Police Psychology: Stress Management and Crisis Intervention for Law Enforcement*, explains the need for the psychological testing of police officer candidates:

> Police officers are charged with the responsibility of making life-and-death decisions in a short period of time under dangerous and stressful circumstances. It's understandable, then, that some form of psychological screening for basic mental stability and judgment be a regular part of the recruitment process for new officers.

The next rounds of tests are assessments of the candidate's physical strength, stamina, and agility. The candidate is required to run long distances, perform as many push-ups and sit-ups as she can within a specified time frame, jump over ditches, crawl under barriers, and effectively drag a life-size, 150-pound dummy over and through a short obstacle course. The tests are the same for both male and female candidates.

Finally, the candidate who successfully makes it through the rigorous testing process is brought before a review panel for a face-to-face interview. The panel consists of ranking officers from the department, members of the city council, possibly the mayor or mayor's representative, and sometimes people selected from the general public. Each member of the review panel questions the candidate. At the end of the interviews, the panel makes its recommendation to the officer in charge of hiring—usually a major, captain, or police chief.

The successful candidate is notified within a few days about when he's to report for his uniform and bullet-resistant vest fitting. The recruit is also given a date to report to work, his shift assignment, and his date to report to the police academy. Police academies normally offer basic officer training either once or twice a year, so a recruit could actually work for several months before receiving formal academy training. In these instances the recruit is usually paired with a certified field training officer until the date of his scheduled training.

In order for a recruit to make a lawful arrest, she must first raise her right hand and swear an oath promising to uphold the laws of the United States, the state where she's employed, and her local jurisdiction. Once this ceremony has been completed, the recruit is considered a sworn officer. Civilian employees of police departments, such as clerical workers, records clerks, computer technicians, and some crime scene technicians and criminalists aren't sworn officers and have no powers of arrest.

SHERIFFS' OFFICES

As noted at the start of this chapter, a sheriff is an officer of the court who's elected by the voting public of a county. Sheriffs normally serve a term of four years, and it's not uncommon for a sheriff to hold office for several terms. Sheriffs are constitutional officers—their positions are created by a constitution, not by legislation—and they have no supervisors other than voters.

The responsibilities of a sheriff are a bit more complex than those of a police chief. A police chief is only responsible for the enforcement of local, state, and federal laws and for the protection of citizens and their property. A sheriff is not only accountable for the enforcement of those same laws, but he's also charged with the service (delivery) of criminal and civil documents, courtroom security, jail and lockup operations, prisoner transports, and the supervision of deputies who are law enforcement officers. Sheriffs also have authority in the county in which they were elected, and in all cities, towns, and villages located within that county. This means that, even though a city has its own police force, county sheriffs and their deputies have jurisdiction in that city and can make a lawful arrest there.

Even though all deputies wear the designated uniforms of their departments, not all deputy sheriffs are police officers. Deputies assigned to work in county or city jails are corrections officers, sometimes referred to as jailers.

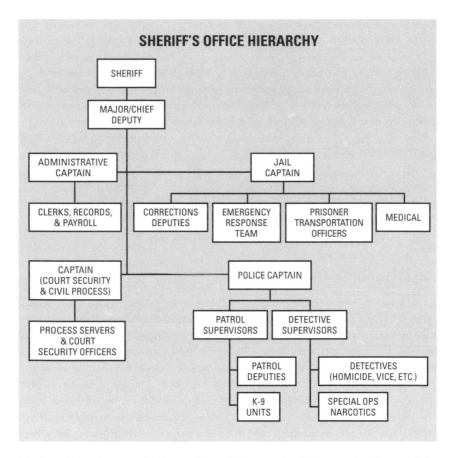

SHERIFF'S OFFICE HIERARCHY

- SHERIFF
  - MAJOR/CHIEF DEPUTY
    - ADMINISTRATIVE CAPTAIN
      - CLERKS, RECORDS, & PAYROLL
      - CAPTAIN (COURT SECURITY & CIVIL PROCESS)
        - PROCESS SERVERS & COURT SECURITY OFFICERS
    - JAIL CAPTAIN
      - CORRECTIONS DEPUTIES
      - EMERGENCY RESPONSE TEAM
      - PRISONER TRANSPORTATION OFFICERS
      - MEDICAL
    - POLICE CAPTAIN
      - PATROL SUPERVISORS
        - PATROL DEPUTIES
        - K-9 UNITS
      - DETECTIVE SUPERVISORS
        - DETECTIVES (HOMICIDE, VICE, ETC.)
        - SPECIAL OPS NARCOTICS

Their training is very similar to the training received by guards who work in the state and federal prison systems. Their sole duties are to supervise inmate activity and maintain order and security within the jail facility.

Deputies working in county and city courthouses are courtroom security officers and are trained to serve as bailiffs and to provide protection for court employees and judges. They're also responsible for the safety of trial evidence, witnesses, jurors, and prisoners within the courthouse.

Deputies who travel the countryside delivering court papers such as jury summonses, lien notices, divorce papers, and eviction notices are called process servers. These deputies, through the authority of the court and the sheriff, are also responsible for the eviction of delinquent renters and people whose property's been foreclosed on by banks and mortgage companies.

The training for jailers, courtroom security officers, and process servers is limited to their areas of expertise. They don't attend police academies and aren't certified police officers. Some sheriffs' offices cross-train their deputies so they may be certified to work in two or more areas of the department.

The ranking structure for a sheriff's office is similar to that of a police department, with the exception of the second-in-command. The person who serves directly under the sheriff is the chief deputy who, like her police department counterpart, normally holds the rank of either a major or captain. It's the chief deputy's responsibility to assume charge of the department in the sheriff's absence. The chief deputy is responsible for managing the entire department until either the sheriff returns to duty or, in the event of his death, until an election is held to name a new sheriff. The judge of the highest court within the jurisdiction may appoint the chief deputy, someone else from within the department, or someone from the community as acting sheriff until the next election.

The chief deputy reports to the sheriff and is the direct supervisor of all department heads. Each division supervisor—normally a captain—is responsible for the operation of the various subdivisions within the sheriff's office. These captains oversee the operation of the county jails, courts and courtroom security, civil process, police patrols, detective and traffic divisions, jail medical departments, and inmate transportation.

The administration of county jails is an enormous responsibility. These facilities are subject to the same rules, laws, and procedures as state prisons—a few have inmate populations with numbers equal to some prisons. The deputies who supervise these facilities are sometimes called jail administrators, and some are even called wardens. They're not only responsible for the supervision of around-the-clock staff but for the control and well-being of the jail inmates as well.

The jail administrators must ensure that prisoners' rights are protected, that they're properly fed and exercised, that their religious beliefs and activities aren't restricted, and that security isn't compromised at any time. They're also responsible for inmate transportation to the various courts and to medical appointments for needs that can't be addressed by the jail's medical staff, such as surgery. If a jail inmate is required to stay in the hospital, around-the-clock security must be provided; therefore, at least two deputies per shift are normally assigned to guard the prisoner. Most hospitals are equipped with special security wings or floors that are designed to house prisoners. It's also the duty of the jail administrator to oversee the hospital security assignments.

To assist with this daunting responsibility, jail administrators have shift supervisors who report to them. Shift supervisors are normally lieutenants or sergeants, and it's their primary duty to oversee the day-to-day activities of the inmates and to supervise all jail deputies.

Majors or captains in charge of the police department divisions within each sheriff's office manage all patrol units, detective divisions, K-9 squads, and SWAT teams. Each shift supervisor—the lieutenant or sergeant—oversees the line officers of his unit.

Large sheriffs' offices sometimes utilize substations located in various areas inside the county limits. Each subdivision is supervised by a commanding officer who reports directly to an administrative major or captain within the main sheriff's office.

Courtroom security and civil process divisions are managed by a supervisor who sees to it that the deputies carry out their duties in the timely manner prescribed by law. These supervisors also are also the sheriff's liaisons to the courts, judges, and attorneys.

SHERIFF'S OFFICE HIRING PROCESS

Since sheriffs are elected into office, they can't be fired for any reason. The only way to remove an elected sheriff from office is through impeachment or a new election. Sheriffs' deputies are appointed, not hired, by the sheriff, and they can be legally dismissed at any time without cause or reason. The qualifications to become a sheriff in many areas of the country are modest. Normally, a candidate needs only be eligible to vote in the community where she's seeking office and to have lived in that community for at least one year. Prior law enforcement experience isn't a requirement.

Ohio is one of the few states in the country that requires a candidate for sheriff to be a sworn police officer. He must also be certified to carry a firearm and have at least a two-year college degree. All sheriff candidates are also required to submit to a thorough background investigation.

Candidates for the position of deputy sheriff can be subjected to the same intense background investigation and testing procedure as applicants for city police departments, but since they're political appointees, this practice isn't always carried out—especially for candidates who are friends or family of the sheriff.

STATE POLICE

The first law enforcement agency with statewide jurisdiction was the Texas Rangers. In the early 1800s, ten men were employed to protect the area around a Texas colony from Indians. This group of men furnished their own guns, horses, and supplies, and they worked for just over one dollar a day while enforcing their unwritten policy of "Shoot first and ask questions later."

When the Rangers waged a war against the Cherokee Indians, they quickly developed a reputation for their aggressive and often brutal style of law enforcement. They continued that same vicious style of fighting in the Battle of Plum Creek with the Comanche Indians. This style of law enforcement earned them worldwide recognition during the Mexican War.

After the Texas Rangers, the first professionally organized state police department was the Pennsylvania State Constabulary, an agency that was actually formed to quell the state's coal miners' strikes. Soon other states began to follow suit and formed their own state police departments.

Today, each state has its own police department that's responsible for enforcing the laws of that state, as well as the laws of the United States. State police officers (also called State Troopers or Highway Patrol) have jurisdiction in any city or county within the state where they're employed. They're also authorized to make arrests for any crime that's committed within the state. In most areas, the state police are primarily responsible for enforcing traffic laws; however, they have their own fully functional criminal investigative divisions, undercover investigators, crime labs, and crime scene technicians and equipment. They also assist local departments when needed.

State police departments normally have one large, central center of operations located in the state's capital. The state is divided into districts, each having a district headquarters that's responsible for several counties. Some state police departments have smaller field offices located within the individual counties.

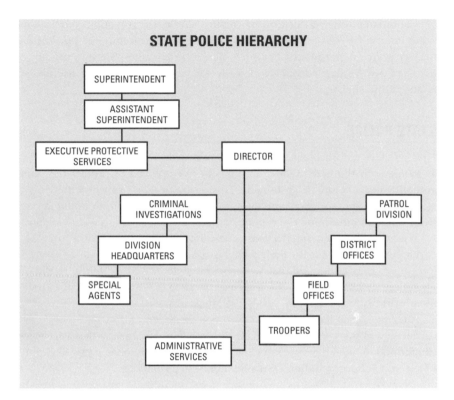

STATE POLICE HIERARCHY

SUPERINTENDENT

ASSISTANT SUPERINTENDENT

EXECUTIVE PROTECTIVE SERVICES

DIRECTOR

CRIMINAL INVESTIGATIONS

PATROL DIVISION

DIVISION HEADQUARTERS

DISTRICT OFFICES

SPECIAL AGENTS

FIELD OFFICES

TROOPERS

ADMINISTRATIVE SERVICES

The Virginia State Police (VSP) has grown from a one-man department that began in the early 1900s to a department that's currently over three thousand strong. In the early days, Virginia troopers patrolled a highway system of dirt roads that had a maximum speed limit of fifteen miles per hour. One hundred years later, the VSP is responsible for patrolling nearly 30 million miles of highway while responding to well over 1.25 million incidents annually.

In 1922, Virginia troopers, or inspectors as they were then called, earned around $1,500 annually. In 2006, a trooper's starting salary was over $33,000 with an additional benefits package worth approximately $26,000. They're also provided take-home patrol vehicles, which allow the troopers to respond quickly during emergencies.

At the onset of Virginia's state police department, a single plainclothes police inspector watched over a mere handful of automobiles traveling on seven miles of hard-surfaced roads. Troopers today are outfitted in handsome blue-and-gray uniforms styled after the colors of the Confederate and Union Armies—gray for the Confederate Army and blue for the Union.

In 2004, Virginia state police officers, for instance, responded to approximately 1.3 million incidents, and they investigated nearly 43,000 traffic accidents; made 65,000 traffic arrests and more than 21,000 criminal arrests; assisted police and sheriffs' offices more than 40,000 times; seized narcotics worth more than $130 million; and conducted 345 search-and-rescue missions. Each state's police department has a similar record of advancing with the times.

FEDERAL LAW ENFORCEMENT AGENCIES

The U.S. Government employs more than 106,000 full-time, sworn law enforcement officers. Each of these officers carries firearms and may legally arrest criminals anywhere within the United States and its territories.

FEDERAL BUREAU OF INVESTIGATION

The primary law enforcement agency of the United States government is the Federal Bureau of Investigation (FBI). The FBI was originally established in 1908 to defend the United States against attacks by terrorists and to enforce the criminal laws of the United States.

The responsibilities of the FBI have expanded greatly since its early days. Not only is the FBI the chief investigative arm of the federal government; today's agents are assigned many duties, such as assisting local and state agencies with laboratory testing, narcotics trafficking, and Internet and cyber investigations. The FBI also assists in protecting the civil rights of American citizens and maintains the Integrated Automated Fingerprint Identification System (IAFIS)—an electronic exchange of fingerprint identification.

The FBI operates its own training academy at the U.S. Marine Corps Base in Quantico, Virginia. New agent trainees—NATS—receive 643.5 hours (17 weeks) of intensive basic training. During their training, NATS divide their time between the classroom and practical, hands-on exercises. As weeks go by, NATS are expected to improve on their strength and stamina. They're given physical training tests during the first, seventh, and fourteenth weeks to determine their individual progress in performing sit-ups, push-ups, pull-ups, and distance running.

NATS practice their newly learned skills through repetition and role-playing. The training academy at Quantico features a mock town named Hogan's Alley, complete with buildings and city streets. This lifelike depiction of Anytown, USA, is where NATS are given the opportunity to come face-to-face with armed robbers, killers, and fleeing bandits—all of whom are instructors and actors role-playing as bad guys. NATS are assigned crimes to solve that have been "committed" within the city limits of Hogan's Alley. They're then graded on their ability to put their newly acquired skills to practical use.

NATS must undergo a rigorous schedule of defensive tactics training. They're graded on their expertise in grappling, handcuffing, takedown and control techniques, weapons retention, and suspect disarming. They must also complete driver training and a basic firearms course in which they're trained to fire an assortment of weapons.

During FBI firearms training, NATS must demonstrate the ability to properly handle and fire thousands of rounds of ammunition from each of the weapons used by the FBI, including a submachine gun.

The FBI operates fifty-six field offices with four hundred satellite offices within the United States. The bureau also maintains forty-five international offices called Legal Attaché offices, or Legats. These worldwide offices prevent foreign crime from making its way to the United States. The Legats work closely with their foreign hosts and don't conduct solo operations or intelligence gathering.

BUREAU OF ALCOHOL, TOBACCO, FIREARMS, AND EXPLOSIVES

The Bureau of Alcohol, Tobacco, Firearms, and Explosives (ATF) was first established as a tax-collecting and law enforcement agency. Today, since the inception of the Homeland Security Bill, the law enforcement duties of the ATF have been assigned to the U.S. Department of Justice. The tax-collection functions of ATF remain under the control of the U.S. Department of the Treasury.

ATF special agents follow a chain of command similar to the FBI, with field agents reporting to either an assistant special agent in charge or to the special agent in charge. Large-area field offices, called posts of duty, employ group supervisors who report to the agents in charge.

Agents receive basic and advanced training at one of the many Federal Law Enforcement Training Centers (FLETC) located throughout the country. The first FLETC was established in Glynco, Georgia, where many federal officers still receive their basic training.

Another FLETC located near Roswell, New Mexico, specializes in training courses for government agencies, including the ATF, the U.S. Border Patrol, the Bureau of Indian Affairs, Federal Air Marshals, and the Transportation Security Administration. In addition, the New Mexico facility offers advanced certification training for driving, physical fitness, and firearms instructors.

There are many police agencies within the boundaries of the United States. Each of these agencies employs sworn police officers who are authorized to enforce the laws of the United States and of their individual bailiwicks.

OTHER FEDERAL POLICE AGENCIES

Bureau of Engraving and Printing Police
Department of Homeland Security
Diplomatic Security Service
Federal Protective Service
Federal Reserve Police
Hoover Dam Police
Internal Revenue Service
Museum Police Departments
National Institutes of Health Police
Pentagon Police Department
Tribal Police Departments
U.S. Citizenship and Immigration Services
U.S. Coast Guard Police Department
U.S. Defense Protective Service
U.S. Department of Energy
U.S. Drug Enforcement Administration
U.S. Environmental Protection Agency
U.S. Marshals Service
U.S. Mint Police

U.S. Park Police
U.S. Postal Police
U.S. Secret Service
Walter Reed Hospital Police

OTHER POLICE DEPARTMENTS

Some individual communities and most government agencies maintain their own police and/or security departments to preserve and protect individual laws and property. An example of a police department operating independently, but within the jurisdictional limits of another locality, is a college or university police department. In these cases, the physical locations of universities obviously lie within specific cities or counties that are normally policed by a city police department or a county sheriff's office. However, due to on-campus housing, large student populations, and the potential for criminal activity outside the normal course of duty for existing local departments, colleges have established their own individual police departments called campus police departments.

CAMPUS POLICE DEPARTMENTS

College campuses are sometimes large enough—housing student populations well into the thousands—to warrant having their own campus police departments. These police departments operate exactly as any city, town, or village police department, with the exception of their possible need for officers with a more sympathetic, understanding nature than is normally required. The quest for candidates who possess this desired trait makes the hiring process of a campus police department a little more difficult than its municipal counterparts.

College life presents a somewhat different type of criminal activity than is normally found in most cities and counties. The majority of the crimes committed on college campuses are crimes of a petty nature, such as vandalism, annoying phone calls, and larceny. Although fewer in number, crimes of a more serious nature do occur and are often crimes against a person, such as sexual assault and rape.

Campus police officers undergo the same training as officers with city, town, and village police departments. In fact, some campus police departments send their officers to the academies of those other departments. Campus police officers are sworn police officers. They're authorized to carry firearms and have the power to make arrests and serve warrants. A campus police officer's authority is limited to the geographical boundaries of the university where he's employed unless he's in pursuit of a fleeing felon.

CAPITOL POLICE DEPARTMENTS

Capitol police officers are responsible for the security of state-owned buildings located on state capitol property. These officers enforce the laws of their states, and they investigate all crimes that occur within their jurisdiction—all property owned by the state. They provide security for the governor, the lieutenant governor, the attorney general, state Supreme Court justices, members of the general assembly, and their families.

The U.S. Capitol Police, established in 1828 for the purpose of providing security for congressional buildings, is in charge of protecting the members of Congress, the Senate, the House of Representatives, and their families.

Capitol officers enforce traffic and criminal laws within all congressional buildings and property. During times of civil unrest capitol police officers must maintain order during demonstrations, protests, and rallies. They're also responsible for regaining control during riots. Other local and state police agencies are often called on to assist in these situations.

In the early days of the U.S. Capitol Police, officers earned meager salaries. Today, capitol police officers earn more than $50,000 annually along with a generous benefits package.

PORT AUTHORITY POLICE

Officers who are employed by port authorities enforce the laws of their respective states and localities. In addition to normal police activity—with the ever-present threat of terrorism in and around our nation's transportation hubs—port authority officers must be ever vigilant for terrorist-related activity.

GAME AND FISHERY DEPARTMENTS

Game wardens enforce the hunting, fishing, trapping, and boating laws of their respective states. They're authorized to arrest criminal suspects for any crime, and they have statewide authority and powers of arrest. Since these officers constantly patrol wooded areas, they're often assigned to state and local drug task forces, especially task forces that are responsible for marijuana eradication.

ALCOHOLIC BEVERAGE CONTROL

Some states, such as Virginia, North Carolina, Washington, and Oregon, require that all alcohol-related sales be controlled by the state government. In fact, in some of these states, such as Virginia, citizens can only buy liquor by the bottle from a state-owned-and-operated store.

These states have special law enforcement agencies responsible for enforcing the state's alcohol laws. For example, the Virginia Department of Alcoholic Beverage Control (ABC) manages more than three hundred ABC stores throughout the state. In 2005, Virginia's state-run ABC stores collected more than $268 million from alcohol sales.

The Virginia Department of ABC employs sworn police officers called ABC special agents. These agents have authority and arrest powers anywhere within the state.

ABC special agents monitor the sale of alcoholic beverages in stores, trains, airplanes, wineries, restaurants, and nightclubs. In many states laws mandate that all establishments selling alcoholic beverages must also serve hot food. In these states food must be sold in a predetermined ratio to the establishment's alcohol sales.

The sale of mixed beverages may also be prohibited in any nightclub commonly called a strip club where partial or full nudity is permitted. Undercover ABC agents often patrol these clubs searching for violations of the law. ABC agents may also be assigned to work with local and other state police departments for the purpose of investigating criminal activity, such as narcotics crimes and the manufacturing of illegal liquor (moonshine).

CHAPTER 2

THE POLICE
ACADEMY

Training is without a doubt the most important investment that a police department can make. With ever-changing tools, techniques, and laws, it's imperative that today's police officer is constantly afforded the best training to provide the best service possible to the public that they serve.

—SERGEANT ED BUNS, TRAINING SUPERVISOR,
HAMILTON, OHIO, POLICE DEPARTMENT

Large law enforcement departments normally maintain their own police academies. Smaller agencies sometimes pool together and operate multi-jurisdictional academies, where candidates from various police departments and sheriffs' offices attend the same classes.

Each police academy teaches the fundamentals of law enforcement. Recruits are schooled in areas such as basic law, driving, firearms, officer safety and survival, defensive tactics, accident investigation, human behavior and psychology, crime scene management, and interview and interrogation.

Recruits participate in mock exercises simulating nearly every possible scenario they might one day encounter in the field, from shootouts to hostage situations. They're graded through practical and written exercises and exams. The training is extremely extensive and stressful.

Academy life is similar to military boot camp training, and police recruits are often pushed to the limits of their physical and mental capabilities. All prospective police officers must undergo and pass a physical examination prior to their enrollment in a police academy. My academy instructors insisted that recruits run everywhere as their primary mode of transportation. We ran to meals and to classes; we even ran to the streets and forest trails where we were to begin our daily five-mile run.

There's no room in a police academy for someone who's not willing to put 100-percent effort into every assigned task. Instructors actually expect a 110-percent effort—they want to see the extra effort. In fact, they demand it.

The men in our class had to keep their hair closely cropped. The women wore theirs pinned up or cut short. No one was allowed to have hair touching his shirt collar.

We all were required to keep our shoes shined to a glossy sheen.

Dress uniforms, Class A as they're called, had to be neatly pressed, with creases nearly sharp enough to slice bread. I even saw instructors looking into the ears and noses of recruits, searching for a stray hair. The consequence for any infraction of the dress code by any recruit was hundreds of push-ups for the entire class. Needless to say, we were a self-policing group that groomed one another, like monkeys, prior to inspections.

The length of training time varies for different academies. Some police officer certification courses last for as little as thirteen weeks, while others last for as long as thirty-six weeks or more, depending on individual departmental requirements.

The police academy course of instruction begins with an orientation much like any high school or college. Recruits sit at desks, poised to take notes from instructors who are either permanent employees of the academy or volunteers from various police departments and sheriffs' offices. The instructors are experts in their various fields, and most are certified as academy instructors by the U.S. Department of Justice.

The recruits are first given a broad overview of their chosen career. They're told of the dangers, the accompanying anxiety, and the long hours that come with the job. Instructors stress that new officers will be loved by some and hated by others. Recruits are taught to be fair and just, and they're hit with the cold, hard fact that some of them may not make it to see retirement alive.

Recruits stand ready for inspection.

Training begins with instruction on local, state, and federal law. The recruits are taught only the very basics in areas such as search and seizure, arrest, liquor laws, and motor vehicle laws. This portion of the training lasts for approximately forty hours, and the recruits take a written test at the end of the week—the first of many weekly tests. Recruits must pass each written exam with a perfect score of 100 percent. If a recruit receives anything less than the required 100 percent, she's given two additional attempts to correctly answer each missed question. If, after the third try, her final score is still less than perfect, the recruit is immediately expelled from the academy, resulting in the loss of her job. The pressure to perform is tremendous.

ACADEMY COURSES

Police academies vary depending on their local jurisdictions, but the schedule of classes for most academies is similar to the following schedule.

INTRODUCTION TO LAW ENFORCEMENT

- Orientation to Basic Training
- Note Taking and Study Habits
- History of Law Enforcement
- Police Ethics and Moral Issues
- Police Authority and Discretion
- The Criminal Justice System

POLICE AND THE LAW

- Constitutional Law
- State Liquor Laws
- Civil Liability
- State Criminal Law
- Laws of Evidence
- Laws of Arrest
- Search and Seizure
- Search Warrant Preparation
- Use of Force
- Hunting Laws
- Weapons and Permits
- Courtroom Testimony and Demeanor
- Mock Trial

PRACTICAL POLICE SKILLS

- Firearms
- Shooting Decisions
- Tactical Use of Weapons
- First-Responder Course
- Water Safety
- Officer Safety/Mechanics of Arrest, Restraint, and Control
- Handcuffing
- Defensive Tactics
- Police Baton Training
- O.C. (Pepper) Spray

- Practical Skills Day
- Driver Training
- Physical Fitness

HUMAN RELATIONS

- Human Behavior/Interpersonal Relations
- Stress Management
- Police and the Public
- State Juvenile Law/Dealing With Juveniles
- Suicide Recognition, Management, and Intervention
- Supervisor-Subordinate Relations
- Substance Abuse Issues
- Career Development
- Victim/Witness Advocacy
- Law Enforcement and Citizens With Special Needs
- Conflict Management
- Cultural Awareness and Diversity

CRIMINAL INVESTIGATION

- Principles of Investigation
- Crime Scene Processing
- Interviewing Techniques and Skills
- Admissions and Confessions/Criminal Statements
- Fingerprinting
- Photography
- Surveillance
- Alcohol, Tobacco, and Firearms
- Explosives and Incendiary Devices
- Identification and Handling of Drugs
- Narcotic Field Testing
- Criminalistics
- Sexual Assault/Rape Crisis
- Counterfeiting
- Gambling and Organized Crime
- Case Preparation

- Informants and Intelligence
- Motor Vehicle Theft
- Child Abuse
- Identification of Suspects
- Arson Awareness
- Death Cases
- Crimes Against People
- Crimes Against Property

PATROL PROCEDURES

- Accident Investigation
- Community Policing
- Crime Prevention
- Crimes in Progress
- Building Search
- Stopping Suspicious Persons/Suspects
- Handling Animals
- Crowd Control and Civil Disorder
- Domestic Violence
- Hazardous Materials
- Electrical Emergencies
- Principles and Operation of Radar
- Impaired Driving
- Breathalyzer/Intoxilyzer 5000 Certification
- Motor Vehicle Law and Enforcement
- Radio and Telephone Procedures
- 10 Codes
- Diplomatic Immunities
- Vehicle Stop Tactics
- Low-Risk Stops
- High-Risk Stops
- Civil Complaints and Service
- Note-Taking and Report Writing
- Roadblocks
- K-9 Teams

- Seized Property
- Traffic Direction and Control
- Gangs

Police academy coursework is grouped by subject and is normally taught in weeklong blocks. As with any other type of classroom training, recruits can become quite bored while sitting behind a desk for hours each day. However, there are certain subjects and practical exercises that can be quite entertaining, and they're a welcome break to the long days spent in warm classrooms.

DUI/DWI TRAINING

As demanding as it is, even academy life has its better days, like the week of Breathalyzer or Intoxilyzer5000 certification, when half the class spends a day getting drunk and the other half tests them for intoxication at various stages of drunkenness. The two groups switch places on the following day, and those with the hangovers now conduct the testing. After weeks of arduous training, these two days are a great stress reliever.

I should mention that many patrol vehicles wound up being driven home by drunken recruits at the conclusion of each of those days. The idea of driving a police car while drunk was cool—playing with the lights and sirens—but I look back on this dangerous and foolish exercise and wonder if these days are the beginning of the high substance-abuse rate among police officers. I should also mention that this particular exercise isn't practiced at all police academies.

The DUI/DWI training continues as the recruits conduct mock traffic stops of intoxicated drivers. Some academies use volunteers to represent drunk drivers. These volunteers are often off-duty police officers, attorneys, academy instructors, and even civilians. They consume alcoholic beverages in varied proportions and the recruits carry out the necessary procedures to apprehend and arrest drivers who are under the influence of either alcohol or drugs.

Prior to actual contact with a drunken subject, recruits are taught the various means of detecting a person who's driving under the influence. For instance, they're taught to look for certain behaviors, such as crossing the center line of the highway, weaving within the traffic lane, excessive braking, driving on the shoulder of the road, stopping too far away from a crossing where a stop sign or traffic light is present, running red lights or stop signs, and hesitating before or not dimming bright headlights when meeting oncoming traffic.

OFFICER SURVIVAL

Weeks pass, and recruits see their waistlines become slimmer as their endurance to physical exercise becomes greater. Their attitudes change. The class as a whole takes on the persona of a tightly knit family, each member of which would do almost anything for the others. They help each other through tough times. They study together, eat together, run together, relax together, and sweat together. They learn that they need each other to survive. Cops are taught early on to depend on one another for everything. A bond is made in the police academy that can almost never be broken.

Survival is a word that's drilled into the heads of academy recruits. They're taught that they'll survive no matter what kind of situations they're forced into. During the weeks of practical exercises, instructors set up staged scenarios both day and night, in which the recruits are placed into every situation imaginable, such as shootouts with armed robbers, assaults, sniper fire, fistfights, and stabbings. At every phase of the exercises, their teachers methodically and monotonously repeat the phrase, "You will survive."

Police training is based on repetition. Recruits are made to practice each exercise or drill over and over again, much like an animal being trained to perform a trick. These repetitive exercises are designed to cause the recruit to revert to her training—reacting instinctively and without contemplation—during stressful or emergency situations. The split second it takes to gather one's thoughts and then pull a gun in self-defense can be the difference between life and death. At the conclusion of each exercise, the recruits are graded on their performance and their ability to react appropriately for each situation.

At the close of each day of academy training comes the dreaded physical training. Recruits run miles upon miles during the many weeks of training, and they perform thousands of sit-ups and push-ups. Stamina, perseverance, and control of emotions are pushed to their limits by this point in time, but nothing they've gone through yet can compare to the week of defensive tactics training, otherwise referred to as Hell Week.

DEFENSIVE TACTICS

Hell Week is the forty-hour defensive tactics training period. During this course of instruction, recruits are taught how to defend themselves from attackers and how to subdue unruly suspects. They're taught proper handcuffing and arrest techniques, effective uses of nonlethal weapons, and personal-weapon retention.

Police officer defensive tactics techniques are based on the pain compliance techniques of the martial arts. The Japanese martial art of Aikido and the Chinese martial art of Chin Na are two of the styles used to develop those skills. Chin Na means to seize (Chin) and lock (Na). Aikido, the more modern of the two martial arts, is defined as a union of universal energy, way, and harmony. Both styles focus on controlling an attacker by locking the joints and redirecting the attacker's energy. Pain is the force behind both.

To truly learn the effectiveness of each technique, recruits must practice, and demonstrate, the painful procedures on their partners. The pain that one experiences from the application of these practical exercises is truly excruciating.

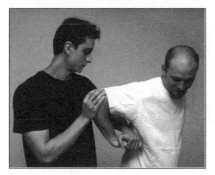

Officers practice wrist-control techniques.

When the Kotegaeshi Nage (wrist turnout) technique is correctly applied, the officer's thumb is placed on the underside of the wrist and acts as a lever. The other four fingers apply pressure to the joint.

Each recruit must successfully display his ability to perform the required techniques on both armed and unarmed attackers, and on arrest suspects. Four of the basic techniques, the wrist turnout (Kotegaeshi Nage), the twisting wrist lock (Sankyo), the gooseneck lock (Kote Mawashi), and the straight-arm bar (Ikkyo) must be learned and learned well. Other movements, techniques, and procedures are derived from these four basic fundamental maneuvers.

Each technique is practiced through repetition and normally begins with both the recruit and suspect in a standing position. A correctly performed technique ends with the criminal's hands safely handcuffed behind his back. The recruit can accomplish this from either a standing position or by performing a complete takedown to the floor, whichever the situation requires. The most effective means of subduing and handcuffing an unruly subject is for the recruit to force the suspect to the ground and hold him in a control technique.

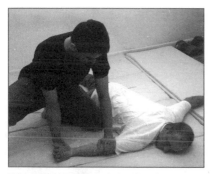

Using a combination wrist lock and arm bar, the recruit forces his partner to the ground. From this position, the recruit can easily move the controlled hand to the small of the suspect's back and apply handcuffs.

Throughout Hell Week, the recruits repeatedly strike each other with batons and fists and stretch their opponents' joints to the maximum. They toss their partners around, throw them to the floor, and handcuff them over and over again. They're kicked, pushed, pulled, and slapped, and they spray each other with pepper spray. They must also learn to disarm criminals who are wielding knives, handguns, and shotguns. They do whatever it takes to simulate any possible scenario a police officer may encounter during the course of a shift. The good guy must always win.

No matter how grueling a day of Hell Week training may be, and no matter how tired the recruits may be, when the day is over, with body parts still sore and aching, the recruits still have to run, and they still have to exercise.

DRIVER TRAINING

Driver training is in direct contrast to Hell Week. This week of driving a police car at top speeds through obstacle courses is a fun week for most of the recruits. It's almost like spending several fun-filled days at an adult theme park. This is the first time most of the recruits experience driving with lights and sirens going at full blast. They take turns chasing one another at speeds some-times more than one hundred miles per hour. It's the first taste of a real action-packed street experience for the anxious officers-to-be.

An abandoned airport runway is often the stage for police driver training. The near-mile-long stretches of pavement are dotted with hundreds of orange traffic cones that are placed into various patterns to simulate city streets, high-ways, and parking lots.

To assure the practice sessions are safe, each recruit is required to wear a crash helmet and a seat belt. The car's tires are overinflated to prevent the rub-ber from separating from the metal rims in case a driver loses control of her vehicle at a high rate of speed. A car that's sliding sideways on a rim without a tire can overturn quite easily. The metal wheel gouges into the pavement, causing the vehicle to stop abruptly and the car's momentum tips it over. The overinflation of the vehicle's tires allows the rubber to tightly grip the rim and causes the car to slide and spin like a top instead of turning over.

In case of an emergency, and for further safety, a police driver-training in-structor rides with each recruit at all times. All recruits must spin their cars out of control at some point during the driver-training portion of the academy so they can learn the correct way to regain control of their vehicles.

Some academies have the recruits attempt to maneuver their cars on a "skid pad," a section of pavement covered with water or a slippery substance, such as a mixture of water and transmission fluid. The slimy, pinkish-red flu-id simulates an icy surface. Instructors sometimes aim large streams of water from fire hoses at the recruit's windshield to reduce his visibility as he at-tempts to make his way across the skid pads.

Some academies, such as the Federal Bureau of Investigation training acad-emy in Quantico, Virginia, use specially designed skid cars on these unique driver courses. A skid car has an extra wheel at each of the four corners of the training vehicle. These wheels are attached to hydraulic cylinders which, when activated, raise the car off of the ground a few inches to render the car's normal wheels inoperable. The use of skid cars allows recruits to experience the sensation of losing control of a vehicle.

Recruits are taught to drive with their hands at the 10 and 2 positions on the steering wheel, and they're instructed never to cross one hand over the other; in-stead, they're taught to "feed the wheel" from one hand to the other as they turn. They learn to repeatedly tap the breaks when attempting to stop or slow down from high rates of speed, such as during pursuit driving. Brake pads get very hot from the friction caused by constantly applying pressure to the brake pedal.

Overheated brake pads reduce a vehicle's ability to stop. This "stab and jab" method, as it's called by some older instructors, reduces the amount of friction to the brake pads and allows them to cool down a bit between braking periods. The practice also prevents brakes from "locking up," which can cause a vehicle to skid out of control. Cars today are equipped with antilock breaking systems that are designed to automatically "stab and jab" when the need arises, especially on wet pavement.

Recruits are taught that most suspects who flee from the police during high-speed chases almost always make right-hand turns, but instructors throw in several left turns on the pre-staged courses to keep the recruits alert. Recruits are also trained to never follow the taillights of another car in case the vehicle that's being chased runs off the road or crashes. Officers have been known to follow a crook's car into ravines, ditches, lakes, and even into the path of oncoming cars. Instead, officers should always follow the course of the road and stay far enough behind the suspect vehicle to allow for emergency maneuvering and braking.

As dangerous as all this sounds, it's not unusual to hear giggles and laughter coming from inside a recruit's car as it spins violently out of control. Even rough-and-tough cops enjoy a good rollercoaster ride.

The recruits must complete each of the courses within a specified time limit and must achieve a satisfactory score on their driver tests. Time limits and acceptable scores vary for different academies and jurisdictions. As difficult as it is to avoid doing so, striking the traffic cones with the vehicle isn't permitted; if, at any time, a cone is struck, points are deducted from the driver's final score. The worst drivers of the group easily stand out, because their cars display many well-earned battle scars. When a cone is struck, the orange color rubs off, leaving a telltale mark on the car's paint.

Final practical testing is done on the last days of driver training week. Recruits who have received failing scores are allowed a final attempt to achieve a satisfactory grade after all other trainees have completed their testing. It's a daunting experience to gaze down a mile-long stretch of pavement at hundreds of traffic cones, knowing that a group of inanimate objects is standing in the way of a lifelong dream. Those who fail on their final effort are sent home to join the ranks of the unemployed.

During this week of training, the prevailing message to the recruits is again, no matter how dangerous the situation, they'll survive.

TRAFFIC DIRECTION

Directing traffic is a task that looks quite easy until an officer walks into a busy intersection for the first time and faces ten or twelve lanes of honking, fume-spewing, tire-squealing cars driven by tired, angry, and impatient drivers. I've heard a few well-seasoned officers comment that it's safer to be in a gun battle than to direct traffic.

Recruits are taught the proper methods and procedures of traffic direction, and they're schooled on what to expect when they finally set foot in a busy intersection. Then, in full uniform with brand new whistles, they're sent into an actual intersection with real traffic—sometimes even at night. Occasionally, but not often, an instructor has to untangle a mess when a nervous recruit has signaled for several opposing lanes of traffic to all proceed at once.

MOCK COURT

Another interesting and fun session for most recruits is the time spent learning to testify properly in a court of law. Recruits are taught courtroom procedures and what to say and when to say it—mainly, they're taught only to speak when spoken to. After the course, the recruits are given the opportunity to sharpen their skills in an actual courtroom setting. The recruits each participate in a mock trial. The trial is normally carried out with real attorneys and experienced officers who portray defendants, attorneys, and judges. The mock trials are sometimes videotaped to allow recruits to observe their individual performances.

GRADUATION DAY

Finally, after many weeks of grueling studies and with muscles wracked with pain, the recruits reach graduation day. They march into a banquet hall or auditorium, dressed in their best Class-A uniforms, to receive their diplomas. Some receive special awards for top academic achievements, top shooting, and top driving. At the end of the ceremony, the realization hits—they're now real police officers.

FIELD TRAINING

After graduation from the academy, each officer is required to complete many hours of field training, with a certified field training officer (FTO). Some departments mandate a field training period of up to four hundred hours. The field training program was developed by the San Jose, California, Police Department and is now the standard for most FTO programs in the country. With the field training period complete, the officer moves on to his individual assignment, which for nearly all new officers is an assignment as a patrol officer, and begins the day-in, day-out routine of answering complaints and calls. For eight hours every day, the officer responds to drunk and disorderliness, domestic disputes, fight calls, stray dogs, he said-she saids, burglaries, robberies, shots fired, false alarms, speeders, drunk drivers, child abusers, bad-check writers, and shoplifters. The next day, the routine begins all over again—nine times out of ten with the same suspects.

CHAPTER 3

POLICE OFFICERS:
THEIR DUTIES AND EQUIPMENT

Movies and television have so infused our ideas of law enforcement, giving us, again and again, this well-worn image of the archetypal, nightstick-swinging patrol officer on the beat. It is a big challenge for crime writers and readers to untangle fact from this cultural fantasy and reach something approximating (to paraphrase Raymond Chandler) the "tangled woof of fact": the actual day-to-day experience of frontline officers.

—MEGAN ABBOTT, AUTHOR OF DIE A LITTLE,
THE SONG IS YOU, AND QUEENPIN

The business of solving crimes and protecting the lives and property of American citizens is the responsibility of law enforcement. Each law enforcement agency is comprised of various divisions that function according to the individual needs of the agency's jurisdiction.

The front line of defense against criminal activity is a division of police officers called patrol officers, who are the first responders to accidents and criminal activity. Before patrol officers can respond to a crime, they must first learn of its occurrence. Officers receive the majority of their information and direction via police radio, which is normally transmitted to them by police dispatchers. A dispatcher's job begins with the ring of a 911 call—the first step in solving a crime.

POLICE DISPATCHERS

Good communication is the key to a well-run police department. Officers can't respond to calls and complaints if they don't know where to go or what to expect when they get there. It's the duty of the police dispatcher to maintain the 911 emergency terminals, answering the flood of calls from citizens. It's the dispatcher's job to obtain enough information so he can direct patrol officers and other emergency-response personnel to the scene of a crime or other emergency, such as an automobile or industrial accident or a health-related problem.

Calls pour into police station communications centers, sometimes at a rapid-fire pace. The dispatcher must sort through the caller's information— information that's often provided by callers who are irate, angry, frightened, irrational, upset, and hysterical—to determine the nature of the emergency. She must then decide what type of response is needed and by whom. Assignments are normally doled out to patrol officers, who are the first responders, on a rotating basis.

Dispatchers receive training and certifications in all phases within the scope of their job assignments. Most dispatchers attend specialized training at a police academy; however, some states allow dispatcher training and testing to be completed online.

Dispatchers are also responsible for submitting data for entry in the National Crime Information Center (NCIC) regarding wanted persons, missing persons, stolen property, emergency broadcasts, and criminal histories.

NCIC is a computer database maintained by the Federal Bureau of Investigation at their Criminal Justice Information Services Division in Clarksburg, West Virginia. It's accessible only by law enforcement agencies and is open for business around the clock, 365 days a year.

The NCIC system occasionally goes offline for maintenance, file upgrades, and purging. Downtime is brief and normally scheduled during the wee hours of the morning when officers are least likely to need instant access to information. However, many officers working the graveyard shifts during these downtimes—especially the Sunday night/Monday morning shift—often run into the problem of stopping a car for a minor traffic infraction and having no way to verify if the vehicle is stolen or if the driver of the car is wanted. Situations such as this can be highly dangerous for officers who are left without the necessary information.

The NCIC database contains information about wanted persons and stolen vehicles as well as information regarding missing persons, violent offenders, gang member identification, terrorists, embezzled or counterfeit securities, foreign fugitives, criminal histories, stolen firearms and other property, and descriptions of unidentified homicide victims.

PATROL OFFICERS

Patrol officers are the police officers with whom people are most familiar. They wear the uniform of their departments and display the badges and patches of their city, county, or state. They're the backbone of every police department, and they're the front-line defense against crime. These officers protect citizens and their property from criminal activity. Patrol officers must be constantly alert to all suspicious activity; they must be ever-vigilant for crimes-in-progress, and they must be the first responders to crime and accident scenes. Their jobs aren't easy.

Officers assigned to a patrol division or patrol units, whichever name is designated by an individual department, conduct their day-to-day business from the front seat of a patrol vehicle, a bicycle, a horse, a motorcycle, or on foot as beat officers. Their responsibility is twofold. To ensure the best use of manpower, police departments usually divide their patrol officers into two distinct divisions: routine patrol (criminal apprehension and prevention) and traffic.

It's the duty of the routine patrol division to proactively prevent crime from occurring through methods such as patrol, community policing, and surveillance. They must also react to crimes as they occur by responding to citizen complaints and through their own observations.

A traffic division is responsible for motor vehicle law enforcement and for the prevention of and investigation into all traffic accidents. The traffic division is also in charge of DUI/DWI offense enforcement and prevention.

Each division makes use of any specialized equipment, tools, and training that's available to them, such as bicycle patrol, mounted patrol, and motorcycle patrol.

Some larger police departments assign two patrol officers per vehicle. Smaller departments simply don't have the manpower to do so, and officers must rely on experience, know-how, and a quick response to calls for assistance to keep them safe. Depending on individual department policy, partner assignments may or may not be permanent. In fact, the assignment may be doled out on a day-to-day basis by the shift supervisor.

SHIFT ASSIGNMENTS

Patrol officers normally work eight-hour shifts. Those shifts divide the working day into three segments: 8:00 A.M. until 4:00 P.M., 4:00 P.M. until 12:00 A.M., and 12:00 A.M. until 8:00 A.M. Each department sets its own shift hours, and each of those individual shifts is a world all its own. The types of calls answered by officers during the 8:00 A.M. to 4:00 P.M. shift are different than those answered by the 4:00 P.M., or second-shift, officers; and the midnight, or graveyard shift, calls are even more diverse than those on either of the other two shifts.

Day-shift patrol officers resolve more issues related to nonviolent crime, such as fraud and bad-check writing, than the other shifts. Second-shift patrol officers answer the most crime-in-progress calls such as burglary and robbery. Graveyard shift patrol officers work the most violent crime cases, such as rape, homicide, and assaults. It's been my experience that the majority of serious crime occurs between the hours of 10:00 P.M. and 2:00 A.M. To effectively thwart crime during this time frame, some departments have added a fourth shift from the hours of 8:00 P.M. until 4:00 A.M. This extra shift doubles the manpower on the street during the time when criminal activity is at its highest.

Shift assignments are normally based on seniority. The newest, or rookie, patrol officers are assigned to the midnight shift; those with more years of service work the second shifts, and the senior patrol officers are given the opportunity to work the day shift. Not all patrol officers want to work during day-shift hours. There's a general consensus among patrol officers that they encounter as much, if not more, stress from their superiors as they do from criminals; therefore, some officers prefer to stay away from the 8:00 A.M.

shift when the ranking day-shift patrol officers, the mayor, and city council members are out and about observing the day-to-day operations. Each shift is supervised by either a sergeant or lieutenant.

OFFICER APPAREL

Uniformed patrol officers must wear protective clothing and gear, such as bullet-resistant vests, which can weigh between five and ten pounds. The protective clothing is often uncomfortably warm because of the clay-like density of the bullet-resistant vests worn beneath their outer garments. The vests are secured tightly around their torsos with wide Velcro straps. When the officer sits, any extra body fat or skin around his waistline is almost always pinched between the semi-rigid bottom of the vest and the top of the sturdy, leather gun belt.

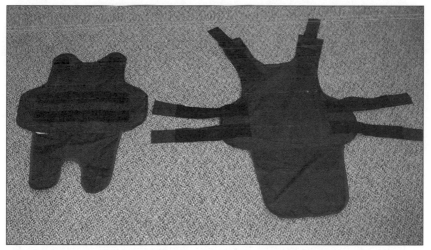

The front and rear panels of a bullet-resistant vest.

Fire-retardant shirts and pants made from thicker-than-normal material can scratch an officer's skin, and their shiny, black or brown patent leather shoes make it nearly impossible to chase a suspect who's fleeing on foot. Some departments have relaxed their strict military-type dress codes and are allowing officers to wear more practical footwear, such as walking or running shoes.

Shirts worn by uniformed patrol officers sometimes have military creases sewn into the front and back. The shirts have a built-in stain-resistant finish and a special badge tab, and the shoulders are adorned with epaulets that are sometimes used to display the pins that signify the officer's rank. Shirts are available with either button-up or zippered fronts. The zippered front permits the officer to remain neat and tidy even at the end of a scuffle. Neckties are the clip-on type to prevent an officer from being choked by suspects.

Most departments have set times of the year when particular clothing is required. Long-sleeved winter shirts and ties are worn during the winter months, and it's only on a predetermined day that officers are allowed to switch to cooler short-sleeved summer shirts. An early spring or summer can provide very uncomfortable working conditions for an officer wearing thick, long-sleeved shirts in combination with an already hot bullet-resistant vest.

Coats, jackets, and raincoats are equipped with side zippers that allow the officer easy access to her sidearms and other accessories.

TOOLS OF THE TRADE

Patrol officers carry an assortment of items on their belts that assist them in the performance of their duties. The weight of the equipment can easily exceed ten pounds and, in many cases, tops fifteen.

• **Sam Browne belt.** The Sam Browne gun belt worn by patrol officers derived its name from General Sir Sam Browne of the British Army in India. General Browne designed the heavy leather belt in the late 1800s or early 1900s to help carry the weight of the heavy pistols and sabers used by the soldiers of the day. A shoulder strap was added to the belt to assist with carrying the load.

Today's patrol officers carry much more weight on their belts, but they no longer need the shoulder straps to hold up the added weight. Instead, thin, four-inch-long leather or nylon straps, called belt keepers, circle around both the Sam Browne belt and the regular dress belt that's worn through the belt loops of the officer's pants. The belt keepers snap into place firmly and hold the gun belt around the waist. Without belt keepers, gravity would quite easily pull the Sam Browne belt, along with all its attachments, to the officer's knees.

The Sam Browne belt is made from thick leather or nylon and is approximately two and one-quarter inches wide. The buckle is removable so its wearer can slide on attachments. The leather belt can be ordered in either a basket-weave pattern, as shown here, or in a smooth black or brown finish.

Some police departments are replacing leather gear with nylon because nylon is much lighter. In addition, nylon tends to repel contaminates, such as body fluids.

Sam Browne belt.

- **Pepper spray and case.** The chemical spray used by patrol officers is oleoresin capsicum (O.C. spray), more commonly called mace. Mace is actually a company brand name assigned to a number of police-related supplies and equipment. Mace products are so widely used by patrol officers that the name has become a nickname for all chemical sprays.

Oleoresin capsicum, or pepper spray, is made from peppers in the chili-pepper family, such as jalapeños and habaneras. Capsicum, an alkaloid, is extracted from the vegetable's stem just above the seeds. This alkaloid produces the "heat" in pepper sprays.

Pepper sprays have become a very popular nonlethal tool for patrol officers. The spray is used in situations where there's a probability of the officer becoming injured by a violent suspect, or when a suspect is resisting arrest. When sprayed, a violent suspect is normally incapacitated for a few minutes, which allows the officer to effectively apply restraints.

- **Semiautomatic pistol and security holster.** Modern-day police arm themselves with semiautomatic pistols, which are capable of storing and firing multiple rounds of ammunition. Most semiautomatics carried by patrol of-

.40 caliber semi-automatic pistol and security holster.

ficers hold a total of fifteen or sixteen rounds. Patrol officers wear security holsters to prevent a prisoner or criminal from removing their weapons during a scuffle or escape attempt. Officers must perform a series of actions to take their guns out of the holsters. This secret sequence is known only to the wearer of the holster.

- **Magazines (clips) and magazine holders.** Patrol officers must carry spare ammunition with them at all times in case they get involved in a gun battle with criminals. Officers who carry semiautomatic handguns carry their extra ammunition in preloaded magazines. Each magazine holds multiple rounds. The double magazine pictured below holds two magazines and allows easy access by its wearer. The officer normally wears the holder on the front of her gun belt.

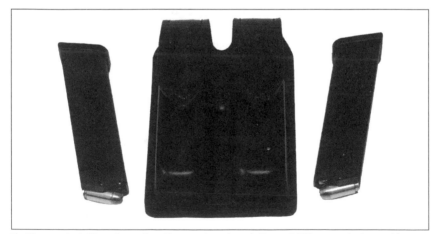

Double magazine holder and magazines. The magazines shown hold a total of fifteen rounds of ammunition.

- **Speed loaders (six rounds each).** Speed loaders were designed to assist with the loading of six-shot revolvers. Each speed loader holds six rounds of ammunition. Bullets for the revolvers are placed and clipped into the loader in slots that correspond with the bullet chambers of a revolver's cylinder. Once the bullets are in place, a twist of a tiny, knurled knob releases the rounds, enabling the shooter to load all six bullets in a single motion.

Speed-loader pouches are designed to carry two fully loaded speed loaders. The double pouches are normally carried on the front of the Sam Browne belt for easy access by officers.

- **Flashlight.** Flashlights are a must-have tool for all patrol officers. They come in all shapes and sizes and are made from either metal or heavy plastic. Some patrol cars are equipped with rechargeable flash-

Speed loader.

lights, assuring the officers of a flashlight that's ready for use at all times.

Patrol officers have sometimes used metal flashlights as weapons. To eliminate the possibility of inflicting severe harm on suspects, some departments require their officers to use only plastic flashlights. Some police academies have training sessions on how to use flashlights as weapons, while others forbid their use for that purpose.

Flashlights are worn on a belt ring located on the opposite side from the officer's service weapon (handgun). Officers are taught to hold flashlights away from their bodies to prevent criminals from using the light source as a target during a nighttime gun battle.

- **Mini-flashlight.** Patrol officers carry mini-flashlights as a spare source of light, in the event their main flashlight becomes inoperable or broken. Pressure-point tactics allow mini-flashlights to be used on a suspect's fingers, wrists, chests, ankles, nose, and ear lobes as pain-compliance and distraction devices. Officers are taught how to use these techniques during their police academy training.

• **PR-24 or side-handle baton.** A PR-24 is a restraint-and-control device that can be used as both an offensive and defensive weapon. The side-handle baton's main use is to allow an officer to gain control of a suspect by using leverage combined with takedown maneuvers.

Striking a suspect with a PR-24 isn't generally permitted by police agencies because of the severe amount of force that can be delivered while executing any of the various techniques. Officers are trained to use striking techniques only in life-or-death situations or where there's a possibility of serious bodily harm to the officer or an innocent person. The baton is made from a high-density plastic called polycarbonate, and it can withstand five thousand pounds of force. An officer must attend training and be certified to carry and use a PR-24.

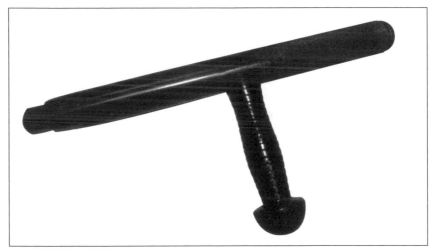

PR-24 or side-handle baton.

• **Portable radio and holder.** Communication equipment is a must for all patrol officers. Handheld portable radios are part of a police officer's arsenal. Today's portable radios can reach far greater distances than the old two-way walkie-talkies. Police departments use a series of communications towers equipped with "repeaters" that relay, or repeat, radio signals. The signals are first sent from the portable unit to a trunk-mounted repeater located in the patrol car. The transmissions are then relayed from the car's repeater to a tower, where the message is repeated from one tower to another until it reaches its destination. This process is completed instantly, without delay. Some portable radios are equipped with a panic button. A wounded officer can simply depress the button to summon aid. His location is identified on an electronic map using global positioning technology.

• **Taser.** Tasers are a nonlethal alternative for use by officers attempting to subdue violent suspects. The device fires two barbed probes capable of delivering eighteen to twenty-six watts of electricity (fifty thousand volts). The probes can penetrate up to two inches of clothing. Each unit is powered by a combination of several AA batteries and two compressed-air cartridges containing 1800 pounds per square inch (PSI) of compressed nitrogen or carbon dioxide. Two types of cartridges are available, which allow the device to propel the probes at distances of either fifteen or twenty-one feet.

Tasers are designed to override the central nervous system of a disorderly suspect by delivering electricity directly to the skeletal muscles. Those muscles contract until the target suspect can no longer stand. In fact, the suspect usually ends up lying on the ground in a fetal position.

Tasers are effective against suspects who are under the influence of drugs such as PCP, and, unlike lethal weapons, the takedown capability of Tasers remains the same no matter where the probes contact the body.

Taser.

There's been some recent controversy regarding Taser use by patrol officers. Some say officers are too quick to use the devices, and several deaths have been thought to be directly related to Taser use. These incidents are rare and are currently under investigation. Most police departments, police instructors, and the weapons' manufacturers still insist that the Taser is a safe and effective tool for use by police departments.

• **Handcuffs.** Handcuffs have been around in various forms for hundreds of years. Before the mid-1800s handcuffs were only available in one size. The universal cuffs were simple metal rings that looped around an offender's wrists and locked at the point where the loops joined. These one-size-fits-all handcuffs were very uncomfortable for large people and they allowed slender people an excellent opportunity to escape custody.

Chain-link and hinged handcuffs, leg irons, waist chain.

In 1862, a man named W.V. Adams saw the need to make handcuffs adjustable and designed a ratchet locking system that could accommodate wrists of all sizes. The first patent for handcuffs was issued to Adams and his partner, Orson Phelps, in 1874.

The two most popular handcuff styles used by law enforcement are the chain link and the hinged. Both are made from carbon steel and can withstand a pulling pressure of more than one thousand pounds.

Chain-link handcuffs are the most widely used by street cops because the single connecting chain allows for the easiest application. Hinged cuffs are somewhat difficult to apply during a struggle because of their lack of flexibility. They're more widely used in transporting felons from jails, prisons, and lockups. The hinge that separates the two cuffs greatly restricts the movement of a suspect's hands.

Both styles of handcuffs feature two locking systems. One is the familiar ratchet lock (two sets of interlocking teeth) that automatically catches when the cuffs are placed around a wrist. The second is a push-pin lock that serves as a safety, locking the ratchet in place and preventing the handcuffs from tightening further.

- **Handcuff keys.** Handcuff keys come in all kinds of shapes and sizes. The L-shaped end of the key is inserted into the keyhole to release the locking devices. The pin protruding from the opposite end of the key activates the small push-pin lock located on the handcuffs.

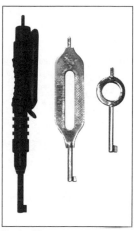
Handcuff keys.

To unlock handcuffs that have been double-locked with both the ratchet lock and the push-pin lock, the officer inserts the L-shaped portion of the key into the keyhole and turns it to the left, ninety degrees. This action releases the ratchet. The officer must then rotate the key in the opposite direction a full 180 degrees to release the push-pin lock. Simply put, the officer turns the key first to the left as far as it will go, then back to the right as far as it will go.

- **Handcuff case.** Handcuff cases are designed to hold either one or two pairs of chain-link and/or hinged cuffs and are usually worn on the rear of the gun belt—in the center—to allow for access with either hand.

PATROL VEHICLES

Officers rely on many tools in the performance of their duties, and one of the most important tools at their disposal is the patrol vehicle. The majority of a patrol officer's time is spent behind the steering wheel of this car. The patrol vehicle isn't just a means of transportation—it also serves as the officer's mobile office, a storage area for equipment, a safe haven from dangerous situations, and an observation post to watch for criminal activity.

The brand of vehicle used by police departments is determined by a bidding process. The manufacturer that can meet the production specifications and departmental demands with the lowest price will normally receive the contract.

A patrol vehicle isn't all that different from a normal passenger car. Patrol vehicles are regular cars that have been equipped with a "police package" that's comprised of heavy-duty suspension, brakes, tires, cooling system, and transmission. The engines are usually the same engines that are installed in an average high-performance car.

Patrol vehicles are also modified to accommodate the extra wiring requirements of lights, antennas, and sirens. They can also be equipped with rear-door and window locks that can only be operated by the driver. Patrol vehicles assigned to canine officers are often equipped with rear doors that lock and unlock and open and close via remote control. This feature allows the officer to release her dog from a distance should she need assistance with apprehending a suspect or controlling a dangerous situation.

Other equipment such as push bumpers, hidden lighting, radio equipment, computer terminals, shotgun mounting brackets, weapon lockboxes, light bars, radar equipment, sirens, and camera equipment is often installed by the department's vehicle maintenance technicians or motor-pool mechanics.

Screens made from a combination of steel mesh, aluminum, and Plexiglas separate the rear passenger compartment of patrol vehicles from the front driver's seat. The heavy screens provide a secure area in the rear compartment for the transporting of prisoners. The compartment also provides safety for both the driver and the prisoner. Before the safety screens were available an extra officer had to ride in the back seat to prevent the prisoner from interfering with the driver and to prevent offenders from harming themselves.

Older patrol officers often reflect on the days when the screens were fabricated from welded-wire mesh, much like grates over storm drains. These old-timers frequently used the dog-in-the-road trick to bring unruly prisoners under control. The driver would slam on the brakes saying, "Did you see that dog?" The handcuffed prisoner's unprotected face would smash into the steel barrier. Any disruptive behavior ceased immediately. The dog-in-the-road trick was much more effective when it was implemented in a paddy wagon or a transport van, in which the traditional seats had been removed and replaced with smooth, wooden benches. Not only was the metal screen a hazard, but prisoners were often tossed and rolled about in the back of the van. Needless to say, this practice is dangerous, cruel, and illegal.

The interiors of patrol vehicles are equipped with oversized, extra-bright, overhead dome lights. These provide proper lighting for officers when they're completing reports and filling in the blanks on a traffic summons. Officers activate these lights with a switch on the light itself that operates independently from the normal on-off switch in the door frame. For the safety of the patrol officers, the lights that normally come on when car doors open are often disconnected in patrol vehicles. These lights can illuminate officers at inopportune moments, making them targets for criminals.

Officers use toggle-type rocker switches to operate the various strobe lights and rotating beacons mounted in the roof light bars, rear windows, dashboards, front grill, headlights, taillights, and any other place of possible concealment.

TRAFFIC DIVISION

Patrol officers who work in the traffic division are responsible for the enforcement of motor vehicle laws. These officers work radar and DUI/DWI enforcement and investigate traffic accidents. Their primary duty, through the enforcement of traffic codes and laws, is to reduce the number of accidents on the roadways of their jurisdictions. They're also responsible for a great deal of extra municipal income from the fines they collect for various infractions of the law.

Traffic fines can increase a city or county's revenue by millions of dollars. The lure of that much extra money has some departments paying patrol officers a higher rate of pay during their off-hours to catch speeding motorists. Many communities have become known nationwide as speed traps due to their very aggressive speed enforcement.

Radar is an acronym for radio detection and ranging. The radar devices most often used by patrol officers—Doppler radar units—emit a continuous frequency and then receive that frequency's echo after it has reflected from the target vehicle (the speeder). Doppler radar units are capable of determining the speed of moving vehicles while the patrol vehicle is sitting still (stationary radar) and while it's in motion (moving radar).

In stationary radar, the radar unit instantly calculates the difference between the two frequencies. That variation is then converted into miles per hour—the target vehicle's traveling speed.

In moving radar, the unit must process more than one reflected signal. To do so, it first determines the patrol vehicle's rate of speed. This is accomplished by the radar unit transmitting a signal that reflects from the roadway surface

Radar units display both the target vehicle's speed and the speed of the officer's patrol vehicle.

and the surrounding landscape. The signal is reflected back to the unit's antenna where it's converted into the patrol vehicle's miles per hour. That speed is displayed as *patrol speed* on a small digital screen on the front of the radar unit. Simultaneously, the radar unit sends another signal that reflects from oncoming or receding vehicles. These signals are reflected back to the unit. The two speeds are combined by the unit, which then calculates the difference between the patrol vehicle and the speeding car. The speed of the target automobile is then displayed in the *target* window on the face of the radar unit.

If the patrol vehicle and the target vehicle are moving toward one another at identical speeds, no speed displays in either the patrol speed or target windows. Since moving radar is based on the patrol vehicle's speed, all patrol vehicle speedometers used for radar operation must be regularly calibrated for accuracy.

Radar units can pick up a vehicle's speed at distances as close as one hundred feet and as far away as one mile. Smoke, dust, and moisture don't affect the accuracy of the units, only their range.

Patrol officers who operate radar units are required to successfully complete and pass a basic radar operator's training course. The course is normally a forty-hour class with instruction on motor vehicle law regarding speed and the proper operation of various types of radar units.

Officers are required to calibrate each radar unit at the beginning and end of their shifts. To do so, they strike a tuning fork that's designed to simulate a vehicle's speed, such as sixty miles per hour. Then they hold the vibrating tuning fork in front of the unit's antenna (the part we see mounted on the outside of the patrol vehicle or the handheld radar gun). The tuning fork's frequency is received by the antenna and is converted into traveling speed. A reading of sixty miles per hour should be displayed on the unit's dash-mounted digital readout. A second tuning fork is struck, simulating thirty-five miles per hour, and the same procedure is followed. If the machine accurately displays both speeds, it's deemed to be operating appropriately.

Patrol officers aren't required to show the digital readout to speeders. Most states require patrol officers who are working radar to be in full uniform, and they must display their badges of authority in plain view.

Laser radar operates on a much simpler principle than Doppler radar. It simply emits a short burst of infrared light, and the light travels to the targeted vehicle where it's reflected back to the radar unit. The laser unit then calculates how long, in nanoseconds, the light took to travel to and from the speeding car.

Laser radar is accurate and easy for officers to use. They simply point the device at a car that's suspected of speeding and

Laser radar unit.

then pull a trigger that operates like the trigger on a pistol. Almost instantly the car's speed and its distance from the officer are displayed numerically on a digital readout on the rear of the unit. Laser radar units are a bit more expensive than other radar devices, but their accuracy and ease of use often justify the price.

DUI/DWI ENFORCEMENT

DUI/DWI (driving under the influence or driving while intoxicated, depending on the state) is a criminal offense—a misdemeanor that can carry a penalty of up to one year in jail with the possibility of accompanying fines. A DUI/DWI conviction can result in the loss of driving privileges, and the offender's driver's license may be revoked.

In most states, it's presumed that a person is legally intoxicated when his blood-alcohol concentration (BAC) is 0.08, meaning when the ratio of alcohol in his bloodstream is 0.08 grams of alcohol per 100 milliliters of blood.

A person's level of intoxication can be amplified by synergism, the multiplicative effect of combining alcohol and drugs. Genetics and a person's chronic use of alcohol can also alter the effects of alcohol.

Once alcohol is consumed, nothing can remove it from the person's system except time and normal digestion, metabolism, evaporation, and excretion. The metabolism (the body's means of converting food into energy) of alcohol begins immediately after consumption. Typically the body metabolizes approximately .015 of blood alcohol per hour; therefore, someone who has a BAC of .15 after his last drink will have no measurable alcohol in his body after ten hours.

The level of alcohol in a body can be measured as soon as forty to seventy minutes after the person has consumed one drink. Excretion of alcohol through urine begins in about forty to fifty minutes after the drink has been consumed. The body breaks down approximately 90 percent of alcohol in the liver and 1 to 3 percent of alcohol through the elimination of urine; a scant 0.5 percent is eliminated through sweat and tears. The rest is released by evaporation through breathing.

People try many things when attempting to fool the police and the machines they use to measure a suspect's BAC. They place copper pennies in their mouths, chew gum, eat candy, and spit. They even try eating raw onions.

None of these methods are effective. Coffee won't make someone sober; it only increases the drinker's need to use the restroom.

Patrol officers are trained observers, and they're not easily deceived when driving behind a drunk driver. They're taught to be aware of certain signs that show a person is driving while intoxicated or under the influence of drugs. Some of the indicators of a drunk driver include:

- crossing the center line
- weaving within the travel lane
- excessive braking
- failing to dim headlights when meeting oncoming cars
- driving somewhere other than a designated roadway
- straddling the center line
- stopping in the middle of the roadway for no apparent reason
- almost striking other cars or stationary objects
- driving with headlights off
- traveling above or below the specified speed limit

Sometimes officers pass a suspect vehicle close enough to see a driver displaying certain physical signs that indicate a drunk driver. An intoxicated driver sometimes grips the steering wheel much too tightly; her gaze is often unwavering and fixed straight ahead; she may sit with her face too close to the windshield as if attempting to see better; and she may even be drinking alcoholic beverages as she drives.

When patrol officers initiate a traffic stop, they begin to look for signs of drunk driving. Drivers who are under the influence of drugs and/or alcohol sometimes swerve abruptly from one side of the road to the other when they first notice blue lights flashing behind them. They may not respond to lights and sirens. They sometimes drive for miles before finally realizing a patrol vehicle is behind them. I've been behind a suspected drunk driver who, when I activated my blue lights and siren, instantly slammed on his brakes, causing his car to come to a sudden stop just inches in front of my patrol vehicle. I've also witnessed inebriated drivers hit the curb when they tried to stop; they've driven onto sidewalks, and they've pulled their cars into ditches thinking they were parking on the shoulder of the roadway. They stop and, thinking they're shifting into park, put their car into reverse; then they step out of the car while it moves slowly backward.

Erratic driving provides patrol officers ample probable cause to conduct a traffic stop. Once the stop is made, officers begin to look for other telltale signs of a DUI/DWI offense, such as a red, flushed face; slurred speech; the odor of alcoholic beverages coming from the driver's breath or elsewhere inside the car; bloodshot or watery eyes; and difficulty communicating. The odor associated with alcoholic beverages isn't the aroma of the actual alcohol; it's actually the combined scents of additives that are mixed with the beverage during the fermentation process. Toxins that are produced as a result of fermentation also provide their own smells. Pure alcohol is nearly odorless.

Drunk drivers may also exhibit difficulty maintaining balance, and they may stumble or sway when they attempt to walk. Inebriated drivers frequently place a hand on top of their cars in an attempt to steady themselves when talking to the officer. They often provide inappropriate or unusual answers to officer's questions.

One of my standard questions to ask suspected drunk drivers was, "Have you been drinking any alcoholic beverages?" Surprisingly, many people answered the question truthfully, which is great evidence in a court proceeding. One man in particular was a little too honest for his own good. He looked hurt and appalled that I would ask him such a question. His response, complete with a roll of the eyes accompanied by a condescending, disgusted tone of voice, was, "No sir. I don't drink. That stuff'll kill you. I just smoked a little marijuana and snorted just a wee bit of coke before I left the party."

Drunk drivers also can run the gamut of emotions from being overly cheerful and happy to acting rude and combative. Officers frequently ask suspected drunk drivers how much they've had to drink, and the most common response is, "Two beers (drinks)." I've seen drivers who were barely able to stand due to the extreme amount of alcohol they'd consumed, and their responses were the same.

When an officer suspects a driver is under the influence of either alcohol or drugs, he may ask the driver to step outside of the car and perform a series of field sobriety tests, such as standing on one leg for a short period of time or reciting numbers or the alphabet in succession. The officer may ask the driver to walk several steps away from him, pivot, turn, and return to the original spot. Another test is the well-known process of having the driver close his eyes, tilt his head back, and touch the tip of his nose with the tip of his right index finger, then repeat the step with his left hand.

Patrol officers who have received the appropriate training have yet another tool in their arsenal against drunk drivers—they're qualified to test for a person's horizontal gaze nystagmus (HGN). Human eyes have a natural ability to track objects moving in any direction. Alcohol consumption slows this ability to track and causes an involuntary jerking of the eyeball called nystagmus. Nystagmus can be horizontal, vertical, rotary, or a combination of either, but it's usually the onset of HGN that's of interest to patrol officers.

Alcohol stimulates nerve endings in the eyes, causing nystagmus to become more pronounced in intoxicated people. As the level of alcohol in the body rises, the eyes' reaction to tracking side-to-side movement occurs sooner—the more intoxicated a person is, the less the eyes move to either side before the jerking motion begins.

Officers test a suspect's HGN by first verifying that both pupils are of equal size. When the officer's satisfied that both eyes function equally (if not, there may be a medical condition present and the test must be aborted), they hold an object such as a pen approximately twelve to fifteen inches in front of the suspect's nose, keeping the pen's tip slightly above eye level. The suspect is instructed to focus on the tip of the pen, face forward without moving, and follow the movement of the pen with her eyes.

The officer then slowly and smoothly moves the ink pen forty-five degrees to the left, then back to the front. He then performs the same movement to the suspect's right side. During the pen's movement, the officer looks at the suspect's eyes, watching as she pursues the progress of the pen. If the suspect has consumed alcohol, her eyes will normally begin to show signs of nystagmus at some point as they move to each side.

The officer is looking for three signs of intoxication in each eye—the eye's lack of smooth tracking, obvious nystagmus at the forty-five degree angle (maximum deviation), and the onset of nystagmus prior to the maximum forty-five degree angle. If four or more signs are present, that person is considered to have a BAC of .10—well above the legal limit of .08. An officer should conduct an HGN test at least three times to provide consistency.

These hand-eye coordination, balance, and thought processing tests are designed to provide officers with more evidence toward proving the driver is intoxicated.

There are many people who have various illnesses, impairments, or difficulty with the performance of this type of physical testing; therefore, drivers

A holding cell or "drunk tank." Solid doors with tray slots have replaced bars.

aren't required by law to perform any field sobriety tests. However, most states have implied consent laws, meaning that any person operating a motor vehicle on the roads, streets, and highways of the state must submit to either a breath or blood test when instructed to do so by a patrol officer. Refusal to do so is usually a misdemeanor that carries penalties and fines similar to DUI/DWI offense. A refusal to submit to either a breath or blood test may also result in the revocation or suspension of a driver's license.

The DataMaster, Breathalyzer, and Intoxilyzer 5000 are machines used by police to measure the amount of alcohol in the blood. These machines don't detect alcohol that's in the air or in the suspect's breath; instead, they measure the ratio between the concentration of alcohol in the blood and the concentration of alcohol in deep lung air. When someone drinks alcohol, the alcohol is dispersed from the bloodstream into tiny air sacs in the lungs called alveoli. It's at this exchange point that the machines calculate the ratio and convert it into the percent of alcohol that's in the tested person's bloodstream. The average ratio of breath alcohol concentration to blood alcohol content is 2100:1.

Operators of the breath-testing devices must complete a certification course and must recertify regularly. Officers who haven't attended training may not perform breath testing on a person suspected of a DUI/DWI offense.

A DUI/DWI arrest can result in the driver spending at least a few hours in a jail cell. In fact, it's not unusual for the offender to be incarcerated overnight while he waits for a family member or friend to post bail and assume responsibility for him. Magistrates can also order the drunk driver to be held without bail until he's had time to sober up, meaning the alcohol and its side effects have been purged from his system.

Holding cells for those who have been arrested for DUI/DWI, or for being intoxicated in public, are usually large cells—often referred to as drunk tanks in TV shows—capable of holding several prisoners at once, and some facilities are reserved just for drunks. The concrete-walled cells are often overcrowded, forcing many inmates to sleep on the floor, on a single mattress coated with hard plastic, or—if mattresses are in short supply—a folded wool blanket. Two-inch-thick pillows made from the same hard plastic are handed out on a first-come, first-serve basis, and drunks are usually last in line to receive pillows. A solitary stainless steel combination sink and toilet is shared by all. It stands in full view of everyone, prisoners and jail employees alike.

The constant influx of new arrivals and the release of offenders sometimes prevent proper cleaning and disinfecting of holding cells, and more often than not the cell floors and walls are littered with a concoction of debris, urine, hair, blood, fecal matter, and spilled food. To spend even one minute in a small, dirty jail cell is bad enough, but falling asleep or passing out while drunk and then waking up with a hangover in that same cell makes matters even worse.

Wall-mounted steel plates serve as "beds." When all beds are full, prisoners are forced to sleep on the concrete floor.

Hangovers are the result of the body desperately trying to rid itself of toxins by producing enzymes that attempt to purge the poisons. However, when the toxin level reaches a point higher than the body's ability to remove it, the stomach becomes irritated, the person feels sick, and headaches and vomiting can occur.

Alcohol is a diuretic, which means it increases the body's

urine output. The body is then depleted of water, which further complicates the problem and increases the effects of the hangover.

A person who's been convicted for driving under the influence of drugs and/or alcohol faces the possibility of a suspended driver's license, court-ordered rehabilitation, a fine, jail time, and—if his drunk driving resulted in the injury or death of another person—a prison sentence.

A single toilet/sink combination is shared by all.

MOUNTED PATROL

Patrol officers assigned to mounted patrols must attend a ten-to-twelve-week training period in addition to their basic academy training. After their training, they conduct their routine patrols on horseback.

Several breeds of horses are used in police work, such as Morgan horses, Arabians, Percheron draft horses, Percheron/Thoroughbred cross horses, and Tennessee Walking horses. Horses chosen for police duty are large (15.2 hands or taller), strong animals with even temperaments. Most departments find it best to use animals between the ages of eight and twelve years old.

The horses selected for service can be donated to or purchased by the departments, and they must have a suitable disposition for the work they're required to perform. These animals are often subjected to large crowds of unruly people, gunshots, and having objects thrown at them. It can take special police-equestrian trainers anywhere from four to six months to train a horse to be street-ready.

Officers on horseback are able to patrol areas not normally accessible to vehicles, such as park trails. Mounted police patrols are highly visible and are often used daily as part of regular patrol assignments. They're also very effective for crowd control and special events.

Police horses are very well cared for. They're fed twice a day, exercised, given supplemental vitamins, petted, groomed, and checked regularly by veterinarians. A horse and its police officer rider quickly form a bond and become a team.

During inclement weather, officers assigned to a mounted patrol detail may be reassigned to a patrol vehicle or other duties as needed.

BICYCLE PATROL

Officers selected for bicycle patrol duty must be in excellent physical condition. They spend their eight-hour shifts patrolling areas that are normally not accessible to officers in vehicles, such as walking trails, public bike paths, parks, and areas where special events and public gatherings take place. Bike patrols are not only effective because of their off-road abilities; they're excellent in situations that require a stealthy approach.

Bike patrol officers are highly visible, and their presence within the communities they patrol creates safer neighborhoods. They're also able to supply a more personal approach to law enforcement because they're essentially outside—not confined to a vehicle—and can converse with people as they ride through their patrol districts.

Bikes used by departments for patrol are often mountain-type, multi-speed bikes made from lightweight aluminum with heavy-duty suspensions. They're equipped with containers for various police equipment and are painted in matte or flat-black finishes for stealth-type patrol or in bright colors for high-visibility community relations and policing.

Officers working bicycle patrol normally have a patrol vehicle assigned to them as well. The patrol vehicles are equipped with bicycle mounting racks, which allow officers to transport their bikes from one location to another.

SWAT

Special weapons and tactics, or SWAT, units are specially trained teams of police officers (both patrol officers and detectives) who respond to particularly dangerous situations. SWAT teams are equipped with high-tech weapons and equipment, such as machine guns, concussion grenades (flash-bangs), high-powered rifles used by SWAT snipers, and night-vision scopes and goggles. Some SWAT

SWAT sniper.

units are equipped with armored vehicles and aircraft.

These highly skilled officers are combat trained, much like the military. They undergo rigorous physical training and are required to maintain a regular physical fitness program. SWAT officers must be extremely proficient in their use of firearms and hand-to-hand combat.

SWAT team membership begins with an officer's application to the unit. The application must be accompanied by a letter of interest stating why the officer wants to join the SWAT team. A letter of recommendation from the officer's supervisor must also be provided to the SWAT team commander.

Officers who are selected as members of the team must be proficient with firearms. They must regularly shoot an average score of 80 to 90 percent during their first year as a SWAT team member. Each year thereafter, their scores must average at 90 percent or better on each of the required courses. The scoring requirement to become a sniper is even higher. Team members train regularly with handguns, rifles, shotguns, and submachine guns (subguns). Each member is trained and practices to become quite skilled in firing the .223 caliber semiautomatic M16 Bushmaster rifle.

Snipers are trained to fire rifles such as the Remington 700, which is sometimes equipped with a night-vision scope. The Remington 700 is a favorite weapon of the U.S. Marine Corps. It's a bolt-action rifle that weighs approximately four kilograms without the scope and fires .223 caliber ammunition. Under good conditions—clear weather, no wind or smog—a sniper can fire the 700 with accuracy at a range of more than 860 yards, the length of nearly nine football fields.

SWAT training is intense and extremely demanding. Standards for SWAT teams nationwide were established in 1983 by the elite SWAT team of the Los Angeles County Sheriff's Department. Along with the standards, they also formed the National Tactical Officers Association (NTOA), which is responsible for the basic and in-service training of SWAT teams all across the country.

At least once each year SWAT teams renew their certifications, and at other times they undergo specialty training. Areas of special SWAT training include:

- booby trap and explosive recognition
- use of ballistic shields
- covert operations
- building searches
- room clearing
- warrant service
- shooting at moving targets from various locations
- shooting from various angles
- shooting in dim or no light
- counter-ambush tactics
- quelling critical situations in special areas, such as hospitals, schools, and factories
- prison cell extraction of violent inmates
- ground fighting
- knife fighting
- stick fighting
- rappelling
- neutralizing suicide and homicide bombers
- chemical agents
- counterterrorism
- counteracting barricaded suspects

SWAT teams are normally deployed for high-risk search warrant service, hostage rescues, building searches, manhunts, armed robberies, and drug raids. Teams use speed and stealth to quell volatile situations; their presence reduces the risk of injury to police, citizens, and criminals. Canine units are often assigned to SWAT units to assist with criminal apprehension and building searches.

A SWAT high-risk entry team normally consists of six to ten officers (preferably ten). The first officer on the team strikes the door with a battering ram and steps to the side to allow the rest of the team to enter. That officer then brings up the rear. The next officer tosses in a concussion grenade, or flash-bang, which generates a small explosion and emits a small amount of smoke. Its purpose is to distract the occupants of a house and provide enough cover to allow the officers to enter safely.

Simultaneously, as the front door is breached and the flash-bang explodes, other officers who've been stationed at other doors and windows initiate their part of the entry procedure—the rake and break. Raking and breaking is the breaking in of all the other doors and windows of rooms where there are no exits to the outside. Officers who break in the other doors secure those areas by aiming their automatic weapons through the open windows. Anyone in those rooms are ordered to lay on the floor with their arms outstretched—palms facing upward—so officers can see what, if anything, is in their hands. All suspects are held at gunpoint until the entry team arrives in each of the rooms to handcuff them.

The entry team divides into teams of two and moves from one room to the other, making sure there's no one in the room. The team supervisor normally remains in the first room entered and choreographs the search via radio, sending team members to wherever they're needed. Each SWAT team member has a hands-free microphone positioned near his mouth. The radio activation button is mounted on the chest area of his level-three ballistic vests (on the non-gun-hand side) for easy access. A single touch allows him to contact team members.

When the entire dwelling has been given the "all clear" by the SWAT commander, detectives who've been waiting outside enter the house to begin their investigation, evidence collection, and interrogations and interviews.

CHAPTER 4

DETECTIVES

Ever see a cartoon character run off a cliff? He runs beautifully—until he looks down. Writing a novel is like running through the air; it's all about confidence. Confidence is the key requirement for crime writers lacking a background in law enforcement. Without it, no one will believe our stories. In this chapter, we are effortlessly taken through every facet of a detective's job. Sure, we get the facts—plenty of them. But the facts are integrated in such a way that we begin to understand the culture behind the detective. This is what gives us the self-assurance to make the detective's world our own.

—J. CARSON BLACK, AUTHOR OF DARKNESS ON THE EDGE OF TOWN
AND DARK SIDE OF THE MOON

Many uniformed police officers who work their way up the chain of command strive either to obtain the position of a uniformed supervisor or move into what some officers think of as the ultimate police job—a detective.

How an officer becomes a detective varies with each individual department. Some departments offer the position as a promotion. These departments post the vacant position and officers apply and test for the job, and the most qualified person receives the advancement. Promotions, or assignments to a detective division, aren't normally awarded to officers until they've completed at least five years of service. Other departments take the rivalry between uniformed officers and the plainclothes detectives into account and simply assign officers to a detective's position on a rotating basis, which allows every officer a turn as an investigator.

A detective is responsible for the investigation of both misdemeanor and felony crimes. How each department carries out these investigations depends upon the size of the department. Some departments are large enough to have detectives who specialize in certain areas such as credit card fraud, homicide, juvenile crime, arson, narcotics, rape, vice, etc. (We'll look at some of these areas in greater detail later in the chapter.) Detectives sometimes work in several specialized areas before finding one they like. Once they do, they usually make that area their permanent assignment.

Other departments have only a couple of detectives for the entire agency— if any. In some rural departments where manpower is limited, patrol officers serve as first responders, evidence technicians, and investigators. There are advantages to each situation. The specialized detective becomes very skilled at his particular craft, whereas a detective or patrol officer in a smaller department has the opportunity, out of necessity, to work all kinds of cases.

No matter what the assignment, the duties are the same. Detectives are investigators who gather facts and collect evidence in criminal cases. They conduct interviews and interrogations, examine records and documents, observe the activities of suspects, and participate in and conduct raids or arrests. A detective is usually charged with applying for and obtaining search warrants. To accomplish these tasks effectively, detectives are trained with a more diverse approach than patrol officers.

Both detectives and patrol officers are required to attend, at minimum, semiannual in-service training to stay abreast of new laws and procedures. In addition to the in-service training, a detective's education must be endlessly updated, and his base of knowledge must be constantly expanded. Criminals are continually developing new ideas and methods to get around the law, and the detective has to make every effort to stay one step ahead of them.

Modern criminals are more highly educated than offenders of the past, and today's crooks rehearse and practice every aspect of their craft, like actors studying for a Broadway production. The thugs even hone their shooting skills. I was once searching the trunk of a drug dealer's vehicle and found an automatic weapon, several rounds of ammunition, and a police silhouette target. The center of the target was filled with bullet holes, and *Lee Lofland* was written above the head. That was an eye-opener.

There are many new ways to fight crime in today's computer and technology age, but nothing can compare to the old-fashioned method of the detective getting out and beating the streets for information and clues.

The image of the detective has changed as well. It has evolved from the trench-coat-wearing sleuth to a more stylishly dressed investigator. That image possibly reflects a larger clothing allowance than was once provided by departments. I think, years ago, I wore the long coat not because I was cold, but to cover my outdated cheap suits. All my sport coats had torn linings from years of friction caused by my gun's hammer constantly rubbing against the fabric. When I began my career, the pay was around $8,400 annually, with no clothing allowance. Also in those days, we had to buy our own guns, handcuffs, flashlights, raincoats, ticket books, and shoes. Oh yeah, and bullets. If we thought we might need them, we purchased a handful of those as well.

Today, all expenses are paid by the officer's department, including clothing allowances for undercover officers who sometimes must wear really unusual clothing in order to blend in with their working environment.

A case begins with the commission of a crime. Uniformed patrol officers are often the first officers on the scene, and they gather the pertinent information—the who, what, where, why, when, and how, if available. It's the duty of the uniformed patrol officer to secure the scene until a detective or the officer in charge relieves him. The officer who gathers the information later passes it on to the detective assigned to the case. Cases are usually assigned on a rotating basis, or a detective can be assigned to a particular case based on her particular knowledge and skills that relate to the offense. Once assigned to a case, a detective will follow it through until the case has been solved and the suspect is tried and convicted. The detective may use other officers to assist in the investigation, but the case will remain in her charge.

Fact gathering is a must in police work. Detectives can only relate specific details in a court of law and may not offer opinion, as a rule, for testimony. However, during the investigation, gut feelings and instinct play a large role in the detective's search for information. Years of experience can be, and often are, the most formidable tool in the detective's arsenal.

IN THE LINE OF DUTY
ON BECOMING A DETECTIVE

When I raised my right hand to take the oath to serve my state and my country, I felt a lump rise in my throat. It was such an honor and a thrill to finally be sworn in as a police officer. The feeling of putting on a uniform and pinning a shiny, silver badge to my chest was one of the greatest moments of my life. When the day finally arrived, though, to transition from a uniformed officer to a plainclothes detective, I couldn't wait to trade the uniform for a new suit and to hook a new, gold badge on my belt. After all, my childhood dream was to become an investigator, and I could finally wear cotton again instead of double-knit polyester shirts with fake buttons that zipped up the front and pants that retained enough heat to bake bread. (Of course, that cool stripe down the leg offset all negatives!)

I turned in my marked patrol vehicle and received my first department-issued, unmarked car. It was an old, beat-up Chevrolet Caprice, a car I write about fondly in my books and stories. The car was midnight blue, several years old, and would reach its top speed of eighty-five miles per hour only after going downhill for about three miles. I didn't care. It was mine. I washed it, cleaned the tires and wheels, and put my things—a fishing-tackle box filled with fingerprint equipment, a shotgun with an eighteen-inch barrel, extra ammo, hand cleaner, paper towels, and a roll of crime scene tape—into the trunk. I'd get more tools later as I figured out what I needed. For now, I was ready for my first case.

In my early days as a patrol officer, I looked on with envy as the detectives came in and took over my cases after I'd done the dirty work. They were the guys getting their pictures in the newspapers and getting all the glory for doing nothing ... or so I thought. It took just a few months of being a detective to dream of an eight-hour shift like the old days, instead of a twenty-hour day, and of not being called out in the middle of the night, *every* night! The thought had never occurred to me that it would be irritating to have newspaper reporters snapping photos of me while I struggled to hold in my lunch at a gruesome homicide scene, or that reporters would write things in the paper I didn't say or leave out the important things I did say.

Nobody teaches you how alienated you become from your old co-workers, the boys in blue, once you become a detective. Uniformed officers sometimes feel a bit of jealousy toward detectives, and detectives sometimes experience a bit of an unjustified superiority complex toward uniformed officers. It's a rivalry that's always been in place and probably always will be.

Nobody explains the many hours you'll spend sitting in the woods, or in the bushes, with hungry mosquitoes and spiders and snakes, or in the rain or snow, watching suspects in your attempts to build cases. Nobody tells you how it feels to work undercover and to walk into the middle of a drug deal, unarmed and without a radio. Nobody describes how it feels to be shot at, spit on, beat up, kicked, scratched, stabbed, cut, knocked down, punched, and pepper sprayed (with your own pepper spray), all the while wearing a suit.

Yes, I was finally a detective and it was absolutely ... *Glorious!*

DETECTIVE DIVISIONS

Police departments are divided into various specialized divisions, and those divisions are sometimes divided into even smaller, more focused groups of officers. The chart here shows the various subgroups within a detective division. These subgroups may vary depending upon the needs of individual departments.

VICE

Vice detectives are generally charged with the investigation and prevention of crimes involving prostitution, gambling, liquor, and pornography. Narcotics is also included in this group of crimes of immorality, but, with the increase of drug use and sales, some police departments have a division specifically for drug enforcement and eradication.

Vice detectives maintain files and photographs of all suspected and known offenders. These detectives must be familiar with each of the establishments within their jurisdictions that are licensed to sell and serve alcoholic beverages. They must also periodically inspect these businesses to ensure that permits are current and valid. These inspections are conducted during normal business hours. Officers may also observe activities in these businesses in an undercover capacity.

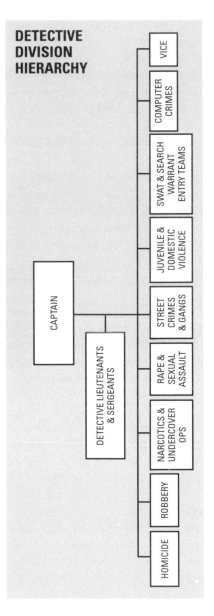

DETECTIVE DIVISION HIERARCHY

- CAPTAIN
- DETECTIVE LIEUTENANTS & SERGEANTS
- VICE
- COMPUTER CRIMES
- SWAT & SEARCH WARRANT ENTRY TEAMS
- JUVENILE & DOMESTIC VIOLENCE
- STREET CRIMES & GANGS
- RAPE & SEXUAL ASSAULT
- NARCOTICS & UNDERCOVER OPS
- ROBBERY
- HOMICIDE

Vice detectives must be willing to work odd hours and under extreme conditions, sometimes undercover. They frequent the areas where these crimes are known to occur, such as gambling establishments, bars, nightclubs, streets, and sidewalks. It's not unusual for female, and some male, vice detectives to pose as prostitutes in undercover sting operations. They must also infiltrate the makeshift unlicensed bars called "juke joints" or "nip joints."

To build their cases, vice detectives rely heavily on information they gather from informants, so it's imperative that they build a certain trust or bond with the people of the street. These street people can sometimes provide the knowledge that could save the life of officers and detectives.

Vice detectives build a network of informants through a variety of means. One such means is by working out "deals" with crooks—no prosecution for their crimes in exchange for solid information about an upper-level criminal. These "snitches" must prove to the detectives that their information is indeed accurate before detectives can make any promises to them.

In most cases, detectives are required to present their potential deals with informants to the prosecuting attorney who either agrees or rejects the plan. First- or second-time offenders are normally given the okay by the prosecutor to work off their charges by helping the police. A repeat offender may not receive a favorable response and must stand trial for his offense.

Detectives must abide by strict rules when using informants to help build a case against a criminal. An informant first must be established as a reliable source of information. To accomplish this, most police departments require the potential informant to fill out a form detailing his reasons for wanting to help the police.

Once the paperwork has been completed, the detective who'll be working with and supervising the informant signs the forms, then presents them to her commander, who approves of and signs the agreement. The informant's activities as they relate to the cases in question are closely monitored by the supervising officer and a second officer who's been assigned to assist. Sometimes male officers supervise female informants and female officers oversee male informants. The second officer is added as a witness and to prevent anything from occurring that could be later described as inappropriate.

The reliability of a confidential informant (CI) in drug cases is normally established by having the informant purchase narcotics from a dealer on three separate occasions, using money that's either been marked or for which the serial numbers have been recorded.

After each purchase, the drugs are delivered by the CI to the detective, who places the narcotics into a sealed container, marks it as evidence, and records the date and time of the transaction. These purchases may be used later as probable cause for obtaining a search warrant for the arrest of the dealer and/or as evidence in court.

If the CI's buys are used to establish probable cause for a search warrant, the marked money will be used as evidence that the transaction took place. This isn't always a good thing to do if the detective is attempting to protect the identity of the CI because the dealer will know that the informant is the person who "set him up."

Informants always live in fear for their safety but sometimes can't stop themselves from continuing their clandestine work, usually because they love the adrenaline rush or because they're in debt so deeply to the police and the prosecutor for keeping them out of jail that they must continue.

Other times, informants are people who simply desire to help police catch bad guys. They have varying reasons—some good and some not so good.

Some have grudges against someone and they want to see that person get into trouble and perhaps even go to prison.

Others may have attempted to become police officers and for various reasons couldn't, such as failing the entrance exam, physical agility tests, or psychological profile. For these people, becoming an informant is the next best thing. They get to hang around police officers and are sometimes exposed to some of the excitement that comes along with the job of a law enforcement officer.

These informants are normally paid a small fee in exchange for their services. That fee can range anywhere from no money—just an assurance of not going to jail for crimes they've committed—to several hundred dollars or more depending upon the value of their information.

STREET CRIMES AND GANGS

Gangs are structured organizations in which two or more people engage in criminal activity as part of that organization's purpose. There are many types of gangs, and they can be found in nearly every part of the world. Gangs are a major source of crime, and gang-related crime has become more and more prevalent in recent years. Members of these organizations hang out in, and control, certain areas of cities and towns. They claim these areas as their own and call them their "turfs." In some cases, gangs have established turfs in outlying areas of counties. Even small areas of prisons and jails have been claimed by prison gangs as their turfs, such as portions of recreation yards, TV rooms, and dining halls. A rival gang member can't cross from one turf into another. To do so is a sign of disrespect to the opposing gang. This display of insolence can result in the death of the trespassing gang member. Gang leaders who have been incarcerated may still run their gang's activities from behind bars by sending out messages, some of which are encrypted.

Gangs usually require prospective members to undergo an initiation before they're allowed into the organization. Often it's mandatory that the initiate spill the blood of another person—usually a rival gang member—through an act of physical violence such a stabbing or shooting. This initiation rite is called a "blood in." To leave or quit the gang, a similar act must be accomplished; this is called a "blood out."

Gang members are seldom allowed to simply quit; therefore, it's not uncommon for the blood spilled during the blood out to be that of the outgoing gang member. The remaining members feel that the member who wants out knows too much about their illegal activities, so they kill him to prevent him from snitching to the authorities.

Members of gangs use certain identifiers to let others know to which gang they belong. For instance, the members of a particular gang may all wear their left pant legs rolled up to mid-calf, or they may all wear their hats tilted to the right side of their heads. They may even always stand with either their right or left hands in their pockets.

Tattoos are also used to identify gang members and are a large part of gang culture, like the "TS" of the Texas Syndicate prison gang or the five-pointed crown of the People Nation gang.

Detectives assigned to work a gang detail or task force have the enormous task of learning the various cultures, identifiers, hand signals, signs, and slang of the gang. They must also be constantly aware of and alert to the gang's activities, since it's sometimes thought to be an honor and a privilege for a gang member to kill a law enforcement officer.

Detectives have worked undercover in an attempt to infiltrate gangs, but their attempts are often in vain due to the blood-in ritual. Officers aren't allowed to participate in any illegal activity that would require them to physically harm another person. If they refuse to perform a particular ritual, they take the risk of exposing their undercover status.

An undercover detective once infiltrated a notorious motorcycle gang and avoided the blood-in ritual by "killing" someone who was already dead. As part of an elaborate illusion, detectives used the body of a John Doe victim as a ruse to make it seem the undercover detective had indeed committed a murder. The detective shot the body several times during a mock drive-by shooting. The scheme worked, and as a result, the detective was allowed into the club as a full member.

WHITE-COLLAR CRIME

White-collar crime derives its name from the particular class of workers who commit these crimes. They're the business people associated with wearing business suits, white shirts, and ties. The crimes they commit are of a nonviolent nature and usually involve bookkeeping or computer use.

Detectives assigned to this area of expertise must be mathematically savvy and computer literate. They're usually college graduates with majors in accounting or computer science, and they're normally considered experts in their fields.

It's the duty of the detectives in this division to track and document the activities of embezzlers, tax cheats, and other business-related criminals.

HIGH-TECH CRIMES

High-tech crime units are fairly new additions to police departments. Their tasks are easily defined—they detect and investigate criminal activity that involves technology, such as computers, laptops, identity theft, digital storage media, camcorders, digital phones, computer-based child pornography, digital cameras, and phishing.

Phishing is a relatively new term for a crime that involves criminals who send fraudulent e-mails to individual parties, requesting their account numbers and passwords for various bank accounts, creditors, and other financial institutions. These e-mails appear to be legitimate.

Criminals fool the recipients of these e-mails because their messages often bear the logo of the institutions they claim to represent. The links they provide to the recipients, however, don't link to the actual institutions. When the recipient of these e-mails fills out the information and sends the replies, the messages transmit directly to the crooks, who then have access to the victim's personal information. They use this information to access the victim's bank accounts, get cash from ATM machines, obtain credit cards, and buy big-ticket items like cars, boats, and jewelry. The losses can be devastating, and it can take victims years to repair their damaged credit histories.

Detectives in this highly specialized field receive their training from various agencies such as the International Association of Computer Investigative Specialists (IACIS) or the National White Collar Crime Center. The IACIS is a nonprofit volunteer organization staffed by law enforcement personnel who help to train, certify, and recertify both new and experienced forensic examiners.

During their training, detectives are taught the laws of search and seizure as they apply to technology. They're schooled on the many aspects of computers and how they're operated—legally and illegally. They learn how data is stored; how to recover deleted files; how to examine boot files, temporary files, cache files, history files, and registry files; and how to search unused or blank space for deleted information.

Other classes instruct detectives on how to examine hard drives for hidden or encrypted messages, how to break passwords, how to detect Trojan horses, and how to discover devices that can destroy a computer and its inner workings.

The fees for a basic training course vary throughout the industry, but they average between six hundred and seven hundred dollars.

Police departments operate on very limited budgets, and the start-up and operation of a high-tech investigative unit can be a burden, especially to smaller departments. For example, a basic forensic computer can cost in excess of five thousand dollars, an additional twelve hundred dollars for the hardware write blockers (devices attached between a suspect's computer and its storage device to monitor the computer's activity), two thousand dollars for forensic software, and two thousand dollars for cables and software. All totaled, equipment and training for just a few officers can quickly total forty thousand dollars or more in start-up costs.

A forensic computer is unlike any other computer. It's designed especially for computer forensics and has a very large capacity for memory. Detective Josh Moulin, a forensic computer examiner and supervisor of the Central Point, Oregon, Police Department's High-Tech Crimes Unit, operates a forensic computer with 1 terabyte of storage, twin nineteen-inch monitors, two gigabytes of RAM, an Intel P4 3.4 GHz processor, and removable drive trays. Detective Moulin's division provides assistance to many other agencies that aren't equipped to investigate high-tech computer crimes. The department also assists the Federal Bureau of Investigation (FBI), the Department of Homeland Security, U.S. Immigration and Customs Enforcement, and various state police agencies.

The hardware write blocker (HWD) is an essential tool for high-tech crime detectives. Its principle is simple: It allows information to flow in one direction only—from the suspect's computer directly into the forensic computer—never in reverse. The information is stored on the forensic computer for later examination and evidence collection.

The HWD functions much like the foot valve in a water line that's connected to a pump and well system. The valve opens when the pump (in this case, the HWD) pulls water (information) toward a house (forensic computer) but closes tightly when the pumping stops so the leftover water in the lines can't return to the well (the suspect's computer).

The one-way action of the HWD is designed to prevent cross-contamination of evidence. It doesn't allow any information from the forensic computer to find its way into the suspect's computer—an incident that an attorney could use as a defense. It could be compared to planting evidence, such as a bloody knife or glove at a homicide scene.

To prevent the police from detecting their illegal activities, criminals have devised several ways to destroy evidence of their crimes. They've attempted to demolish their hard drives by drilling holes into them; they've smashed the hard drives with sledgehammers, and they've submerged them in acid—the only true way to destroy data. Even with several holes drilled into the drive, forensics experts have been able to retrieve some data from the damaged computers.

The Central Point, Oregon, Police Department's High-Tech Crimes Unit is, as are most departments, very proactive when it comes to online investigations. The computer age, along with Web sites and chat rooms, has made it easier than ever for sexual predators to stalk their prey. Men are using computers to find underage sex partners because it's much easier to meet kids online than to approach them in public places like parks and shopping malls.

Departments all across the country have begun to stalk the predators that stalk our children. In the quaint village of Yellow Springs, Ohio, Officer Matt Hoying spends several hours each week online posing as a fourteen-year-old girl in hopes of nabbing a sexual predator. He's been quite successful—since he began the project, he's averaged at least one arrest per week. Men have made the trek from nearby cities to meet the teen girl (Officer Hoying) that they've met online—one even rode a bicycle nearly twenty miles to meet his underage date.

Much of Officer Hoying's time online is spent chatting with adult men in a Web site chat room named "I Love Much Older Men." Using chat room lingo that sounds as if it's coming straight from the keyboard of a giggling teen, he responds to questions asked by the men—some of whom claim to be engineers, truck drivers, and even police officers. Some are young and some are old; some are married while some are single; some are rich and some are poor; some are friendly and outgoing and others are loners. They're your next-door neighbors.

Quite often the men portray themselves as handsome, rich, and successful. They tell the young girls that they drive expensive cars and wear expensive jewelry and clothing. In reality, a lot of the guys are poor, unkempt, and dirty. They live in squalor where their most prized possessions are their computers and their pornography collections.

Officer Hoying's fingers tap out chat room slang such as LOL (laughing out loud), TTYL (talk to you later), MMLOMS (my mom's looking over my shoulder), ROFLMAO (rolling on the floor laughing my ass off), and a/s/l (age/sex/location). Training for detectives who work Internet sting operations involves teaching them how a teen would respond to questions, how to answer those questions without entrapping the suspect, how to properly use online slang, and how to surf the chat rooms frequented by sexual predators.

The conversations are initiated by male suspects almost immediately after detectives log on to a Web site. Usually not more thirty seconds passes before an unsuspecting man makes the first contact. Within ten minutes officers have more requests to chat than they can possibly handle. They pick one or two targets and disregard the rest. They consider a good target suspect to be one who lives close to the detective's jurisdiction. Close proximity means there's more of a chance that the suspect will want to meet the girl face-to-face.

Talk quickly turns to sex. The men ask the young girls if they're virgins (a popular question), if they desire older men for sex partners, and if they've ever given or received oral sex. The next line of questioning usually begins with questions about the girl's parents. Are they home? How long will they be gone?

Within minutes, the questions begin to flow at a rapid-fire pace. Do you have a boyfriend? Is he there? Do you have sex with him? Have you ever had sex with an older man? Have you ever had sex with one of your girlfriends? What are you wearing? Do you like to masturbate? The questions are followed by the men sending photographs of themselves to the young boys and girls. The first volleys of pictures are of men in various poses—fully clothed or shirtless. As they send more and more, the men are posed in less and less clothing, and— in some—they're totally nude.

At this point, the detectives discover whether or not the men want to meet the girl or if they're only looking for a cyber-partner to engage in mutual on-line masturbation. The conversation will either shift to questions about a possible meeting or the men will push the conversation toward just sex talk. If the talk heads into the direction of just sex talk, the detectives save a printed copy of the conversation for future evidence and log off that particular chat. They continue this process until someone asks to meet in person. Each online conversation is saved and printed for later use in court.

The men who are arrested for this crime are normally quite passive at the time of their arrests. They rarely ever resist arrest and seldom attempt to run from the police. They're sometimes open about their intentions, but most try to explain their reasons for wanting to meet an underage girl or boy. They offer explanations of just wanting to talk; they say that they knew the child was alone and only wanted to make sure they were safe from danger. Some freely admit that they were hoping to have sex with the children.

Sexual predators of children are often bold enough to meet the children in their own homes while their parents are away. With the recent attention by police and the media to this type of crime, the offenders have begun to conduct their own countersurveillance. They drive by the neighborhoods or parks where they're supposed to meet their victims, looking for anything out of the ordinary. They search for people who look like undercover detectives. They search for video cameras, unmarked police vehicles, and even media personnel and their vehicles.

Convictions for sex offenders—rapists, child molesters, and child pornographers—generally result in a lengthy prison sentence. At the completion of their sentences, the offenders are required to register with their local law enforcement agencies. They must provide a current address—they're not permitted to live near areas where children are known to frequent, such as schools, parks, and playgrounds—and they must report to their probation officers on a regular basis.

RAPE AND SEXUAL ASSAULT

Detectives assigned to investigate crimes of rape and sexual assault receive specialized training in the investigation of cases involving rape, incest, domestic violence, stalking, and sexual assault. They learn to recognize the signs and symptoms of abuse by family members. They also maintain a close working relationship with local centers for the prevention of domestic and family violence, and with other agencies that provide representatives who serve as victims' advocates.

It's crucial that victims of sexual assault are made to feel as comfortable as possible during the interview process and throughout their medical treatment and examination. It's also imperative for the victim to be examined by a physician or a specially trained Sexual Assault Nurse Examiner as soon as possible after the assault to protect and preserve any physical evidence the attacker might have left behind, such as hairs, clothing fibers, saliva, and semen.

Detectives and the victim's advocate accompany the victim to a hospital or doctor's office for the examination and treatment of injuries. The physician conducts a physical examination of the victim using a prepackaged Physical

Evidence Recovery Kit (PERK). Victims of sexual assault sometimes request that the victim's advocate, who's usually female, and female officers and detectives remain with them during the exam and evidence recovery. It's not a legal requirement for a police officer to be present during the examination. The physician or nurse can be summoned to court to testify regarding the evidence and its collection.

Detectives who work in sexual assault divisions are responsible for monitoring convicted sex offenders and their activities. Task forces within these divisions have been created specifically to supervise and monitor the court-ordered terms and conditions of probation and parole and the release of high-risk sexual offenders from prison.

NARCOTICS

Narcotics officers, or narcs as they're commonly called by criminals, work in one of the most dangerous divisions within a police department. It's their job to prevent or reduce the manufacturing and sale of illegal drugs. To effectively battle this ever-present and increasing problem, it's necessary for these officers to work extremely odd hours, often in harsh conditions.

Detectives who work as narcotics officers receive specialized training in drug recognition, search warrant preparation and execution, rules and laws of evidence and procedure, firearms, and self-defense and defensive tactics. Many narcotics officers are designated to undercover duty. They're schooled in the mannerisms, slang, and cultures of the communities where they're assigned. They learn to walk and talk like their target suspects, which enables them to blend into the local groups or gangs.

Narcotics officers aren't permitted to use, nor do they use, illegal drugs as part of their cover. Obviously, the use of mind-altering substances would reduce the officers' ability to reason and react effectively in emergency situations. In addition, they wouldn't be able to testify in court regarding events that had taken place during the time of their intoxication.

Narcotics officers often wear long hair, beards, and shabby clothing. They sometimes drive old beat-up cars and possess fake driver's licenses and IDs that coincide with their false identities. These officers must live their assumed roles to avoid detection by criminals.

The drug culture is so vast, and covers such an enormous territory, that it's become necessary for police agencies to form multi-jurisdictional task forces. These task forces can be comprised of members from several police agencies, such as police departments; sheriff's offices; state police; the FBI; the Bureau of Alcohol, Tobacco, Firearms, and Explosives; the National Guard; the U.S. Coast Guard; the U.S. Border Patrol; and the Drug Enforcement Administration (DEA).

Joint membership in a federally sponsored task force offers the participating agencies more manpower at no cost to local departments and allows free access to expensive government-owned equipment. Officers who are members of these elite teams can be sworn in by any of the participating agencies. This action provides the members with arrest powers in those jurisdictions, allowing them to travel and work anywhere in the country if necessary.

HOMICIDE

Of all the detective divisions, the homicide division is probably the one most familiar to the general public, due to the ever-increasing popularity of television shows that feature homicide detectives. The specially trained homicide detectives delve into the mysteries surrounding death by unnatural circumstances.

Detectives who work in homicide divisions are afforded unique pieces of evidence—human bodies. A corpse is a macro-environment where countless pieces of micro-evidence lay waiting for discovery. Homicide detectives piece together their cases much like a child assembles a jigsaw puzzle, only in reverse. They begin the investigation with the full puzzle—a body—laid out in front them. Puzzle pieces—evidence—must be carefully removed, examined, cataloged, and filed. These bits and pieces of evidence are the clues that will eventually lead the detective to the murderer.

A clue can be as small as a clothing fiber or a human hair or even smaller, a piece of slimy, coiled DNA. Clues can also be large and obvious, like a person's name tattooed on the victim's skin or a wallet found at the scene filled with a killer's identification.

Detectives must wade through what is sometimes a mountain of evidence, using whatever tools may be available to arrive at their conclusions. They must determine which of the items they've discovered are evidence and which are not, taking care not to discard what could later prove to be a valuable piece of evidence.

Homicide detectives must be alert and extremely observant. Sometimes the tiniest clue solves the case. Detectives assigned to work homicide must also be top-notch interrogators.

A good homicide detective is the chameleon of police officers. He can effectively converse with people from all walks of life. He knows the talk and the jive of the street, and he knows what it's like to wear a suit and tie while sipping the finest wine. He's a good actor and an extremely good liar. He has what it takes to stand toe-to-toe with a cold-blooded killer, look her in the eye, and tell her he has enough evidence to send her to the electric chair—when in actuality the only evidence he has is a gut feeling.

Homicide detectives receive intensive training in crime scene investigations, evidence collection, bloodstain and spatter evidence, crime scene photography, ballistics, and interview and interrogation techniques. They attend the autopsies of their victims and notify their next of kin of the death. They often attend the victim's funerals and graveside services, hoping the killer is doing the same—they often do.

Homicide detectives see life in a way that most people never will. They witness it through the eyes of the dead. It's the job of the murder investigator to discover the identities of killers; sometimes she must even use her skills to learn the identities of the dead.

INTERNAL AFFAIRS

There's a detective for every type of investigation, every crime imaginable, and every donut shop in town. All of those detectives take pride in their work, and they eventually settle into a niche that becomes their area of specialty. The one area of investigation that causes even the most seasoned detective to cringe is that of internal affairs.

An assignment to the Internal Affairs Division (IAD) is often called the "kiss of death." To investigate a fellow officer for anything is considered by some an act of treason. The silent, unspoken loyalty code among officers is one of the most substantial and solid bonds I've ever encountered. No gang on the face of this earth has a more loyal membership. I've seen police officers fight for one another, lie for one another, and cheat for one another. No one, but no one, can say anything bad about one of the men or women in blue and come away unscathed.

Police officers can be a vindictive group. Revenge is the word. Hurt one of their gang, or spew hateful words against the brethren, and see how long it takes to receive a speeding ticket or find your car in the police impound lot. There are rotten eggs in any profession—police agencies are no different. Those bad eggs are the "dirty cops." To ensure that those eggs are gathered before they hatch into evil monsters, a checks-and-balances system must be put into place. The balancing weight in this case is internal affairs.

These specially trained detectives are typically responsible for the required background investigations of police officer applicants, officer-involved shootings, and illegal or corrupt activities by police officers and other non-sworn department employees. The investigations can range from minor matters, such as speeding tickets received by police officers, to homicide investigations. A good means of lessening the animosity toward IAD investigators is to (as some experienced chiefs and sheriffs do) rotate each detective through the IAD department, giving everyone a turn in the dreaded division.

A chief who decides that his IAD detectives and his criminal detectives should become one and the same can cause horrendous problems for those detectives. From the moment the other detectives discover that the criminal detectives have been assigned to the IAD, they begin to shun them. The detectives who were once their close friends soon give the cold shoulder. Requests for backup receive slow responses—if any at all, no matter how urgent the plea. Invitations to go out for coffee or to have a drink after the shift cease. Their workout partners and fishing buddies suddenly have "other things" to do—and their families may soon begin receiving various traffic citations.

Internal affairs detectives are notorious for their secret files of information about each department employee. Rumors are abundant about the content of those files. While it's true that IADs maintain files on officers, the files normally contain only information of officer misconduct, not details about which officer is sleeping with whom. Of course, if the "whom" is another officer, there's a good chance that tidbit is tucked neatly—with pictures—into a private folder deep within the walls of the IAD.

Internal affairs detectives aren't normally assigned to regular criminal cases. They do, however, observe how other detectives and uniformed officers handle their cases. Some internal affairs detectives are responsible for observing and noting special situations, such as officer stress. These investigators are often the source of information for department psychologists regarding an officer's early signs of posttraumatic stress disorder.

Patrol officers and detectives know it's not usually good news to be called into an internal affairs detective's office. Internal investigations are conducted in the same manner as any criminal interview. The officer is read his Miranda warnings and is informed of his rights according to department grievance procedures and union rules. He has a right to have an attorney present, as well as a representative of his choosing for any internal hearing not of a criminal nature, such a departmental rule infraction.

If the IAD finds an officer negligent in her duties, any number of disciplinary actions can be taken. The punishments can range from a simple reprimand to suspension with or without pay to termination of employment. If the offense is criminal in nature, the officer can be arrested. Depending upon the severity of the criminal charge, the IAD detectives decide whether they'll seek an arrest warrant or turn the task over to another agency, such as the state police, FBI, or DEA.

It's never pleasant to see a friend or co-worker break the rules, or the law, and it's even more unpleasant when that particular co-worker is a police officer. For whatever the reason, it happens, and it's left to the investigators of the IAD to bring those rogue cops to justice.

⬡ IN THE LINE OF DUTY
THE SHOOTOUT

How police officers are treated by their own departments has a huge impact on how they bounce back from an officer-involved shooting. This includes access to appropriate psychological debriefing and counseling when needed.

—*Laurence Miller, Ph.D., Clinical, Forensic, and Police Psychologist*

Although detectives are normally assigned to specialized divisions, they're often called on to assist in other areas of law enforcement, such as backing up fellow officers when they're faced with dangerous situations. Such was the case when I, a detective, was called on to back up a group of uniformed patrol officers who were engaged in a standoff with an armed and desperate bank robber.

It was a sweltering August morning when a young man invited me to join the ranks of killers. I never in my wildest of dreams would have thought I'd accept such an invitation, nor would I have thought I could ever take a human life. It was surprising to learn how easy it is to kill.

Less than thirty minutes from the time the robber fled the bank parking lot, with gun in hand, in his father's beat-up station wagon, he had first locked himself out of the car, then wrecked it, lost most of the stolen money, and had a dye pack blow up in his face. Dozens of police officers were speeding toward him from all directions, and he was, unknowingly, moments away from death and from changing the lives of many good people.

I looked on as the robber loaded his weapon while squatting behind the old, beat-up station wagon. To his left, in the midst of a group of small maples, I stood watching his every move, all the while pleading with him to drop his weapon. He didn't acknowledge my presence; in fact, I don't believe he ever knew I was there. He was fixated on officers who had positioned themselves on the crest of a hill, barely in sight of the soon-to-be-dead robber. He appeared to be disconnected from the reality of the circumstances as he calmly turned his gun's cylinder, one click at a time, placing the tiny pieces of ammunition into their respective slots.

Suddenly, and without warning, he snapped the drum back into place and looked up. He was ready.

Using my portable radio, I called to my fellow officers and informed them of the circumstances. The situation was no longer the norm—this bad guy was not going to be coming out with his hands up. This young man was going to shoot it out with the police, and I already felt within my heart that someone was going to die.

The robber squatted at the rear bumper of the car, elbows resting on his thighs and both hands tightly clenching the revolver. His lips moved occasionally, saying something to himself or to an imaginary conspirator.

Suddenly, he stood and fired a shot in the direction of my co-workers. He had offered his formal invitation, and I accepted without a second thought by placing a carefully aimed round through the right rear window of the car and into the side of his head, just below a freckled cheekbone.

As academy students, we were taught to shoot the center mass of our targets, meaning the center of whatever portion of the body that's visible. After firing his first shot, the bank robber ducked behind his car, leaving only his head discernible through the long, rear side glass of the car's window. His head was the target for which I aimed, and that was the target I hit with my first round of return fire. I looked toward my fellow officers to see if the robber had somehow struck one of them with his wild shot. It was this moment when I first became aware of the slow motion and muted sounds.

On the hill to my left and directly in front of the suspect I saw uniformed police officers standing ready, in two separate groups of two, in various stances, some with feet spread and others with one foot in front of the other. All had their weapons trained toward the robber; all used a portion of a patrol vehicle for cover, be it a door or a fender, and all were yelling fiercely for the robber to put down his gun and surrender. It was obvious, by their strained expressions and frantic actions, that they were united by one common element: fear. It was also odd that their every movement was extremely slow and deliberate. They had switched from 78 rpm to 33⅓ rpm in a single muzzle flash.

During the slow motion I took the time to examine the faces of my partners. Terror and foreboding had replaced calm; furrowed brows and clenched jaws replaced composure. My eyes moved, gradually, from one group of officers to the other. Their lips moved, slowly but forcefully, yet there were no sounds. Droplets of spittle trailed silent words, words nearly frozen in place by the horror-induced time warp. I saw tiny blue puffs of smoke waft from the steel barrels of their weapons, but again, I heard nothing. I recall seeing a golden retriever held on a leash by a gray-haired, grandfatherly man. I saw the two, from the corner of my eye, standing on an overpass watching the shootout unfold. The dog's mouth was opening and closing, and his head was jerking violently as dog's heads do when barking. I couldn't hear a single sound.

I turned my attention back to the robber. He stood, with measured erratic movements and blood trickling from the neat little round bullet hole in his left cheek, and fired another round. My stomach turned over once when I suddenly realized he was smiling. He was enjoying the situation and was apparently very pleased with himself.

It seemed five minutes had passed before I finally pulled my gun up from my side and into a firing position. I shot again and the bullet snapped into the man's narrow chest, a little to the left of dead center.

He folded to the ground. His fall resembled the movements of a carpenter's folding ruler. His black T-shirt, with white lettering, began to darken and glisten with wetness. I stood unmoving, with my gun trained on his still body, for what felt like hours, watching the earth around him change colors. Like a twisting and turning kaleidoscope, the soil transformed from its natural color into a glistening, rusty red hue.

The man, destined to depart this life, was so intent on dying that he didn't realize he had nearly achieved his goal, and minutes later he would indeed reach that end. He stood three more times and fired a single round each time, aiming at no one target in particular. I returned fire, round for round, with each of my bullets hitting him each time. When the fifth round from my gun struck him, he fell to the ground for the final time. I called to everyone on the radio and calmly uttered two simple words: "It's over."

The slow motion stopped as suddenly as it had begun, and I remember hearing the tiny chirps of birds in the tree canopy above my head. The retriever's yelping and frenzied barks bounced off my eardrums, and sirens were screaming in the distance as more and more police officers responded to the emergency call.

Together, a sheriff's deputy and I approached the dying man as he lay face down bleeding among the weeds and debris on the roadside. His breathing was labored and sounded as if there was more liquid than air in his lungs. His legs twitched and quivered like those of a deer felled by a hunter's bullet.

His hands were beneath his body and, upon rolling him over to place handcuffs on his bloody wrists, we discovered he was still clutching the gun. His index finger was inside the trigger guard, and he was repeatedly squeezing the trigger of the empty weapon.

He died laying amid blood, garbage, and a million questions. A total of sixty-eight rounds had been fired by police officers, a police vehicle had been nearly destroyed by gunfire, the suspect was dead, and I had a hollow feeling in my soul that hasn't gone away to this day. When he died, he took a piece of me with him that I never regained.

UNDERCOVER OFFICERS

Police officers who work undercover are usually detectives from one division or another within a police department. Any officer, from any section of a police department, may be called upon to work a covert assignment; however, to work in the capacity as an undercover officer (UC), they must first learn to rid themselves of all the habits that would give them away as cops. Police officers have a tendency to walk with their arms out and away from their bodies a bit more than the average person, because they're so used to wearing a gun. If police officers allow their arms to hang normally at their sides, the hammer of their sidearms (pistols or revolvers) will cut, scratch, or scrape the skin near their elbows.

Police officers prefer to sit with their backs to the wall when in public buildings, such as restaurants. This habit allows the officer to watch the entrance and exits of the business, and it prevents a criminal from sneaking up on him. Officers have a tendency to absent-mindedly tug upward on their belts and waistbands—pulling up their pants, because they're used to the weight of the equipment hanging from their Sam Browne belts.

Police officers are naturally suspicious of people, so they have a tendency to examine others carefully with their eyes, watching every move. They stand with a familiar defensive stance—one foot slightly forward with their gun-hand side to the rear. Police officers look people directly in the eyes when speaking, and they wear clothing that almost spells out the word *cop*, such as the combination of black, spit-shined shoes with jeans.

Seasoned police officers ask questions—lots of them. They constantly interrogate people; they're hyperaware of their surroundings, and they drive defensively, always wearing their seatbelts and their hands positioned at the 10 and 2 positions on the steering wheel. These are all great traits for uniformed police officers, but not for cops who are attempting to hide their identities.

Crooks look for these surefire signs of police officers. They watch the actions of anyone new in their group, and they ask questions. They ask if the stranger is a police officer, and they sometimes test the newcomers by asking them to perform illegal acts.

It's an eerie experience to be surrounded by a roomful of some of the most monstrous people on earth and have them ask if you're a police officer. I've encountered this situation on many occasions, and I've managed to convince the thugs that I was one of them simply by laughing and saying, "Hell, no, I'm not a cop. Are you?" I've heard drug dealers make the statement to one another that cops can't lie if asked that question. They couldn't be more wrong. I've attended training given by the DEA and police academies that teaches undercover officers how to lie, and lie effectively.

Officers can be forced to expose their identities, or blow their covers, if a heinous crime is about to take place. They must stop the commission of any capital crime, such as murder or rape. Sometimes the officers are fortunate and can stop the crime by alerting back-up officers and having them foil the crime, which allows the undercover officer to retain his secret identity.

Police officers have been known to work "deep undercover," keeping their identities hidden for periods as long as two to three years. This deep undercover mission is the most difficult assignment an officer can encounter. Working in an assumed role for such a lengthy period can have adverse effects. The officer can easily succumb to a criminal lifestyle. He's surrounded by the criminal element for so long he begins to think and act like the very criminals who are the targets of his investigation. Undercover officers sometimes develop actual friendships with these criminals. It's important for a department to rotate undercover assignments to prevent officers from giving in to the pressures associated with the project.

Police officers are human. They have emotions like anyone else, and they can become sympathetic or emotionally attached to their target criminals; therefore, it's up to supervisors to monitor the officer's well-being and state of mind. In the event that adverse mannerisms or behaviors develop in the officer's character, her assignment to the mission should be terminated immediately.

Undercover officers normally dress like the people they're trying to arrest. If the group in question is a motorcycle gang, the officer will wear jeans and leather; if his target crowd is wealthy, a suit and tie and a Rolex watch (borrowed) might be appropriate.

Carrying a gun can be difficult when working undercover; however, there are many pistols and holsters that make the task a little easier. One officer, whom I'll refer to as Special Agent X to protect his identity, carries a Sig Sauer P232. It's a small pistol capable of holding only seven rounds of ammunition (six in the magazine plus one in the chamber). Special Agent X looks like a typical blue-collar factory or construction worker. He conducts his daily police duties while wearing cargo-style shorts, a cotton T-shirt with a bright green marijuana leaf covering the chest area, work boots, and white crew socks. His long hair is graying and pulled back into a ponytail. He maintains a few day's growth of salt-and-pepper whiskers on his cheeks and chin.

His holster—designed and used by the Israeli army—is sold by Fobus Holsters. It's very compact and fits snugly inside the waistband of his pants. A T-shirt easily conceals the portion of the pistol that protrudes above his waistband. That small handgun is sometimes an undercover officer's only security. Many undercover officers aren't even allowed that option—criminals often pat down newcomers to their group. Strangers aren't allowed to carry guns until they've proven their loyalty.

Undercover officers participate in the service of search warrants and in the arrests of the criminals they've been observing. Normally, when the arrests and search warrants are carried out, the officers wear

An undercover officer wears a mask to protect his identity.

masks to hide their identities. Officers are also required to attend and testify during the court proceedings of the criminals they've arrested. Some judges will close their courtrooms to the public during those trials. Others permit the undercover officers to testify while wearing masks.

CHAPTER 5

ARREST AND
SEARCH PROCEDURES

Being an investigative reporter is just like being a cop—you ask questions, examine the evidence, search for clues, interview the suspects. The big difference: there's no journalism Miranda warning. If the bad guys don't already know their rights, we don't have to tell them.

—HANK PHILLIPPI RYAN, EMMY AWARD-WINNING INVESTIGATIVE REPORTER
AND AUTHOR OF PRIME TIME AND FACE TIME

Law enforcement agencies and departments have minimum standards of operation as delegated by the U.S. Department of Justice, the U.S. Constitution, and local governing bodies. These standards are specific rules, regulations, and laws that direct the actions of law enforcement officers. These regulations also protect the rights of law-abiding citizens and the rights of those who stand accused of crimes.

TYPES OF CRIME

Crime is divided into two types—felonies and misdemeanors. *Felonies*, such as rape, robbery, and murder, are the more serious of the two types of crime and are punishable by death or one or more years in a penitentiary, also known as a state or federal prison (county jails are not prisons). *Misdemeanors* are crimes that aren't considered felonies. Misdemeanors, such as trespassing and simple assault, are less serious in nature than felonies and are punishable by fines, probation, and/or imprisonment in a county or city jail for a period of up to twelve months. Unless otherwise authorized by special provisions in the law, a police officer may only make an arrest for a misdemeanor when the offense has been committed in her presence.

To ensure an offender answers for a misdemeanor committed outside her presence, the officer must either issue a summons for the accused criminal or obtain a warrant for his arrest. To obtain an arrest warrant, she must present the facts surrounding the case to a judge or magistrate, who determines if enough probable cause exists to issue the warrant.

An officer may issue a written summons for a misdemeanor offense, and, as with traffic citations, the suspect must sign the form indicating his promise to appear in court to answer the charges. Signing a citation isn't an admission of guilt; however, a suspect's refusal to sign a citation gives the officer grounds to take him into custody (a traffic stop is considered an arrest).

If the suspect refuses to sign the summons and is arrested (the actual arrest is based upon the original offense, not the refusal to sign), the officer handcuffs him and brings him before a magistrate. The magistrate sets a dollar amount for bail. In some states, the bail is a predetermined amount and can be collected at police headquarters by the arresting officer. The offender is held in police custody until the bail has been paid.

Some states have authorized exceptions to the law that says an officer can only make an arrest for a misdemeanor offense committed in her presence. Exceptions have been made for offenses such as driving under the influence of drugs or alcohol, in which case further harm or damage may occur if the officer doesn't make an immediate arrest.

An officer may make a warrantless arrest for a felony as long as he has sufficient probable cause to believe a felony has been committed and that the person he's arresting is actually the person who committed the felony.

Most states prefer that officers obtain arrest warrants whenever possible. (Having an actual warrant in hand seems to somewhat pacify a bad guy—he tends to offer less resistance than those who are arrested for a crime-in-progress). However, if an officer believes the situation requires a warrantless arrest, she must be able to effectively articulate, in a court of law, the conditions and facts that led to that arrest. If her explanation for the arrest doesn't provide ample probable cause, a judge may deem the arrest illegal. The suspect may bring civil proceedings and/or criminal charges against the arresting officer.

An officer's most important tool is his credibility. If he falters in the course of his duties by performing an illegal arrest, exposing his lack of knowledge of the law and his ability to follow and enforce the law, his career as a police officer will begin to decline. His testimonies will become questionable and he'll begin to lose court cases, which sends guilty suspects back onto the streets. It's essential for a police officer to make every effort to be certain of the facts when making an arrest. Cutting corners doesn't pay.

ARREST WARRANTS

Once an officer presents the facts in a criminal case to a judge or magistrate and receives an arrest warrant, she may then legally take the suspect into custody. The difficult part of serving a warrant (other than the danger factor) is that criminals aren't always home when police arrive to serve them with an arrest warrant. Sometimes it takes several days or more to locate a suspect.

If an officer can't locate a suspect, he returns the warrant for her arrest to the police department, where it's placed on file. The warrant is now considered an outstanding warrant. Officers working the next shifts pick up any leftover warrants and attempt to serve them. If, within a few days, the suspect still can't be located, her information (name, birth date, a physical description, social security number, driver's license number, and nature of offense) is entered into the National Crime Information Center (NCIC) database. Then, if the suspect is stopped by the police for any reason, including a traffic offense, officers will know she's a wanted person.

ROUTINE TRAFFIC STOPS AND PENDING WARRANTS

To outsiders a traffic stop seems like a routine procedure, but it can be an adrenaline roller-coaster ride for police officers because of the many moments of high-to-low-anxiety.

When stopping a driver for a traffic infraction a police officer automatically does two things: She checks to see if the car's license plate is valid and she checks to see if the driver's license is legal or restricted. When the officer pulls up behind a car, she reads the license number (in some departments, a 10-28 is a request for a vehicle license check) to the dispatcher, who enters the information into the NCIC database. Almost instantly, all information regarding that particular license number (type and color of car, who the car is licensed to, if the car is stolen or wanted, and the dates of license validity) is relayed back to the dispatcher. He then provides the information to the officer.

If the response indicates that the car and driver are wanted, the officer requests assistance and simply follows behind the car until her backup arrives. If no "wants" are reported, the officer activates her lights and siren to begin the traffic stop.

During the beginning of her traffic stop the officer must be constantly aware of her surroundings. She must run through a complete mental checklist of "What if?" questions: *Is the driver dangerous? Has he been drinking? Does he have a gun? Does he have a hostage? Is this a setup? Could there be someone waiting in the trunk for an ambush? Is the car carrying illegal drugs or weapons? How will the driver react to receiving a traffic citation? Will he become combative?* The officer has only seconds to complete this entire evaluation.

During her approach to the car the officer places her hand on the trunk lid to make sure it's tightly closed (no ambush), glances into the back seat (no one there, no dead bodies, and no large satchels full of cocaine and machine guns), and then approaches the driver's side of the car (if the stop is made in heavy traffic, she may approach the passenger's side). Her initial conversation with the driver determines if he's under the influence of alcohol or drugs. If he's unusually nervous it can be a good indicator that he's just committed a crime or is wanted by the police. She must rely heavily on her instincts and gut feelings while still following the letter of the law. She must protect the driver's rights while making sure she's able to go home, alive, at the end of her shift.

A police officer automatically has the right to ask a person to step out of his car. This right ensures the officer's safety. Believe me, there's nothing worse for a police officer than stopping a car with tinted windows, in the middle of the night, and not being able to see what's going on inside the vehicle. Having the person step outside *can* be the difference between the officer living or dying. If every person could experience that gut-wrenching feeling, they might feel a little less inconvenienced when ordered out of their cars by police officers.

When she performs the last item on her checklist and decides this is just a normal traffic stop, the officer asks to see the driver's license (some states call them operator's licenses) and proof of insurance. She takes both back to her patrol car and makes a second call to the dispatcher—a 10-27, the check of a driver's license. The dispatcher enters the driver's license number and issuing state into the computer, and a reply is once again returned almost instantly.

The check reveals a person's entire driving history, such as the number of traffic citations received nationwide, and it confirms that the person's license is either valid, suspended, or that he actually has no license. Simultaneously, the dispatcher runs a check to see if the driver is wanted by police. If the check reveals that the driver has outstanding warrants, the dispatcher must immediately notify the officer without alerting the suspect that they're on to him. Instead of using the word "wanted" over the radio, the dispatcher makes the announcement using the 10-code. In some locations 10-99 means "wanted person." If a want is returned, backup is sent to the officer's location to assist her with arresting the driver. For her safety, she should remain in her patrol car until help arrives. (For more on 10-codes, see appendix B.)

If the driver is charged with any type of infraction, including speeding, the officer requests that a printout of all the driver's records be held for her. This is done because the officer will need to enclose the printouts in her files for use as evidence in later court hearings.

The NCIC printout also serves as a temporary arrest warrant for a wanted person and provides the officer with just cause to detain him until he's picked up by the department that's looking for him.

Any police officer who makes an arrest based upon an arrest warrant or NCIC printout is doing so in good faith and may not be charged with making an illegal arrest.

In order for an officer to legally arrest someone, he must make the person aware that she's "under arrest." The officer must make it clear to the suspect that he's a law enforcement official and has the proper authority to make an arrest. Officers are required to identify themselves as police officers. Undercover officers must give verbal identification and show their badges of authority. When a uniformed officer makes an arrest, his uniform and badge is evidence enough of his authority.

INITIAL SUSPECT ENGAGEMENT

The rules concerning the initial engagement of a suspect depend upon the officer's knowledge of that suspect and the crime at the time of the confrontation. The rules vary, depending upon whether the officer suspects the person of the crime or simply believes the person knows something about the crime but isn't involved. Either way, a law enforcement officer may stop and hold, or detain, someone if she has a reasonable suspicion that the person is involved in a crime or has knowledge of a crime. For her own safety, the officer may handcuff the suspect, but if at any time she decides the suspect has no knowledge of criminal activity, she must release him immediately.

Every person in the United States, resident or visitor, is required to supply basic information, if asked, to a law enforcement officer. Courts have ruled that an officer may legally ask for a person's name, address, and social security number, and the person is required to supply that information upon request.

An officer who has personal knowledge of the facts of a crime, but doesn't have probable cause to make an arrest, may *briefly* detain a suspect for the sole purpose of answering general questions—name, address, social security number. For example, let's say an officer knows that a robbery has just occurred at a convenience store. The clerk states the suspect was wearing a white T-shirt and jeans. Upon his arrival, the officer sees a young man walking away from the scene of the crime wearing a white T-shirt and jeans. The officer has the right to stop, hold, and question the suspect.

If the officer detains the suspect longer than is reasonably necessary to obtain general information (name, address, etc.), the stop becomes an arrest, and the rules of search and seizure based upon the Fourth Amendment—protection against unreasonable searches—as well as the rules of the Fifth Amendment—protection against self-incrimination—go into effect.

THE STOP AND FRISK SEARCH

If an officer believes a suspect may be concealing or carrying an illegal weapon, he may go one step further and frisk, or "pat down," the suspect. Keep in mind that officers must have facts to conduct a search, not merely a hunch, a gut feeling, or even a really good guess. The pat down search must be quick, and the officer may only perform it to search for weapons. Any other items discovered during this brief search may not be used as evidence, since their seizure would be considered the fruit of an illegal search, even if those items were later determined to be key items of evidence in a major case. Even if officers found a key piece of evidence that solved a string of murders, it couldn't be used. A pat down search may be conducted without arresting the suspect.

The rule of law that authorizes the stop and frisk of a suspect for weapons is based on the ruling in the precedent-setting case *Terry v. Ohio*. In this case a police officer observed a group of men pacing back and forth in front of a store. Upon each passing, the men would stop, peer into the windows, and then confer with one another. Soon they were joined by another man who also began to peer into the store.

Based on his years of experience and training, the officer believed the three men were acting suspiciously and were possibly planning to rob the store. He thought a proactive approach was best in this instance, so he walked over to them. In light of the situation, and for his own safety, the officer decided to frisk the men for weapons. During the pat down search, he discovered two handguns and charged the men with carrying concealed weapons. They were each convicted and, during the appeal process, their convictions were affirmed by the Supreme Court of the United States.

The court determined that a police officer need not be concerned with normal probable cause standards if she believes someone is illegally carrying concealed weapons. The officer need only consider the reasonableness surrounding the situation—and if she believes a crime has been, or is about to be, committed that could jeopardize someone's safety—she may legally conduct the pat down search without violating the suspect's rights. The Fourth Amendment of the U.S. Constitution guarantees this.

THE ARREST PROCESS

An arrest can be defined as an incident in which a person's freedom has been denied or reduced by law enforcement. An arrest doesn't always mean that a person is handcuffed or placed in a jail cell. An act as simple as telling a suspect that he's no longer free to leave the police station may constitute an arrest. Once a person's liberty has been denied, he must be formally charged with a crime. If not, he must be released.

The law doesn't specify a length of time that law enforcement may hold a suspect prior to issuing official charges, but it does state that the time frame must be reasonable. It's a very gray area of the law. A person who is held without cause or without being formally charged may file suit against the officers and/or the department where she was held. However, since the law is so vague, it's difficult to win a case of this nature unless the suspect can prove that the period of time was extensive and unreasonable.

A police officer may not remove a suspect from the place of questioning without making an arrest or without the suspect's permission. For example, if an officer shows up at a suspect's house, he can't legally force her to accompany him to the police station. She must either go with the officer voluntarily, or he must place her under arrest.

A person taken away in a police car does not, no matter how amiable the circumstances, normally feel free to leave. During the ride to the police station, the feeling of loss of liberty is reinforced because she's seated in a caged compartment. She's also separated from the officers by a heavy screen, and she can open neither the rear doors nor the windows from the inside. At that point, many people begin to feel that they're in police custody even if they've agreed to go with the officer.

To some people, a mere visit to a police station constitutes a feeling of imprisonment, especially police stations and sheriff's offices that also contain county or city jails. The individual must pass through electronically controlled gates, fences topped with razor wire, and steel doors that lock behind him after he passes through.

Inside is a flurry of activity. A suspect is often asked to empty his pockets and is searched for weapons and contraband. Armed police officers are everywhere—walking from office to office, escorting handcuffed prisoners, and talking to one another in cop lingo. Masked, undercover officers (undercover officers wear masks inside police stations to prevent the general public from learning their identities) gather weapons and restraints from the armory. Somewhere deep in the building, officers and prisoners can be heard arguing. An inmate wearing an orange jumpsuit scrubs the floor. Dozens of police radios constantly crackle and hiss canned voices. It's all very intimidating, especially for a first-time visitor or offender.

RESISTING ARREST

People are required by law to comply with an officer who's making a lawful arrest. Any attempt to physically defy that arrest can, and usually does, result in the officer charging the suspect with the crime of resisting arrest. Law enforcement officials may escalate their level of force to meet the resistance and to bring the subject under control.

A person who hasn't committed a crime and runs away or hides from police isn't resisting arrest. The resistance must be some form of physical contact, such as hitting, kicking, or in some way struggling to avoid the arrest.

In the case of an unlawful arrest (when a police officer attempts to arrest an innocent person), the suspect has the legal right to resist, but she'd better be prepared to offer the judge a very good and believable reason for her resistance. Defendants in resisting cases rarely ever prevail. On the other hand, just because a suspect can't be found doesn't mean she's a fugitive. She must know the police are actively looking for her to be labeled and charged as a fugitive. For example, the suspect may have been formally charged for a crime, arrested, and then released on bond. If she doesn't appear for her trial, she'd be considered a fugitive.

An undercover officer who doesn't properly identify himself may cause a person to resist arrest, thinking she's being improperly detained by someone other than a law enforcement officer. Sometimes even those officers who do offer proper identification find themselves in the middle of a scuffle. Some offenders find it difficult to be arrested by a man with long hair and a beard or a petite woman wearing a miniskirt.

For the safety of the officer, it's best to force combative suspects to the ground. Handcuffing is also easier when an aggressive suspect is in a prone position.

USE OF FORCE DURING AN ARREST

An officer may use whatever force is necessary to make an arrest. If all that's needed to get a suspect to comply is a verbal command to place his hands behind his back for handcuffing, that's all the force necessary. If a suspect becomes combative or resists arrest, an officer may escalate her use of force to meet the level of the suspect's resistance. If at any time she feels that her life or the life of another is in jeopardy, she may resort to the use of deadly force.

There are more nonlethal weapons available today than ever before in a police officer's arsenal. The devices listed below provide officers with many options before they're forced to use deadly force.

- **Concussion grenades.** Small, explosive devices commonly referred to by police officers as flash-bangs. Search warrant and special weapons and tactics (SWAT) teams toss these grenade-like devices into houses and buildings. A team's goal when using concussion grenades is to divert the criminal's attention away from the police officers, allowing the officers safe entry to the structure.

- **Shock sticks.** Nightstick-like weapons, also known as electric batons, with two electrodes on one end capable of delivering a low-voltage shock with the push of a button. The stick is used in a manner similar to a cattle prod.

- **Beanbag projectiles.** Cloth sacks filled with lead shot that are designed to be fired from twelve-gauge shotguns. They're normally used during riot situations.

- **ASP expandable batons.** Metal batons with retractable sections that fold inward like a telescope. When the baton is in its fully retracted position, an officer can carry it in a small leather case on his gun belt, or, if he's a plainclothes officer, inside his back pocket.

- **Two-handed riot batons.** Thirty-six inch batons made from wood (hickory) or hardened plastic. Officers and tactical response teams (TRTs) normally use these sticks for crowd control and riots. (Note that tact teams are used for riot and crowd control, duties not normally assigned to SWAT teams.) Prison guards often use them during prison riots.

- **Electric police jacket.** Jackets worn during riots to protect police officers against a hand-to-hand attack. The jackets shock anyone who touches them.

- **Stun belt.** Device placed around the waists of prisoners to prevent combative behavior. Officers carry a remote control device that, when activated, delivers a debilitating electric shock to the prisoner. This device is often used on jail and prison inmates, or by police officers when transporting violent suspects.

- **Noise- or sound-impulse devices.** Devices that deliver loud, repetitive audio impulses, noise, or even annoying music. Irritating noises will often cause suspects to surrender to police just to get away from the intense sounds.

- **Pepper spray (oleoresin capsicum).** An inflammatory agent derived from the fruits of capsicum (chili-pepper) plants. When a suspect is sprayed, his eyes close immediately and he begins to cough uncontrollably. The effect of the spray lasts for approximately thirty to forty minutes.

- **Freeze Plus P spray.** A combination of pepper spray and tear gas (orthochlorobenzalmalonitrile). This combination creates a synergistic effect, with each chemical magnifying the other. Freeze Plus P will penetrate wet or greased skin, as well as entering the body through inhalation.

- **The Wrap.** A nylon restraint device that can be wrapped around the torso and arms and legs of a combative person, rendering her almost motionless. The Wrap is held securely in place by wide strips of Velcro. Smaller versions of the Wrap are also available for use on just arms or legs. Police officers often use the Wrap when dealing with extremely violent suspects. The device allows officers to safely transport their prisoners to a nearby jail.

- **Rubber bullets.** A nonlethal means to disperse riots. The bullets are made from rubber and are fired from many types of firearms. Death can occur if the rubber projectiles are fired at someone at close range.

THE RIGHT TO REMAIN SILENT

The Fifth Amendment of the U.S. Constitution protects citizens against double jeopardy (being tried twice for the same offense). This amendment also provides citizens with the right to due process of the law and the right to just compensation in the case of eminent domain, in which the government takes a person's property for public use. Finally, the amendment protects citizens against self-incrimination, giving them the right to remain silent during questioning by police.

THE FIFTH AMENDMENT

No person shall be held to answer for a capital, or otherwise infamous crime, unless on a presentment or indictment of a Grand Jury, except in cases arising in the land or naval forces, or in the Militia, when in actual service in time of War or public danger; nor shall any person be subject for the same offence to be twice put in jeopardy of life or limb, nor shall be compelled in any criminal case to be a witness against himself, nor be deprived of life, liberty, or property, without due process of law; nor shall private property be taken for public use without just compensation.

In the course of any given day, police officers all across the country stop people just to talk to them. They ask questions, and they ask citizens for their permission to search them, their vehicles, their property, and their homes. This is all part of a proactive attempt to enforce the law and is quite legal.

No one who is not, or has not been, engaged in criminal activity is required to answer any officer's questions, except to provide basic information, such as his name, address, and social security number (although, believe it or not, not everyone knows his social security number). Criminals are expected to answer an officer's questions, although they rarely do. No one is required to allow officers to search him or his property without a warrant. On the other hand, since these people aren't in custody, officers aren't required to tell them they have the right to remain silent. Thinking they have to answer, and knowing they possess illegal items, many people admit their wrongdoings and grant officers permission to conduct searches. And every day officers make arrests for the contraband they find.

MIRANDA WARNINGS

On June 13, 1966, the four Miranda warnings (the right to remain silent; anything said can be used in a court of law; the right to the presence of an attorney; and if an attorney cannot be afforded one will be appointed *prior to any questioning*) were mandated by the Supreme Court of the United States as a means of protecting a criminal suspect against self-incrimination, a right guaranteed us by the Fifth Amendment of the U.S. Constitution.

Miranda warnings originated with a precedent-setting court case, *Miranda v. Arizona*. Ernesto Miranda was arrested for the slaying of a young woman in the mid-1960s. Miranda was taken into custody for the murder and later confessed, in detail, to the killing. During the questioning, detectives didn't tell Miranda that he didn't have to talk to the police, nor did they tell him he could have an attorney with him to aid in the questioning process.

In 1966, on appeal, the Supreme Court of the United States, with a 5-4 vote, ruled it unconstitutional that Miranda hadn't been advised of these basic rights. They went even further to rule that Miranda's statements couldn't be used against him in court. The prosecution had other evidence sufficient for a conviction, so, in a second trial, Miranda was convicted and sentenced to serve time in the penitentiary. (An interesting fact: Ernesto Miranda was released from prison after time served and was killed in a barroom fight. Ironically, his killer was advised of his rights according to *Miranda v. Arizona*. He chose to remain silent.)

We've all watched TV police detectives and patrol officers slap cuffs on a suspect and immediately begin advising the person of his rights. This is a TV falsehood that's designed to provide action for our entertainment. An officer is only required by law to read the Miranda warnings before questioning a suspect in police custody, not immediately upon arresting him. In fact, most officers don't advise a suspect of Miranda warnings at the time of arrest. I can think of many words that are exchanged between officers and suspects during and after a scuffle, but Miranda isn't one of them. Many of the words used during the heat of the moment are of the four-letter variety.

The law draws no firm line that determines when a person is in police custody. The rule of thumb is that a person is in police custody when she no longer feels she can leave the immediate area. A suspect who is handcuffed or sitting in a locked room inside a police station obviously can't leave and is definitely in custody.

Miranda warnings don't apply if an officer is speaking with a suspect and gives him no indication that he's in custody. This is true even if he's the sole suspect in a crime. Suspects sometimes claim they were tricked or coerced into talking with the police. They rarely ever win this argument.

It's common practice for police departments to have a preprinted waiver-of-rights form for the suspect to sign, stating she's been advised, agrees to waive her rights, and wishes to speak with the officers. The suspect, the questioning officer, and a witness—usually another officer—sign these forms.

An officer must obtain an affirmative answer from the suspect for all of the above before he may begin questioning. Should the suspect request an attorney, the officer may not question her, and the interview must cease. No further questioning of the suspect is permitted without her permission and/or the permission of her attorney.

Even if a suspect initially agrees to talk to an officer, he can change his mind at any time during the investigation and assert his right to remain silent. If an officer persists in questioning a suspect after he has asked for his attorney, any statements he makes after that point must not be used against him in court. This scenario does occur—officers sometimes become excited or get

---

WAIVER OF RIGHTS

1. You have the right to remain silent. Do you understand this right?

2. Anything you say can and will be used against you in a court of law. Do you understand this right?

3. You have the right to speak with an attorney and have him present with you while you are being questioned. Do you understand this right?

4. If you cannot afford to hire an attorney, one will be appointed to represent you before any questioning if you wish. Do you understand this right?

5. Do you understand each of these rights I have explained to you?

Having these rights in mind do you wish to talk to me (us) now?

Accused	_Officer_

Witness

---

carried away during stressful cases and continue their attempts to pry a confession from a suspect. Sometimes their illegal efforts are successful, but the cases are often overturned on appeal. This is a very difficult case for the defense to prove, but it does happen.

The officer should repeat the reading of these rights prior to each session of questioning or after any lapse in questioning, such as a lunch break.

If a person is merely a witness (not a suspect at this point in time) to a crime, an officer doesn't have to advise her of the Miranda warnings during questioning. However, if at any time the person shows involvement in the crime, she immediately becomes a suspect, and the officer must advise her of her rights according to *Miranda v. Arizona*.

There are certain instances in which a person can be interviewed and interrogated without being in police custody, such as when a suspect initiates the interview. If a suspect voluntarily comes to a police station, asks to speak with investigators, and provides details of his involvement in a crime, he's not considered to have been in custody during the questioning.

Incriminating statements made voluntarily don't fall under the custody rule of thumb; therefore, these statements are normally allowed into court as evidence, as are statements that are deemed to be spontaneous or excited utterances.

A spontaneous utterance is a statement made by someone in an animated state as part of her reaction to a particularly exciting event, such as a murder or an armed robbery. Courts have found that statements made during times of excitement are statements of truth. Lies take time to formulate.

It's good practice for a police officer to advise a suspect of the Miranda warnings each time he questions her to avoid problems in court. It's better to be safe than sorry, or to see a killer walk away free because of something the officers did or didn't do.

Once a person appears in court, he's no longer considered a suspect in the crime. He has become a defendant, and the officer can no longer question him without his attorney's permission.

Prisoners are incarcerated twenty-four hours a day and are definitely not free to leave their surroundings. However, courts have ruled that Miranda warnings and the custody rule-of-thumb don't automatically apply to prisoners who commit crimes while incarcerated, since they're free to move about the prison grounds and aren't always confined to a cell. If an interview takes place in a cell, the "in-custody" rule applies.

It's a different story if the interview is conducted in the prison recreation yard or other areas where prisoners are free to roam at will. In these areas, prisoners aren't technically considered to be in custody according to the rule; therefore, officers may ask general questions without advising the prisoner of his rights according to Miranda.

IN THE LINE OF DUTY
"MOUNTAIN MAN"

For all writers, character development is critical. For mystery writers, delving into every character's life, no matter which side of the crime line that character stands on, is crucial. If we don't understand the experiences of criminals and convicts, we cannot add the depth to our stories that our readers deserve.

— BECKY LEVINE, WRITER AND EDITOR

There was a powerhouse of a man we called "Mountain Man." This giant redneck lived in the country and, for his weekend recreation, loved to come into the city and drink, which always resulted in a fight he never lost. I saw many officers try to arrest him, and they were constantly tossed around like flies.

I had the unfortunate task, one fall night, of responding to a complaint from a local bar. The owner called to say that there was a monster of a man inside who was extremely intoxicated. The bartender had refused to serve the man, who then became violent. The club's three bouncers had tried to toss him outside, but that proved to be an enormous mistake. The man threw two of the bouncers through the glass front door, and the other wound up in the hospital emergency room with an assortment of broken ribs.

I was the first officer to arrive. I called in via radio to see how long before my backup would arrive, and I found out that everyone was tied up on a shooting complaint. Deciding I had no choice, I grabbed my flashlight, swallowed really hard a couple of times, felt to be sure my gun was on my side, and went inside. My fears were correct. It was indeed Mountain Man, and he'd already destroyed the inside of the bar. I don't think he'd left a single table or chair standing.

He saw me and grinned. Backing into a corner, he motioned with both hands for me to come and get him. The jukebox behind him glowed eerily through a cloud of cigarette smoke, and the mood lighting from the dance floor did nothing to tone down the situation. It was time to swallow hard again.

Everyone in the bar was waiting to see what I would do. It was pretty well known in the area that I held a black belt in the martial arts. I owned my own gym and martial arts school where I taught classes, and I was an instructor for defensive tactics at the police academy.

The room was silent, and I could hear Mountain Man breathing. In the distance, I actually thought I heard a drum playing, but soon realized that the sound was my own heart pounding inside my chest. I think it wanted to get out so it wouldn't have to be a part of the beating I was about to receive. Between snorts and snarls, the big man again motioned for me to come to the corner and get him. I took a couple of steps in his direction before I stopped and told him he was under arrest—that I didn't want to hurt him and he needed to make it easy on himself. I told him, in my most authoritative voice, to turn around so I could put the handcuffs on him. Right! But it sounded good.

A couple of people in the crowd chuckled at hearing my brave words. I actually grinned a bit, too. It was a dumb thing to say, given the circumstances.

I knew I would only have one chance at this guy, so I walked toward him until I was within arm's distance and looked him directly in the eyes. His breath reeked of alcohol, stale cigarette smoke, and onion dip. I could feel a faint hint of a breeze around my knees because my legs were shaking just enough to make my pant legs flutter.

We stared at one another like gunfighters in an Old West town.

Without another word, I hit him as hard as I could right between the eyes with my flashlight. The metal light broke into two pieces, and the four batteries tumbled to the floor. So did Mountain Man. I rolled him over, clicked on the cuffs, and called for the dispatcher to send an ambulance. Being the tight-knit group that cops are, and given the fact that the dispatcher had sent me to arrest the giant single-handedly, she asked if I was all right, instantly assuming I was the injured one. When I told her the ambulance was for the suspect, the male voice of a co-worker came across the radio. "What happened, did he pass out before you got there?"

The flashlight incident was talked about for several years and, to this day, I still hear an occasional comment about it. I do know that, from that night forward, whenever we were dispatched to arrest Mountain Man, I never had any further trouble from him. He would stop in mid-fight or argument when I arrived and would immediately turn around to allow me to place the leg irons around his wrists. (That's right—regular handcuffs wouldn't fit his massive wrists.)

They don't teach you the flashlight move in the police academy or in the martial arts, but they didn't tell me I should come in out of the rain, either.

Some things you just know.

SEARCH AND SEIZURE

The Fourth Amendment of the U.S. Constitution governs and restricts the powers of law enforcement officers to conduct searches of persons and property. Police officers are thoroughly trained in the laws of search and seizure. An officer has a very simple rule to follow when conducting searches: She must have a reasonable belief, based on reasonable sources of information, that evidence of a crime is located within the area to be searched. The search can't be based on a mere suspicion, but the officer doesn't have to be completely certain that the information prompting the search is a fact.

THE FOURTH AMENDMENT

The right of the people to be secure in their persons, houses, papers, and effects, against unreasonable searches and seizures, shall not be violated, and no Warrants shall issue, but upon probable cause, supported by Oath or affirmation, and particularly describing the place to be searched, and the persons or things to be seized.

Search warrants are much more difficult for a police officer to obtain than television would lead us to believe. Strict requirements, governed by the U.S. Constitution and the courts, must be met. The time and location of the search must be very specific. The items the police are searching for must be detailed on the warrant, and the persons they're searching for must be accurately described and identified by scars, marks, tattoos, and social security numbers, if available.

The rule of thumb for obtaining a search warrant is simple. If a police officer can't readily see an item and has to move something to see that item, his action is considered a search, and he needs a warrant. If an object is in plain view, the officer doesn't need a warrant (as long as he has just cause to be in a position to view that item).

For example, let's say that an officer is dispatched to a residence where domestic violence has occurred and—in the course of speaking with the residents—she sees a stack of microwave ovens in the corner. She knows a thief has been stealing microwave ovens in the neighborhood, and she even has the list of stolen serial numbers in her notebook. However, she can't touch the ovens to turn them over and check for matching numbers. She'll need a search warrant to do so. Now, I believe there would be enough probable cause to get that warrant, but the officer must leave the premises to do so. Were I in this position, I'd call for backup and have other officers stand guard outside and around the residence to assure no one disposed of the microwave ovens until I returned with the search warrant.

The officer applying for a search warrant must state under oath that the facts in the affidavit are true. The judge reviews the document, questions the officer regarding the reliability of the information, and issues and signs the search warrant. The entire search warrant process could take anywhere from a couple of hours to several months depending on the complexity and extensiveness of the investigation. The actual paperwork and approval by a judge can be completed in less than an hour.

Once the search warrant is signed by a judge, the officer's work has only just begun. There's a stringent time frame that must be followed to execute and serve the search warrant. There are hard-and-fast rules of law governing how the warrant must be served.

A search warrant, to retain its effectiveness, should be served as soon as possible after the court has issued it. Any delay could provide the suspect ample time to hide, destroy, alter, or dispose of the sought-after evidence. After servicing the warrant, the officer must fill out a detailed inventory of the items seized and return that list and the warrant to the court within three days (seventy-two hours) after executing the search (the seventy-two hour time limit may vary depending upon the locality).

How the officer must serve, or execute, the warrant depends entirely upon the situation. The knock and announce rule of law requires an officer to knock first and then announce (through a closed door) her intention to serve a search warrant. She must then wait a reasonable time (a specific time frame hasn't been ruled upon) for someone to answer the door before resorting to extreme methods of gaining entry (we'll look at the exception to this rule shortly).

EXCLUSIONARY RULE

The exclusionary rule is a protection of a suspect's rights against illegal searches and the illegal seizure of property and evidence during that search. The rule simply states that no illegally obtained evidence may be used against a defendant.

If the officer checks the serial numbers on the aforementioned microwave ovens without first obtaining the warrant, and if she finds the entire stack to be stolen property, she can't use this information, no matter how incriminating, as evidence in court. The evidence is inadmissible because it was obtained during an illegal search.

The defense attorney would file a motion to suppress the evidence, and the court would be forced to grant the motion. This situation could very well result in nonprosecution, and the defendant would be set free as if nothing had happened. An illegal search can also result in civil or criminal proceedings against the officers involved and the department or disciplinary proceedings against the officers. Termination of employment is another possibility for the officers.

A search warrant is normally written to cover a suspect's entire house and property. Judges normally require separate warrants to search people other than the residents of the home. However, for safety purposes, officers may handcuff and frisk everyone inside the house. Any people not listed on the warrant or who aren't involved in the crime in question may be released as soon as it's safe to do so. Separate warrants are also required for vehicles located on the property.

Some courts have ruled it unconstitutional for police officers to search the room of a minor child if the child keeps his room locked, preventing parents from having ready access. The same holds true for people who rent a room in someone's house. Police may not search the room of a tenant without a separate search warrant.

An officer can only conduct a search until she's found the item, or items, listed in the search warrant. If the officer is looking for a stolen gun and finds that gun beside the front door, she can't go any further into the residence. However, officers may seize any illegal items, in addition to the items listed on the warrant, found during a legal search.

At the time of arrest, a police officer may search the arrested person and the area immediately surrounding the suspect without a search warrant. This search is allowed for the officer's safety and to eliminate the suspect's means of escape. Any evidence the officer seizes at this time isn't subject to the exclusionary rule.

An officer doesn't need a search warrant if the owner of the property, or any person (including a husband or wife) having control of the property, gives consent for the officer to search. The officer should obtain consent in writing to avoid possible disputes. Most departments have preprinted consent-to-search forms available.

The word *curtilage*, another important term used by police and other law enforcement officials, is found quite often in the body of a search warrant. Curtilage refers to the area surrounding a house or home, such as a wooded area or toolshed, which is frequented by the homeowners or residents.

CONSENT TO SEARCH

I, _____, authorize Detective _____ of the Anytown Police Department to search my property located at _____, Anytown, America. I further authorize Detective _____ to confiscate and remove any and all items found that are either illegal to own or to possess.

No threats or promises have been made to me in return for my granting consent to search my property.

_____   _____
Property Owner   *Witness*

AFFIDAVIT FOR SEARCH WARRANT

To obtain a search warrant, the requesting officer must submit a sworn affidavit for search warrant before a judge or an appropriate officer of the court, such as a magistrate. The affidavit is a very precise and a very detailed document, and it must contain clear-cut information based upon specific facts, not assumptions.

An affidavit for search warrant is divided into sections, with each section pertaining to a specific item of the desired search.

AFFIDAVIT FOR SEARCH WARRANT

1. A search is requested in relation to an offense substantially described as follows: _____ _____.

2. The place, person, or thing to be searched is described as follows: _____.

3. The things or persons to be searched for are described as follows: _____.

4. The material facts constituting probable cause that the search should be made are: _____.

5. The object, thing, or person searched for constitutes evidence of the commission of such offense: _____ _____. (List offense and code section here.)

6. I have personal knowledge of the facts set forth in this affidavit, OR I was advised of the facts set forth in this affidavit, in whole or by part, by an informer. The informer's credibility or the reliability of the information may be determined from the following facts: _____ _____.

_____   _____
Affiant   *Judge or Magistrate*

SEARCH WARRANT FORM

The wording of a search warrant varies from jurisdiction to jurisdiction. The sample below shows the basic wording common to all search warrants.

SEARCH WARRANT

To any policeman of the county, city or town:

You are hereby commanded by the State of _____ to forthwith search either in the day or night _____ (detailed description of the person or property) located at _____ (precise address) and its curtilage.

You are further commanded to seize said property, persons, and/or objects if they be found, and to produce before the _____ (name of issuing court) an inventory of all property, persons, and/or objects seized.

This warrant is issued in relation to an offense described as follows: _____. (Code section for the law governing the particular offense. Code sections differ in various states.)

_____   _____
Affiant   *Judge or Magistrate*

EXIGENT CIRCUMSTANCES

The *only* exception to the knock and announce rule is found in exigent circumstances. Webster's dictionary defines *exigent* as demanding, exacting, or requiring immediate action. Obviously, if a SWAT team is serving a search warrant at the residence of a suspect who has shot and killed three police officers, the SWAT supervisor won't knock on the front door and politely wait for the suspect to answer. This type of search warrant service involves exigent circumstances, and an officer may serve it under cover of night and with a heavily armed, well-protected entry team. This team would likely set off flash-

---

bangs for diversion and then enter the residence by force, taking the suspect—hopefully—by surprise. The safety of all involved, including the suspect and innocent bystanders, is the ultimate goal for the officer, along with achieving the purpose of the warrant.

Gathering the information needed for the affidavit can take days, weeks, months, and even years. The process can involve long hours of surveillance, covert undercover operations, and vast hours of manpower. Obtaining a search warrant is one of the most arduous duties of any detective, but also one of the most rewarding, when she recovers the murder weapon or stash of drugs.

Television and movies depict cops stampeding their way into the homes and warehouses of the drug dealers and their labs. There's always a shoot-out and the good guys always win. There *are* times, unfortunately, when a search yields nothing at all, except embarrassment. There's no worse feeling than to conduct numerous hours, days, and even months of surveillance on the property of a suspected criminal and then—when you think the time is right—kick in the door and rush in, followed by the entire entry team with weapons drawn, only to find that you've accidentally gone into the neighbor's home. It happens.

Day after day, police officers throughout the country serve search warrants. Sometimes they find what they're looking for; other times they don't. Patience is a huge part of the search warrant game. The investigator who gathers intelligence is like a spider waiting for a fly—sooner or later, the insect will make a mistake and fly into the web of the spider. Then, like the spider, the officer must move quickly and capture his reward. That's how a cop feels when a well-planned raid is properly executed—like she's received a reward.

WARRANTLESS SEARCH AND SEIZURES

A search warrant isn't always required to make a lawful search and seizure. Let's take a closer look at the exceptions.

PLAIN VIEW

An officer doesn't need a search warrant to view something that's in plain view. In fact, many narcotics arrests stem from suspects leaving their "stash" lying on a car seat or console where an officer can readily see it during a common traffic stop. The plain view rule even extends to an officer seeing illegal items through the windows of a suspect's home, as long as the officer has a just reason for being in a position to see inside the window. For example, let's say an officer approaches someone's front door to ask him a question regarding something that's happened in the neighborhood. While standing on the front porch she can clearly see inside the house through a glass storm door. Inside the room she sees a kilo of cocaine, scales, and packaging material lying on a table. She may use that sighting as probable cause for a search warrant. The plain view rule even extends so far as to allow the officer to go into the home without a search warrant if there's reason to believe the evidence will be destroyed or removed before a warrant can be obtained.

PLAIN TOUCH

During pat down searches for weapons, an officer often discovers items that aren't guns or knives. If, based on his training and years of experience, he immediately recognizes that an object is illegal, he may seize it. However, he must be able to satisfactorily articulate what led him to that conclusion.

Officers are taught the word *articulate* and its meaning early in police academy training. More often than not, unclear testimony leads to the dismissal of the suspect's charges.

CHAPTER 6

HOMICIDE, MURDER, AND
MANSLAUGHTER

Murder: a life extinguished, mid-sentence. It's a police officer's job to work the crime scene, pursue the truth, and respect the dead; a writer would do well to treat his own scenes with as much consideration—a little less CSI, a lot more compassion. After all, cops and writers share the same goal: to find the best way to finish the victim's sentence.

—THERESA SCHWEGEL, EDGAR AWARD-WINNING CRIME-FICTION AUTHOR OF
OFFICER DOWN, PROBABLE CAUSE, AND PERSON OF INTEREST

We are a society that's obsessed with death. Scores of movies, TV shows, and books are written with murder as their point of interest. People are fascinated with how, why, and when killers commit their crimes. Entire families structure their evenings around reality police shows. During the day, we tune our sets to coverage of the real-time murder trials of the rich and famous. Newscasters describe overnight slayings while we eat our breakfast and drink our coffee. And in the evenings, we watch procedural crime dramas play out on prime time.

We can't seem to pass by an automobile crash without slowing down to look for blood and amputated body parts. Our kids play video games in which the object is to kill as many people as they possibly can in one sitting.

We watch it, we read it, and we dream it, and a lot of people still get it wrong—murder and homicide aren't the same. All murders are homicides, but not all homicides are murders.

CRIMES INVOLVING DEATH

Taking the life of a human being is considered taboo in most cultures. When a killing occurs, it's normally left to the courts to decide the fate of the killer. To do so, judges and juries must first examine the circumstances surrounding the death.

Murders are like snowflakes—no two are exactly the same. The facts surrounding each case must be thoroughly scrutinized by authorities before they can decide what charges may apply. There are several criminal categories involving death, and each category is accompanied by its own individual criminal charge. Once the crime has been assigned to an appropriate category, authorities can proceed with issuing warrants that correspond to the crime.

The categories of criminal death are (charges may vary in some courts):

- capital murder
- first-degree murder
- second-degree murder
- third-degree murder
- manslaughter

To better understand how police and the courts decide which charges apply to a killing, one must understand the meaning of the term *homicide*.

Homicide, simply put, is the killing of one human being by another. Homicide is not always considered a crime, as in the case of self-defense or in the instance of a police officer who uses deadly force to defend himself or someone else. These instances are considered justifiable homicides.

When killings aren't justifiable, they're considered illegal and are classified as murder. The crime of murder is a felony that some people believe to be the ultimate crime. The absence or presence of malice is the determining factor as to whether a homicide is deemed a murder.

A death that results from negligence, such as a death resulting from a traffic accident, is considered illegal homicide, but it's not necessarily murder. Any killing that occurs during the course of robbery, rape, or burglary is also an illegal homicide, and the killer is normally charged with murder. As always, the burden of proof to provide evidence that the act wasn't criminal lies solely on the accused, although in some cases, the evidence shows beyond a shadow of doubt that the killing was in self-defense, the defense of others, or an accident.

Punishment for murder is based upon the level, or degree, of murder for which the defendant is convicted. The distinctions between the different classes of murder are based on the circumstances in which the crime was committed. The most severe class of murder is capital murder, in which a guilty verdict for certain offenses, or a combination of offenses, demands a punishment of life in prison without the possibility of parole, or death.

Let's take a closer look at each type of murder charge.

CAPITAL MURDER

Most states require that, before a person can be charged, tried, and convicted of capital murder, he must have committed one or more of the following offenses:

- Premeditated and planned the killing of a person, or willfully and deliberately killed a person during the course of an abduction, rape, armed robbery, attempted armed robbery, sodomy, attempted rape, or murder for hire.

- Premeditated the killing of an officer, or willfully and deliberately killed a law enforcement officer during the performance of his duties when that killing was for the purpose of interfering with his official duties as a law enforcement officer.

- Premeditatedly, willfully, and deliberately killed a corrections officer while incarcerated as a prisoner in a jail or prison.

- Premeditatedly, willfully, and deliberately killed more than one person during the commission of one crime or crime spree.

- Premeditatedly, willfully, and deliberately killed a person during the course of an illegal narcotics transaction, when that killing was for the purpose of continuing that crime or drug transaction.

- Premeditatedly, willfully, and deliberately killed a child under the age of twelve, when that killing was part of an abduction or part of an attempted abduction.

Note the use of the terms *premeditatedly, willfully,* and *deliberately* in each of the above capital murder offenses. A murder that's committed with the absence of willfulness, deliberateness, and premeditation can't be considered capital murder. In other words, to be convicted of capital murder, the killer must have shown forethought, planning, and intent to commit one of the above listed offenses.

Forethought can be something as simple as looking at Web sites, such as when convicted murderer Scott Peterson used his computer to research tide patterns in the San Francisco Bay. That bit of research indicated that he may have been planning to dispose of his wife's body in those waters.

FIRST- AND SECOND-DEGREE MURDER

The law normally specifies two classes of murder other than capital murder—first- and second-degree murder, although some states have a provision for third-degree murder, which applies to the indirect and unintentional killing of someone, such as a drug dealer who supplies drugs to an overdose victim. (Contact your local clerk of court, prosecutor, or police department to learn of specific charges for your area).

First-degree murder involves a killing during the commission of lying in wait, holding someone against her will, poisoning, or starving, or during the acts of robbery, inanimate-object sexual penetration, forcible sodomy, burglary, or abduction.

All other murders are considered second-degree murders. Second-degree murder is a murder committed due to the reckless indifference for human life, such as in the case of a death resulting from an accident where the driver of the car who initiated the accident was intoxicated.

The charge of second-degree murder can vary in some states, and, interestingly, some states consider *all* murders to be second-degree murders until the state (prosecution) proves that aggravating factors are present. Only after that proof is presented does the charge elevate to first-degree or capital murder. In most states, the act of illegal homicide is always considered second-degree murder.

MANSLAUGHTER

Although not all homicides are illegal, such as in the case of self-defense or the defense of others, those that are committed outside the law are considered felonies (crimes punishable by one or more years in a state or federal prison). Any homicide that occurs accidentally, but occurs during the commission of another crime, is considered to be illegal.

Manslaughter is a criminal homicide that's without deliberation, malice, or premeditation but that has occurred during a reckless, careless, or otherwise unforgivable act of irrational behavior. It's a killing in which no excuse can describe or explain away the actions of the accused.

Voluntary manslaughter occurs most often during the heat of the moment, such as during a scuffle when one person kills another accidentally as a result of the fight.

Involuntary manslaughter occurs when someone kills another while committing an unlawful act without intending any bodily harm to another other person. The homicide is an accident, such as during a fatal automobile accident.

MURDER METHODS

There are different means of committing murder. Not all murders involve the victim and the killer being at the same place at the same time, but all murders are the result of a person's indirect or direct action. A murder by direct action occurs when a killer, by his own hand, causes the death of a victim by using a weapon or his own bare hands.

An indirect murder is usually the result of a scheme or convoluted plot to kill someone—a plot where the murderer causes a person's death either by the hand of a third party, by using a method like poisoning, or by staging an accident in which the victim dies. Some would-be killers have even used scare tactics in attempts to cause their victims to suffer a heart attack.

Killers have used an array of far-out schemes to stop a heartbeat, such as taking advantage of their victim's phobias. Desperate criminals have attempted murder by placing claustrophobic victims in close, tight areas. People who are arachnophobic (afraid of spiders) or ophidiophobic (afraid of snakes) have been forced to be in close proximity to spiders and snakes. Killers have even tossed live reptiles onto their victims. Would-be murderers have dressed up as clowns to frighten those who are coulrophobic (afraid of clowns), and they've even tried to kill by shutting someone in total darkness who suffers from achluophobia (the fear of darkness). These methods are rarely successful, but they're occasionally attempted.

The most common types of murder include:

- **Crime of passion:** occurs suddenly and in the heat of the moment when anger is provoked by an act, actions, or words. The killer is often someone whom friends and family would never think of as a criminal, and whom they'd definitely never consider capable of murder. Crimes of passion often involve infidelity, financial troubles, and/or bad business deals. Crimes of passion are normally direct murders.

- **Murder for hire:** a crime that involves two or more parties who engage in a business transaction in which one person hires another to kill a third person. The reasons a person hires someone else to do his dirty work vary. Either the instigator doesn't have the nerve to do the deed himself or he wants the trail of evidence to point away from himself. Hiring a third party to kill allows him to establish an alibi. These alibis are often so airtight that it's difficult for investigators to prove the suspect had any involvement with the crime. As always, though, when more than one person is involved in the commission of a crime, that crime becomes easier to solve as time passes. Detectives and criminals alike share a saying: The only way two people can safely share a secret is for one to kill the other. A murder for hire can be either a direct or indirect murder.

- **Poisoning:** normally an indirect method of killing. Although the killer usually feeds the victim her lethal dosage by placing a toxic substance in her food or drink, a murderer may sometimes inject his victim with an overdose of legal or illegal drugs. An injection of this type deems the murder a direct homicide.

- **False or staged accidents:** another indirect method of killing. The killer is usually not around when her victim succumbs to the effects of faulty automobile brakes or a partially sawn rung on a ladder.

- **Implied malice or extreme neglect:** occurs when someone does something so hurtful to another person that the act alone would shock a normal person, such as feeding harmful substances to a helpless infant or violently shaking an infant until death results. Killings that fall into this category can be either direct or indirect.

- **Irresistible impulse:** when the killer knows what he's doing is wrong but feels the uncontrollable need to commit the act regardless of the consequences. The killer seems to have no mental control of his actions. This killer normally relies on a defense of insanity or diminished mental capacity at the time he committed the crime. An irresistible impulse can be carried out directly or indirectly.

- **Murder while under duress:** occurs when someone feels that legitimate threats of death or physical harm have been made against himself or members of his family, such as the case in which a child has been abducted and the kidnappers tell the father he must kill someone in exchange for the release of the child. This type of murder can be direct or indirect.

- **Lynching:** an act of violence by a group of people that can be described as a mob, which results in the death of a particular individual. Lynching is a felony and is considered a direct murder.

INVESTIGATING MURDER

Murder investigations are conducted much like any other investigation—the crime occurs, the police respond, investigators process the scene and collect the evidence, and *then* the real work begins. It's often said on television, and even in some real police departments, that a murder must be solved within the first forty-eight hours after its occurrence or the chances of it being solved are reduced to almost zero.

This is partially true, but not always. First of all, the forty-eight-hour rule can apply to any situation in which humans are involved. People have a tendency to forget things as time passes. They also have a tendency to allow their imaginations, families, friends, and co-workers to get in the way of their recollections. Sometimes even a person's own fears can skew her memories.

The best possible time for detectives to interview a witness to a crime is immediately after the offense has occurred, while the events are still fresh in the witness's mind. At this point he hasn't had time to let nature take its course and let doubt overtake fact. *Maybe he was tall, or wait, maybe he really wasn't. Could he have had a beard, or was it just a moustache? Red hair or blonde? Caucasian, Hispanic, African-American, or maybe Asian?* The first description of a suspect by a witness is usually the best description.

As time passes, witnesses also have a tendency to back off from being involved in the situation. Sometimes the perpetrator may have even contacted the witnesses and warned them against speaking to police about the case.

Evidence from the crime scene itself can grow stale, old, or even be misplaced or accidentally destroyed if too much time elapses. There's no better time for an investigator to begin her detective work than when the case is hot. Even investigators can become can bored with a case if the excitement of the moment wanes and they don't make any progress.

Pride sometimes plays a large part in a detective's decision to slow his work on a case that's not showing signs of progress. Efficiency statistics can be a very important part of a police officer's record, and those same statistics can be a factor in promotions and raises. A detective with a poor crime-solving record and low arrest numbers may soon find himself back in uniform patrolling a high-crime area on the midnight shift. Unsolved cases can reflect poorly on detectives. This can cause a case to be written off as unsolved or cold so the detective can move on to a case that's fresher or more active—and possibly easier to solve.

Some departments have special divisions or task forces dedicated to solving unsolved, or cold, cases. These investigators don't have to worry about case clearance rates or other statistics, so they can devote all their attention to a single case.

TV shows such as *CSI: Crime Scene Investigation* depict crime scene detectives and investigators in the best possible light. Unlike real-life detectives, the TV homicide cops always dress impeccably and have the finest tools of the trade available to them at all times. Their highly complex crimes are solved within sixty minutes, minus commercial breaks—forty minutes with TiVo. In reality, nothing can be further from the truth.

A murder scene, like any crime scene, is secured by the first officers to arrive. Detectives and, if available, crime scene technicians are called to gather evidence. In many cases police departments don't have specialized crime scene investigators or technicians. Crime scene investigators are normally police detectives. Crime scene technicians are normally civilian employees who have received specialized training in the field of evidence collection.

The two best tools a detective has in his arsenal are a good pair of shoes and the gift of gab. The detective must be willing to get out, walk door-to-door, through alleys, up and down streets, through the projects, and through high-class neighborhoods, all while walking the walk and talking the talk of everyone he meets. The detective must constantly ask question after question after question. Most crimes are solved this way. Physical evidence, such as hair, DNA, and fingerprints are all icing on the cake.

DESCRIBING THE HOMICIDE SCENE

There are no textbooks or instruction manuals that can accurately describe to you, the writer, what stimulates you or your readers' senses. Books can't bring forth real smells and sounds, and they can't activate a person's taste buds. Words can, however, bring forth memories, and those memories force our brains to associate words with familiar sights, sounds, and tastes. It's the writer's job to use the proper adjectives that best arouse a reader's senses.

A description of the dew-dampened petals of a wildflower may rekindle the memory of the rainy day when a thoughtful husband sent his wife a dozen roses for no reason at all other than to offer a gesture of love. Words describing the pops, flashes, and bangs of Fourth of July fireworks may renew a police officer's memories of the sounds heard during a shootout with an armed robber. Officers must write their reports without the words that so vividly animate sentences; they aren't even allowed to describe obvious things, like blood and tissue.

There's a distinct difference between the way a writer describes a murder scene and the way that police officers are trained to record the same picture. A police officer's job is to document the facts and then use those facts to solve crimes. Prosecutors use those facts to convict the perpetrators of crimes. Only after an examination by a trained professional working in a laboratory can a substance discovered at a crime scene be positively labeled as blood, saliva, or semen.

The following sample narrative report by a police officer is an example of how an officer might write his official account of a homicide case.

On August 25, 2004, at 1604 hours my partner, Detective Ben There, and I were dispatched to 1234 Grave Street, Anytown, USA, a dead-end street. Upon arrival I met with Officer W.A. Happened, the first officer on the scene, who told me that an apparent homicide had occurred inside the master bedroom of the residence. He thought the murder weapon could possibly have been an ax. Officer Happened also advised me that he had sealed the perimeter of the entire scene with crime scene tape and had called the coroner and emergency medical personnel. He further stated that he had posted Officer J. Smiley at the rear door of the house to maintain the crime scene log book.

At 1617 hours, Officer Happened relinquished control of the scene to me, Detective I.N. Charge. Detective There and I approached the crime scene from the rear door of the residence, where Officer Smiley was stationed. He had each of us sign the log before entering the house.

The body of a female was found lying supine on the master bedroom floor surrounded by a liquid substance which was brownish red in color. Dr. Idun Feelsogood, county coroner, stated the victim was indeed deceased and had died of what appeared to be several wounds inflicted by a large edged weapon. The doctor stated that an autopsy would be performed to determine the actual cause of death. There were no people present at the house other than law enforcement and medical personnel. The coroner's investigators placed the victim into a body bag and then transported it to the morgue. Dr. Feelsogood advised me that he would contact the family.

The scene was cleared and released at 2007 hours.

Detective I.N. Charge
Badge number 153

Writers use words not only to deliver facts but to provoke a reader's senses. The paragraphs below describe the same murder scene as the officer's report above, but using words that energize a reader's sensations. This scene is real, and many years later I can still taste, touch, feel, hear, and smell the murder in my mind.

The first officer on the scene said the killer had used an old ax with a rough oak handle—the kind that would leave splinters in your hand if you didn't wear gloves. I'd already noticed a chop-marked stump next to a small mountain of split, red oak. The ax that had made those cuts wasn't anywhere in sight.

The victim's house, a run-down Victorian, with its cracked windows, peeling paint, torn shingles, and general gloom and despair, gave me the creeps. When I was a kid, I'd have thought the place was haunted.

My partner and I stepped onto a back porch that had once been screened-in. The screens were gone, and all that was left in their place were a few tattered corners of the rusted, woven-metal mesh. The wood that had once held the screens in place had rotted long ago and succumbed to insects, termites I supposed. A white garbage bag sat next to the door. Some sort of liquid had escaped the bag and left a sticky-looking, wet trail across the painted floor where it disappeared beneath a lopsided washing machine.

We were met at the door to the kitchen by a uniformed officer. He handed me a clipboard that held the sign-in sheet—a page torn from a spiral-bound notebook. I scribbled my initials and badge number on the second hand-drawn line; the only name before mine was the coroner's.

Inside, the first two rooms appeared normal. Thick candles scented with something tropical—coconut and mango maybe—sat burning on the tiled countertop; soft, light jazz spilled from a portable radio. A faint hint of spoiled milk struck my nose as we passed the sink. Two dirty glasses. A trace of cola in the bottoms.

A ceiling fan twirled slowly, slightly off balance. It clicked softly with each oblong rotation. Its light, spring-like breeze didn't match what we found in the next room.

The body lay on a hardwood floor—whitewashed oak. Her eyes were open and seemed to look through me. It felt as if her gaze paused briefly at the core of my very soul, as if attempting to see my innermost thoughts, before moving on into infinity. I had to look away.

Puddles of blood (don't step in the blood puddles was a thought that kept swirling through my mind) had begun to dry and were the consistency of warm pudding just as the skin begins to form on top. The color of the syrupy liquid had already transformed from bright red to the brownish red of burnt transmission fluid.

The air was filled with the scent of human tissue and blood. It was the stench that we investigators associate with violent death and its ingredients. The scent is that of a butcher shop combined with corroded, green copper. It's an odor that's not quickly forgotten.

Even though I knew she was dead—hacked to death with an ax—I placed a gloved finger on the dead woman's throat where her pulse should have been. Her cool flesh was like firm Jell-O.

> The coroner's attendants waited until I stood, and then they loaded the body—that's what she was now, just a body—onto a gurney.
> I turned to the task at hand. It was my job to find her killer.

A death scene, such as the one described in the paragraphs above, is a sensory mix of sentiments that lay heavily on one's mind. The mingled odors can be tasted when you inhale, and that scent clings fiercely to the taste buds. Sometimes forever.

The taste and smell sensations of a murder scene can be closely mimicked by touching your tongue to a penny and holding it there for a second or two to allow the taste to firmly embed itself in your mind. Then, with that tang fresh on your tongue, open a package of "reduced for quick sale" hamburger and draw a long whiff deep into your lungs. That's the combination. That's the taste and smell of murder. Sometimes you can detect a faint whiff of burnt gunpowder wafting through a death scene, even hours after the killing has taken place.

The silence at murder scenes is sometimes overwhelming for detectives as they scour through evidence while looking for clues. It's not unusual for even the most experienced detectives to hear their own hearts beating. Talking among the detectives is often reduced to whispering—the whir and flash of cameras are amplified.

Death itself is quite loud. It's heavy, and it smothers the living with unanswered questions. Homicide detectives are often asked how they deal with the day-in and day-out carnage. Their responses are usually similar in nature—they leave their work at work. They don't talk about it. Instead, each detective deals with the situation in her own way.

Some go home after work and put on running clothes and headphones and go out for a jog; others engage in hobbies, lift weights, cook, garden, or bowl. Sadly, some turn to drinking and drug use to relieve their minds of the stress that's associated with their jobs. Those who can handle it do, and they return to face it yet again another day.

CHAPTER 7

CRIME SCENE
INVESTIGATION

Detectives and crime scene investigators often think of each other as "highly overrated." In reality, both are "highly dependent" on the other to successfully solve and prosecute crimes.

—LIEUTENANT DAVID SWORDS, RETIRED,
SPRINGFIELD, OHIO, POLICE DEPARTMENT

It's important for writers to know that not all crime scene investigators are sworn police officers. Many years ago, before technology was so very important in police investigations, crime scene investigators were always police officers. Now, many departments hire civilian specialists whose duties are to collect and examine the evidence that's found at various crime scenes. It's easier to separate the two positions—police officer and crime scene investigator—because of the difference in training and salaries. Sworn police officers generally earn the higher salary.

The job description of crime scene investigator is wide-ranging. These highly skilled workers are trained in areas of expertise such as crime scene photography, latent and patent fingerprinting, computer technology and electronics, blood-spatter examination, firearms and ballistics, and tool and tool-mark examinations. Police detectives, especially homicide detectives, normally receive training in all the above areas.

To understand how a crime scene investigation is conducted, one must understand the difference between a crime scene and the scene of a crime. The scene of the crime is any area where a crime has been committed. A crime scene is an area where evidence from a crime can be found. For example, let's say a store clerk is robbed and killed during a robbery. The store where this incident took place is the scene of the crime.

Hours later, the robber is driving the getaway car down a deserted country road. He rolls down the car window and tosses the murder weapon into the bushes, where it's later found by a farmer. The area where the gun is found is now a crime scene because evidence of a crime is located there. Police detectives seal the area surrounding the gun and gather any evidence that can be found. Both locations are crime scenes, but both aren't the actual scene of the crime.

Investigators handle the scene of a crime differently than crime scenes because the danger level is often higher. Responding officers must be alert for the presence of the perpetrators and their accomplices.

THE CRIME SCENE

Death comes in many forms and is accomplished by many methods. A killer, or would-be killer, sometimes uses a weapon other than the traditional gun or knife. A killing that takes place on the spur of the moment can force a murderer to become quite creative with his choice of weapons.

When approaching a crime scene, officers should never rule out any one object as a potential murder weapon. People have killed with hammers, baseball bats, poisons, electric shocks, knives, forks, needles, drugs, reptiles, automobiles, trains, planes, water, pillows, wire, axes, hatchets, nail guns, screwdrivers, and their bare hands.

At all costs, officers should avoid adrenaline-induced tunnel vision. Once the blue lights begin to flash and the sirens start to wail and yelp, excitement makes it quite easy for officers to lose track of their surroundings. Their heartbeats become rapid, and their tone of speech sometimes climbs another octave (the voice change is evident to anyone who's listened to a police radio or a scanner). However, when officers are traveling to the scene of a crime or a crime scene, especially a crime in progress, they should always take the time to scan the area on the way. They should look on both sides of the road, on walkways and sidewalks, in parking lots, in neighbors' lawns, beside bushes, in wooded areas, and at passing cars. It's quite possible they'll see the criminal departing the scene or hanging around to watch the police arrive. Criminals often like to watch the police conduct investigations.

Police officers are schooled to protect all evidence, but protecting human life comes first. In most instances, an officer should wait for backup before proceeding into a crime scene, but when someone is ill or injured she may have to enter to administer first aid.

Once an area has been established as a crime scene and they've provided any necessary first aid, officers should set up and secure a perimeter, allowing only necessary personnel—the detectives investigating the case, the medical examiner, and the crime scene and evidence technicians—inside the crime scene. A chief of police, sheriff, and the mayor of the city don't count as necessary people, although they seem to think they are, especially during election years or when members of the press are present.

THE FIRST OFFICER ON THE SCENE

The first officer on the scene of a homicide, or any crime scene, is most often a uniformed patrol officer. The dispatcher receives a 911 telephone call, and he assigns the case to the next patrol officer on the rotation. Depending upon the severity of the crime and the danger level, more than one officer may be assigned to the same case.

Upon her arrival at the scene of a crime, a responding officer must first, if necessary, defend herself or others against attackers. It's then her responsibility to provide first aid to the injured and protect the scene and the remaining victims, or witnesses, from harm. It's her duty to make the necessary arrangements to contact emergency personnel, the medical examiner, the crime scene investigation team, and the detectives on duty or on call.

Each patrol car should be equipped to properly safeguard a crime scene, and each responding officer should have the knowledge and ability to process the entire scene in the event that all detectives or crime scene investigators are busy elsewhere. The following basic crime scene equipment can be found in each responding police vehicle:

Patrol officers carry basic crime scene equipment in the trunks of their vehicles.

- consent-to-search forms
- crime scene barricade tape
- personal protective equipment
- first aid kit
- paper bags
- flashlight
- flares
- notebook or note pad
- tape recorder
- camera
- plastic bags
- knife/scissors
- tape measure
- traffic cones
- hand cleaner
- cell phone

THE CRIME SCENE INVESTIGATOR

Upon arrival at the crime scene, the investigators, or detectives, assume charge of the scene. They may require the assistance of the uniformed officers for perimeter control, crowd control, media access, and security. If they require no further assistance from the uniformed officers, the detective in charge may dismiss them to continue their patrol duties. At this point the investigation begins.

Detectives use a variety of means to solve crimes of all types. Those means can be as simple as speaking with witnesses. Investigators can also use any number of scientific tests to aid them in their quests for a killer's identity.

The chart below describes some of the duties and responsibilities of the crime scene investigator.

DUTY OF A CRIME SCENE INVESTIGATOR	ACTION TAKEN
Respond to the call.	Record time, date, and location. Record names of all persons present.
Establish the perimeter.	Assure that the scene is safe and first aid is rendered. Seal the area. Allow no one to enter or leave unless authorized by detectives.
Survey the crime scene.	Determine the type of search to be used. Call for assistance if needed.
Check the body for signs of life and for evidence of the murder method.	Check the pulse, pupils (touch eyes for response), bleeding, wounds, livor mortis, and rigor mortis.
Respond to the medical examiner's arrival.	Note the time of arrival. Also note the medical examiner's opinion as to the cause of death. Arrange to meet with the medical examiner for autopsy, etc. Arrange to obtain a copy of the death certificate.
Photograph the crime scene.	Take overall photographs of the scene from all angles.

Make a crime scene sketch.	Take measurements and sketch the crime scene, identifying each item of evidence.
Note all observations of the scene.	Light switches on or off, weather, heat settings, windows open or closed, doors locked or unlocked, pets, ashtrays and contents, beverages, food, refrigerator and freezer contents, food in the oven or microwave, mail, computers, answering machine messages, TV/radio on or off, cell phone/pager messages, address books, cash, credit cards, etc.
Look for the obvious.	Sometimes we get caught up in the excitement and overlook simple things, such as a wallet left by the killer on an end table, or a medicine bottle prescribed to a person other then the victim or the victim's family.
Look for things that should be there but aren't.	Wallets, watches, keys, wills, purses and pocketbooks, children, pets, firearms, etc.

TOOLS AND EQUIPMENT OF THE CRIME SCENE INVESTIGATOR

Each police investigator has her favorite method and means of evidence collection, although the end result must remain the same. All samples must be presented to the laboratories in a similar manner. The equipment used by these specialists is standard. Below is a list of items typically found in the toolboxes of a crime scene investigator. You'll notice some of these items are a repeat of the responding officer's equipment. Sometimes the detective is the first officer on the scene. A first-responding uniformed officer may also collect evidence if detectives aren't available.

- bindle paper
- biohazard bags
- blood-test supplies
- body-fluid collection kit
- business cards

- camera (35mm or digital) with flash/film/tripod (some courts won't accept digital photography as evidence due to the possibility that the images may be altered)
- casting materials
- cell phone
- consent-to-search forms
- crime scene barricade tape
- cutting instruments (knives, box cutter, scalpel, scissors)
- disinfectant
- evidence-collection containers
- evidence identifiers
- extension cords
- first aid kit
- flares
- flashlight/batteries
- gunshot residue kit
- high-intensity lights
- latent-print kit
- magnifying glass
- marking paint
- measuring devices (tape measure, ruler)
- mirror
- narcotics test kit
- permanent markers
- personal protective equipment
- photographic scale (ruler, engineer's scale)
- sealing tape
- shoeprint lifting kit
- sketch paper (graph)
- string
- templates
- thermometer
- tire-impression kit
- tool kit (screwdriver, pliers, etc.)

- traffic cones
- tweezers
- tape recorder
- UV light (black light)
- video recorder

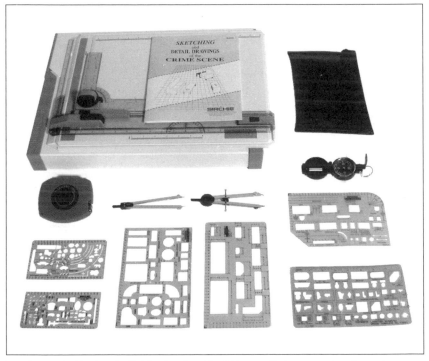

Investigators should make a detailed drawing of each homicide scene. To do so, many detectives and technicians prefer to use a crime scene sketch kit such as the one pictured above.

CRIME SCENE LOGBOOK

A uniformed officer is normally assigned to maintain a logbook at the entrance to the scene of a major crime. The logbook is used to record the names, dates, and times of those persons entering and exiting the sealed area. This record is necessary for future comparison of evidence, such as footprints. The log is admissible in court as an accurate depiction of events, such as the removal of the body by the medical examiner's office and the arrival and departure times of investigators.

CRIME SCENE LOG

Name and Agency	Date	Time In	Time Out	Purpose of Visit	Signature and Rank
Joe Cop Anytown P.D.	6-7-07	1030 hrs	1330 hrs	Investigation	Joe Cop, Det. Sgt.
Hugh S. Body Office of M.E.	6-7-07	1047 hrs	1133 hrs	Exam and body transport	Hugh Body, Medical Examiner

It's imperative that investigators minimize foot traffic in crime scenes to prevent the removal or destruction of evidence. It's also possible for people to add unwanted items to a crime scene that could be mistaken for evidence. Photographers drop film canisters and paper, reporters smoke cigarettes, and mayors and police chiefs chew gum. One piece of chewing gum found at crime scene can result in many hours of wasted laboratory testing and paperwork. It's best to eliminate the problem before it begins by refusing entry to the scene unless a person's presence is absolutely necessary.

Uniformed officers are often stationed outside and around the crime scene to prevent anyone who isn't a police officer from entering the scene. Crime scene tape is often used as a barrier; however, other items can be used as well, such as folding road signs, police vehicles, and even people.

Homicide scenes inspire passionate emotions, especially from family and close friends. Often family members feel they have the right to be inside a house, or particular piece of property, where their loved one was killed. Not true. Family and friends are normally not allowed inside a crime scene.

Once a crime scene is established, no one is allowed to be on the premises without the permission of the officer in charge. The officer in charge is more often than not a detective.

CRIME SCENE SEARCH PATTERNS

Crime scenes must be searched effectively and meticulously. The illustrations that follow are examples of search methods taught in police academies and crime scene workshops and schools. The four most common search methods used by police are:

Spiral Search Pattern

A single officer searching a crime scene will often use a spiral search pattern. The officer begins the search at the body—or other source of a crime or piece of evidence—and begins the search by walking away from, and simultaneously circling, the body, as in the drawing below. He continues this pattern until he's searched and examined the entire scene for evidence.

Block Search Pattern

Officers often conduct searches by sectioning and numbering an area that contains a crime scene. In the figure at the top of the next page, two rooms of a house have been sketched and sectioned, and each section has been assigned a corresponding number. These number assignments aid the police and court in determining the exact position of a body or evidence.

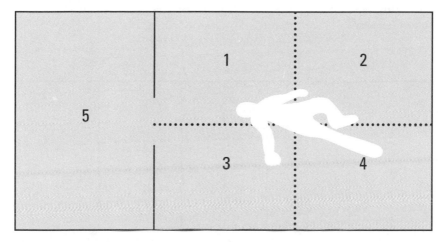

Grid Search Pattern

Officers can divide a crime scene into grids and search the individual grids for evidence. Imaginary lines mark the area deemed the crime scene, and the officers travel through the entire location in a manner such as that shown below.

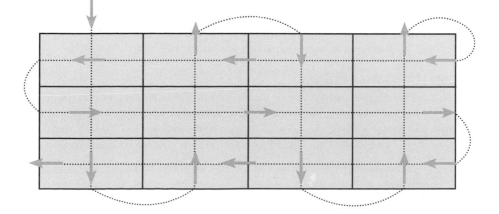

Strip Search Pattern

Officers can divide narrow crime scenes, such as an alleyway or a hallway, into strips for searching purposes. The individual blocks can be numbered for future reference.

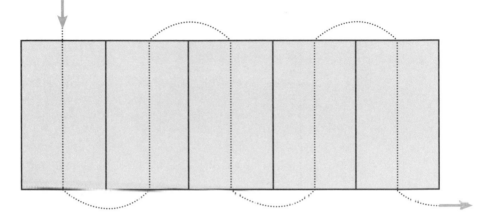

INSIDE THE CRIME SCENE

What goes on behind the yellow crime scene tape isn't the flurry of activity portrayed on television. In fact, the yellow crime scene tape isn't even used at every crime scene. Larger departments normally use the tape as a means to keep people out of a crime scene and to keep evidence in, but smaller departments may not use the tape at all. In fact, there are small departments that have never used crime scene tape to barricade a scene. Their budgets don't allow for the purchase of items that aren't absolutely necessary.

COLLECTING THE EVIDENCE

Dr. Edmond Locard, the director of the first crime lab in France, formed the basis for forensic sciences. His work became known as Locard's exchange principle and remains the cornerstone of today's investigations. In *Crime Investigation, second edition*, by Paul Leland Kirk and John I. Thornton, Locard states:

> Wherever he steps, whatever he touches, whatever he leaves, even unconsciously, will serve as a silent witness against him. Not only his fingerprints or his footprints, but his hair, the fibers from his clothes, the glass he breaks, the

tool marks he leaves, the paint he scratches, the blood or semen he deposits or collects. All of these and more bear mute witness against him. This is evidence that does not forget. It is not confused by the excitement of the moment. It is not absent because human witnesses are. It is factual evidence. Physical evidence cannot be wrong, it cannot perjure itself, it cannot be wholly absent. Only human failure to find it, study it, and understand it can diminish its value.

A crime scene investigator or detective must be cautious—not only in her efforts to protect and preserve evidence but to protect herself from coming in contact with the body fluids of the victims and their attackers. All police officers and investigators should carry protective equipment in their vehicles. Uniformed officers wear a pouch attached to their gun belts that contains at least one pair of latex gloves. They also wear the gloves when performing pat down searches as a barrier between their bare hands and the skin and clothing of suspects.

It's important that nobody disturb a crime scene until the entire area has been photographed and sketched. Detectives often stand in or near a scene and allow their eyes to examine in the entire area. Their minds form possible scenarios as to what happened, how it happened, and why. Who was standing where when the death blow was dealt? It is here, looking and thinking, that detectives achieve some of their best work.

The actual collection of physical evidence is a slow, arduous task. Investigators must be organized and careful when approaching the scene and collecting all the evidence they discover. All evidence must be properly photographed and accurately identified along with its corresponding location before it's bagged, tagged, and removed from the scene.

Detectives must be systematic and methodical, yet they must keep an open mind. A good detective can effectively mesh together science and imagination.

INDOOR CRIME SCENE

A murder that occurs within the home of a victim will instantly set off a detective's internal alarm system and guide his radar to the spouse as the initial suspect. When a detective approaches an indoor crime scene, he should first look for the obvious, such as footprints in the carpet. These prints can be of tremendous value in the later investigation. The size of the killer's foot can eliminate or identify potential suspects. The detective must photograph the area from all angles before allowing evidence to be moved or gathered. Thermostats should be checked and their settings recorded. The inside and outdoor air temperatures should be compared and recorded as well. All doors and windows should be checked for lock tampering and pry marks. The presence of insects should be noted, and detectives should make a note of the presence or absence of family pets.

A search of the kitchen provides investigators with some very important information. Food left out on countertops or stove tops can reveal the contents of a victim's last meal. The number of glasses and utensils could indicate the number of people who shared a last meal with the victim. A knife missing from a countertop knife block could be the missing murder weapon. Garbage disposals and sink traps can contain body tissue and fluids. The same is true for bathroom drains and showers. The wall behind a toilet or urinal is an excellent source for finger and palm prints (some men have a habit of leaning or placing a hand against the wall in front of them while urinating).

Murder weapons and other evidence have been discovered in toilet tanks, septic tanks, freezers, refrigerators, ovens, and pots on the stove; under rugs, carpeting, and beds; between and inside mattresses; inside floor, ceiling, and wall vents; inside light switches and receptacles; taped to the bottom of drawers; inside secret wall and floor panels, safes, and light fixtures; and even inside a human body. X-rays have shown many strange things inside the human body, such as lightbulbs, keys, knives, drugs, and bullets. An entire hacksaw blade was once discovered in the rectum of a prison inmate..

OUTDOOR CRIME SCENE

In an outdoor crime scene, an officer must establish and secure a perimeter, and she must make sure the entire area is searched for evidence, such as foot-

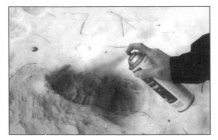

Snow impression wax allows investigators to make shoe and tire impressions without melting surrounding snow.

Dust and dirt hardener for making tire and shoe impressions.

prints, discarded papers, wrappers, cans, bottles, insects, the victim's belongings, clothing, and tire impressions.

Detectives must keep in mind that a crime scene can possibly be altered by weather conditions. Wind can blow away trace evidence, rain can wash away fibers, and sunlight can destroy DNA. Therefore, investigators must take appropriate steps to protect crime scenes. For example, during a rain shower, a body can be covered with a tarp to prevent it from the elements.

Crime scene investigators should always be completely aware of their surroundings. Evidence can be located in odd places, such as in trees and shrubbery (clothing can snag on overhanging branches), and animals can drag it away to areas many feet away from the actual scene.

BLOOD-PATTERN EVIDENCE, INTERPRETATION, AND ANALYSIS

Patterns created by blood that's been transferred from a human body to another object or surface can be instrumental in solving a murder case. It takes a trained eye and years of investigative experience to decipher the meaning that's hidden in wet evidence. There are three basic types of bloodstains—passive, projected, and transferred.

Passive bloodstains are created by a wound that drips or seeps, allowing gravity to pull the droplets downward naturally. When a drop of blood strikes a surface, it's called spatter. The force of impact sometimes causes the spatter to divide into several much smaller droplets called secondary spatter. Some droplets are so tiny that they're barely able to be seen with the naked eye.

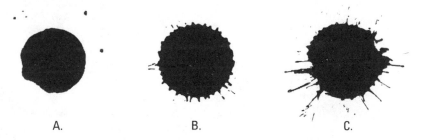

A.   B.   C.

A. Bloodstain from a single drop of blood striking a smooth surface, after falling from a distance of eight inches.

B. Bloodstain from a single drop of blood striking a smooth surface, after falling from a distance of forty-two inches.

C. Bloodstain from a single drop of blood striking a smooth surface, after falling from a distance of seventy-two inches.

Projected bloodstains occur when blood is forced in a direction other than the downward path caused by the natural pull of gravity. Blood can be propelled away from a body in many ways: from severed arteries that spurt blood with each beat of the heart; centrifugal force from a moving or flailing lacerated body part; and injuries that force blood away from injured body parts, such as a blow from a hammer or baseball bat.

Transferred bloodstains are caused by a wet, bloody object touching another surface, such as a bloody hand that touches a painted wall or door. The stain that's left on the wall is a transferred stain.

Projected bloodstain from ten milliliters of blood thrown slightly upward onto a smooth vertical wall. The original stain is in the classic teardrop shape because gravity pulls cast-off blood downward.

A victim transfers a bloody handprint—a transfer stain—to a nearby surface.

Crime scene investigators are able to determine the positions of the victim and the killer at the time of impact by establishing the angles of bloodstains. The shapes of the stains are also keys to determining the point of impact.

A drop of blood that's circular in shape has fallen straight down from a ninety-degree angle to the surface where it landed. Blood spatter that strikes a surface at less than a ninety-degree angle has a distinct teardrop shape. The smaller, more pointed tip of the drop serves as an indicator of the direction of the droplet's travel—it (the tip) always points away from the position of impact. As the angles of travel decrease, the bloodstains become less circular and much longer.

Scientists and detectives use a standard trigonometry formula to calculate the exact angle of travel for individual blood droplets. To make the calculations, investigators first measure the length and width of the droplets in question.

After obtaining the measurements of the blood drops, detectives can calculate the angle of impact. The formula for determining the angle of impact is:

$$\text{SIN} < = \frac{\text{width (a) 1.5cm}}{\text{length © 3.0cm}}$$

$$\frac{\text{width (a) 1.5cm}}{\text{length © 3.0cm}} = \text{SIN} <$$

$$0.5 = \text{SIN} <$$

$$< = 30 \text{ degrees}$$

A blood drop that's 1.5 centimeters wide and 3.0 centimeters long can be determined to have traveled at a thirty-degree angle away from the victim to the point of the drop's impact.

As the illustration on the next page shows, the point of impact (where the victim was struck) can be determined by simply drawing a line from each of the furthest droplets in a row to the closest droplet in that row. The point where the lines intersect is the point of impact.

Surface textures can greatly affect the appearance of spatter. A slick, dense surface causes a blood drop to break apart, spraying smaller droplets in the same direction of travel as the larger drop.

An investigator must examine these smaller droplets closely when attempting to determine the speed of the impact. Speed of impact can aid in determining the type of weapon used. Tiny droplets that have been sprayed throughout the room at great distances from a body indicate a very high-velocity impact, while large drops that have landed close to the victim's body indicate free-falling, gravity-pulled blood.

The fly in the ointment to this detective's rule of thumb is actually a fly. Flies of all types feed on the blood of the dead. After they've consumed the blood, they move to a warm area of the room—around lamps, windows, and other heat sources—to regurgitate their meals as part of their digestion process. This part of the digestion allows enzymes to break down the blood into a more easily digestible substance. The flies make several trips to and from the body, repeating the regurgitation process. Then they come back to the regurgitated blood at later times to feed on their prepared food. During this course of action, tiny blood specks are transferred throughout the room from both the flies' feet and from regurgitation—the more flies, the more blood specks.

These minute specks of blood left behind by feeding flies have the appearance of high-velocity blood spatter and can be confusing to investigators. A close examination can reveal patterns and spots of fly defecation. The presence of a fly is indicated by dark swiping patterns (defecation) mingled among the tiny blood droplets. Houseflies are suckers and lappers, not biters like horseflies, and that lapping action creates small craters in dried blood spatters. The craters are proof of fly activity. A misidentification of this false spatter can lead investigators to incorrect conclusions about the course of events that occurred at a crime scene.

Murderers have been known to try to cover their tracks by hiding and destroying evidence. Blood evidence is no exception. They've tried to wash it away, scrub it away, remove contaminated carpeting and bedding, paint over the stains, and even burn it away.

When an investigator feels strongly that a murder's been committed and he can't locate any of the usual blood evidence, he turns to Luminol for help. Luminol is a chemical that reacts with blood—specifically, the iron that's found in hemoglobin.

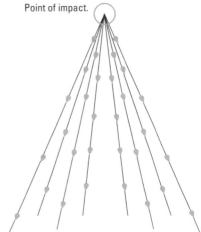

Point of impact.

When the chemical comes into contact with blood, it causes the blood to luminesce with a bright, blue-green glow that can be seen in a dark room with the naked eye. Luminol is so sensitive that it reacts to one drop of blood in a container filled with 999,999 drops of water.

The use of Luminol by investigators at crime scenes can not only show that there's human blood at the scene, but it can also point to where within the scene the victim was attacked. It can show the direction of the force of impact; what type of weapon was used—a knife, blunt instrument, or gun; the direction the suspect was standing or walking (traces of bloody footprints); and the direction in which the suspect dragged or carried the victim.

As with other chemical agents used by law enforcement officers, Luminol has some drawbacks—it can mar or destroy other trace evidence, and it reacts to other materials, such as horseradish, copper, and some common household bleaches. However, the glow produced by Luminol's contact with blood is quite a bit brighter than the glow it generates when in contact with other substances. Detectives should always conduct all other investigations before they employ the use of Luminol.

The glow produced by Luminol's contact with blood last only for a few minutes, so investigators should photograph the tested areas as soon as possible for later reference.

EDGED WEAPONS

Edged weapons are some of the earliest weapons known to mankind. Most people think only of knives when they talk about edged weapons, but the category also includes axes, razors, hatchets, scalpels, and swords. In fact, any item that can be sharpened or honed is considered an edged weapon.

A good knife blade is easily sharpened, doesn't rust, and polishes well. The steel used for a high-quality knife blade is high-carbon steel with a high-chrome content, such as 440C, a type of steel that's capable of achieving a maximum hardness.

An ax can deliver blunt trauma as well as the lacerations associated with any other edged weapon. It also can be responsible for torn flesh.

Wounds caused by edged weapons can have more stopping power than a firearm. One important thing for a detective to remember is that a knife never runs out of ammunition. Attackers have the ability to strike again and again and again.

Knives of all types are carried by a large number of street criminals as weapons of self-defense or aggression. Many assaults and robberies are carried out by knife-wielding suspects, and the damage inflicted by those knives can be deadly.

Unlike gunshot wounds that are sometimes so small the extreme heat seals the hole, a knife wound can be deep enough to cut large muscles, bones, internal organs, arteries, and veins—all from a single slash.

A knife attack by a suspect can come as a complete surprise. Knife attacks are silent, giving no warning. There's no identifiable sound, like that of a gunshot. Quite often an attacker will approach her prey, stab him, and walk away before the victim has the time to react. Assailants can easily conceal almost any size knife.

Some attackers stab their victims a multitude of times. Either way, the wounds are usually inflicted quickly, sometimes without the victim ever seeing the weapon. Even if a victim is aware that the attacker has a knife, it's still difficult to defend against a knife attack. The blows are usually delivered in a hammer-type strike—either a downward stab or a diagonal slashing. A lunging stab is a favored method of street fighters.

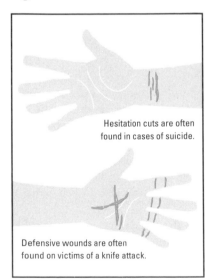

Hesitation cuts are often found in cases of suicide.

Defensive wounds are often found on victims of a knife attack.

Officers are trained to pay particular attention to the direction of the cuts. The type of wound can show the investigator a possible positioning of the suspect and victim when the attack occurred. For instance, a blade entering the flesh at less than a right angle makes a beveled wound. A blade piercing the flesh at a right angle creates an oval wound. A twisting of the knife blade as it penetrates the flesh creates a scrimmage wound.

Defensive wounds are often found on the palms and forearms of the victim of an edged-weapon attack. When attacked, a human's natural instinct is to put her arms and hands between her face and the attacker's weapon. This action causes the initial blows to be dealt to those unprotected body parts. Defensive wounds can also be found on the arms and hands of gunshot victims.

People who are contemplating suicide often attempt to do so by cutting or slashing their wrists with knives or razor blades. Sometimes it takes the person several attempts before he gets enough nerve to make deep enough cut. The shallow "practice" cuts are called hesitation cuts.

ENTOMOLOGY OR INSECT EVIDENCE

All too often, patrol officers, detectives, and emergency personnel accidentally destroy some of the most important evidence at a crime scene. During the examination of a body, I've seen emergency medical personnel and other detectives wipe away maggots and wave flies away in disgust. These insects can be important determinants of the time of death, and it's essential that the detective and medical examiner make note of and collect samples of each individual species found on or around the body.

The presence of blowflies and/or houseflies indicates a body is in the first stage of death, the fresh or recently deceased stage. These large, green or black flies are usually first to arrive and lay their eggs in open wounds or cavities and in places such as the eyes, ears, nose, penis, and vaginal openings.

During the examination of the body as evidence, it's important to note the presence of other insects other than those directly on the body. There may be ants darting about, carrying away live maggots, or there may be wasps feeding on the flies.

The fresh stage of the body begins to attract the first insects approximately ten minutes after death, depending on the climate and weather conditions.

After a period of time, the body will enter the second stage, the bloated stage, in which gases build up inside the body cavity as a result of decomposition. Live bacteria feeding on human tissue cause the decomposition. Maggots, during their feeding, also contribute to the decomposition and speed up the process. The presence of maggots is key to determining the time of death. During the decomposition stage, the body temperature can be elevated to temperatures much higher than when the body was alive. The temperatures can rise to points exceeding 120° F.

It's important for the detective to note the ambient air temperature when a body's discovered. Should the temperature be below the point that maggots prefer to exist, the insects will move to a warmer location inside the body to protect themselves from the elements and will continue to feed. A body found outside, and decomposed only on the inside, indicates the presence of maggots inside the body during cold winter months. The insects use the body as a shelter from the elements and feed on the corpse, from the inside, until only a hull, or thin shell of skin, surrounds the skeletal remains.

When approaching an outdoor murder scene, a detective must do so cautiously. I preferred to begin my search for insect activity, relative to the victim, at a distance of approximately thirty feet from the victim. In the third stage of decomposition, the decay stage, maggots will depart from the body and seek shelter under leaves or plant material. At this point, the investigator should begin to, literally, leave no stone unturned. I have often seen large black and/or green beetles crawling in and out of body cavities and on the surface of the body as well.

Immediately following the decay stage is the post-decay stage, and the insect most often found on the body at this point is the beetle. Keep in mind, there may still be other insects lingering as well, but the beetle is the predominant one.

The final stage is obvious. It's the skeletal stage, and only insects that live in the earth will feed upon these remains. Detectives should obtain soil samples from beneath the body; it's a good rule of thumb to sample the earth surrounding the body up to three to four feet away.

I have observed different methods of collecting insects at murder scenes. Different investigators use different methods, but the end result must be the same. One particular detective I recall used a net designed for skimming pool water to sweep through the air and collect flying insects. It looked a bit silly but was very effective. Officers should collect samples of live, crawling insects, place them into containers filled with local material or sand, and then transport them immediately to a lab for testing.

Lack of insects on or in a body can be a sign of freezing. The killer may have kept the body in a freezer and later moved it to the location where it was discovered.

The soil above a buried body may provide clues as well. Certain moths burrow into freshly loosened soil, and they're indicators of a fresh grave.

Killers sometimes go to great lengths to disguise the time and method of death, but wrapping the body in plastics bags, rugs, drums, or other containers doesn't prevent insect penetration and activity.

During the course of a criminal investigation, a detective may need to know the content of the victim's stomach. The deceased's last meal may indicate evidence of a particular restaurant, or, more importantly, the presence of a poison may indicate the cause of death.

As the body deteriorates and decomposes, body organs and fluids become unattainable, making testing impossible. The presence of maggots and their cast-aside shells revives the probability of obtaining the needed information. A scientist can trace chemical compounds from the victim within the bodies of the maggots. Testing on maggots has proven to be quite effective and has produced findings of chemicals such as heroin, cocaine, amitriptyline, mercury, and phenobarbital, to name a few.

CHAPTER 8

FINGERPRINTING

It's a challenge to write crime scene investigation that's authentic; it's harder still to make it believable when everyone's become an "expert" watching the folks on TV get it wrong.

—HALLIE EPHRON, AUTHOR OF WRITING AND SELLING
YOUR MYSTERY NOVEL: HOW TO KNOCK 'EM DEAD WITH STYLE

Fingerprinting is a valuable tool for law enforcement because no two people in the world have identical prints. Even though identical twins have identical DNA, they have markedly different fingerprints. The basics of fingerprinting are taught to all police officers, but a fingerprint technician practices her craft daily. It takes a delicate touch and a keen eye to be the best, and a good fingerprint technician can sometimes make or break a criminal case.

A BRIEF HISTORY OF FINGERPRINTING

The ridges that cover the surface of fingertips and palms first caught the eye of University of Bologna professor Marcello Malpighi in the late 1600s. The worth of those looping crests was of no importance to him at the time, however, so he conducted no further research, and more than one hundred years passed before the subject of finger ridge patterns was addressed.

In the mid-1800s, Sir William James Herschel served as a British chief administrative officer in Bengal, India. His method of fingerprinting for the purpose of invoking honesty among the Indian natives would eventually spark the idea of using fingerprints for the purpose of identification. Herschel thought that requiring someone to place a fingerprint beside his signature would reduce a person's inclination for deceitfulness because of the intimacy associated with touching the paper.

Three years after Herschel began his quest to standardize a fingerprint honor system, Dr. Henry Faulds of Tokyo, Japan, realized the importance of using fingerprints not only for identification purposes but as a means of solving crimes. He also introduced the use of printer's ink as an excellent medium for transferring prints from fingers to paper.

The late 1800s was a busy time for those who studied fingerprinting. Mark Twain wrote of identifying a murderer by his fingerprints, and Charles Darwin's cousin, Sir Francis Galton, wrote the book *Finger Prints* in 1892. Also in 1892, Argentina claimed the first use of a fingerprint to identify a murderer. In 1893, Twain's *Pudd'nhead Wilson* thrilled readers with its accounts of murder, court trials, and the use of fingerprint identification.

England and Wales began the first fingerprinting for criminal identification in the early 1900s. Shortly afterward, the New York Civil Service Commission adopted the fingerprinting process as a means of identification for job applicants.

Around the same time, the New York state prison system began using fingerprints for the identification of criminals, and they officially adopted the first fingerprint system in 1903. A year later, the U.S. penitentiary at Leavenworth, Kansas, established its own fingerprint bureau. The penitentiary in Leavenworth also began to exchange fingerprint information with other law enforcement agencies and police officers.

Prior to 1903, the Leavenworth prison used an identification system designed by French anthropologist Alphonse Bertillon. Bertillon's system measured the bony parts of the body, inserted the measurements into a formula and calculated the results, which supposedly applied only to one person.

Bertillon's method was used for approximately thirty years before encountering its first major problem. A man named Will West was arrested and sentenced to serve time at the federal penitentiary at Leavenworth. When officials completed the measurements of West's personal identification features, they discovered that those measurements were almost identical to another man, William West, who was already serving time at Leavenworth.

Officials compared photographs of the two men and were astounded to see that they could be mistaken for identical twins even though they weren't related. Prison employees took fingerprint samples from each of the men and compared them—they were different. After this discovery, fingerprinting became the official means for the identification of prisoners.

Within twelve months of the Leavenworth fiasco, the U.S. Army began using an official fingerprint system for identification purposes. The U.S. Navy followed suit and, in as many months, was followed by the U.S. Marine Corps in adopting the system.

MODERN-DAY FINGERPRINTING METHODS AND USES

Fingerprint technology has come a long way since the days when detectives had to wait months for laboratories to return fingerprint comparisons from crime scenes. It wasn't unheard of for fingerprint comparisons to arrive after criminals had been arrested, tried, and convicted based on evidence other than their fingerprints.

Sometimes, criminals had actually served their time in jail when detectives received a positive match from the labs. It was a very slow and tedious process to examine individual fingerprints and then compare them to hundreds of possible suspects.

Today, fingerprinting has moved into the world of computer technology. With the 1999 inception of the Integrated Automated Fingerprint Identification System (IAFIS), prints can be compared to a database of thousands of fingerprints in mere seconds. Now, it's possible for investigators to learn the identity of a criminal suspect on the same night he committed a crime, possibly preventing him from continuing a potentially dangerous crime spree.

FINGERPRINT PATTERNS

Human fingertips are covered with convoluted ridges and grooves. The raised ridges are called friction ridges and are formed prior to birth. Fingerprints consist of two layers: The top layer is called the stratum corneum and the lower layer is called the stratum mucosum.

Fingerprints are permanent, and slight injuries and cuts won't deface the pattern. However, a serious wound that damages the stratum mucosum can leave a permanent scar that alters a fingerprint. Each fingerprint is composed of several identifiable characteristics that make fingerprints unique to each individual.

Television and movies sometimes suggest that criminals can conceal their identities by sanding or burning away their fingerprints with sandpaper or acid. Not so. Sanded fingertips still reveal the original print patterns, and permanently burned or disfigured prints become the suspect's permanent fingerprints, which are still unique to that person. The vast majority of burned or scarred fingertips still exhibit some or all of the original print patterns.

The identifiable characteristics of fingerprint patterns are:

- **Delta:** the point on a ridge that's on or is nearest to the point of divergence of two lines.

- **Divergence:** the point where two parallel lines begin to separate.

- **Core:** the center or approximate center of a fingerprint pattern.

- **Comparison:** matching the similarities and differences of the ridge patterns of two fingerprint patterns.

- **Bifurcation:** a forking or dividing of one line (ridges or grooves) into two individual lines, which appears like a fork in a roadway.

- **Common:** a ridge that runs in a continuous line with no breaks.

- **"T" junction:** the point where a ridge ends at another ridge that runs at an angle to the first ridge, forming a "T" intersection.

- **Dot:** a tiny ridge that looks like a small dot or period.

- **Row of dots:** a continuous line of two or more dots.

- **Trifurcation:** occurs when a ridge divides into three separate ridges.

PLAIN ARCH
The ridge enters on one side of the finger, rises gently in the center, and falls gradually as it reaches the other side of the finger.

TENTED ARCH
One ridge rises upward, bisecting other arches.

LOOP
A pattern formed by recurving ridges.

WHORL
Two deltas with a recurve in front of each of the deltas.

COMPOSITE
Consists of two or more patterns.

ACCIDENTAL
Two deltas with one recurving ridge and one up-thrusting ridge.

CENTRAL POCKET LOOP
Consists of one recurving ridge with two deltas that have no recurving ridges within the center of the pattern

There are three major types of fingerprint patterns—arches, loops, and whorls. Each of those categories can be subdivided into even more distinguishable categories, such as tented arches, double loops, and accidental whorls.

LATENT, PATENT, AND IMPRESSED PRINTS

Latent prints, the prints most often mentioned by police officers or crime scene investigators, are prints that are accidentally or unintentionally left at a scene or on an object. Normally invisible to the naked eye, latent prints are made by someone touching an object and leaving behind natural body secretions like oils and sweat. Latent prints become visible when contacted by fingerprint powders.

Patent prints are made when a person touches a surface with a bloody or greasy finger; these prints are readily visible. A third type of prints—impressed prints—are formed when a person touches a moldable material, such as clay, caulking, drying blood, or paint.

DEVELOPING AND LIFTING LATENT PRINTS

All police officers are trained in fingerprinting. Some departments employ crime scene investigators whose main duty is fingerprinting. However, most small police departments don't have the luxury of specialized crime scene units; therefore, fingerprinting may be performed by the uniformed officer who first answered the call. In most cases a detective performs the fingerprinting duties.

The ideal method for protecting print evidence is for the investigator to seize the entire object containing the suspect's prints, place the object in appropriate packaging, and deliver it to a testing facility. This method eliminates the possibility of destroying good evidence. Unfortunately, it isn't always possible to physically deliver large, heavy, and bulky objects, such as a refrigerator or built-in range, to a laboratory, so the technician must dust for and lift the prints from those items in the field.

In the best possible scenario, investigators could fingerprint every single surface and object in a crime scene. Unfortunately, to do so would be highly impractical. The practice could produce hundreds of prints left by anyone from the TV repairman to former owners of the property. Instead, investigators normally process items in the immediate area of the crime scene and use their common sense and intuition regarding other items in other areas. For example, a

Technicians use a combination of gentle brushing and swirling motions to develop latent prints.

murder victim may have been found stabbed to death in the bedroom, but investigators may fingerprint items in the kitchen if they noticed a butcher knife missing from a knife block on the kitchen counter. Good old-fashioned common sense is a large part of police work.

Investigators find it helpful to take photographs of all developed prints before lifting them in case something happens during the lifting process to alter or destroy a print. Lifting tape, which is similar to wide transparent tape, can form an air bubble beneath the surface that doesn't allow the entire print to be lifted. The tape can also slide, and the technician can accidentally touch the print. If the printing is taking place outdoors, weather can become a factor. Rain can erase an impressed print entirely.

All these problems can result in a distorted or destroyed print. Photographs of fingerprints can be used for comparison at the testing labs. They can also be enlarged for enhancement purposes. Photographed prints can be entered in the IAFIS system just as easily as the actual print.

Brushing fingerprint powder on a surface in an attempt to develop a visible fingerprint is sometimes called dusting for prints. There are a few ways to dust. The first method comes into play when investigators discover a suspect's prints already in dust or dirt, such as on a windowsill or furniture that hasn't been cleaned for a while. The investigator should photograph these prints prior to lifting them, and she shouldn't use any additional powders to assist in the developing.

There are various assortments of print powders available. The basic colors are white, for use on dark surfaces, and black, for use on light-colored surfaces. Some technicians also use a mixture of approximately 60 percent black and 40 percent white for use on surfaces where neither of the two standard colors is effective, such as on stainless steel. In most cases, one of the three will do nicely.

Some multicolored surfaces require a fluorescent powder, and a technician must use an ultraviolet light source, such as the Krimesite Imager, to see the developed print. Other items such as biological fibers and trace evidence also become visible when exposed to this type of equipment, which uses an alternative light source similar to a black light and is capable of capturing digital images of fingerprints that are difficult to lift by traditional means. A well-prepared detective or crime scene investigator would carry an alternate light source or a Krimesite Imager in their vehicle at all times.

Fingerprinting brushes are normally made from fiberglass, camel hair, squirrel hair, or—as most technicians prefer for larger surfaces—marabou feathers. Marabou feather brushes are made from the feathers of the African marabou, the largest bird in the stork family. Camel hair brushes aren't actually made from the hair of camels; they're fashioned from a combination of hair from squirrels, ponies, sheep, goats, and other animals.

When not in use, fingerprinting brushes are stored in small plastic tubes to protect the hairs and feathers from becoming frayed or bent. Feather brushes should be used for one color only because they retain powder; other types of brushes can be readily used for multiple powder colors. A simple shake or twirling action will remove excess powder to prepare the brush for use with another color. Most investigators prefer to use separate brushes for each color powder to avoid cross-contamination of conflicting colors.

Marabou feather fingerprinting brush.

Also, detectives and investigators normally have a favorite type of brush and powder that they prefer to use for individual or unique situations.

A detective begins developing a print by using a small amount of dusting powder on the tip of a fingerprinting brush. He shakes off any excess powder before applying the brush to the area he's to print. A very light, delicate touch must be used to develop a latent print. Investigators alternate techniques between brushing and swirling motions. The procedure requires practice to be performed properly and effectively.

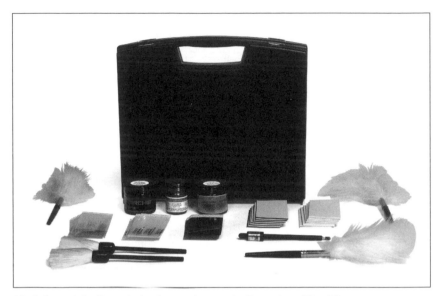

A basic fingerprinting kit contains brushes, powders, tape, backing cards, and hinged lifters.

To lift the print, the detective uses either hinged lifters—factory prejoined pieces of lifting tape and backing—or lifting tape that resembles a wide roll of packing tape. The detective places the tape, or the taped portion of the hinged lifter, over the dusted print and then rubs the tape gently to smooth out all wrinkles and tiny air bubbles. He then grasps one corner of the tape and peels it away from the printed surface. The print should be perfectly preserved on the sticky side of the tape. The detective then carefully places the tape on a firm surface, such as an index card, for preservation. The card serves as a backing and as a place to record notes about the print, such as the date, time, and location from where the print was lifted. In the case of hinged lifters, the backing is already attached so the detective needs only to stick the two pieces together. He can record all necessary information on the rear of the backing or at the top of the lifter.

Prints are difficult to lift with tape from some surfaces, such as paper, but they can be easily lifted with chemicals. One such chemical is ninhydrin, a ready-made chemical available to law enforcement through police supply houses. It can be found in ready-made aerosol form or as a crystalline powder that's ready for mixing. For less than twenty dollars, detectives can purchase a sixteen-ounce aerosol can of ninhydrin. Twenty-five dollars will get detectives a jar of ninhydrin crystals, which will last much longer than the aerosol spray.

In either form, ninhydrin is easily applied, but it's also very harmful to the human body. Ninhydrin is an amino-acid reagent and, therefore, adheres easily to the body surfaces and eyes of anyone in the presence of the spray. Fumes may also be inhaled. All persons present when ninhydrin is being used should wear protective gear.

Standard latex gloves can allow seepage of some chemicals, so detectives should wear nitrile gloves in combination with goggles, breathing masks, and a protective outer garment, such as coveralls or a lab coat.

To develop prints with ninhydrin, the detective either sprays or paints on the chemical, or dips the paper into it. She then exposes the paper to moist heat. One way to do this is to hold the paper near a hot steam iron. The purplish tinted print develops in front of the detective's eyes.

Some detectives prefer to mix and use their own solutions of ninhydrin. The mixing formula is simple: twenty-five grams of crystalline ninhydrin per four liters of solvent (acetone or methyl alcohol).

A ninhydrin-developed print fades over time, so it's always a good idea to photograph the developed print and place the original into a sealed plastic bag. The bag will increase the longevity of the print. Ninhydrin has been used effectively to develop two-year-old fingerprints and, in some experimental cases, to develop prints that were fifty years old.

Chemical print developing has other drawbacks—the chemicals can alter or even destroy other types of evidence, such as handwriting and ink from a printed document. The solvents used for mixing with ninhydrin can actually cause ink to run or dissolve. All documents should be copied before they're tested for fingerprints.

When all else fails, detectives have another trick up their sleeves—cyanoacrylate fuming. Cyanoacrylate is an instant adhesive better known as Super Glue and Krazy Glue. It's used by physicians to seal wounds and by funeral directors to permanently close eyelids and lips, and to hold fingers together.

Cyanoacrylate can be a very effective tool in developing hard-to-get fingerprints on nonporous materials. The investigator positions the object in question into a specially designed fuming chamber, such as the CyanoSafe. The CyanoSafe fuming chamber heats the cyanoacrylate to the proper temperature,

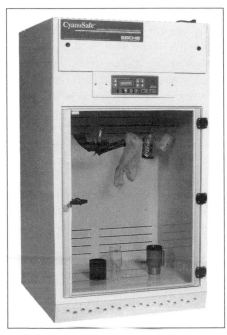

CyanoSafe, a cyanoacrylate fuming chamber.

allowing the release of the necessary fumes. The chamber automatically filters exhaust fumes and monitors the exhaust process. Sensors activate humidity controls, and the chamber features a glass front to let investigators visually monitor the print development process.

The investigator squirts a dab of the glue into a round metal cup and then places the cup atop a small hot plate inside the fuming chamber. The heat from the hot plate causes the glue to produce fumes that react with the amino acids, fatty acids, and proteins contained on latent fingerprints. This chemical reaction forms a sticky substance along the ridges of the latent finger print, making the print visible to the naked eye. The drawback to the cyanoacrylate method is that, as with ninhydrin, the print fades over time and doesn't leave a permanent record; therefore, the print must be photographed. Although a photograph is never as good as the actual evidence, it's still enough for a conviction.

A CyanoSafe can cost nearly ten thousand dollars, so it's not usually found in smaller police departments. Detectives in those departments often fabricate their own versions of the chamber, sometimes out of aquariums with tightly fitting tops and a portable hot plate. Portable, disposable fuming chambers are also available.

Other specialty items or powders used by the police for the development of fingerprints are:

- **Hungarian Red:** used for staining print impressions found in blood. The prints show up under a green alternate light source. Gel lifters are used to lift the developed prints.

- **Basic Yellow:** a fluorescent dye used to enhance cyanoacrylate prints. These prints fluoresce under ultraviolet light.

- **Iodine crystals:** sold in prescored ampoules, these crystals are used for the development of prints on paper and some porous materials. They're not used for metals.

- **Fluorescent powders:** used on multicolored backgrounds.

- **Rhodamine 6G:** used for the enhancement of cyanoacrylate-developed prints.

- **Aqueous Leucocrystal Violet:** a highly sensitive testing compound that detects the presence of blood.

- **Crystal Violet:** a dye used to enhance sebaceous sweat residue in latent prints.

- **Silver nitrate:** used for the development of latent prints on porous surfaces. It won't dilute or cause inks to run.

FINGERPRINT ANALYSIS

Investigators spend sixteen hours in training classes learning to use the IAFIS system, forty hours learning to properly classify fingerprints, and an additional forty hours becoming certified in fingerprint comparison techniques.

The IAFIS system is online 24 hours a day, 365 days a year. In the days before IAFIS became available to all law enforcement agencies (that can afford it), submitting a hard copy of a print to the Federal Bureau of Investigation (FBI) for possible suspect identification was a long and drawn-out process. It could take months before the submitting agency received a response. IAFIS now makes it possible to submit a print and receive a confirmation (a "hit") in a matter of minutes. Some responses have been received as soon as ten minutes after the technician hit the "send" button on the IAFIS computer terminal.

Response time for IAFIS can be slower depending on the day of the week the request is sent. Mondays offer the slowest response times due to the normally high volume of fingerprint evidence submissions gathered from week-

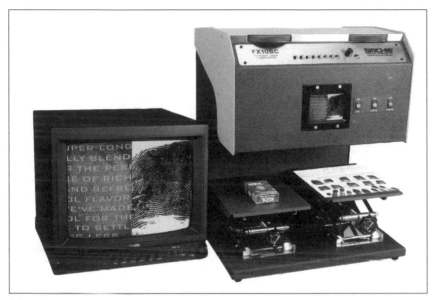

A fingerprint comparator.

end crimes. The time of day is also a factor. Nighttime submissions receive quicker responses than daytime requests. In short, the more people using the system, the slower it operates.

Television rarely gets the fingerprint process exactly correct. TV detectives send a print over the wires and instantly receive the name, address, phone number, social security number, and shoe size of their suspect. IAFIS is fast and very accurate, but it's not quite that fast; in fact, it doesn't deliver a perfect match to a suspect's prints. It sends a list of the best and most probable matches on file. From that list, detectives must examine, by hand, each of those prints and compare them to the fingerprints of the suspects.

Before fingerprint technology received a boost from computers, detectives had to painstakingly scrutinize each print with a magnifying glass and a tiny metal pointer. Today, Cogent LiveScan, a computer linked to IAFIS, is a favorite tool of many law enforcement agencies. The 250-pound machine is a hefty piece of equipment standing over five and a half feet tall, two and a half feet wide, and nearly three feet deep. It has its own thermostatically controlled, self-contained cooling system and is built to withstand the abuse that combative suspects often deliver to police equipment.

LiveScan has the ability to capture and transmit flat and rolled prints, as well as a suspect's palm prints. In most areas, the terminal is set up to instantly send images from a police department to the state bureau of investigation and the FBI.

Some departments even have their own intradepartmental fingerprint computer, such as the Live-ID system employed by the Hamilton, Ohio, Police Department. The in-house system stores the fingerprints of local offenders and can be quite useful when officers arrest someone who refuses to tell them his name. If the person has ever been arrested by the department, a quick scan by the system will provide officers all the details about him. Jails also use the system to prevent the release of the wrong person. A person's fingerprints must match the fingerprints in her file before she can be released.

Fingerprint technicians and detectives who have the painstaking task of comparing fingerprints use fingerprint comparators to help them. A fingerprint comparator is designed to illuminate and project images to two side-by-side viewing screens. These machines have zoom capability and are also used for the comparison of counterfeit currency and handwriting samples.

ROLLED PRINTS

Rolled prints are taken from fingers of actual humans, such as after an arrest or during an autopsy. Each suspect who's been arrested must submit a copy of his fingerprints during the booking process. If the arrest is for a misdemeanor, the print cards remain with the arresting agency. In the case of a felony arrest, a suspect is required to submit two sets of her prints. One set is sent to the FBI for entry into IAFIS (the FBI has been maintaining an official database of fingerprint records since July 1, 1921). The other set is kept and filed by the arresting agency. Departments equipped with computerized fingerprint terminals have all but eliminated the use of manually rolled fingerprint cards.

To obtain a rolled print, a technician or officer grasps a subject's finger, presses it against an inked pad, and rolls the first joint of the finger from side to side on a fingerprint card. The ink isn't permanent and can be quite messy, so most police departments keep a jug of hand cleaner and a roll of paper tolls on hand to allow suspects and officers to clean their hands after the printing process is complete.

Fingerprinting the dead isn't always an easy task. Fingers of the deceased can be badly damaged, decomposed, dry, and brittle. Investigators sometimes have to employ the use of special techniques to assist them with fingerprinting a corpse.

The hands of the dead are often found with clenched fingers. Finger-straightening tools—zinc-coated steel strips that fit over the fingers—are used to straighten the fingers by force. Tissue builders and finger softeners are used to return the flesh to a more pliable state.

When all else fails, technicians use bone cutters to remove the fingers. Some investigators have even skinned the fingers and placed the skin over their own fingertips to complete the printing process.

Rolled prints are often taken from the hands of children and kept on file to be used in the event the child becomes missing or is kidnapped. Rolled prints are used for identification purposes and are usually entered into IAFIS.

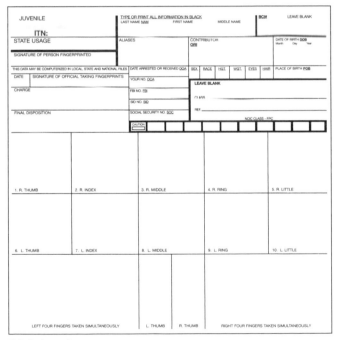

Rolled print card.

CHAPTER 9

DNA

The science of DNA profiling is sound. But not all DNA profiling is sound.

—DR. DAN KRANE, *CEO, FORENSIC BIOINFORMATICS, INC.*

Essentially, humans are all the same. We're only separated genetically by a scant 0.5 percent of our total DNA. The remaining 99.5 percent is identical. That 0.5 percent, however, has taken the world of crime solving by storm. Although DNA is fairly new to law enforcement, its roots have been firmly implanted within the scientific community for more than a century.

Over the years, DNA evidence testing has become a valuable tool for law enforcement. It has aided detectives in cases that were otherwise impossible to prove. Items once thought to be too small for testing, or even for use as clues, are now the solid foundation of murder and rape cases.

DNA evidence tests are capable of providing us with invaluable scientific proof of physical contact between an assailant and a victim. The tests can also be used to eliminate a person as a suspect or to link several crime scenes to the same perpetrator.

DEOXYRIBONUCLEIC ACID (DNA): THE NEW EVIDENCE

Tough-guy police detectives who strong-armed confessions from two-bit thugs are things of the past. The investigators of today have not only filled their crime-solving toolboxes with the standard hammer and nails of law enforcement (guns and search warrants), they've also tossed science and technology into the mix. For the first time in the history of policing, cops have begun to use words like *mitochondria* and *electropheragram*. Not only do they say those words, they also know what they mean.

For the past two decades, more and more crimes have been solved not in back alleys, poolrooms, and crack houses but in laboratories filled with whirring and buzzing machinery. Forensic scientists—the law enforcement officials who wear white lab coats, safety goggles, and paper booties—are discovering the answers to some of the world's most heinous crimes, and they're doing it with something that's barely visible to the naked eye: deoxyribonucleic acid, or DNA.

To better understand how crimes are solved using science, the law enforcement community (police officers, prosecutors, defense attorneys, judges, investigators, crime scene technicians, and laboratory personnel) must know what DNA is, how to collect it, and how to test it so it can be used as a tool for suspect identification or elimination. They must also know how to present their findings in a court of law.

DNA is the genetic blueprint for building a person. It's inherited from both the mother and the father and is found in almost every cell of the human body (except for red blood cells).

The combination of DNA found in the nucleus of each cell is what gives each individual the characteristics that make him uniquely different from the next person. The human genome—the body's entire collection of genes—is composed of three billion base pairs. The specific order of these pairs makes up a gene, and a gene's specific location on a chromosome is called a locus (plural: loci). A variation of a particular gene (the genetic marker) at any given locus is called an allele.

Each cell in the human body is composed of twenty-three pairs of chromosomes—one set from the mother and one from the father—for a total of forty-six chromosomes. Twenty-two of those pairs are called autosomes; the final pair is the sex chromosomes, XY in males and XX in females. The Y chromosome is the male chromosome that differentiates the two sexes. It determines how much, if any, facial hair is present, the tone of voice, and the differences in genitalia.

Both males and females have the X chromosome. Females begin life with two active X chromosomes, but in early embryonic stages one of those X chromosomes becomes inactive. The process that causes the inactivity of the X chromosome forms what's known as a Barr body. Under a microscope, a Barr body has the appearance of a small appendage that's attached to the cell's nucleus. Barr bodies make it possible for forensic scientists to learn the sex of a badly decomposed or dismembered body by looking at the nucleus of a single cell. Barr body testing is also used in some sporting competitions to ensure that everyone who claims to be a female is indeed a female.

DNA SEQUENCE (GENETIC FINGERPRINT)

DNA is rather long as molecules go: It's a polymer composed of sugars, phosphate, and other organic bases that form a twisted ladder-like configuration that we all recognize as the double helix. Within the helix, the ladder rungs are comprised of four paired molecules called bases. The bases are adenine, guanine, cytosine, and thymine (AGCT). These four bases can only pair together in certain patterns—T only bonds to A, and C only bonds to G, so the only possible combinations are CG, GC, TA, and AT.

Each human cell is composed of three billion base-long DNA sequences. When forensic scientists look at someone's DNA, they only look at a short sequence of the base patterns, such as the sequence, CACGATACTTATTTATT-TATCCGAGCCTA. When scientists look at that sequence more closely, they see that a grouping of bases (TTAT) is repeated, CACGATACTTATTTATTTATCC-GAGCCTA. These repetitions are called short tandem repeats, or STRs. That pattern of STRs is what identifies someone as an individual. That unique and repetitive pattern is a person's genetic fingerprint.

IDENTICAL DNA

Normally, no two humans have the same DNA, except in the case of identical twins. The exception to this rule, according to Wright State University professor and world renowned DNA expert Dr. Dan Krane, is that out of every 459,000 pairs of siblings, 3 of those pairs should have matching DNA at all 26 loci. Dr. Krane further states that there are five thousand pairs of nontwins in the United States whose DNA matches identically, which could cause the police to arrest an innocent person. A mistake such as this could also send the wrong person to the electric chair.

WORKING WITH DNA EVIDENCE

The DNA collection and testing process is complicated and can take many weeks or months to complete. It can also be very expensive for police agencies (sometimes more than two thousand dollars per test), especially if a detective has submitted several articles of evidence. Law enforcement usually requires and relies upon testing to be completed at twenty-six (thirteen pairs) specific loci on the DNA.

An investigator can obtain DNA samples from various places on or in the body such as saliva, skin tissue, sweat, bone, blood, earwax, mucus, urine, semen, vaginal cells, rectal cells, and the shaft of a human hair. Unless the sample is given voluntarily, a court order or search warrant is required before evidence may be collected. A warrant isn't normally required when DNA samples are collected from a murder victim during an autopsy.

A detective can also collect a suspect's DNA evidence from items such as dirty laundry, cigarette butts, hats, gloves, and bite marks. She can find samples under a victim's fingernails, on the victim's body, or on bedding or clothing. Only an extremely small sample is required for testing purposes.

ACCIDENTAL TRANSFER OF DNA EVIDENCE

Laboratory technicians and evidence collectors must protect the evidence at all times. There are many possible means by which evidence can be exposed to cross-contamination—the mixing of one person's DNA with that of another. It's actually quite easy to transfer DNA evidence. When evidence is transferred from a person to an item, it's called a primary transfer of evidence. When evidence is transferred from one item to another, it's called secondary transfer. Tertiary transfer occurs when the DNA that's been transferred to a second item is again transferred to a third item.

Coughing, sneezing, or touching one's mouth or nose then touching the area to be tested are all means of cross-contaminating a sample. DNA can also be transferred to an item simply by a person touching that item. That same DNA can be transferred to people who then use that item, such as a towel that's been used by someone else. DNA can even be transferred from one article of clothing to another in a washing machine.

Evidence that's been cross-contaminated will exhibit false results and could be used to convict the innocent and allow the guilty to go free. To prevent these false results, detectives must wear gloves when handling evidence, and they must change them frequently to prevent the transmission of trace material from one item to another. Evidence collection tools and equipment have to be thoroughly cleaned or disposed of after each crime scene. Also, detectives, first responders, evidence technicians, criminalists, patrol officers, news reporters, and anyone else who may have reason to be in or around a crime scene should take care to protect themselves against the possibility of exposure to blood-borne pathogens such as HIV and hepatitis.

PRESERVING DNA EVIDENCE

Investigators must preserve and protect collected DNA evidence from contamination and degradation. DNA samples can deteriorate over a period of time, but a refrigerated sample may be preserved for years. Heat, humidity, exposure to ultraviolet light, and the presence of bacteria can increase the breakdown of the sample. Samples that have been properly preserved can be tested with positive results tens of thousands of years later. On the other hand, a body that's been dumped into a swamp during the heat of the summer may only retain DNA worthy of testing for mere days. Bacteria that feed on a body produce liquid waste, and once DNA has been broken down by bacteria it's no longer a link to the body from which it came. Trying to extract a victim's DNA from a bacterium would serve no purpose; the DNA simply wouldn't be there.

An investigator should never package an item of evidence for DNA testing in plastic. Plastic encourages a growth environment for harmful bacteria, which can destroy the sample, rendering once-good evidence impossible to test. The Nicole Brown Simpson murder case provides a good example. Wet evidence was accidentally allowed to sit for hours in the back of the crime scene investigation truck in the California heat. O.J. Simpson's defense team jumped on this oversight, creating a reasonable presumption of evidence degradation and contamination for the jury to ponder.

All items containing possible DNA evidence should be carefully collected and packaged in *new* paper bags or paper packaging material. The evidence should also be kept away from moisture and allowed to air dry.

DNA evidence has to be kept at room temperature and away from direct sunlight. Investigators should transport evidence in a manner that prevents it from contacting moisture, and they should never place the evidence package on a car seat where it could be possibly come into contact with spilled coffee, soft drinks, or rain from an open window.

Police officers should never assume that an item doesn't contain DNA evidence. Anything is a potential source for that case-solving piece of DNA— hats, used tissues, condoms, toilet tissue, drinking glasses, hairbrushes and combs, dentures, and even carpeting (which can contain dandruff, skin cells, and body hair).

DNA TESTING

The sole purpose of DNA testing in criminal cases is to include or exclude people as suspects in a crime. Forensic scientists spend hours running DNA tests just to be able to report one of three things: Yes, this person can be *eliminated* as a suspect; yes, this person can be *included* as a suspect; or, this person can neither be included nor excluded as a suspect.

DNA testing has come a long way in a very short time. Scientists are constantly working on ways to make the process of analyzing DNA faster, less costly, and more accurate. Each of those elements can be factors in the outcome of a trial.

RFLP TESTING

One method of DNA analysis used by law enforcement is restriction fragment length polymorphism (RFLP). The RFLP method of DNA testing is a time-consuming and expensive method of DNA testing. It's become a bit outdated but is still used.

RFLP is used for the identification criminal suspects and for paternity testing. Forensic scientists use RFLP analysis to examine evidence samples for the presence or absence of DNA sequences. The test separates the sites by a technique called gel electrophoresis. A scientist mixes a solution, which later hardens into a clear gelatin-like substance. Once it's thoroughly mixed, the scientist pours the gel solution into a heat-resistant glass dish where it's allowed to set into a slab of gel (slab gel testing), usually overnight.

The next day, the technician injects radioactive-based DNA into the gel and applies an electrical charge to the entire blend. The electricity causes the DNA to move, breaking it apart. The smaller, lighter pieces move farther away from the source of electricity, leaving the larger, heaviest pieces behind.

An X-ray film is placed over the gel and photographed. The radioactive bases produce a picture called an autorad, which depicts the image of the classic DNA bar code, a person's DNA fingerprint. The autorad image is eventually used by prosecutors as evidence in court proceedings.

RFLP testing requires very large amounts of DNA, about 100,000 cells, or a drop of blood approximately the size of a dime. Crime scene evidence collection methods are often less than satisfactory for gathering completely non-contaminated samples, and samples that have been introduced to things such as mold and dirt won't test adequately using RFLP.

PCR AMPLIFICATION

To analyze a piece of evidence, scientists must first extract DNA from the item, and because DNA's so tiny, they then must divide that piece of DNA into several exact copies to ensure there's enough material on hand for testing. To make copies of DNA, scientists perform a procedure called polymerase chain reaction (PCR) amplification.

PCR amplification is used to amplify, or increase, the number of available samples of DNA. Using PCR amplification, technicians can duplicate millions of copies of a piece of DNA, which allows deteriorated samples to be salvaged and tested.

Scientists begin the PCR amplification process by heating a sample of DNA and then pulling it apart. During this initial process a synthetic primer (a short, artificial strand of DNA) binds to the DNA and begins to duplicate it. In the final step, technicians apply heat to the sample, which activates an enzyme to produce an identical copy of the original DNA strand. This procedure can be performed repeatedly, creating billions of perfect copies.

There can, however, be a problem with cross-contamination using PCR amplification. There's so much scientist-to-DNA-to-equipment contact that it's imperative the technician wear protective gear such as gloves. To further alleviate the risks of cross-contamination, all tools and instruments must be sterile.

ELECTROPHEROGRAM

Slab gel testing for DNA—used in the old RFLP testing—has been all but replaced in modern laboratories by machines. One of those machines, the ABI Prism 310 Genetic Analyzer, was developed by the Foster City, California-based company Applied Biosystems.

According to the Bureau of Justice Statistics, the ABI Prism 310 is one of the most widely used types of equipment for DNA testing in the United States. Its popularity is followed by another of Applied Biosystems' analyzers, the ABI 377. A third favorite is Hitachi's FMBIO.

Each of these machines, or analyzers, uses a set of genetic probes, such as the Profiler Plus probes, which examine ten DNA loci. COfiler, another brand of software probes, examines fourteen DNA loci. Alleles, the small sections of DNA on the human genome, are detected by the probes during DNA testing. During the tests, the computer software assigns each allele a number at each locus. Each locus usually has two alleles, one inherited from the mother and one from the father.

An electropherogram is a graph depicting peaks that correspond to the amount of DNA that passes through the analyzer. To produce an electropherogram, a forensic scientist or technician places a DNA sample into a small well in the analyzer. The rest of the process is fully automated. The technician switches on the analyzer and the process begins.

Just as is needed in the manual tests, the DNA must be amplified (replicated), so the machine uses primers and the PCR amplification method of replication to duplicate DNA segments. For identification purposes, the loci are separately dyed blue, yellow, or green. (The loci will then show up as colored peaks on paper.)

Electric current separates the DNA and sends it through a narrow, straw-like capillary tube. As with the slab gel tests, the shorter, lighter portions of DNA move through the tube at a much quicker pace than the longer, heavier fragments. A laser light causes the colored loci to fluoresce as they pass by, which allows a computer-operated camera to capture their images. The images show up as peaks on the electropherogram.

The height of the peak, which is measured by reflective fluorescent units (RFUs), depicts the amount of DNA at that particular location. A noticeable difference in the heights of peaks in any given sample indicates the possibility of a second suspect—a mixed sample.

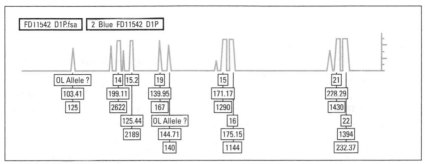

Peak height differences indicate a possible mixture of two people's DNA.

A degraded sample of DNA evidence can show up as gradually declining peak heights across the electropherogram. If the peaks get short enough (caused by badly degraded samples), they can easily be interpreted as "noise." They may also be disregarded as a low peak.

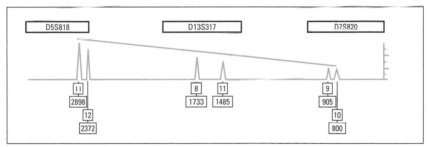

Diminishing peaks caused by a degraded sample.

Spurious Peaks

Spurious peaks are peaks that show up on the electropherogram but aren't an actual allele. These false peaks are generally caused by a side effect of the testing process itself. They can be caused by the amplification of the DNA—stutter peaks—or from sample degradation, urea crystals in the sample, or tiny air bubbles in the samples. These pollutants cause small "noise" peaks that occur all along the baseline of the electropherogram. Once in a while, one of these impurities can cause the laser to create a large enough flash that it records nearly as large as a true peak. These peaks can be wrongly interpreted by scientists.

A pull-up is simply a glitch in the computer software that causes the machine to misread the dye colors, which in turn can cause the technician to misread the results of the test.

Spiked peaks can be caused by voltage surges in the laboratory's power supply, such as a sudden lightning storm.

Blobs occur when the colored dyes somehow become separated from the DNA. When that dye passes by the laser, the analyzer records it as an allele. Blobs are normally depicted as really wide peaks and are obvious to experts; however, an inexperienced scientist might interpret the blob as a true peak.

Short peaks are, as their name suggests, peaks that are shorter in height than those normally found during the testing process. Oddly enough, there's no standard "low" threshold for scoring alleles. If a sample has been even slightly degraded, it can show up during the testing, but it may only show up as a small (short) peak. Some experts may simply disregard these low peaks as "noise" or as a stutter peak when in actuality they could be dismissing the most important piece of evidence in the entire case. Some labs even set their software to ignore or even disregard these short peaks. The ABI Prism 310 Genetic Analyzer in combination with the Profiler Plus probes uses thresholds as low as 40 RFU. Other labs that don't use the same standard may not count the same peaks and could result in an entirely different interpretation of the same test results.

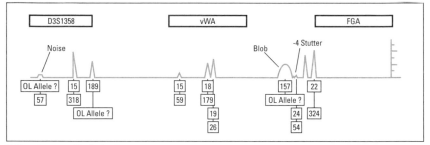

Odd peaks caused by "noise."

Sample Mixtures

Since DNA testing can now be conducted with very small samples, it's become even easier to obtain a suspect's DNA that's been mixed with more than one other person. DNA is being retrieved from places as small a light switch and even from single fingerprints. There's probably enough of your DNA on the cover and pages of this book to collect as a sample, but think about how many people have touched this book, the light switch, or the very spot from where the fingerprint was lifted. A mixture of your DNA with the DNA of a total stranger—perhaps even a serial killer—is very possible, even probable.

An evidence sample that contains DNA from more than one source is very difficult to interpret. A person should, at best, contribute only two identifying markers at each locus. More than two peaks at any given locus indicate the contribution of DNA by more than one person. Some laboratories attempt to distinguish the difference in the peaks by stating that one suspect has a higher peak than the other, in other words, saying that the two individuals are distinguishable. It's not that easy. There can be other causes of additional peaks.

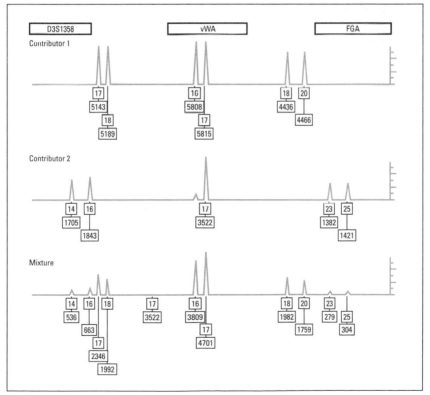

Mixed sample showing multiple peaks.

MITOCHONDRIAL DNA TESTING

Another method of testing is mitochondrial DNA (mtDNA) analysis, which can be used to connect a suspect with his crime. Each person can be traced to his mother through mtDNA analysis, which looks only at the X (female) chromosomes. DNA samples can be obtained from human remains and compared to other people for possible maternal matches. The bodies of Laci and Conner Peterson (the wife and unborn child of convicted murderer Scott Peterson) were both identified by matching their DNA to the DNA of Laci's mother using mtDNA analysis.

Mitochondria are found within cells and are used by the cells as a source of energy. MtDNA is inherited only from the mother, who passes it on to her offspring. MtDNA testing can be used on areas of the body where there's little DNA available, such as hair, bone, and teeth; this testing is also useful if samples have degraded. Detectives find mtDNA analysis particularly useful when a case has remained unsolved or "on the shelf" for many years. It's also helpful when the only evidence is a body part, such as a leg, arm, or even a single fingertip. DNA extracted from the tissue of those limbs can be tested and linked to family members of the victim. There are very few mtDNA testing sites available, which can delay the examination of evidence. This type of DNA testing is quite expensive.

STR TESTING

The method used most commonly in current law enforcement is short tandem repeat (STR) analysis. STR testing is based upon the repetition of alleles (remember the TTAC, TTAC, TTAC pattern) on any given suspect sample. That consecutive repetition sets apart one person's genetic mapping from another (each person has her own individual repetitive pattern).

To clarify the difference between PCR amplification and STR testing, PCR amplification is like running DNA through a copy machine, which duplicates the sample as many times as needed. STR testing doesn't duplicate a sample; it's used to identify someone by isolating a particular pattern of alleles.

Any variance of a person's normal pattern of alleles indicates the presence or a mixture of a second person's DNA—a difficult sample for scientists to interpret.

STRs can even be performed on degraded samples because the amount of DNA needed to conduct the analysis is small compared to the dime-sized drop of blood needed for the RFLP analysis.

CODIS

STR results can be entered into the Combined DNA Index System (CODIS), the database of DNA profiles comprised of samples taken from crime scenes and individuals convicted of certain crimes, such as sex crimes and other violent crimes. CODIS is operated by the FBI and is available to all levels of law enforcement—local, state, and federal.

Technicians and scientists working in law enforcement labs enter DNA profiles into the CODIS database from crime scenes and from offenders who have been arrested for sexual (rape and sexual assault) and other violent crimes, such as homicide. Some states even collect DNA samples from people who have been convicted of other felonies. CODIS searches its database and returns positive results to the submitting agency.

The FBI started CODIS in the early 1990s as a pilot program and began full swing operation in 1998. Software, training, and installation are provided free of charge to any law enforcement agency that is equipped for DNA testing. Today, the DNA profiles of approximately three million felons are on file in the CODIS system.

FAMILIAL SEARCHES AND CODIS

A current and quite controversial means of DNA sampling is called a familial search. Law enforcement officials use familial searches to locate offenders by tracking the DNA of family members. For example, let's say a rape occurs and police enter DNA from the semen sample into the CODIS system. CODIS returns information about someone in prison whose DNA closely, but not exactly, matches the rape suspect's DNA. Through further investigation, police learn that the DNA of a family member of the prisoner is an identical match to the DNA from the rape suspect. Police are presently able to conduct these familial CODIS searches without search warrants.

DNA AND THE PROSECUTION

DNA evidence can provide detectives with scientific proof of physical contact between an assailant and a victim. Likewise, DNA tests can also be used to eliminate a person as a suspect or, in some cases, to link several crime scenes to the same perpetrator.

DNA is an excellent tool for the prosecution, if it's used correctly. Attorneys who rely on DNA as a sole means for prosecution just may find themselves hearing the words, "not guilty." They also may find a case they win overturned later on appeal. Criminal cases must be built on the totality of *all* the circumstances that surround a criminal act, not on DNA alone. In other words, the more truly credible evidence that's presented to tie a suspect to a crime, the better.

Just because someone's DNA is found at a crime scene, or even on or in the body of a victim, doesn't mean that person committed the crime. The location of DNA can, however, help prosecutors figure out the chain of events surrounding a murder. A combination of DNA evidence from a victim and another person found in places other than where the victim's body was discovered can suggest a struggle between those two people at that location.

A combination of incriminating evidence offers the best case against a suspect. For example, a perpetrator's DNA found in the home of a rape victim along with the discovery of burglary tools and restraints (rope, handcuffs, and duct tape) in the suspect's vehicle is much more powerful than either of the two circumstances alone.

For a prosecutor to be sure his case is solid, he must be certain that DNA evidence has been preserved properly and hasn't been contaminated. The attorney must also be able to convince a judge and/or a jury that the collection and testing procedures are sound. He must prove that the DNA evidence he's presenting does indeed implicate the suspect on trial, without any doubt whatsoever.

The use of DNA technology is rapidly closing the gap between unsolved crimes and closed cases. As proficiency in testing increases, cases will be solved more rapidly, allowing police detectives much-needed time to work on other cases.

DNA AND THE DEFENSE

There are two sides to the DNA coin, and when tossed, it doesn't always land heads up. More and more cases are being overturned based upon improper or nonexistent DNA evidence, and more and more prisoners are being released from prisons all across the country as a result.

In the past, defense attorneys have seemingly just accepted DNA evidence as pure and undisputable fact, but research today by firms such as Forensic Bioinformatic Services, Inc. (FBS) of Fairborn, Ohio, have discovered that what was once thought of as the perfect law enforcement tool isn't quite so perfect. FBS scientists are some of the world's leading experts on DNA and are quite often found testifying as expert witnesses in very high-profile cases, such as the Alejandro Avila murder case (victim: five-year-old Samantha Runnion); the O.J. Simpson murder trial (victims: Nicole Brown Simpson and Ron Goldman); the Dr. Dirk Greineder murder trial (victim: Mabel Greineder); the case of Lee Boyd Malvo, one of the D.C. snipers (multiple victims); the case of the Green River Killer (multiple victims); and the Monica Lewinsky "blue dress" case.

FBS founder Dr. Dan Krane suggests that defense attorneys should follow a simple formula for presenting arguments on behalf of their clients. Following a simple three-tiered, inverted pyramid formula could mean the difference between life and death for a defendant.

The major obstacle for presenting a strong defense is the cost of that defense. DNA testing is expensive, but not as costly as paying for the time and knowledge of expert witnesses. Offenders who are indigent and have had attorneys appointed for them by the court simply don't have the means to pay for private investigators and DNA experts.

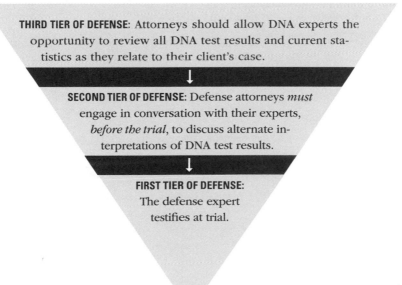

THIRD TIER OF DEFENSE: Attorneys should allow DNA experts the opportunity to review all DNA test results and current statistics as they relate to their client's case.

↓

SECOND TIER OF DEFENSE: Defense attorneys *must* engage in conversation with their experts, *before the trial*, to discuss alternate interpretations of DNA test results.

↓

FIRST TIER OF DEFENSE: The defense expert testifies at trial.

A simple day's testimony from an expert witness can cost approximately three thousand dollars plus travel and lodging expenses. Additional time—further testimony or testing interpretation—can be billed at fifty to three hundred dollars per hour, depending on the expert. Needless to say, the more test results and samples, the more time is needed by the experts and the attorneys. Sometimes experts offer their services pro bono (without charge), especially if the case is a high-profile case where worldwide exposure for their companies can be achieved.

Defense attorneys have the task of presenting evidence that exonerates their clients or, at the very least, instills reasonable doubt about their clients' guilt into the minds of jury members. Attorneys for the defense can make use of sources of uncertainty in DNA testing and DNA test results.

INTERESTING DNA FACTS

- All plants and animals have DNA.

- Humans have 46 chromosomes; carp have 104.

- Human and mouse DNA are nearly identical.

- A person's blood type can change after he receives a bone marrow transplant. DNA in blood cells also change, but saliva and other areas remain the same.

- The total length of human DNA is thirty-nine inches. The total length of corn DNA is sixty-seven inches.

- Ultraviolet light and chemicals can damage DNA. These changes are called mutations.

CHAPTER 10

AUTOPSY

If a medical examiner were allowed to do only one thing during an autopsy, that one thing should be to weigh the heart of the victim. The weight of a heart is the key to most of death's mysteries.

—RICHARD BURKHARDT, M.D., CORONER, BUTLER COUNTY, OHIO

An autopsy is the postmortem examination performed on a body to determine the cause of death. The word *autopsy* means "to look for one's self," and people have been doing just that—peering inside dead bodies—for a long, long time.

The dissection of dead bodies can be traced to at least 3500 B.C. These early examinations were conducted, not for medicinal or forensic research, but for the purpose of predicting the future. Early people thought that internal organs, such as the liver and intestines, contained messages from spirits.

The father of medicine, Hippocrates, theorized that illness was caused by a person's superstitious beliefs, by something the sick had done to displease the gods, or by dark and evil spirits possessing the ailing person. Hippocrates also believed that for a person to remain in good health, his four circulating humors (phlegm, blood, yellow bile, and black bile) must be in perfect balance.

Those who practice traditional Chinese medicine still believe in the importance of balance between the four bodily humors. Traditional Chinese medicine places *qi* (air and breath), life's energy, as the foremost of the humors, followed by blood, vital essences, and fluid. Although these four humors differ a bit from those listed by Hippocrates, the Chinese also believe that any imbalance of the humors can cause a person to suffer extreme adverse effects and illness.

Somewhere around 135 A.D. a young scholar and disciple of Hippocrates named Galen began his studies of medicine at the age of sixteen. Galen became a surgeon to the gladiators and believed that all those who studied medicine should learn anatomy through autopsy and dissection. Galen was the first person to discuss a four-chambered human heart, and he believed in a "balance treatment" of disease—if a person was cold, he prescribed giving him something hot; if he was wet, he prescribed drying him off.

In the late 1200s, the University of Bologna's law faculty ordered autopsies to help solve legal troubles within the community. In the 1500s, autopsy became a standard practice in the studies of human pathology, even though it was a crime to dissect a human corpse. Grave robbing became commonplace among some medical students.

Giovanni Battista Morgagni is considered one of the first great pathologists. His book *The Seats and Causes of Diseases Investigated by Anatomy* is considered one of the most significant works in the history of medicine.

In the 1800s, autopsies became one of the most important courses of study at the Pathology Institute in Vienna. In fact, dissection was so important to the school that almost every cadaver in the entire area was autopsied there. The head of the institute, Karl Rokitansky, alone observed over seventy thousand autopsies during his tenure. Of those seventy thousand, Rokitansky performed thirty thousand. During his near half-century at the institute, Rokitansky participated in some form of autopsy at the rate of two per day, seven days per week, for forty-five years.

In the 1920s, Charles Lindbergh flew from America to France, a Model T Ford could be purchased for $350, and refrigerators became an integral part of U.S. households. Women were also allowed to vote for the first time. Things looked bright for what was still a young country, but little did Americans know that bleak times were coming. The Great Depression was on its way.

In spite of the impending doom, more historical milestones entered the history books in the 1920s. Alongside George Eastman's discovery of the camera and the first-ever radio broadcast was a monumental Massachusetts study of three thousand autopsies. The study generated alarming news that rocked the medical world. The medical community learned that doctors had been regularly misdiagnosing illnesses and disease. As a result of the eye-opening Massachusetts study, autopsy became a regular part of medical education.

THE MODERN AUTOPSY

In the United States, it's the duty of either a coroner or a medical examiner to perform examinations of the dead for the purpose of discovering how a person died. It's also the duty of a coroner or medical examiner to decide if and when an autopsy is needed. The rule of thumb for determining if an autopsy is warranted is whether or not the cause of death is at all suspicious. Individual locales decide which to utilize, a coroner or a medical examiner.

THE CORONER

A coroner is an elected official who has the responsibility of investigating all circumstances that surround a suspicious death. U.S. law doesn't mandate that a coroner be a medical doctor. In fact, the only requirements for being a coroner in most states are that the candidate be a citizen of the jurisdiction where she's running for office, be of legal voting age, and be a registered voter.

The state of Ohio is one state that requires all coroners to be licensed medical doctors. In some areas, the coroner's job is part-time, so, in addition to her official duties, a coroner normally has another full-time job. In some states, the sheriff or a local funeral director serves as coroner. In others, perhaps a gas station attendant or even the ticket-taker at the local movie theater may hold the position. Idaho's coroners aren't required to have any experience or qualifications at all. Some counties in the state of Washington even allow their prosecutors to serve as coroners.

It's the coroner's duty to sign all death certificates. Since some coroners aren't medical doctors, they must employ or subcontract the services of forensic pathologists, who perform the actual autopsies and make the determination as to how the victim died. The coroner then records the official cause of death on the certificate.

THE MEDICAL EXAMINER

Medical examiners (or M.E.s), like coroners, are also responsible for determining the cause of unnatural or sudden deaths. Chief medical examiner is an appointed position for the most qualified person hired by city, county, or state officials. The person hired for the job must be a licensed medical doctor and forensic pathologist. In turn, the chief medical examiner may appoint deputy chief medical examiners to work in other facilities throughout the state or districts.

Depending on the laws of the individual state or county, medical examiners are supervised by government officials or governing bodies. For example, in King County, Washington, the medical examiner works for the director of public health. In Spokane, Washington, the medical examiner works at the will of the board of county commissioners. In other areas of the country the medical examiner may even work for the county sheriff.

California has different systems of operation from county to county. Counties in the state of Washington with a population of 200,000 or more can actually place the medical examiner issue on the ballot and have voters decide whether or not to have a medical examiner or a coroner.

Like coroners, medical examiners are responsible for determining the cause of death in all suspicious circumstances, and they sign all death certificates. Unlike coroners, however, all medical examiners are medical doctors/pathologists, and they or their assistants—who are also pathologists—perform all autopsies.

COLLECTING A BODY FROM A CRIME SCENE

The police are in charge of all crime scenes, but the coroner or medical examiner, depending which official serves the area, is in charge of the body. That body may not be moved without their permission. The police or emergency personnel should call the medical examiner or coroner to the scene in the case of any death that occurs outside of a hospital or a medical facility. The medical examiner or coroner can then make the determination if any further investigation is warranted.

The Spokane County Medical Examiner's Office in Spokane, Washington, has a policy in place, as do most medical examiner's offices, that requires the medical examiner (or a designated assistant) to respond to all death scenes within one hour from the time the death is reported. A timely investigation normally provides the most accurate results. It also allows detectives to begin their investigations more quickly.

Spokane Medical Examiner Sally Aiken, M.D., requires that she or someone from her staff respond to each scene where a death has been caused by suspected suicide, homicide, or as a result of a traffic accident. The presence of Dr. Aiken's staff is needed for all deaths in which the deceased is under the age of eighteen; for deaths that occur within a prison or jail; accidental deaths; and for any unusual and/or suspicious deaths, especially in cases where the victim has had no prior history of medical problems. Medical examiners and coroners are also called to the scene where a body has been discovered that's so badly decomposed the police can't properly identify the remains.

Coroner's/medical examiner's investigators have the duty of gathering information surrounding a scene where a body's been found. They only collect facts about the decedent's medical history, the circumstances that led to the death, and sometimes the scene where the death took place. They search for clues regarding the cause of death, not necessarily for clues that lead to the perpetrator of the crime. Coroner's/medical examiner's investigators don't conduct criminal investigations. That's the job of the police.

Coroner's/medical examiner's investigators aren't normally sworn police officers; therefore, they don't have the power to arrest or detain witnesses and suspects. When the time comes to make an arrest, a warrant is issued by the court, and the police are charged with serving it on the appropriate suspect.

The duties of the coroner and medical examiner are specific. They're to determine the cause and time of death. To make these determinations, the body must first be examined for rigidity (the stiffening of the muscles after death) and lividity (the purplish coloration of the skin caused by the pooling of blood at the lowest points on a dead body).

The positioning of the body is also an important factor in determining if the victim was found where he was killed or if he was killed elsewhere and moved after death.

DETERMINING THE TIME OF DEATH

Investigators can make close determinations as to the time of death. The rule of thumb is that a body begins to stiffen (rigor mortis) two hours after death, beginning with the facial muscles then moving downward to the larger muscles of the lower body. As rigor mortis progresses, the body becomes more and more rigid until it's completely stiff, usually about eight to twelve hours after death. After rigor mortis reaches its peak, it remains that way for approximately sixteen to eighteen hours. The stiffness begins to dissipate in the exact order it began until the body returns to its normal flaccid and pliable condition in about twelve hours.

Lividity begins immediately after the heart stops functioning. The cessation of the heart's pumping action allows gravity to pull blood to the lowest points of the body. There, in those low areas, the tissue begins to take on a purplish tint, much like a dark bruise. In fact, lividity appears so much like a bruise that laypeople and police officers who see a dead body for the first time sometimes think the victim has been badly beaten, especially if the victim is discovered lying facedown. When the body's rolled over, the face is sometimes badly discolored due to the collection of blood in the tissue.

It's possible to see the effects of lividity within thirty minutes after the victim's heart stops beating. The pooling of blood reaches its peak eight to twelve hours after death. Lividity becomes fixed in six to eight hours; deterioration of blood vessels causes blood to leak into the surrounding tissue, permanently staining it. Until that process is complete, lividity can shift from one area of the body to another if the body is moved or turned. A body found lying face down with lividity on the back and buttocks is a clear indicator to detectives and medical examiners that the body has been moved at some point after the lividity became fixed.

The police have the responsibility of securing the scene and protecting the body and evidence. They must provide security for the medical examiner and her staff as they conduct their examination of the body and the crime scene. The police don't conduct any physical examinations of the body other than to check for signs of life, such as pulse and respirations. Taking and recording body temperature isn't the responsibility of a police officer.

Medical examiners and coroners use the interior temperature of the body and its surroundings as another means to determine the time of death. The normal temperature of the human body is approximately 98.6° F. When a person dies, his body begins to cool at a rate of approximately 1.5 degrees per hour until it reaches the same temperature as its surroundings. (If a person dies in a room where the temperature is 75° F and the body is discovered with a temperature of 86.6° F, investigators can conclude that the person has been dead for approximately eight hours.)

Several factors can accelerate or reduce these results, such as extreme heat or cold. A body that's left outside in frigid weather cools much faster than one left in desert heat. Investigators should make note of the temperature of the area where the body was found so pathologists can take that into consideration when making their time-of-death calculations.

TRANSPORTING THE BODY

Investigators should photograph the victim and the surrounding area where the body was discovered. All items of possible importance to identifying the victim (wallets, purses, clothing, identification cards) and the cause of death (medications and poisons) should be collected and transported, along with the body, to the morgue for examination. Any items deemed as evidence in the criminal investigation should be transferred to police investigators on the scene. It's important for the investigators and the medical examiner to work closely together.

Coroner's/medical examiner's investigators should collect all medications found near the victim. They should place these items inside the body bag for transportation along with the body. Any ligatures (rope, wire, or cord used for strangling or choking) still attached to the body should be left in place. Under no circumstance should investigators cut or disturb these parts at the crime scene. The medical examiner doesn't normally collect weapons, such as guns and knives. These, along with any other hazardous materials such as explosives, narcotics, and syringes, are retained by police officers.

Investigators (police, medical examiner, or coroner) should cover the hands of all victims of homicide or suicide with clean paper bags and fasten the bags with either tape or string. This procedure prevents the contamination or loss of evidence that could be found on the fingers, palms, or under or around the fingernails.

The body of a homicide or suicide victim is removed from the scene under the direction of the medical examiner or coroner. Accident victims or people who died of natural causes may be picked up and transported by ambulance or funeral home personnel.

Before the body is transported to the morgue, it's photographed and then placed in a heavy, plastic-coated body bag in front of witnesses. The leak-resistant bag should be sealed with a tamperproof seal. The victim should be transported to the morgue in the clothing that was found on the body. Forensic scientists could discover trace evidence on these items.

Bodies are stored in walk-in refrigerated coolers.

The body is removed and delivered to the morgue by the ambulance crew or coroner's/medical examiner's investigators. At the morgue, autopsy technicians receive the body, sign the appropriate receipts, and then transfer the body from the transport stretcher to a stainless steel gurney (still inside the sealed body bag). With the paperwork complete, they roll the gurney to a set of scales mounted into the floor. The body and the gurney are weighed together. The weight of the gurney is deducted (morgue gurneys weigh approximately 142 pounds), and the true weight of the body is recorded in the permanent record of the deceased.

After weighing and measuring the body, autopsy technicians record the victim's personal information (name, weight, height, date and time of death, case number, etc.) on a toe tag. Then they tie the tag to the big toe of the victim. The remains are then placed into a cooler that's much like the walk-in coolers found in grocery stores or butcher shops. Refrigerated air retards the rate of decomposition of a body, which allows the medical examiner's team ample time to conduct any necessary investigations prior to autopsy. It's possible to keep a body refrigerated for several months before performing an autopsy.

THE AUTOPSY PROCESS

In most morgues, several autopsies are scheduled throughout the day. At the appropriate time, an autopsy technician (or *diener*—the proper name for an autopsy technician, which means "servant") retrieves the corresponding body and delivers it to the autopsy room.

A medical examiner, assisted by one or more autopsy technicians, performs the autopsy. Any tasks carried out by the autopsy technicians are done only under the direct supervision of the attending pathologist.

The morgue staff usually includes a chief medical examiner, one or more autopsy technicians or deputy medical examiners (depending upon the size of the jurisdiction), and one or more autopsy technicians. The medical examiner and the autopsy technicians conduct the autopsy. Medical students may be present during the autopsy, as observers, along with visiting doctors. Police academies sometimes require recruits to attend an autopsy as part of their basic training.

The autopsy room is generally—as one would probably expect—windowless, quiet, and eerie. I've witnessed several autopsies in different jurisdictions, and the experience is always the same. The odor of raw flesh meanders among stainless steel

Autopsy room.

tables and jars of formalin. White lab coats soiled with brownish red bloodstains hang loosely beside a doorway that houses a pair of electronically controlled doors. Florescent fixtures hum softly overhead and fill the room with cold light. Tiled walls and floors are dull and dingy from years of spilled blood. Banks of cabinets stand at the rear of the room. Glass-front doors expose an electric saw and other bone-cutting tools. Disposable face shields, similar to welding helmets, line the shelves beside the various other supplies. Polished steel sinks stand along the wall behind the row of autopsy tables. Over the years, I've noticed that, no matter how many attempts are made to mask the purpose of autopsy rooms, they all wind up looking exactly the same. Morbid.

Sometimes, police investigators are present during the autopsy of homicide or suicide victims. Their presence isn't required unless they're there to take possession of evidence. It's a good idea, however, for police officers to attend an autopsy as a learning experience. The procedure enables the officer to see how physical evidence is retrieved from a body and what he can do at the crime scene to protect and preserve that evidence.

THE EXTERNAL EXAMINATION

Once the body has been delivered to the autopsy room (sometimes called an autopsy suite), it is removed from the sealed body bag and again weighed and photographed. Technicians position the body on a stainless steel autopsy table. The metal tables are equipped with running water and several holes for drainage. They're also tilted to allow fluids to run off and into the drainage holes.

With the body in place on the table, the autopsy technician places a hard rubber body post beneath the victim's back. The post raises the head and chest area upward to allow better access to the upper body. It also allows the arms and head to fall backward, slightly out of the way. The pa-

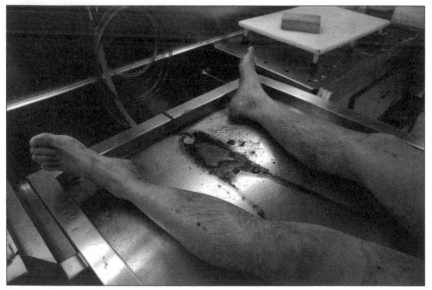

Autopsy table.

thologist compares the information on the body bag seal, the toe tag, and the paperwork to ensure that she has the correct body before her. If all's well, the autopsy begins.

The pathologist observes and notes any evidence of prior medical treatment on the victim, such as gastric and endotracheal tubes (life support may have been attempted on the scene by emergency medical personnel).

In the case of an autopsy for a suspicious death, the autopsy commences with the tedious task of collecting trace evidence, such as hair and fibers. This examination is sometimes enhanced by the use of alternate light sources, such as black light.

Bags are removed from the hands and labeled, right and left. Each bag is marked with a corresponding case number and the victim's name. The bags are packaged and retained for evidence.

The victim's fingernails are trimmed to the quick, and the trimmings are collected and placed into paper evidence envelopes. The envelopes containing the nail clippings are also marked with the corresponding left and right hand. Some pathologists place the nail clippings from each finger in separate packages.

The medical examiner examines the victim's clothing prior to removing it from the body. She looks for foreign particles and other trace evidence. She also searches the clothing for evidence of gunshot residue and holes and tears that could have been made by cutting implements such as knives, scissors, hatchets, and other edged weapons. If any breaches in the clothing are found, they're photographed, measured, and marked as evidence.

Head and pubic hair are combed, and the loose hair, along with the comb, is packaged in paper containers. The packaging is labeled for future testing and comparison. Hair samples are plucked from the scalp in a systematic manner. They're plucked from each side, the top, the front, and the back of the head. The goal is to pluck approximately fifty hairs from each of the sites. These hairs are also packaged in paper containers such as envelopes. Random samples of beard and moustache hair are also plucked and saved.

The victim's mouth is swabbed with sterile swabs. The swabs are used to make slides for examination under a microscope. These slides can be used for the detection of foreign elements, such as sperm. DNA testing may also be performed later, if necessary.

To preserve the slides, the medical examiner sprays them with a fixative and allows them to dry. The slides are then packaged in paper or cardboard containers and sealed with evidence tape. The packaged slides are labeled with the appropriate case number.

If the victim is female, the medical examiner must perform a vaginal examination. This exam is conducted much in the same manner as a normal gynecological exam. The medical examiner examines the vaginal area via speculum. Cotton swabs are used to conduct both vaginal and cervical smears, and slides are made from both locations. The slides are sprayed with fixative, packaged, and labeled. The same procedure is carried out in the anal area of both male and female victims.

Sometimes insects are discovered when a body is presented for autopsy. If the time of death isn't known, the medical examiner may collect samples of each insect, such as maggots and beetles. Live bugs are collected and placed into suitable containers to preserve them. The cartons (half-pint containers are ideal) are filled with an inert material, such as vermiculite or loose soil. The insects must also be provided a food source, such as beef liver or pieces of raw meat.

Dead insects are preserved by placing them into hot water (about the temperature of water used for a cup of hot tea or coffee) for two to three minutes, then transferring them to a 70 percent ethanol or isopropyl alcohol/30 percent sterile water solution. A forensic entomologist, who may be called into court to testify to his findings, examines both live and dead insect specimens.

Body fluids, such as vitreous humor, blood, and urine, are collected and preserved for examination and testing. The policies of each morgue determine when these fluids are drawn and by whom. Some medical examiners insist upon drawing the fluids themselves, while others allow the collection to be performed by their autopsy technicians. Some fluid, such as vitreous humor, may be collected prior to the actual autopsy to save time.

Vitreous humor is the transparent, gelatinous fluid that fills the space in the eyeball between the lens and retina. The fluid helps maintain the shape and pressure of the eyeball. During autopsy, a 10cc syringe is used to collect a sample of vitreous humor from each eye. A few drops of the fluid are deposited on a factory-prepared analysis strip to test for the presence of alcohol, dehydration, ketones, and glucose (high or low levels of blood sugar). The remaining fluid is placed into a red-topped vial and sealed.

Scientists and medical professionals use vials topped with various colored stoppers to identify their contents and purpose. These vials come from the factory with certain additives for various functions.

- **Red-topped vials:** contain no additives and are used for specimens that don't require any added preservatives.

- **Blue-topped vials:** contain sodium citrate for coagulation studies.

- **Gray-topped vials:** contain potassium oxalate, another anticoagulate for collecting plasma.

- **Orange-topped vials:** contain thrombin and are used for inducing coagulation, usually within five minutes.

- **Yellow-topped vials:** contain acid citrate dextrose, which prevents coagulation, and are for use in paternity testing and transplant capability.

- **Green-topped vials:** contain heparin for anticoagulation studies.

- **Purple-topped vials:** contain ethylenediaminetetraacetic acid (EDTA) for hematology (blood) studies and for potential DNA testing. (You may remember the purple-topped vial from the O.J. Simpson case. Blood droplets were found at the scene that contained small amounts of EDTA. The defense raised the issue that police officers had possibly brought blood to the scene—hoping to frame O.J.—that had been stored in a purple-topped vial, even though human blood naturally contains small amounts of EDTA.)

The medical examiner measures the length of the victim's body, and then one of the technicians cleans the body. The cleansing process is simple—the body is rinsed off with a water hose. If needed, X-rays of the body are taken at this time.

THE INTERNAL POSTMORTEM EXAMINATION

The internal examination begins with the medical examiner or an assisting autopsy technician making a "Y" incision. A "Y" incision is actually a series of either two or three individual cuts. The technician inserts a scalpel at the front of one shoulder and slices from that point to the tip of the xiphoid process (the lowest point of the breastbone). She can either stop the incision there or curve downward toward the feet, continuing the cut until she reaches the area of the pubic bone (making a slight detour around the belly-button). She then makes another incision into the opposite shoulder, slicing until the incision meets the previous cut at the xiphoid process. The resulting cuts form the "Y."

The technician then peels the skin and surrounding tissue away from the chest area, exposing the ribs. To completely expose the ribcage, she may have to slice away any connecting tissue remaining between the flesh and rib bones. The loose skin and muscle tissue now hang freely to the sides of the chest.

Using an electric bone saw or a manual bone cutter (which resembles a gardener's pruning shears), the technician severs the ribs and chest plate. When the cut is complete, the chest plate and ribs are lifted out of the upper body in one solid triangular-shaped piece and laid to the side until the autopsy is complete. The muscle wall of the abdomen is also severed from the lower portion of the ribcage. The interior organs of the body are now fully exposed and ready for examination. The odor that's emitted from the interior portion of a human body closely resembles that of the inside of a butcher shop. Its scent is quite similar to raw animal meat.

Blood that's seeped into the chest and abdominal cavities is scooped out with a plastic cup and measured in a tall, flask-like container, called a graduated cylinder. If the victim's been dead for a while, the technician may need to collect decomposition fluids from the body cavity as well.

All internal organs (including the testes) are removed, weighed, and dissected. They're sliced much like one would slice a loaf of bread and are examined for any abnormalities such as necrosis (dead tissue) or for any foreign objects such as bullets. Gunshot wounds are examined for a bullet's path of travel, if possible. This information can sometimes assist investigators in determining the position and location of the shooter in relation to the victim.

After dissection, portions of each organ are placed into containers filed with formalin. The medical examiner performs a microscopic examination of each organ and tissue sample sometime after the autopsy is complete.

The brain is the last organ to be examined, and this is part of the autopsy where the lay observer usually becomes the most squeamish. The autopsy technician uses a scalpel to make a cut through the scalp behind one ear, and then slices around the back of the head to the other ear. The scalp is then stripped away from the skull and peeled over the top of the head until it comes to rest over the face. The top of the skull is now exposed and ready for cutting. To make the cut into the skull, the technician uses an electric saw, sometimes called a Stryker saw—named after a particular brand name of an electric bone saw. Another popular brand of bone saw is the Thermo Shandon autopsy saw.

The technician guides the saw all the way around the head, pausing only once to form a triangular notch in the back of the skull. This notch ensures that the top portion of the skull is properly aligned when it's replaced after the brain cavity examination. The technician must take care not to cut so deep that he cuts into the soft tissue of the brain.

The sound made by the saw is quite similar to, but much louder than, a dentist's drill. The high-pitched whirring combined with the stench of hot, burning bone is an experience many police officers never forget.

After the skull cut is complete, the technician uses a small, stainless steel hammer and chisel to tap the top portion of the skull loose from the bottom half. The sound that's made when the technician removes the top portion of the skull closely resembles the noise made when pulling a foot free from sticky mud, or by pulling apart two halves of a piece of juicy fruit.

The top section of skull is laid to the side. The victim's brain is partially exposed but is still covered by a clear, tough membrane called the dura. The technician strips away the dura with a plier-like device called dura strippers. The brain is now ready for removal. The final step in the removal of the brain is to sever the spinal cord. The technician cuts the cord and pulls the brain free from the skull.

The brain is a very soft and spongy organ. In fact, it's so soft that dissection of it at this point is sometimes difficult. In this case, the technician places it into a brain bucket (a plastic bucket that's the perfect size to receive and contain a human brain) filled with formalin, where it remains for several days. The formalin fixes (firms up) the tissue, allowing for proper dissection and slicing. If the brain is ready to dissect at the autopsy, it's placed on a cutting board much like the ones found in most home kitchens and is cross-sectioned.

When all organs are outside the body, the medical examiner can examine them thoroughly. The medical examiner's job is done when the last organ has been dissected, with individual sections prepared for microscopic study or preservation for future reference. Even then, though, the autopsy process itself is far from over.

Obviously, a body obviously can't be left as it is after an autopsy. A standing joke among medical examiners and autopsy technicians is that bodies make really great "human canoes" because all that's left after an autopsy is an empty hull.

The autopsy technician must reassemble the body before it's picked up by funeral home personnel. He begins by replacing the top of the skull (sometimes minus the brain), lining up the precut notch to prevent slipping, pulls the scalp back into place, and sews it together with a very heavy twine. The stitched wound can't be seen once the body is resting in a casket, with its head on a satin pillow. The internal organs are dealt with in different ways. Some medical examiners put the remaining sliced organs back into the chest cavity, while others place them in a garbage bag and position the entire bag inside the empty body. The ribs are returned to their proper places, and the trunk is stitched with zigzag stitches (like the ones on baseballs), leaving behind a huge "Y"-shaped, stitched wound on the front of the body.

The autopsy technician is now responsible for cleaning the body and the autopsy room, using a sponge and a water hose for the body and a mop and bucket for the room. After cleaning, the body is placed into a thin, paper body bag that's used mainly for transporting bodies from the morgue to a funeral home.

The funeral home selected by the family is notified by the medical examiner that the body is ready to be picked up. If the family of the deceased isn't known, the body is kept in the cooler at the morgue for a period of time in case someone shows up to claim it. If the body remains unclaimed, it's either buried in a state cemetery or incinerated.

After the final testing of the organs, the toxicology, and the other testing is complete, the medical examiner issues a formal report stating the cause of death. In the event of a homicide, the report is forwarded to the investigating officer, and the murder investigation has another chapter in the file.

Family members may request an autopsy, but if the coroner or medical examiner hasn't ordered it, they may have to bear the entire cost of the procedure. The fee for a private autopsy in one rural Ohio county is $1,500—$500 for the use of the coroner's facility and equipment, $250 for the coroner's autopsy technician (clean up and suturing of the body upon completion of the autopsy), and $750 for the forensic pathologist's fee. There are additional fees for toxicology testing and transportation of the body. A basic toxicology panel (drug and alcohol screening) costs approximately two hundred dollars. Transportation fees vary but include the salaries of two employees and vehicle and equipment use. There would be other fees for additional laboratory testing.

Family members may also request that an autopsy not be performed due to their religious beliefs. Medical examiners and coroners try to honor these requests but are sometimes unable to due so because of pending criminal proceedings. Judges sometimes order autopsies to be conducted in cases where the only means to catch a dangerous criminal suspect would be through autopsy.

IN THE LINE OF DUTY
HOLD THE LIVER ...

I witnessed my first autopsy during my training in the police academy. It was a shocking event, to say the least. I can still smell the stench of death in the far corners of my mind and, I don't hesitate to say, the odors of that day will never leave my memory.

My entire class and I were paraded through the cold room where the bodies were kept as they awaited their turn on the "table." Each of the dearly departed was wrapped in heavy, translucent plastic, which did nothing to prevent me from seeing their gaping mouths and the lavendar-gray skin of their naked torsos.

We exited, one by one, from the cooler into the actual autopsy suite where the medical examiner stood waiting. She was dressed in full medical examiner attire, complete with little paper booties. She answered a couple of questions from our group and then turned her attention to her attendant who, honestly, looked as if he belonged in a Frankenstein movie.

I sensed the coldness of the room for the first time when the medical examiner's attendant removed the covering from the body—an elderly man who had died from a gunshot wound to the chest. His toothless mouth was frozen open, and his eyes stared upward. He was naked, and I couldn't help thinking how humiliated he would be were he alive. The medical examiner began to speak into a microphone hanging from the ceiling. The autopsy had begun, and the realization hit me that I was standing in a human butcher shop.

The morgue attendant pushed a cart into the room and left it beside the table; the cart held stainless steel instruments designed for cutting, sawing, prying, and tearing. The medical examiner spoke out loud, announcing the date, time, and the name of the victim, as well as the names of all persons present. She began to examine the body from head to toe and front to back. The others and I listened as she described, both to us and to the microphone, each of her findings. She completed the initial external examination and, without hesitation, made the "Y" incision into the chest. Her gloved hands deftly pulled a large scalpel through the flesh, creating a gaping, bloodless wound beneath the steel blade.

With the aid of her assistant, the medical examiner peeled the skin back and away from the man's skinny chest, with the upper flap resting near his face. The morgue attendant cut apart the exposed ribs with a tool specifically designed to cut bone. The instrument looked like a gardener's tree-limb lopper or tree pruner. When he pulled the victim's ribs apart, a new stench seeped into the room. It was nearly overwhelming, and a couple of my classmates had to leave the room quickly.

A small amount of flesh remained attached to the man's exposed ribs. The medical examiner cleanly sliced away those tiny bits and removed the ribcage. The heart and lungs were now exposed. The medical examiner used both gloved hands to reach inside the chest cavity to palpate the organs, attempting to detect blood clots or other abnormalities. Apparently satisfied there were none, she removed the organs, one at a time. Positioning each organ on the scales, she announced their weights into the microphone. One by one, I noticed more of my classmates leaving the room. When they returned, moments later, they stood just a little farther away from the table, and each looked a little woozy.

The medical examiner was pulling on a portion of the liver with a pair of "pick-ups," or forceps, when a tiny piece of the slimy organ meat broke free and landed squarely on my cheek. Two additional class members headed for the door, and the rest stood staring at me, wondering what I was going to do about the situation. For a moment I just stood there. My stomach was telling me what it thought I should do, but that wasn't an option in front of all these people. Besides, the medical examiner performing the autopsy was very famous. I simply wouldn't allow myself to be sick in front of such a high-profile doctor.

She casually pointed, with a blood-covered hand, to a roll of paper towels on the table beside her. I tore one from the roll and wiped away the tiny piece of human liver. She watched me, from behind a surgical mask and protective glasses, as I deposited the soiled paper into a stainless steel garbage can. The room was totally silent. The medical examiner raised her eyebrows. I took the gesture as her way of asking if I was all right. I nodded; she turned around and continued the exam as if nothing had happened. Apparently, I passed the test, but to this day I have a difficult time eating liver and onions.

THE FUNERAL HOME

Once the body's been released to the family, funeral home representatives are dispatched to the morgue to pick up the remains. They're required to sign a receipt for the body and for any personal effects the family hasn't already retrieved. Evidential items are turned over to the investigating police officers. The mortuary employees take the body to the funeral home to prepare it for viewing and burial.

Once the body has arrived at the funeral home, it's removed from the body bag and placed on a stainless steel table much like the one in the autopsy room.

The funeral director (mortician) washes the body with a mixture of insecticide and germicide. The body is positioned on its back, with the hands folded across the stomach. The director's next step is to shave the face, if that's the desired look. Then, he packs the nose with cotton filler so it retains its shape, and rounded, plastic eye-caps are placed beneath the eyelids. Super Glue is sometimes used to keep the eyelids tightly closed. Cotton or gauze is packed into the throat and other openings of the body to prevent fluid leakage. The mouth is kept closed by thin wires twisted together and attached to a tack on each jaw. The lips are held in place with thin sutures or glue. A moisturizing cream is applied to the lips to prevent them from appearing too dry.

EMBALMING

Now, with all the preparations complete, it's time for the director to introduce the embalming fluid into the body. (Note that although no law states that a body must be embalmed, tradition nearly mandates that the process be performed unless the family chooses to cremate their loved one.)

The practice of embalming doesn't stop the process of decomposition. It merely slows it down and changes the way a body decomposes. Instead of rotting away (putrefaction), it oxidizes (components of the body lose their electrons) and basically dissolves. Like the process where the forensic pathologist preserves tissue samples for examination by "fixing" them in a solution of formalin, a funeral director temporarily preserves the cell proteins of the body by injecting a formaldehyde solution. The chemical causes the dissolvable proteins in blood to turn into a gel. Simultaneously, formalin kills bacteria, which further slows the decomposition process.

If possible, the director makes an incision in the carotid artery located in the notch between the Adam's apple and the large muscle of the neck (sternocleidomastoid muscle). If not, he makes the incision in the femoral artery in the upper thigh near the groin. One end of a flexible tube is inserted into the artery. The opposite end of the tube is attached to the embalming machine. Another tube is inserted into the artery's corresponding vein. The opposite end of that tube is placed into a drain that leads directly into the city sewer or septic system. There are no laws that prevent a funeral home from dumping body fluids into public utility systems.

With all tubing securely in place, the director switches on the embalming machine. The machine instantly pumps the pinkish embalming fluid into the

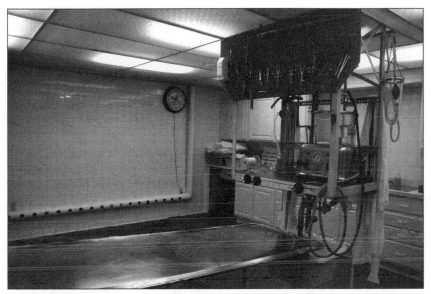

The director fills the three-gallon reservoir of the electric embalming machine with a mixture of water and embalming fluid (eight ounces of water per one gallon of fluid).

body's vascular system. The pumping action forces the fluid in through the artery and pushes blood out the tube attached to the vein. The discarded blood flows into the sewer system. The machine is turned off when the color of the exiting fluid turns from blood red to embalming-fluid pink. That color change is the indication that embalming fluid has replaced the blood in the body.

When the vascular system is full of embalming fluid, the director withdraws each of the tubes and sutures the incisions to prevent leakage of the solution. A chemical preservative is injected into the abdominal cavity, unless the body has undergone an autopsy. In this case, the director removes the autopsy sutures from the "Y" incision and introduces the liquid preservative directly into the plastic bag containing the organs. The director then resutures the opening in the abdominal cavity. Funeral directors may elect to incinerate the internal organs or leave them in place, but if they're removed, a filler material must be used to "inflate" the chest wall to its normal position before viewing.

After the completion of the fluid transfer, the body is again thoroughly cleaned. Muscles, stiffened by rigor mortis, are massaged to make them more pliable (for the application of clothing and proper limb positioning), and a skin softening cream is applied to the face and hands to prevent drying. Missing tissue and flesh are repaired with molded wax.

The next step is the placement of the body into a casket that's been selected by the family. Once the body's been placed into the casket, the funeral home staff applies flesh-colored makeup to disguise any imperfections on any parts of the body that may be visible during the viewing. Some funeral homes employ makeup and hair specialists, while others call in outside cosmetologists from local salons.

CHAPTER 11

DRUGS, NOT MONEY,
ARE THE ROOT
OF ALL EVIL

Drug addiction has only three exit strategies: recovery, insanity, or death. Along the way, incarceration is a real possibility.

—D.P. LYLE, M.D., AWARD-WINNING AUTHOR OF
FORENSICS FOR DUMMIES

Wherever major crimes such as larceny, simple assault, robbery, rape, and murder appear, drugs seem to be in tow. I've arrested countless suspects who were under the influence of many types of illegal drugs. In the majority of those cases, the use of at least one of five drugs surfaced—crack cocaine, methamphetamine, alcohol, marijuana, or ecstasy. The type of drug and its side effects varied, but the end result was usually the same—destruction of the user, destruction of the family unit, and incarceration of the addict or recreational user.

Police officers and courts are discovering more and more people who are committing crimes and blaming their actions on their use and abuse of physician-prescribed medications, such as hydrocodone (Vicodin), oxycodone (OxyContin), oxycodone with acetaminophen (Percocet), methylphenidate

(Ritalin), and clonazepam (Klonopin). These medications are all highly addictive drugs that, either separately or in combination, are known for their mind-altering capabilities. All these drugs are prescribed by doctors for various physical ailments and mental disorders.

Mind-altering and mood-enhancing drugs of all types have been used and abused in America since the days of the early settlers. From the early marijuana farms of colonial times to the elaborate clandestine laboratories of today, people have sought ways to achieve new highs. Millions of dollars are spent each year to fight the government's war against drugs. For instance, the U.S. government spent more than nineteen billion dollars on the drug war in 2003, and the Drug Enforcement Administration (DEA) alone had an operating budget of nearly two and a half billion dollars for the year 2006.

Statistics from the U.S. Department of Justice report that more than 50 percent of all state and federal prisoners admit to having been under the influence of either drugs or alcohol at the time of their offenses. Sixty percent of mentally ill prisoners admit that they, too, were under the influence of alcohol and drugs at the time of their offenses. Seventy percent of people receiving probation for their crimes, in lieu of jail or prison time, acknowledge the use of drugs or alcohol at the time of their offenses.

Sometimes a court will allow a defendant one chance at rehabilitation in lieu of going to jail for committing a minor offense. If a judge elects to do so, she may order the offender to attend an alcohol or drug treatment program. When the defendant successfully completes the program, his record is cleared. If the defendant fails to complete the program, he must serve the original jail sentence imposed by the court.

DRUG SCHEDULES

The U.S. Attorney General's office is charged with the task of evaluating each drug according to its potential for abuse, its pharmacological effects on the body, the current state of scientific knowledge regarding the drug, the extent of risk to public health, and the potential for physical or psychological addiction. Once the evaluation is complete, each drug is listed in a drug schedule maintained by the DEA—a system of categorizing drugs for use by courts to determine the severity of the offense and punishment for the possession or sale of a particular drug.

Drugs and other substances that carry a risk of abuse are divided among five specific categories: Schedules I, II, III, IV, and V.

- **Schedule I:** includes drugs such as PCP and ecstasy that have an extremely high potential for abuse and addiction by their users. Drugs in this category aren't recognized in the medical community as having any value; therefore, they're considered to be dangerous or harmful to the human body.

- **Schedule II:** includes drugs such as heroin and cocaine that also have a very high potential for abuse, but these drugs are recognized as valid medications for medical treatments. The dispensing of these medications is closely supervised and monitored. As with the drugs in Schedule I, Schedule II drugs are highly addictive.

- **Schedule III:** includes drugs such as anabolic steroids and codeine that are further down in the schedule yet still have the potential for abuse. The drugs in this category are most often prescribed by doctors and are generally not as addictive or habit-forming as the drugs in the higher categories.

- **Schedule IV:** includes drugs such as diazepam (Valium) and phenobarbital that have similar characteristics to Schedule III drugs but have a lower potential for abuse. There's a limited potential for dependence on the drugs in this schedule, although psychological dependence is a possibility

- **Schedule V:** includes all other drugs, such as cough syrup, that aren't listed in any of the upper four categories. The drugs in this category have a very low potential for abuse and addiction.

The classification of these drugs by schedule also provides a guideline for the level of severity of an offense and a corresponding punishment for that offense. Illegal possession and distribution of Schedule I drugs is the most severe crime, and subsequently, carries the stiffest penalty for those who violate the laws regarding the drugs in this category. Schedule II is the next most severe category followed by III, IV, and finally Schedule V, which carries the least amount of penalty for the possession, use, and abuse of the drugs listed within.

In addition to the drugs and substances listed in the drug schedules, law enforcement officials have found it necessary to monitor the legal sales and possession of certain chemicals that can be used for the manufacturing of illegal drugs, such as methamphetamine and crack cocaine. Vendors such as agricultural supply companies are required by law to keep records of the type, quantity, and the DEA number of each of the listed chemicals they sell. They must also keep accurate records of whom they've sold the chemicals to. The scrutinized chemicals are placed into two groups: Level I, the more closely monitored that includes benzyl cyanide, hydriodic acid, and nitroethane; and Level II, the lesser-supervised group that includes iodine, sulfuric acid, acetone, and benzyl chloride.

DRUG USE IN AMERICA

During my career as a police officer I devoted much of my time to the enforcement of narcotics laws. I felt that illegal drugs were the source of most crimes, and I decided early on that the eradication of them would lower the crime rate. It didn't take long for me to realize that the elimination of illegal drugs is an impossible task. The drugs in the following paragraphs are ones that seem to pose the biggest problems for law enforcement officers.

MARIJUANA

Marijuana is a Schedule I drug. According to the U.S. government, it has no known medical value. The controversy about whether marijuana should be legalized in the United States is a long-standing argument. Many supporters of the

Marijuana.

legalization of pot believe that the drug has medicinal value or that it simply causes no harm. Supporters also argue that smoking the dried plant leaves causes no more harm to society or to the human body than does alcohol or tobacco; therefore, marijuana should be legalized.

The U.S. government wholeheartedly disagrees and still enforces laws prohibiting the use of marijuana for any reason, even in states that have laws permitting the use of marijuana for certain medical conditions, such as chronic pain and glaucoma.

Marijuana is most commonly smoked in hand-rolled cigarettes (joints), pipes, water pipes (bongs), or blunts. Blunts are hollowed-out cigars that have been repacked with marijuana. The original thought behind smoking pot in blunts was to disguise the act. Hand-rolled joints are pretty obvious to police officers and to the general public. Now, drug enforcement officers look for people smoking faux cigars as well.

In many areas, paraphernalia laws make it illegal for individuals to sell any gadgets (bongs, pipes, and rolling papers) that can be used for the consumption of marijuana and other drugs. It's also illegal in those areas to for people to sell or possess devices used for weighing or packaging any type of illegal drug. Paraphernalia laws can also prohibit legitimate businesses from selling or possessing of any of these objects. However, in some locales these devices are readily available. To dance around the law, shop owners who sell these products simply post signs indicating that their products are for the consumption of tobacco products only.

Effects of Marijuana Use

According to the Partnership for a Drug-Free America, marijuana use can cause impaired memory, distorted perception of the senses, some loss of motor function, rapid heart rate, and anxiety. The Partnership also reports that marijuana smokers who smoke the drug on a regular basis over a long period of time may be taking in many more cancer-causing substances than cigarette smokers who inhale equal amounts of tobacco smoke.

The active ingredient in marijuana is delta-9-tetrahydrocannabinol (THC). When marijuana is smoked or ingested, the THC binds to certain receptors in the brain. This combination sets off cellular reactions that produce the high experienced by users.

Smoking marijuana produces a high that can last for several hours. Immediately after smoking marijuana, blood vessels in the eyes begin to enlarge, causing the classic "red-eyes." The user's heart rate can increase from a normal 60–80 beats per minute to as much as 100 or 120 beats per minute. In some cases, a user's heart rate has even been increased to double the upper range of the normal rate.

With the ingestion of marijuana, the brain is tricked by the THC into rewarding the body's pleasure system. As a result, the brain sends signals to release increased amounts of dopamine, causing the user to experience feelings of euphoria. Users say they begin to feel extremely pleasant, and things like colors and sounds are amplified or are more intense. They also say that things may begin to move in slow motion, as though time has become very sluggish and unhurried. Other side effects of smoking marijuana are an almost uncontrollable urge to laugh, loud and/or rapid talking, anxiety, and sometimes an extreme sense of paranoia. Later stages of the intoxication usually bring on periods of sleepiness and an increased inability to judge how time passes.

Perhaps one of the more classic effects of marijuana is what its users call the "munchies"—the almost uncontrollable urge to eat. And eat they do. The craving for food is normally a craving for sweets and other junk food, such as candy, chips, ice cream, hot dogs, etc. The urge to eat things in odd combinations that aren't normally part of a person's regular diet is also common. In fact, this occurrence is one thing that sometimes draws a police officer's attention to pot smokers.

For example, let's say an officer in the checkout line in a convenience store observes a group of people enter the business. He first notices that their eyes are unusually red. Then the group begins selecting a vast assortment of candy, chips, and soft drinks. To top off their shopping spree, one of the group picks up several jars of pickled pigs' feet. The entire time they're shopping, they giggle and look around nervously.

It's a safe bet that the officer will watch the group as they leave the store. If he feels the situation warrants further investigation, he may approach the group and ask them some questions to determine the extent of their intoxication or influence from the drug. He may also ask permission to search the individuals and their vehicle.

This type of proactive action by a police officer is quite legal and is often very effective in the prevention of traffic accidents. The action also often leads to arrests for the possession of drugs.

Police Efforts Against Marijuana Usage

Police academy recruits are taught to recognize some of the symptoms of marijuana use to assist them in identifying motorists who are possibly driving under the influence of the drug. Some academy instructors also burn thin wafers that mimic the odor of pot smoke so rookie officers will later be able to recognize the scent of burning marijuana.

Law enforcement officers, especially those assigned to a drug task force such as a marijuana-eradication unit, are trained to look for signs of marijuana-growing operations. These special task forces are often comprised of officers and agents from a variety of law enforcement agencies, such as local police departments, sheriff's offices, state police, the Federal Bureau of Investigation, the Drug Enforcement Administration (DEA), the Bureau of Alcohol, Tobacco, Firearms, and Explosives, the National Guard, Game and Fisheries departments, the U.S. Marshals Service, and Alcoholic Beverage Control. Some of the key things eradication unit officers watch for are:

INDOOR MARIJUANA-GROWING OPERATIONS

- Air-conditioning units installed in storage buildings or other outbuildings and sheds.

- Water sources, such as new plumbing or water tanks attached to sheds and other outbuildings.

- Large supplies of potting soil and fertilizers stacked around sheds and outbuildings, or outside entrances to basements.

- A house, shed, or other outbuilding with an unusually high number of roof vents or fans.

- Someone who purchases a large number of heat lamps or indoor grow lamps. (Postal workers have been known to report deliveries of these items to police.)

- Someone other than a farmer who purchases large amounts of potting soil and fertilizer. Miracle-Gro is a popular fertilizer among marijuana growers.

- Extension cords running to outbuildings.

- Someone who has a very large electric bill. Utility companies often contact police if customers suddenly have a large increase in their electricity use.

- Utility meters that have been altered or tampered with. The seals on meter boxes are often cut to allow the suspect to disconnect the meter and replace it with copper bars. This illegal and highly dangerous act allows the thief to use electricity without the power company's knowledge.

- Windows that sweat. Grow rooms have an extremely high humidity.

OUTDOOR MARIJUANA GROWING OPERATIONS

- People who purchase farmland but aren't farmers. Drug dealers often pay cash for property.

- Farmland with gates that are always locked with heavy chains, cables, and padlocks.

- Lots of in-and-out traffic to a particular tract of land.

- Well-worn walking trails throughout a tract of land. The paths are clearly visible from the air.

- Camouflage netting covering large areas of land tracts. Marijuana has a very distinctive blue-green color that's quite visible from the air.

- Large purchases of PVC pipe, fertilizer, and potting soil.

- Water bottles and jugs placed along footpaths.

- Large purchases of chicken wire. Marijuana growers place chicken wire around their plants to prevent rabbits and other animals from eating the leaves and stalks.

- An abundance of security signs. Marijuana growers often place several security-type signs around their property, such as Beware of Dog, Video Surveillance in Use, Keep Out, and No Trespassing. Many times the owners place so many of these signs it becomes obvious to police officers that something odd is going on.

- Purchases of machetes, garden hoses, large garbage bags, staking material, green tie wraps, and green spray paint (to ensure that all things blend in to their surroundings). Many store owners cooperate with police and notify them of purchases of such materials.

- People who pay cash for nearly all their purchases.

- People who visit a certain area of the woods at regular times of the day (to water and tend to their plants).

COCAINE

Cocaine is a Schedule II drug. It's highly addictive and acts as a stimulant to the central nervous system. Dopamine, the naturally produced chemical, offers up feelings of pleasure and enjoyment. Those pleasing sensations make users want to do things that make them feel good, such as having sex and eating great food. When cocaine is consumed, the drug begins to interfere with how the body reabsorbs dopamine. The drug actually increases the amount of dopamine in the body by as much as 150 percent.

Powdered cocaine.

Hydrochloride, the powdered form of cocaine, can be introduced into the body by snorting (inhalation) or injection (via needle). To inject cocaine, a user must first dissolve the drug in water. To snort cocaine, the user inhales the powder directly into her nose..

Cocaine use seems to be most prevalent among users between the ages of eighteen and twenty-four. Unfortunately, U.S. Department of Justice (DOJ) statistics show that a substantial group of school-age children are users of cocaine. A 2005 DOJ poll indicates that 3.7 percent of our nation's eighth graders abuse the drug as well as 5.2 percent of all tenth graders. An alarming 8 percent of high school seniors use cocaine on a regular basis.

Effects of Cocaine Usage

When cocaine is introduced into the body, its effects begin almost immediately and last only for a few minutes. The drug causes a distinct constriction of the blood vessels and dilates the pupils of the eyes. The heart rate becomes rapid, body temperature goes up, and blood pressure increases. Hyperactivity is a classic symptom of cocaine use. The drug gives its user a sense of sudden energy and a boost in fighting fatigue. Sleep is normally out of the question during cocaine use, especially during a period of prolonged use, which sometimes lasts for four or five days.

At the end of a cocaine binge, which is sometimes called "feeming" or "rocking out," an addict will be so exhausted from lack of sleep and hunger that he simply passes out and remains unconscious for many hours. Sometimes he even requires hospitalization. Large dosages of cocaine have been known to cause users to exhibit episodes of extremely violent behavior. Death has also been known to occur as a result of cardiac arrest.

Long-term cocaine use can cause hallucinations, extreme paranoia and psychosis, depression, and respiratory problems.

Cocaine also induces antisocial behavior. Addicts and users miss a lot of time from work, they're often caught lying, and they steal to support their very expensive habits. Police officers are sometimes alerted to a person's addiction by their patterns of thievery. A cocaine addict, as well as addicts of other drugs (this behavior is more often associated with addicts of stimulants), often steals things like DVD players, VCRs, televisions, guns, money, and jewelry—individual items they can sell for at least twenty dollars, the amount of a single hit of cocaine.

People who buy these items from cocaine addicts usually know the cost of the drug and rarely ever offer the seller any more than twenty dollars per item. They know the addict will settle for that amount. They also know the addict will be back later in the day or night with another stolen item for sale. This is a never ending cycle for the cocaine addict.

CRACK COCAINE

Crack cocaine is one of the most addictive illegal drugs of all time and is one of the easiest to make. Smoking a crack rock takes only a minute or so and the high can last for as little as a few seconds. Unfortunately, unlike other drugs that require prolonged use to create physical dependency, crack cocaine can create an addiction the first time a user smokes it.

The intense rush experienced with the use of crack cocaine together with the powerful need to smoke more only minutes later causes a quicker addiction to crack cocaine than users experience with powdered cocaine. In a few minutes the user will return, looking for the same runner from whom to buy more crack.

Crack cocaine, because it's not pure, is less expensive than its original powdered form. The drug was once thought to be a drug of choice for the lower class, but not anymore. The drug is found in every neighborhood in America.

Crack Cocaine Dealers

A major drug dealer sells powdered cocaine to street dealers; those street dealers then make the more addictive crack cocaine by combining cocaine with baking soda and water. The dealer cooks the blend for a few minutes in a microwave oven and then air-dries the mixture so it cools and hardens. After the mixture cools, the dealer lays out the drug in sheets resembling thin, flattened cookie dough. As the sheet of crack cocaine cools, it pops and crackles, much like Rice Krispies cereal does when milk is added to

Crack cocaine.

it. The name "crack" was derived from these sounds. The dealer then cuts the crack with a razor blade, dividing it into pea-sized pieces called "rocks" because they resemble small white pebbles. The dealer wraps each rock individually with aluminum foil, cellophane, or corners torn from plastic baggies and sells them for twenty dollars each. Crack rocks are also packaged in tiny, factory-made ziplock bags.

The sale of crack cocaine is quick and discreet. Potential customers ride through a neighborhood known for drug sales. They stop beside anyone standing along the street and simply ask if they "have anything" or if "anything's going on." If the person they've approached is indeed a runner, he'll ask what they want. If the user is looking for only one rock, as is often the case, he'll respond by saying, "a twenty." A runner sometimes keeps one twenty-piece inside his mouth and, to complete the transaction, spits it into his hand, exchanges the aluminum-foil-wrapped rock for a twenty-dollar bill, and walks away. This entire business deal takes a matter of seconds. The driver pulls away and goes to the first spot he can find to smoke the rock.

Crack Cocaine Users

A user, or "crackhead," high on crack cocaine exhibits signs of extreme nervousness and agitation. She's normally very talkative, and her actions are jerky and erratic. She experiences sudden and sometimes extreme mood swings. Chronic users show signs of rapid weight loss, malnourishment, tooth loss, and premature aging.

Crack addicts quickly find themselves in constant trouble with family, friends, and eventually the law because of the stealing and shoplifting they must do to support their habits. Users sometimes turn to prostitution as a means of financing their habits.

Users smoke crack from objects like empty beer cans and cut-off boombox antennas. To use a can for a pipe, the smoker lays the can on its side and makes a small dent with his thumb on the side of the can near the bottom. He then makes a circular pattern of tiny holes in the indented area using a nail or other sharp object. The holes must only be large enough to allow smoke to pass through. The crack rock is placed onto the indented area above the holes. Holding the tab opening to his mouth the smoker can now apply a flame to the crack and inhale the smoke as it passes through the can.

Crack doesn't remain lit like tobacco or marijuana, so the smoker must constantly apply a flame to keep it burning. This constant source of heat causes the thin metal holding the crack to become very hot and often results in burns or blistering on the smoker's fingers and lips.

To use the antenna as a pipe, the smoker breaks off a six-inch section of the antenna and packs the largest end with a small piece of steel wool or any other type of porous, metal scouring pad. The user places a piece of crack cocaine against the scouring pad and then holds the flame to it while inhaling from the smaller, opposite end of the "pipe." These makeshift pipes become hot quickly and have been known to burn the lips and fingers of smokers. Those burn marks are telltale signs of a crack smoker.

The user never seems to buy more than two or three rocks at any one time. I've been told by addicts they do this because they hope they can find the willpower to stop after smoking only one or two. Most users never do. Obviously, going through twenty dollars every few minutes for hours at a time is expensive. Addicts do whatever it takes to get their next hit, and crime is often the only option.

IN THE LINE OF DUTY
A PORTRAIT OF AN ADDICT

I recall standing in the courthouse speaking with a prisoner who was charged with possession of crack cocaine, breaking and entering, and grand larceny. The inmate sat on a wooden bench awaiting his trial. Sweat dotted his forehead, and he constantly wrung his hands together, almost as if he was trying to warm them. Clearly that wasn't the reason—it was mid-July.

His wrists were tightly handcuffed and the pant legs of his orange jail-issue jumpsuit were rolled up a couple of turns to prevent them from getting caught in the chains that connected the shackles circling his ankles. His right foot acted as a lever while his leg bounced up and down. He was visibly anxious about the impending legal proceedings.

It's a common occurrence for inmates to talk about their troubles while waiting for their turn in front of the judge. Some talk to police officers because they have no one else to talk to; others talk because thoughts of long prison sentences rattle their nerves. This man was obviously nervous about the impending legal proceedings, and he began to speak quite openly and freely to me about his drug use.

The man, thin and malnourished, began by describing the intense hold the drug had over him. He told me that he knew better than to do the things he did, like stealing and prostitution, but he simply couldn't stop. The drug controlled him and his mind. I asked him what the high felt like, and he told me to imagine the most intense orgasm ever, then multiply that by one thousand and maybe, just maybe, that would be close to describing how good it felt to be high on crack.

He and I had gone to the same high school and had played side-by-side on the same championship football team. In those days, he had been muscular in body and strong in mind. He'd been an honor roll student and a star, three-letter athlete. He was assured of a college scholarship for football. He had had a future, a real future, a chance to be someone in this world. Instead, he sat before me facing several years of confinement in a state prison.

My old friend was pitiful. His body could only be described as skeletal. His arms were thin rails. His cheeks and eyes were sunken from months of going without proper meals. He had lost several teeth (another classic sign of chronic crack cocaine use and something police officers watch for), and he'd developed a palsy-like shake in his right hand. He was a crackhead—an addict.

I listened while he described his drug habit. He told me he smoked crack cocaine every day, as often during the day as he could. I asked him how long he waited after each hit before he smoked again. He said that when he put the lighter to a crack rock to smoke it, he was already thinking of where to get the next hit and how he was going to get it.

He told me he had more than a thousand-dollar-a-day habit and was unemployed; he had been for years. He'd lost his job to excessive absenteeism months prior to his arrest. He'd sold all his personal possessions, had no home, and had even been forbidden to visit the homes of his entire family. They could no longer trust him around their personal belongings. He'd stolen everything he could get his hands on. He'd even started taking things from his beloved grandmother, the woman who raised him and went without so that he might have a chance in life, something she'd never had. He'd been caught breaking into her house to steal her VCR. This was the event that caused him to be awaiting his day in court.

Police Efforts Against Cocaine and Crack

Crack cocaine and the problems that arise from its sales and use are some of the biggest issues facing drug cops today. Crack is more addictive, easier to hide, and easier to make than many other drugs.

Unlike methamphetamine, crack manufacturers don't need large, complicated laboratories to make their product. All that's needed to make crack is a small microwave oven or a cooktop, a box of baking soda, a little water, and some powdered cocaine. Since the drug can be made in any bedroom, bathroom, kitchen, or toolshed, finding a crack dealer's lair can be nearly impossible.

Crack cocaine carries a much stiffer penalty than powdered cocaine. In fact, the federal mandatory minimum sentencing ratio between crack cocaine and powdered cocaine is 100:1, meaning it takes one hundred times more powdered cocaine than crack to receive the same sentence. For example, five grams of crack will earn an offender five years in federal prison. It would take five hundred grams of powdered cocaine to receive the same sentence. Incidentally, before the five grams is cut into the smaller pieces dealers sell to their users, it's worth a little over one hundred dollars. After the five grams is cut into individual pieces (approximately thirty pieces), its return value is about six hundred dollars.

The sentences for crack cocaine are so harsh that some law enforcement officers have actually waited until a suspect has cooked cocaine into the more dangerous and addictive crack before arresting him because the penalties are much higher for crack cocaine than powdered cocaine.

According to the Federal Sentencing Guidelines, which we'll discuss on page 232, the mandatory minimum sentence for the possession of five grams of crack cocaine is five years in federal prison. If the defendant had a firearm in his possession at the time of the drug offense, he automatically receives an additional mandatory five years in prison, for a total of ten years.

METHAMPHETAMINE

Methamphetamine is a Schedule II drug. Often called "The Devil's Drug" by its users, methamphetamine, like cocaine and crack cocaine, is highly addictive. Users and abusers find themselves consuming it more frequently and in larger doses with each use. Other names for the drug are meth, crank, crystal, hillbilly crack, buzzard dust, booger sugar, poison, Satan dust, Scooby snacks, and shit.

Effects of Methamphetamine Usage

Methamphetamine, like crack cocaine, is a stimulant associated with extremely violent behavior in its users and abusers. The drug deadens pain receptors, enabling the user to hyperextend her joints into abnormal positions. These individuals also seem to have above-average strength when high on the drug.

Sometimes users are so extremely violent it requires several police officers to physically maintain control of a criminal who's high on methamphetamine. Officers are often forced to use weapons such as Tasers and chemical sprays to subdue these violent offenders, and sometimes even these methods are ineffective.

Methamphetamine reduces the levels of dopamine in a user's brain by damaging the brain cells contain-

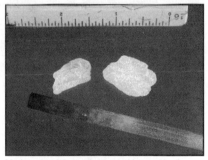

Methamphetamine and pipe used for smoking it.

ing neurotransmitters. Dopamine is crucial to the functioning capabilities of the central nervous system. The damaged cells can result in an involuntary-movement disorder similar to Parkinson's disease.

Methamphetamine use can cause an increased heart rate and raised blood pressure. This explains the "wired" effect police officers so often encounter when dealing with a subject high on the drug. The user can't seem to sit still; she talks nonstop like a 45 rpm record played on the turntable at 78 rpm, and her movements are rapid and jittery. It's as if the user has an electrical charge hooked to her that she can't turn off. Large doses of meth can cause an extreme rise in body temperature.

Meth Dealers

Drug dealers use ephedrine or pseudoephedrine to produce methamphetamine in makeshift laboratories. Ephedrine is a controlled drug found in many over-the-counter medications available for coughing and weight loss. The recipe for methamphetamine also includes anhydrous ammonia, a colorless gas used as an industrial refrigerant and in chemical fertilizers. Anhydrous ammonia (anhydrous means without water) is a regulated chemical requiring a license to possess, so drug dealers must steal it. To obtain it, they usually go to agricultural supply warehouses at night and transfer the gas from large storage tanks to smaller propane tanks. During the theft, gas often leaks into the atmosphere, exposing the community to its fumes.

Drug dealers who manufacture methamphetamine constantly place themselves in harm's way. Not only are they at immediate risk of going to prison, but the health hazards associated with making the drug are enormous. Contact with the vaporizing liquid can cause frostbite, which can lead to a loss of fingers, hands, or entire limbs.

Anhydrous ammonia reacts with any moisture; therefore, when it contacts human tissue, which is comprised mostly of water, the reaction begins instantly. This reaction causes severe chemical burns to the skin. Other dangers of contacting anhydrous ammonia are a rapid swelling of the throat, laryngeal spasms that can lead to asphyxia, lung damage, blindness, chemical burns to the lungs, and pulmonary edema (fluid in the lungs).

Other chemicals used in the production of methamphetamine are ether, sulfuric acid, lithium (usually obtained from lithium batteries), iodine crystals, hydrochloric acid, muriatic acid, sodium hydroxide, acetone, and Coleman stove or lantern fuel.

Drug dealers blend and cook a combination of these chemicals to produce the desired product. This cooking process produces a number of hazardous, toxic fumes such as invisible phosphorous gas and hazardous waste such as lye, hydrochloric acid, cyanide, and chlorinated solvents. Many of these chemicals are highly flammable and often result in fires and explosions within the makeshift labs. Drug dealers are very often badly burned or killed. The odor emitted from these labs is frequently compared to rotten eggs.

In the United States, meth laboratories normally produce anywhere from ten to fifty pounds of methamphetamine in a few hours, usually overnight. The larger, better-equipped laboratories in Mexico can produce anywhere from 150 to 200 pounds in the same amount of time. Clandestine labs in the United States can be set up almost anywhere and at any time. Police officers find them in places like trailers, storage sheds, mobile homes, houses, basements, attics, caves, shacks, and even underground rooms. One meth manufacturer buried a shipping container and used the trailer-like structure as an underground laboratory. Meth laboratories are usually set up so the dealer can pack up and leave in a hurry in case the police are about to close in on the operation.

Meth Users

There are often visible sores on a methamphetamine user's face, hands, and arms from prolonged use of the drug. Those in drug circles refer to these as "crank craters." These open sores and scarring of the skin are self-inflicted wounds the user creates when he picks hallucinatory "crank bugs" from his skin. Users can experience irreversible damage to the blood vessels in their brains, sometimes producing strokes, and can suffer from respiratory problems, irregular heartbeats, collapse of the entire cardiovascular system, anorexia, and even death.

Addicts and users have nicknames for themselves such as battery benders, go-go losers, neck creatures, shadow people, tweakers, and wiggers. Their terms for getting high on methamphetamine are amping, rolling hard, spun, wired, zooming, zoning, ring dang do, and pissed.

Users who go on binges, called "runs" or "running," sometimes inject the drug into their systems at a rate of every two or three hours for several days in a row. During this period of time, users normally don't eat, drink, or sleep, causing dehydration, malnourishment, and exhaustion. Hallucinations and psychosis are common.

Methamphetamine users come from no particular group of people. What was once thought to be a drug of the poor is now abused by people from all cultures and ethnic groups. Nearly twelve million people in the United States alone admit to using meth at least once in their lifetime. In the year 2005, 6.2 percent of all high school students admitted to using meth. While that figure is high, it's still much lower than the 9.8 percent of students who reported trying methamphetamine in the year 2001.

Police Efforts Against Meth

Unlike any other drug, methamphetamine poses an unusual problem for law enforcement officers. Not only must they deal with the normal difficulties of employing the use of informants, undercover officers, stakeouts, drug buys, and search warrants, but they're faced with the danger of clandestine drug laboratories that contain gallons of highly volatile materials that can ignite and explode without warning. These materials, acids, and explosives, sometimes called volatile organic compounds, also emit toxic fumes that can cause nausea, breathing difficulties, and even cancer. When dealing with a meth lab, officers must wear full biohazard gear.

In an effort to reduce and control the production of methamphetamine, stores are now required to display and store ephedrine or pseudoephedrine-based medications behind the counter. Those businesses are also required by law to maintain a logbook containing the names of people who purchase these medications.

There were 1,036 people sentenced for methamphetamine-related crimes during the period of October 1, 2004 to January 11, 2005. An additional 3,703 were sentenced for the same type of crime from January 12, 2005 to September 30, 2005. More than 95 percent of these cases involved trafficking, not use, of methamphetamine.

ECSTASY

Ecstasy, or MDMA (methylenedioxymethamphetamine), is a Schedule I drug popular among today's youth. As its name suggests, it's chemically akin to

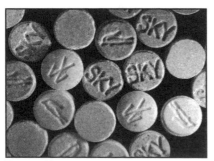
Ecstasy tablets.

its cousin, methamphetamine. It's also very similar to the hallucinogen mescaline. MDMA is a synthetic drug that's available throughout the world. It's very popular with teens and young adults because it reduces inhibitions and isn't known to be physically addictive.

Parties known as "raves" feature ecstasy, also known as E, Cadillac, pink pig, lollipop, smile, snowball, the hug drug, disco biscuit, and California sunshine, as the event's main attraction. The effects of the drug are heightened perceptions of color and sound, hallucinations, and amplification of the sensation of touch, particularly during sex.

Ecstasy was patented in 1914 by the pharmaceutical company Merck but was abandoned for sixty years, then was reintroduced in the late 1970s for use in psychotherapy. Its effects last anywhere from three to six hours, and the drug is considered a mood elevator. Normally, its users are passive; violence isn't a side effect.

Partygoers are known for introducing the drug, also aptly named "The Love Drug," into an unsuspecting person's drink with hopes of taking advantage of that person's drug-induced amorous state.

An ecstasy user must continually increase the amount of drug he takes to feel the same effect. Some possible side effects of ecstasy are elevated body temperature (a danger in the party atmosphere, where hours of dancing contribute to already high body temperature), elevated heart rate, and elevated blood pressure. This type of rapid increase in body temperature can result in damage to the heart, liver, and kidneys and can also cause death. After the effects of the drug wear off, the user may experience periods of extreme depression, confusion, anxiety, paranoia, psychotic episodes, and hallucinations.

The DEA has learned that nearly all ecstasy seized in the United States is manufactured in the Netherlands. The drug is shipped to the United States via cargo containers, luggage, and through express-type mail services.

Ecstasy is so popular among school-age children that recent studies indicate that 40 percent of all eighth graders, 51.4 percent of all tenth graders, and a whopping 61.4 percent of all high school seniors have all tried the drug at least once. Many admit to using ecstasy on a regular basis.

TRAFFICKING

Interstate 95 is a major highway that runs from Maine to Florida and is considered by law enforcement agencies to be the main drug corridor on the East Coast. Any city lying within a few miles of that highway is subject to high drug activity, due the availability of illegal drugs and the easy access for delivery.

Every day, large quantities of marijuana, cocaine, crack cocaine, heroin, ecstasy, methamphetamine, and illegal pharmaceuticals make their way up and down the East Coast inside both passenger and commercial vehicles. The narcotics are hidden within door panels of cars, in secret compartments built into gas tanks and batteries, inside spare tires, and inside trunks.

Unless the driver makes a mistake in driving or becomes involved in an accident, it's very difficult for police officers to detect these shipments. The drivers are usually hired by dealers to make the deliveries and often aren't aware of the cargo. They're sometimes instructed to deliver the car to a specific location and leave it. They can then either return home by plane or bus. These delivery people are called mules.

A mule can also be a person in the permanent employ of a drug dealer, as is often seen in organized crime. In this situation, the mule is usually aware of his goods and of their illegality. Unlike the run-of-the-mill street runners and dealers, a member of an organized crime family usually protects his boss' identity and takes the full blame for his actions. After the arrest of a mule within an organized crime family, the employer usually assumes the mule's financial obligations while he's in prison. The employer sees to it that the mule's family is well taken care of and sends money to the incarcerated mule as well.

Street runners and dealers very often tell or "snitch" on their employers in order to receive a lighter sentence from the courts. If apprehended by the police, these individuals are normally left to fend for themselves; their bosses will sometimes pack up and leave an area entirely to avoid arrest.

Once a shipment of drugs arrives in an area and makes it undetected into the hands of the local dealer, the dealer divides the shipment among his street runners for sale. The runners aren't allowed to handle much of the drug at a time in case they're caught but are normally given approximately three hundred dollars worth of a drug at one time. In the case of crack cocaine, three hundred dollars worth is equal to fifteen "rocks."

The rocks are often carried in a film canister, with the cylinder about half full of crack rocks. When the runners sell that amount, they return to the dealer and exchange the cash for more drugs. This process continues until the entire shipment is sold. On a busy night, this can take only a few hours.

DRUG BUSTS: FIGHTING THE WAR ON DRUGS

Rounding up drug dealers can be an overwhelming task. The process is often a combined, well-orchestrated effort involving dozens of law enforcement officials, such as local, state, and federal police officers (both uni-formed and undercover), informants, entry teams, supervisors, canines, air support, crime scene technicians, magistrates, judges, prosecutors, child protective officers, probation and parole officers, prison officials, and even animal control officers.

The foundation for a drug raid is sometimes laid months and even years prior to the date investigators actually obtain and execute the search warrant. The biggest drug busts can start with something as small as a traffic stop made by a rookie officer who asks the simple question, "Do you mind if I search your car?" A positive response to the officer's question can lead to her finding a single joint in the driver's console. That single joint can start a domino effect that ends up toppling a network of major drug dealers.

Many officers will arrange to make a deal with an offender if he provides the police with the name of the person who sold him the drugs. That information may lead officers to the arrest of the seller, who then can provide the name of his dealer, and so on. Since drug cases can be very time-consuming, uniformed officers normally turn over their information and files to narcotics detectives.

Narcotics detectives try to find someone, either an informant or an undercover officer, who can infiltrate the drug dealer's circle of friends and associates. A likely person to become an informant would be the offender who was initially arrested by the traffic officer for possessing the joint. Police and prosecutors may arrange to have an informant's charges dismissed if she assists the police with their investigation. However, police officers can't promise a dismissal or reduction of any charges without approval from the prosecuting attorney.

An undercover agent participates in a drug raid.

To establish probable cause for the acquisition of a search warrant, narcotics detectives must first determine that a suspected drug dealer is actually selling drugs. The best way to do so is through intensive surveillance and to have informants or undercover officers purchase drugs from the dealer. Most departments have a special fund that's reserved just for the purchase of drugs. In fact, most narcotics officers keep a few hundred dollars on hand at all times. They call this cash "buy money." Buy money can also be used to pay informants a fee for their services. Normally, informants who are "working off" their criminal charges don't receive money for their efforts.

The narcotics detectives must also establish the reliability, credibility, and trustworthiness of an informant. The informant must prove to the detectives that the information he provides is indeed true. He does so by making controlled, supervised drug buys from dealers and then delivering those drugs to detectives. The rule of thumb is that if an informant makes three controlled drug buys and delivers those drugs to detectives, without fail, he's established his reliability. Sometimes, informants wear tiny microphones and transmitters called wires so detectives may monitor their conversations with the drug dealer.

Narcotics detectives either treat money used for drug buys with an invisible marking chemical (which becomes visible when exposed to alternate light sources) or record the serial numbers. Marked money found in the possession of a suspect is proof that he participated in the drug deal.

This process of surveillance and buying drugs could last for a few days or for weeks. When narcotics detectives feel they've established probable cause and are reasonably sure the dealer has drugs in his house, they turn to the official paperwork portion of the case. They fill out the affidavit for the search, detailing all the reasons leading them to believe a crime has occurred and that a search of the dealer's home is necessary to locate his stash of illegal drugs.

At this point, narcotics detectives call in a team of officers who will assist in the execution of the search. Depending upon the danger level of the search, this team can consist of as few as three or four officers to as many as two dozen heavily armed entry-team specialists. Narcotics canine teams are also called in to participate. The team meets at a prearranged place to await the signal to begin the raid. Anxieties are always high during this stage of the process. Officers never know what to expect.

With the search team standing by at a predetermined, secret location, narcotics detectives meet with a judge or magistrate (day or night) to obtain the actual search warrant. The judge reviews the affidavit, and, if she's satisfied that the criteria for probable cause have been met, she approves and signs a search warrant.

Armed with the search warrant, narcotics detectives meet with the search team to brief them on the layout of the suspect's house, the possibility of weapons inside the house (based on the word of the informant who's been inside), and the specific assignment for each team member.

Surprise is the key to a successful raid. The entry team may approach the search area or building in separate groups. Some officers may arrive in old vans or service trucks; others may approach on foot. No matter how they get there, the entry must be quick. If the search is expected to be dangerous, officers will have obtained a no-knock warrant and will normally break in the front and rear doors simultaneously. At the same time, other officers may break out all the lower-level windows and monitor each of those rooms.

For the safety of the officers, everyone inside the house is handcuffed, and they're usually all placed into the same room where they're guarded by an officer who's been previously assigned to that duty. Everyone is patted down for weapons. The target suspect (the drug dealer) is normally searched a little more extensively because officers are hoping to locate some or all of their marked money.

Officers carefully search the entire house to ensure that no one is hiding. Once the all clear is given, the house is turned over to narcotics detectives to conduct a very thorough, detailed search for drugs, drug paraphernalia, records, money, packaging material, and other items associated with drug sales. Detectives may have a narcotics canine search the house before they begin their search. They may also have the dog search again when they're finished.

Narcotics detectives search every square inch of the house, including the inside of the toilet tank and behind each light switch and receptacle plate. They look for hidden panels, trap doors, safes, and secret hiding places. Normally, officers aren't very neat when searching for drugs. Drawers are emptied onto table tops and the floor; mattresses are removed and overturned; closets, boxes, and cartons are emptied; sofa cushions are removed; and the contents

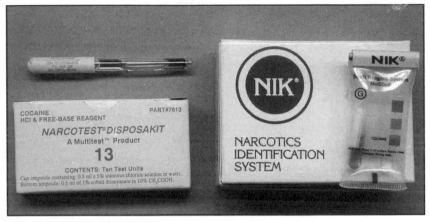

A drug testing kit.

of refrigerators and freezers are removed and searched. Detectives even peer into light fixtures and sink drains.

If drugs are found, the narcotics detectives collect and package them in evidence bags. They may use field tests to determine the type and authenticity of the drugs they've discovered. The drugs will remain in these packages until they're delivered to the laboratory for testing. When the testing is complete, the drugs are placed back into the original evidence container, resealed, and returned to the detectives. If the department is equipped with an evidence locker room, the drugs are kept there until trial. After trial, the drugs are destroyed.

The police aren't required to clean up after a search, nor are they required to put anything back that they've removed. Sometimes, when officers leave, the house looks like a bomb's been detonated inside. Some search warrant teams are neater than others.

It can take several hours to complete a drug raid, so, as a sort of celebration, it's quite common for the entire search team to meet at a favorite restaurant or coffeehouse after a search to unwind, debrief, and offer praises to one another for getting another dealer off the streets.

It is here, at these informal, post-raid gatherings, that stories are told, jokes are cracked, and tensions are allowed to dissipate. But it's the knowledge that everyone made it safely through the danger that feels so good.

In many areas of the country, when a police officer obtains an arrest warrant (subsequent or prior to serving a search warrant) for someone who's accused of a drug crime, the warrant will specify which type of drug is suspected and where in the drug schedule it's listed. For example, the body of a felony arrest warrant (form DC-312) from the state of Virginia reads:

ACCUSED: John D. Crackhead

TO ANY AUTHORIZED OFFICER:

You are hereby commanded in the name of the Commonwealth of Virginia forthwith to arrest and bring the accused before this Court to answer the charge that the Accused, within this city or county, on or about ___June 3, 2006,___ did unlawfully and feloniously in violation of Section ___18.2-248 Sec. A___ Code of Virginia, possess with the intent to distribute a controlled substance, namely cocaine, listed in Schedule II.

Section 18.2-248 Sec.(a) of the Code of Virginia states that it's illegal for any person to make, sell, give, or distribute in any way a controlled substance or an imitation controlled substance. The code section further states that the penalty for violating this particular law is a term in prison of not less than five years and not more forty years. In addition to the prison sentence, a judge may also impose a fine of not more then $500,000. (These laws vary from state to state. Federal sentencing guidelines, which we'll look at next, are different than state guidelines.)

IN THE LINE OF DUTY
THE "DOWNTOWN BOYS"

We had the "Downtown Boys" under surveillance for months. The gang had commandeered an entire section of one the local projects as a base for manufacturing and selling crack cocaine. I'd finally gotten a very reliable informant to gain the trust of these hardened street dealers. He'd been on the inside for months, and they considered him one of their own. Weeks before, I'd instructed

---

a crew to mount a camera that looked like an electrical transformer on a telephone pole, and my partner and I maintained constant surveillance on the area from a monitor in our office. We could pan, zoom, and do everything necessary to build a large library of video evidence on the gang members.

I decided the time was right to raid the gang's operation on a hot summer afternoon. The humidity that day was high enough to make sweat seem dry. I gathered my information and sent the informant to the projects for one last look at the cache of drugs and the location of the drugs within the rooms, and to find out how many people were in the apartment. I wanted to know how many of those people were armed and, if possible, what kind of weapons they possessed. I told my informant to be particularly aware of the presence of innocent children. I wanted to be prepared for the worst.

The other officers and I suited up with vests, shields, and masks to avoid recognition of the undercover guys, and we armed ourselves with shotguns and MP5 automatic machine guns, each with a one-hundred-round magazine. Our adrenaline was soaring as high as the outside temperature. I asked the informant to make a mental note of the correct address on the suspects' front door so I could enter it in the appropriate block on the affidavit and on the search warrant. He returned and was very excited about the news he had to report. The gang had more cocaine inside the apartment than he'd ever seen. They'd just received a fresh shipment of powdered cocaine and were preparing to cook it up into crack. He went on to say that we should be careful because the eight men inside were all carrying, which meant they were all armed. This was going to be a dangerous bust. These guys had killed before and wouldn't be taken easily.

I got the search warrant from the court and had the teams in place by noon. We were all focused on the address followed by "apartment B." I gave the all clear, and the entry team hit the door with a battering ram. We had the apartment cleared and secure in record time without a single shot fired. The only problem was, we were at the wrong apartment. The address should have been apartment *D* instead of *B*. My top-notch informant had given me the wrong address. We had raided the house of an eighty-year-old widow who was seated in her favorite rocker eating ice cream while watching a *Lawrence Welk Show* rerun. Her door exploded, and the apartment was suddenly filled with a dozen masked men brandishing fully automatic weapons, screaming for her to get on the floor.

She never got excited, never raised her voice, and never stopped eating her ice cream. She merely looked at me, pointed to her right with a spoon and, with a deep southern drawl through a toothless mouth, said, "I think ya'll boys want da 'partment next door."

I looked outside and down the walkway. The entire group of Downtown Boys was standing outside of apartment D laughing at us.

Not one of my better days.

Besides having to pay for a new door, new doorjamb, and fresh paint and carpet cleaning, the entire operation cost our department financially and took a toll on many of us physically and mentally. I also bought a half-gallon of Rocky Road ice cream, as a peace offering, for the very understanding grandmother of twelve.

It takes a while to regain ground from mistakes such as this one, but persistence pays off. Drug dealers have an addiction to sell a drug, just as the user has an addiction to use it. Greed plays a large part in drug sales, but a great deal of the need to sell drugs is in the dealer wanting to beat the system. They like the cat-and-mouse game played between law enforcement and the bad guys.

It took many more months to round up the Downtown Boys, but we finally got them—not in a group as I'd hoped—but as individuals. Patience and persistence is the key to really good police work. Oh … and the correct address on a search warrant helps quite a bit.

FEDERAL SENTENCING GUIDELINES FOR DRUG OFFENSES

The U.S. government has developed guidelines for determining what it deems an appropriate and universal system of sentencing people who have been convicted of narcotics offenses. The particular drugs and corresponding amounts of those drugs that a suspect is charged with possessing, selling, or attempting to sell are divided into levels (categories). These levels make up what is known as the Drug Quantity Table (see appendix C). For each level of offense there's a corresponding sentence that's specified in a separate table, the Federal Sentencing Table (see appendix D).

Federal judges use the Federal Sentencing Table to determine the sentence of all convicted federal offenders. Each offender is assigned a number of criminal history points depending on her prior criminal record. The more arrests she has in her past, the higher her point level. When the offender's criminal history category has been determined, the judge compares that number with its corresponding offense level on the chart. The intersection of those two points is the sentence range allowed for that particular drug offense. The same method is used for all federal offenses.

For example, let's say Joe Crackhead is found guilty of possession of 1.5 kilograms of crack cocaine (cocaine base), which is a base offense level 38. It's determined that Mr. Crackhead has never been arrested in the past. His clean record gives him a 0 in the criminal history category. The points intersect at the sentence of 235 to 293 months; therefore, the judge may sentence Mr. Crackhead anywhere within that fifty-eight month range.

CHAPTER 12

TELL IT TO THE JUDGE:
COURTS AND THE LEGAL PROCESS

In our American criminal court system, prosecuting attorneys have a duty to search for the truth. Defense attorneys have a duty to zealously represent their clients. Judges have a duty to ensure that attorneys and witnesses follow the law and at times be a referee in courtroom battles. Jurors have the toughest job of all—to use all their senses including common sense to separate truth from untruth and untangle webs of confusion to result in a just verdict.

—The Honorable Pat Moeller, City Council Member and Former Butler County, Ohio, Assistant Prosecuting Attorney

The U.S. court system can be quite complicated and confusing to a layperson. It can also be quite overwhelming to someone who's been accused of committing a crime. Once a person crosses the line between right and wrong and makes the decision to do something against the law, the wheels of justice automatically begin to spin. There's no turning back. Sure, the offenders can say, "I'm sorry, and I won't ever do it again," but once the system is in motion, the crooks must … *tell it to the judge!*

THE STRUCTURE OF A STATE COURT SYSTEM

The structure of an individual court system varies from state to state, but the idea remains the same—lower courts try minor (misdemeanor) offenses, while higher courts handle the more serious felony cases. Appellate courts, including the State Supreme Court, sit at the top of the organization to oversee and hear all appeals stemming from the lower courts.

MAGISTRATE'S COURT

In some court systems a magistrate is the first court official to see the defendant. Magistrates are specially trained judicial officers who have the authority and power to issue arrest warrants, search warrants, and civil warrants; set bail; commit suspects to jail; issue temporary detention orders (TDOs) for suspects requiring psychiatric evaluation; and administer oaths.

Magistrates are generally appointed to their positions by the chief judge of the area where they're employed. In the case of the state court system in the accompanying illustration, the chief judge of the circuit court would appoint a magistrate. Since the chief judge has the authority to appoint whomever he chooses, the appointments sometimes go to his close friends. Each district in a state has a chief magistrate who supervises the activities of all other magistrates within that particular area.

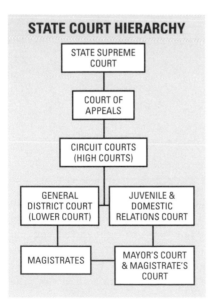

STATE COURT HIERARCHY

In some small rural areas, magistrates work rotating schedules on an on-call basis. This system means that someone (usually a police dispatcher) calls the on-call magistrate from home to report to the law enforcement agency that's requesting her services. In these areas, some of magistrates work on a part-time basis. During the hours when they're not serving in their official capacity as magistrate, they work regular jobs, such as plumbing, driving a tow truck, and farming. Part-time magistrates are required to leave their regular jobs to attend to their magistrate duties whenever they're called. It's not unusual to see a magistrate enter a police station to sign a search warrant dressed in work clothes, smelling like cattle. It's also not unusual for a magistrate's court to be held after normal working hours so the magistrate or mayor may work their normal daytime jobs.

All fines and court costs are a source of revenue for the local community.

MAYOR'S COURT

Mayors' courts are normally held in small communities, such as villages and towns, to relieve caseloads from higher courts. They're also a great source of revenue for the local community.

These informal courts are presided over by the mayor of the municipality. It isn't a requirement that the mayor be a licensed attorney. The presiding mayor is authorized by local law to try cases, such as traffic offenses, minor misdemeanors, minor drug offenses, DUI/DWI cases, and charges involving animals (barking and biting dogs, etc.). A mayor in these courts is even authorized to commit offenders to jail.

JUVENILE COURT

In most states, a juvenile is a person under the age of eighteen. Special courts have been established to handle cases involving juveniles. These courts also handle legal matters for families, abused children and spouses; consent for medical treatment of neglected juveniles; juveniles who are accused of traffic violations and crimes; children in need of supervision; and, in some cases, runaways and truancy. In addition, these courts handle cases concerning child support. There are no juries in juvenile court; all cases must be heard by a judge.

When children are taken into custody by the police, they're brought before an intake officer or a magistrate to determine if the juvenile needs to be held in a detention facility. (Some juvenile probation officers double as juvenile intake officers.) The child may only be held for a short period of time, normally up to seventy-two hours, until he's brought before a judge for an official detention hearing. The purpose of a detention hearing is to determine if the child should remain in custody. Unless the child poses a threat to himself or others, the court almost always attempts to release him into the custody of a parent or other responsible family member.

Children who have been abandoned, abused, or neglected, or whose parents have given up their custody rights, are appointed a *guardian ad litem,* an attorney whose main duty is to protect the legal interest of the child and to see that the child is properly cared for. The attorney is also assigned to represent the child in court proceedings.

Children who commit heinous crimes, such as murder, may be tried as adults; however, some states set a minimum age of fifteen for the point at which the charge may upgraded to an adult offense.

Juvenile judges have a wide range of discretion when it comes to sentencing juvenile offenders. They take into account the offender's prior criminal record, her environmental conditions, her relationship with her parents or guardians, and the circumstances surrounding the crimes she's been accused of committing.

Juvenile courts make every effort to protect the privacy of children by holding private hearings and sealing the court records of children. Most courts expunge the court records of children after they've reached adulthood unless the record contains felony convictions. A felony conviction is sometimes held in the offender's record for as many as twenty years.

GENERAL DISTRICT COURT (LOWER COURT)

Lower courts have many purposes. They also have many names, depending upon the area of the country they're located in. Some areas of the country, such as Florida, refer to their lower courts as county courts. The lower courts in Virginia are called general district courts. No matter the name, the cases heard in these courts are all quite similar. Judges in these courts may hear both civil and criminal cases. They also hear cases involving traffic-related offenses, such as speeding and reckless driving.

Civil cases tried in a general district court typically involve relatively small amounts of money. In many areas that dollar amount may not exceed ten thousand dollars. Some locales have special courts for such cases, called small claims courts.

During the course of their duties, police officers sometimes witness property damage or physical harm to a person, and they can be called as witnesses to testify on behalf of either the plaintiff or the defendant. Testifying in this type of trial isn't a favorite task of police officers. They sometimes feel as if they're selling out to the wrong side if they're required to provide statements in a civil proceeding, especially if they're called on to testify for someone they see as less than law-abiding.

Lower courts, such as Virginia's general district courts, hear criminal cases involving only misdemeanor offenses (punishable by sentences of less than one year in prison). Even though felony cases (punishable by one or more years in prison) aren't tried in lower courts, these courts conduct all preliminary hearings for felony cases to determine if enough evidence exists to justify trying the case in a superior court. If a lower court judge determines that probable cause exists, the case is considered "certified" and is sent to the grand jury for possible indictment (a formal, written accusation of a criminal offense). If indicted, a defendant is tried in a higher court, such as Virginia's circuit court. A grand jury hearing usually takes place weeks or months after the preliminary hearing.

The defendant may or may not be allowed to remain free until the case is heard by the superior court, depending on the discretion of the judge. If the defendant's been allowed to remain free on bond since his arrest and has met all conditions set by the judge at his bond hearing, the judge presiding over the preliminary hearing will more than likely allow him to remain free.

Misdemeanor cases don't require preliminary hearings or jury trials; all decisions are made by the trial judge. Misdemeanor trials are heard on the date that was determined at arraignment (the formal reading of the charges by the court to the defendant).

At the conclusion of a misdemeanor trial, the judge pronounces his findings of either guilt or innocence and imposes a sentence and, if applicable, a fine and/or probation. If the judge imposes a jail sentence, the court bailiff or other courtroom security officers immediately take the defendant into custody. The defendant is held in a small holding cell outside the courtroom where he'll eventually be picked up by sheriff's deputies and transported to the county jail to serve his sentence.

California superior courts are an exception to the rule. Judges in these courts hear all cases—felony, misdemeanor, traffic, and civil.

CIRCUIT COURT

Circuit courts derive their name from the days of the Old West, when each town had a separate jail and court. Judges were assigned to an entire territory and rode either by horseback or wagon throughout their entire circuit, hearing cases. The judges eventually tired of riding the circuit and a single court was established, usually in the county seat. The sheriff of the county then had to bring the criminals to the centrally located courthouse. In many parts of the country, the circuit court system is still in effect.

Circuit court judges in the state of Virginia, for instance, are elected to office by both houses of the general assembly. In other areas of the country, the general public elects circuit court judges to office.

As with the lower courts, the higher courts have many names. Florida and Virginia try felony cases in their circuit courts.

Higher courts, such as circuit courts or superior courts (the two names can be synonymous), receive their cases when a lower court certifies a felony case, a grand jury hands down an indictment, or when a prosecutor bypasses a preliminary hearing and takes her case directly to a high court. (This process is called a straight indictment. It's a ploy the prosecution uses to prevent the defense from hearing state's evidence during a preliminary hearing.) When a circuit court clerk receives a case, she places it on the docket to be tried by a circuit court judge and jury.

Circuit courts also handle all civil cases with dollar amounts exceeding the monetary limitations of the lower courts (dollar amounts exceeding the ten thousand dollar limit). Circuit courts also hear all appeals from the lower courts.

COURT OF APPEALS

The court of appeals, or appellate court, provides appellate review of all traffic and criminal cases heard in circuit courts; in other words, they review all the judgments of the circuit courts. An appellate court is normally presided over by a panel of judges, typically three or more, who are appointed in state courts by the governor of the state. (The president of the United States appoints federal judges.) Defendants don't normally testify before an appellate court. Attorneys for both the defense and the prosecution are given a specific amount of time to present their arguments for the panel of judges. After these arguments, the appellate judges review all trial transcripts, attorney briefs, and testimony. They take this information into consideration and then render their decisions at a later date. These decisions are called judgments and are delivered in writing. It's also a normal practice for appellate court judges to write a corresponding paper, called an *opinion*, which explains in detail the court's reasons for its decision.

STATE SUPREME COURT

State supreme courts have original and appellate jurisdiction; however, the primary function of a state supreme court is to review appeals from lower courts. The supreme court also reviews death penalty cases, cases involving attorney disbarment, and hearings to determine if prisoners are being held legally (attorneys can file a writ of habeas corpus if they feel their clients aren't being held lawfully). Supreme court justices also review other writs, such as a writ of mandamus, which is a mandate for the holder of an office to perform his duties, such as in the case of a judge who's refused to rule on a specific case. In this instance, a state supreme court can order the judge to issue a ruling.

Supreme courts also have the authority to remove judges from office.

THE CRIMINAL COURT CAST OF CHARACTERS

A criminal proceeding can be a long process that involves many people, including judges, jurors, attorneys, police officers, experts, witnesses, security officers, and stenographers. A trial is a multifaceted procedure involving many hours of groundwork by all parties involved. The pretrial activity alone can sometimes take weeks, months, and even years of preparation. The entire complicated process normally revolves around a single person, the star of the show—the criminal defendant.

THE DEFENDANT

All criminal cases begin, of course, with the commission of a crime. As a result of an investigation, police locate the perpetrator of the crime and make the arrest. The moment they place the suspect under arrest (remember, an arrest is when a person is in police custody and no longer feels free to leave) is the moment the court process begins. Every movement and action by both the police and the suspect will now be part of a permanent record. Note, though, that a suspect isn't considered a "defendant" until after the arraignment, at which point he officially becomes a part of a criminal court proceeding. (We'll take a closer look at arraignments on page 256.)

Suspects who've been taken into police custody are handcuffed and searched to make sure they're not concealing weapons, drugs, or other items of evidence. The suspects are then placed into the back seat of a

A deputy sheriff places his weapon inside a lockbox prior to entering the booking area.

squad car and driven to a police station or county jail. In the case of an arrest made by a federal law enforcement officer, such as an FBI agent or a U.S. Marshal, the suspect is normally taken to a federal processing center within a nearby federal courthouse or federal court complex.

Officers escort their suspects inside their respective agency to begin the booking procedure, called processing by many police officers. Prior to entering the booking area, officers remove their weapons from their gun belts and lock them inside a wall-mounted lockbox. This security measure prevents the suspects from having access to a loaded gun. Officers remove the lockbox key and place it inside their pockets until they're ready to leave the processing area.

The next order of business might be for the police officers to interview and interrogate their suspects. It's standard procedure with most police departments for officers to try to obtain a written confession from all suspects, especially those involved in major crimes, such as rape, robbery, and murder.

All statements offered by the suspect at this time should be recorded, transcribed, and then entered into a file that becomes a permanent record. These files are later provided to the prosecuting attorney. Some smaller departments still write all statements and confessions in longhand. Those that do should have the suspect write and sign the document himself to avoid any confusion in the courtroom or accusations that the officers falsified the statement.

If the suspect has recent wounds such as scratches, cuts, and bite marks, police officers use this time to photograph him. These photographs are provided to the prosecutor and can be especially useful as evidence during the trial if the suspect was involved in a crime where a physical altercation took place, such as a rape, assault, or murder.

When the police officers have completed this stage of their investigation, they turn their suspects over to jail or detention center officers, who then begin the booking process. The suspect is required to empty his pockets and surrender all personal property including jewelry, belts, money, and shoestrings. A receipt is issued to the suspect for all property that he's turned over to the booking officers. The suspect is issued jail clothes—normally used (but clean) boxer shorts, used socks, used shoes, used T-shirts, and a used colored jumpsuit, normally orange or black-and-white striped, that's clearly marked with identifying logos or lettering of the detention center or jail.

Jail officers record the suspect's personal information, such as his name, address, all known aliases, next of kin, medical history, and prior criminal history. Officers also make note of any scars, marks, and tattoos that he may have on his body. Tattoos and scars from branding sometimes indicate gang activity. Jail and prison officials make every effort not to place rival gang members into the same cell or cell block.

For the safety of everyone involved, prisoners and jail staff alike, the suspects are asked if they have any known enemies incarcerated within the facility where the booking is taking place. If an enemy is housed at the facility, officials make every effort to keep the rivals apart.

With the paperwork complete, the suspect is moved into a fingerprinting area where he submits copies of his fingerprints, which become part of the jail's permanent record. Larger departments use the computerized Live Scan system, which is capable of transmitting fingerprints directly into the national Integrated Automated Fingerprint Identification System. Smaller departments still use the standard ink-and-ten-print fingerprint-card method of recording fingerprints. Those that still use the cards must make two sets of prints—one for their local records and another that's mailed to the FBI for manual entry into the national database.

After the suspect's prints have been recorded he's allowed to clean his hands with a waterless hand cleaner. Most departments keep a one-gallon, pump-type container of orange-scented cleaner on hand for such use.

Suspects are photographed in the standard, two-picture mug shot fashion—a full face shot and a profile. After the photography has been completed, the suspect is brought before a judge or magistrate to establish the proper amount of bail for the specific crime.

THE DEFENSE ATTORNEY

Police detectives almost always attempt to conduct their interviews before the accused has an opportunity to discuss the case with his lawyer. Why? Attorneys advise their clients not to talk about their involvement in any criminal matters. This advice greatly reduces the officer's likelihood of obtaining a confession.

A suspect in a criminal case has the right to have an attorney with him during questioning, but that doesn't mean a lawyer is going to drop whatever she's doing and run down to the county jail to attend a detective/crook interview session. In fact, suspects aren't normally appointed an attorney until their first court appearance. Many never actually meet their court-appointed attorneys until the day of their trial.

There are three types of defense representation: a court-appointed attorney, a privately retained defense attorney, and self-representation. It is the duty of the defense attorney to represent a client and protect her from miscarriages of justice, police wrongdoings, and illegal prosecution. The defense attorney must protect the client from illegal search and seizures, and illegal uses of force. The attorney must also provide a sound defense, or argument, in response to the prosecutor's case presented against the defendant.

The Court-Appointed Defense Attorney

To qualify for the services of a court-appointed attorney, most states require a defendant to be indigent or otherwise unable to pay for the costs of a court proceeding, including the costs of investigations and laboratory testing. A judge may also consider the severity of the defendant's crime, since a more severe crime may involve a more complex and expensive defense. Court appointments are made on a case-by-case basis.

To assist a judge in making the determination, the defendant is required to complete a form that's much like a credit application. The defendant must list his income, all monthly expenses, the number of dependents, and spouse's income. The court normally doesn't include the income of family members when making its decision whether or not to appoint an attorney. The judge uses the form to make his final decision.

If, at any time during the trial, it's discovered the defendant has improperly reported income or expenses, he'll either be required to retain an attorney at his own expense and/or made to reimburse the court for the expense of the court-appointed attorney. Criminal charges may also be filed for the deliberate attempt to defraud the court.

Court-appointed attorneys are generally chosen from a pool of attorneys who attend court each day waiting to be assigned to a defendant's case. The judge usually chooses the attorneys on a rotating basis and, therefore, shows no favoritism to any one lawyer. Most defendants would like the opportunity to choose a well-established attorney with a proven track record of winning cases; however, they're not allowed to pick their court-appointed attorneys.

Sometimes judges allow an offender to refuse a particular attorney because of a conflict of interest with the attorney. For example, the attorney may have previously represented the victim in the case, or the attorney may herself be a victim of the crime.

Brand-new, unknown criminal defense attorneys don't normally have customers beating down their doors begging for their services. Because of this fact, many attorneys on the rotating list are fresh out of law school and use the appointment process to gain experience and to build a potential list of clients. Court appointments are an almost guaranteed source of income until the new attorneys become established in the community.

In some states, court-appointed attorneys earn approximately fifty dollars per hour for each hour spent in court (some cases last only minutes) and forty dollars per hour for research and other out-of-court time, which is usually only a few hours per case.

Attorneys who are appointed to represent defendants in capital murder cases—cases where the defendant is facing the death penalty—are normally required to spend a great deal of time on the case, due to the intricacy of research and procedure. Two attorneys are always appointed to represent a defendant in a capital case, and their hourly fees can mount up quickly; therefore, most states have a cap on the amount that can be paid to court-appointed attorneys. For instance, in Ohio, that top fee is ten thousand dollars. As with any commodity, this top fee rises with inflation. Any additional expenditure requires the defense attorneys to submit an application to the court for consideration of an increase. It's then up to the judge to decide if the requested increase is justifiable.

In severe cases, such as with a murder case, the court-appointed defense has the option to petition the court for additional expenses to hire private investigators and for the private forensic testing of evidential items. All testing and investigations conducted by the police and state laboratories are done on behalf of the prosecution; the defense doesn't have access to these facilities and investigators. Expenses for these additional services normally range between one thousand and five thousand dollars. All psychological testing, if it's ordered by the court to determine the competency of the defendant, is paid for by the state.

The Privately Retained Defense Attorney

Many defense attorneys in private practice work alone or in small firms, with perhaps only one or two other partners. Attorneys who don't rely on court appointments as a principle means of income have the freedom to pick and choose the clients they prefer to represent. This means that their caseloads aren't normally quite as heavy as those of a court-appointed attorney; therefore, the private attorney can devote quite a bit more time to preparing a defense for her client. As with any other job, the more time spent on it, the better the end result.

Private attorney fees are considerably higher than the fees of their court-appointed counterparts. A privately retained attorney can reasonably expect to receive no less than thirty thousand dollars to defend a client in an average murder trial. In fact, most defendants can expect to spend close to fifty thousand dollars for an attorney with a solid record of achieving acquittals and not guilty verdicts for her clients.

High-profile/celebrity clients and offenders who require the services of more than one attorney can expect to pay millions in legal fees. They must also be prepared to spend similar amounts of money in expert witness fees.

Attorneys in private practice sometimes employ private investigators. Many times these private investigators are former police officers, such as retired detectives and FBI agents. These investigators perform much of the legwork for the attorney. They interview witnesses, conduct investigations, and examine police documents and reports. They even talk to the police investigators who are actively working on the case. A former police officer is more apt to garner information from the investigating officer than a defense attorney. Many police officers feel that talking to the defense attorney is similar to talking to the enemy.

Most defense attorneys require that a defendant pay a retainer fee before they'll begin working on their case. Retainer fees are sometimes in the thousands of dollars, and clients often have to borrow the money from friends and family members. Many attorneys insist that they be paid in full before the trial has concluded.

Since legal fees can mount up quickly, defense attorneys have been known to secure a lien against a defendant's personal property, such as a house or land, to ensure he meets his financial obligations. If the client can't pay the final bill, the lawyer will sell his property, take her fee from the proceeds, and deliver the balance (if any) to the client.

Defense attorneys are permitted to visit with their incarcerated clients. They're not subjected to normal visiting protocol and may conduct their visits outside of normal visiting hours and in private, away from the eyes and ears of jail and prison staff. Wealthy clients have sometimes paid their attorneys to visit them just to have extra contact with the outside world. Some attorneys have been caught smuggling contraband, such as cigarettes, alcohol, drugs, and messages about illegal activities from family and friends.

Self-Representation

Lawbreakers aren't required to have an attorney represent and advise them during their criminal proceedings; however, it's highly advisable for them to do so, especially if they face possible jail or prison time.

Even with the possibility of spending many years behind bars, some defendants insist upon acting as their own attorney. Reading mystery novels and watching reality TV doesn't provide the average person with enough knowledge to defend himself in a court of law. In fact, relying on a work of fiction as a means of legal research can lead to disaster. It takes an appropriate education and many years of experience to offer a proper legal defense.

Defendants who feel the need to represent themselves do so for various reasons. Some have been represented by attorneys in the past and feel they received inadequate service. They think they can do as well or better than the ineffective attorney. Some can't relinquish the control of their future, so they elect to handle their own trials. Others simply don't have enough money to hire an attorney but have income that's too high to justify the court appointing an attorney for them.

The reasons for acting as one's own attorney may seem plausible in the beginning, but as a trial progresses, reasons to hire a skilled attorney soon become apparent. There are countless legal loopholes and rules of law that laypersons aren't privy to—rules and information that could mean the difference between going to prison or not.

Many times a judge won't allow a defendant to represent himself, especially in cases where the outcome may result in substantial prison time, or when the death penalty is a sentencing option. In these instances, a judge orders a court-appointed attorney to represent a defendant, even against his will and protests.

THE PROSECUTOR

It's the duty of the prosecutor to protect the public from wrongdoers and to see that criminals are punished for their crimes. It's the responsibility of the prosecutor to ensure that the police have done their jobs properly and lawfully, and not to present any case before the court that's without merit.

After the police have completed their investigation, the officers present their entire case to the prosecuting attorney. They provide the attorney with a copy of their case files and in many instances they meet with the prosecutor to discuss, in detail, all aspects of the case. They may even hold a mock trial to practice how the officers should respond to questions. However, not all cases require an in-depth, in-person meeting between the officers and the attorneys.

Quite often only the major cases, such as murder, rape, and robbery, receive such intimate attention. In fact, many times police officers don't get a chance to speak with the prosecuting attorney about a minor case (shoplifting, drinking in public, simple assault, minor drug possession) until the day of the trial. Even that meeting may take place just moments before they're to take the stand. Unfortunately, there are just too many cases flowing through the courtrooms to justify anything more.

It's the prosecutor's job to compile the evidence that's been presented to her and bring about criminal charges and proceedings against the accused criminal. The prosecutor presents evidence during the trial, presents arguments, makes motions and objections, and may even take part in the actual investigation of the crime by interviewing potential witnesses and examining evidence. The job is a tough one and requires an extensive knowledge of criminal law.

In many counties and cites, a prosecutor is an elected official who's charged with representing the government in criminal proceedings. In some areas, such as with the U.S. government, federal prosecutors are appointed. Federal prosecutors, called U.S. attorneys, receive their appointments from the president of the United States, and they serve at his pleasure.

The title of state and other local prosecuting attorneys depends upon the rule of the locale where the office is held. In Commonwealth states, such as Virginia and Massachusetts, the prosecutors are called commonwealth's attorneys. Other areas may use the title district attorney, state attorney, city attorney, or county attorney. They're essentially all the same position and have similar duties and responsibilities.

The office of the prosecutor may have a large enough caseload to justify hiring other attorneys who assist the chief prosecutor with her duties. The attorneys she employs are called (again, depending upon the area) assistant U.S. attorneys, assistant commonwealth's attorneys, assistant state's attorneys, assistant city attorneys, assistant county attorneys, or assistant district attorneys.

The chief prosecutor assigns individual cases to her assistants. She may employ one attorney who specializes in sexual assault cases, while another is best suited for homicide cases. A third may handle all drunk driving cases, and another may prosecute only cases involving juvenile offenders. Some chief prosecutors take it upon themselves to prosecute all high-profile cases.

Prosecutors sometimes visit a crime scene to get the feel of the events at the time they took place. This not only enables them to paint a better picture for the jury, but it also gives them the opportunity to instruct police officers as to what evidence they'd like to see collected and preserved.

THE POLICE OFFICER

Police officers are subpoenaed to testify in a criminal case as are any other witnesses. During the trial they're questioned by the prosecutor and cross-examined by the defense attorney. Their duty is to provide truthful testimony regarding their involvement in the case in question. They normally attend the trial dressed as they dress while on duty—patrol officers in full uniform and detectives in suits. While waiting for their individual cases to be called, police officers may be called upon to provide security for the courtroom.

THE BAILIFF

A bailiff is a court employee who is the choreographer and manager of a court proceeding. It's the bailiff's job to ensure all aspects of the trial are carried out smoothly. He may or may not be a sworn police officer; however, many bailiffs are sworn peace officers and have the authority to arrest and detain lawbreakers.

The bailiff calls court to order, maintains security and order within the courtroom, and sometimes has the responsibility for swearing in witnesses. He's responsible for escorting defendants to and from courthouse holding cells, escorting witnesses to and from the witness stand, and handing exhibits and evidence to witnesses, attorneys, jury members, and the judge. During the duration of a trial the bailiff attends to the needs of jury members. He may be required to transport sequestered jury members to and from their hotel, and he may also be required to pick up and deliver meals to the jury members.

A BAILIFF'S CALL TO ORDER

All rise.

Hear ye, hear ye, hear ye. The General District Court of No County, USA, is now in session. The honorable judge Always Wright presiding. All those having pains or suits to prosecute speak now or forever hold your peace. May God save this honorable court. Be seated, please.

THE COURT REPORTER

A court reporter is responsible for recording each and every word that's said during a court proceeding. A court reporter must be properly trained and certified. The training to become a court reporter can vary, but most training periods normally last from two to four years. Upon completion of the training, a skilled court reporter can expect to earn between twenty-five and sixty thousand dollars annually depending on the area where they're employed.

Court reporters are expected to record, at minimum, approximately 225 words per minute. Recording such vast numbers of words so quickly and accurately requires the use of a stenotype machine, which allows the reporter to press several keys simultaneously. Various combinations of keys represent different sounds, words, and phrases. The machine, which is actually a computer, automatically transfers these sounds and phrases into written words.

When a trial is complete, the reporter prepares a written transcript of the proceeding, which becomes a permanent part of the court record.

THE CLERK OF COURT

The clerk of court is an elected official with an enormous responsibility. The office of the clerk generates and maintains all records and paperwork for each civil and criminal transaction within her jurisdiction.

For criminal cases the clerk's office processes all misdemeanor and felony paperwork (warrants, etc.); generates jury summons; issues subpoenas; prepares court dockets; prepares for arraignments; files all motions and warrants; and collects, manages, and maintains all fees and fines paid to the court.

In civil proceedings, the clerk's office is responsible for receiving, filing, and managing all paperwork related to personal injury suits, property foreclosures, judgments, and business-related lawsuits.

Clerks' offices also maintain records regarding all domestic disputes, such as legal separations and divorce proceedings. The offices issue and record marriage licenses, restraining orders, marriage annulments, and child custody suits. Some county and city clerks of court can perform legal marriage ceremonies.

Many clerk's offices are equipped with Live Scan fingerprint technology that enables them to conduct background investigations of employees for schools, employers, coaches of youth teams, and so on. The office charges a small fee for this service.

The amount of paperwork generated by a clerk's office is enormous and grows with each passing year. According to Butler County, Ohio, County Clerk of Court Cindy Carpenter, the number of criminal cases increases at a rate of 12 to 15 percent per year, yet her operating budget increases at the much lower rate of approximately 3 percent each year. Spillover of crime from neighboring Cincinnati, Ohio, has an impact on Butler County's crime statistics, much like all other counties, cities, and towns bordering large metropolitan areas.

Ms. Carpenter oversees a workforce of seventy employees throughout a network of countywide satellite offices. Her staff, like many clerks' offices across the nation, is highly skilled and well educated. Many of her employees have advanced education degrees and extensive experience in the criminal justice system. Others have backgrounds and degrees in bookkeeping and accounting-related fields. Entry-level personnel employed in a clerk's office can expect to receive a salary of approximately seventeen thousand dollars annually. The salary increases with experience and with the level of the position held within the office. The salary of the clerk of court is a fixed salary mandated by the state for which the clerk is elected. The salaries vary depending upon the locale.

The clerk of court has the responsibility for collecting certain fees for the sheriff's office, such as fees for levies, warrant and subpoena services, jury summons services, mileage for serving writs, and court orders. She also collects fees for services performed by the county sheriff's office, such as receiving prisoners, calling witnesses, taking the prisoner before the court, and discharging prisoners. The fees for the sheriff's services vary from locale to locale, but when charged and collected by the clerk, they become part of the court costs that must be paid by the defendant. Fees can include:

- Calling each witness to the witness stand—$3.00
- Taking the prisoner before the court for a hearing—$5.00
- Mileage for summons and writ service—$1.00 for the first mile. $0.50 for each mile thereafter
- Administering an oath—$3.00
- Summonsing a juror—$6.00
- Serving an arrest warrant—$10.00
- Serving a writ of possession (repossession of property)—$60.00

In many courts across the country, the clerk of court sits behind the bench alongside the judge. In these areas it's usually the clerk of court who administers the oath to, or swears in, all witnesses. The clerk also prepares the court docket (schedule of court cases) and calls each case from the docket. The clerk of court reads the jury's verdict aloud at the end of the trial.

THE GRAND JURY

A grand jury is a group of people chosen from the general population to serve the court. It is the grand jury's duty to examine evidence and listen to testimony for the purpose of determining whether there's probable cause to formally charge an offender with a crime.

Grand jury proceedings are secret, informal hearings held prior to trials involving felonies. The only evidence that's presented to the members of the grand jury is evidence that's been gathered by the prosecutor. The defense isn't allowed to present evidence, cross-examine witnesses, or ask questions during a grand jury hearing. In fact, the defense isn't even allowed to attend. A grand jury proceeding is a totally one-sided event.

During a grand jury proceeding, the prosecutor may present physical evidence, such as DNA testing results and fingerprint evidence. She may also summon police officers to testify. When all the evidence has been heard, the members of the grand jury vote to indict (charge with a crime) the offender or not.

A decision of "true bill" means the grand jury's decided there's enough probable cause to indict. A vote of "no bill" means that the prosecutor didn't present enough evidence to go forward with the case, and no charges can be filed against the offender at this time.

Grand juries almost always indict. The chances of obtaining a true bill are so great that most law enforcement officers consider the grand jury process a slam dunk for their side.

THE JURY

Defendants have the constitutional right to be tried by an impartial panel of their peers called a jury. A jury is a group of people (usually twelve) whose duty is to listen to all factual evidence that's presented during a trial and then render a verdict. They may also be called upon to set an appropriate punishment for the defendant.

Jurors are selected at random from local citizens. They're normally chosen through electoral or motor vehicle registrations. Those selected must serve unless they can provide the court with a just reason why they can't. Some of the reasons that jurors may be excused from serving are poor health, work-related issues, and financial hardship. Police officers, other criminal justice officials, and convicted criminals may not serve as jurors.

In the event of a trial by jury, the jury is selected ahead of time through a process called voir dire (pronounced *vwar dir*), which is an examination process that allows both the defense and the prosecution to question each potential jury member and to determine his suitability as a juror. Each side is allowed to eliminate jurors who may be biased or otherwise harmful to their case. After the jury has been selected and sworn in (promising to serve honestly, listen to all the evidence, and make a decision using only the facts presented), the members are seated in the jury box—a separate seating area in the front of the courtroom away from spectators and other court participants. The attorneys present evidence from the trial directly to the jury as well as to the judge.

At the conclusion of a trial the jury meets in secret to decide the fate of the defendant. These secret meetings are called deliberations. During the deliberation process jury members elect a leader and spokesperson for the group called a jury foreman.

When their decision has been reached, the jury foreman sends word to the judge, who orders court to return to session. The jury foreman provides a written copy of the jury's decision to the clerk of court, who reads it aloud. After the verdict has been read, attorneys for both the prosecution and defendant normally ask the judge to poll the jury. Jury polling is simply asking each member of the jury if the verdict that was read aloud was indeed his decision.

At the conclusion of the polling the judge excuses the jurors, thanks them for their services, and excuses them from further duty. The judge then orders everyone in the courtroom to remain standing until the jury has left the courtroom.

Jury Sequestering

In the case of a jury trial, sometimes the judge feels the need to sequester the jury. Jury sequestering prevents jurors from hearing information that hasn't been introduced as evidence. It's also used to prevent media influence over jurors.

Sequestered jury members must stay in the same hotel, eat their meals together, and have no access to the media. They may not discuss the trial with anyone, including family members.

At the end of each court day, court security personnel, such as sheriff's deputies or the bailiff, transport a sequestered jury is transported to a hotel. Security is normally provided for the jury during their stay at the hotel and while they're attending meals. Security is also in place to prevent the jurors from having outside contact with anyone.

THE JUDGE

Everyone is familiar with the man or woman sitting at the raised wooden desk in the front of the courtroom. Those men and women dressed in black robes are, of course, judges. They're the gatekeepers of a courtroom. A judge listens to all evidence presented by both the defense and prosecution; she makes legal rulings regarding whether evidence is admissible, and—during a bench trial (a trial without a jury)—decides the fate of the defendant by determining guilt or innocence. The judge ensures that all rules of the law and the court are properly adhered to by all parties involved. During a jury trial, a judge instructs the jury in all laws pertaining to the evidence they've just heard.

To make their decisions in a bench trial, judges rely on testimony from expert witnesses and examine articles of physical evidence. They must also draw on their own life experiences to assist them in their decisions. For example, a judge who once worked part-time as a bartender during college could more easily determine the truthfulness of a defendant in a murder trial who's currently employed in a local nightclub.

Confessions play a big role in a criminal trial, but they don't automatically mean that a defendant is guilty. A judge must look at all facts surrounding confessions, such as police actions (intimidation and coercion) and the emotional state of the suspect at the time of the confession (depression, mental retardation, etc.).

Judges must also consider the treatment of non-English-speaking defendants at the time of their confessions. Many people born outside the United States speak English fluently; however, not everyone who speaks English can read English. In fact, there are still many people who can't read or write at all, in any language.

Many police officers speak only one language and assume suspects who speak English also understand the English written word. In these instances, suspects are often handed a written statement that was transcribed as a result of an interrogation. They're then asked to sign the document, and many do quite readily without knowing what they're signing.

Many police agencies employ interpreters to assist them in understanding non-English-speaking suspects. Confessions taken through an interpreter sometimes still lose key words during the translation process; therefore, many courts require the entire conversation to be recorded. This allows the defense to object to any inconsistencies.

Judges face many challenges, and one of the biggest problems facing judges is the overwhelming number of cases they're expected to try. To keep up with the ever-increasing workload, many judges are forced to work without a break during the day. Many of those judges who do manage to find time for a moment away from the bench allow themselves only a few minutes for lunch.

My twenty-minute interview for this chapter with Judge Matthew J. Crehan of Ohio took place during a brief lunch recess. The judge kindly answered my questions between phone calls, thumbing through law books, and fielding questions from his clerk and bailiff. Between these many interruptions the judge managed to eat his lunch—half a sandwich and a small cup of Jell-O he'd brought from home. Then he was off for another five or six hours of administering justice. This scenario is typical all across the country. A judge's work day is a hectic day to say the least. A courtroom is a constant flurry of activity.

Another hurdle facing the judges of today has been labeled "The CSI Effect." The CSI Effect is the direct result of jury members—and sometimes even attorneys—relying on popular TV shows as a standard for learning about scientific analysis and other crime scene procedure. Shows of this nature tend to give members of juries a false sense of expectation. Scientific testing is excellent; however, nothing's perfect. Crime scene investigation techniques, tools, and laboratory results assist judges in making their decisions, but judges don't always rely on physical evidence as a means for determining guilt or innocence. Sometimes, for whatever reasons, laboratory test results must be excluded during trial, and judges must look to other areas of evidence.

The position of judge is an extremely commanding one; however, it can also be an extremely lonely and isolated one. Judges often find friends and other attorneys treating them differently once they've received their powerful appointments. Many times the intimidation felt by those who were once close to the judges is due to what some in the legal community call "judge's disease" or, more commonly, "robe-itis." Robe-itis occurs when an individual judge feels superior to others and shows it.

THE TRIAL

A criminal trial actually begins long before the parties involved step into the courtroom. Indictments are handed down from the grand jury; the suspect is arrested; attorneys are appointed or retained; and meetings with witnesses and experts begin.

The suspect is also required to submit to questioning and certain testing by court officials. The process starts with a pretrial investigation—the judge's first glimpse into the life of the suspect.

PRETRIAL INVESTIGATION AND SUPERVISION

Most courts require that a pretrial investigation of the suspect's background and criminal history be conducted before her trial commences. In instances such as these, a pretrial officer is assigned to the suspect. The officer meets with the suspect soon after her arrest and asks questions concerning the suspect's relationship with her parents, spouse, children, and other family members. The officer probes into other areas of the suspect's past, such as elementary, high school, and college performance; church and civic organization involvement; employment history; ties to the criminal community; and past criminal conduct.

During the time the suspect is on pretrial supervision (which lasts until the trial is over), she may be required to submit to drug and alcohol screenings. She may also be asked required to undergo a mental health evaluation by a psychiatrist or psychologist.

At the end of the pretrial period, the pretrial officer prepares a written report for the court to review. The court may use the report for determining bail possibilities, and it's used for determining an appropriate sentence at the end of the trial.

ARRAIGNMENT

The suspect's first appearance in court is for arraignment—to have the charges formally read to him by the court and to have a date set for trial. The law requires arraignment hearings for incarcerated suspects to be held as soon after a person's arrest as possible. In most states, a suspect can normally expect to be arraigned within forty-eight hours, excluding weekends. If a suspect has been released on bail, his arraignment could be held many weeks later.

During the arraignment, the suspect is asked to state his preferences regarding an attorney. If she doesn't already have an attorney, she may ask for a court-appointed attorney or announce that she chooses to represent herself. Privately retained attorneys normally accompany their clients to an arraignment.

Judges may also increase or decrease previously set bail amounts during an arraignment, and the suspect is asked to enter a plea of either guilty or not guilty. After the arraignment, the person is no longer considered a suspect. She's now considered a defendant in a criminal proceeding.

Bail

Bail is an amount of money that the court accepts to allow defendants to remain free until their court cases have concluded. A bail bond is the written agreement between the defendant, the court, and/or a third party, such as a bail bondsman. The bond agreement promises that the defendant will appear in court. If he doesn't appear, the money that was posted as bail is automatically forfeited to the court.

Courts will also accept a property bond, if the value of the property is equal to or greater than the monetary amount of the bail and if the property owner has enough equity to equal the amount of the bail.

Quite often, defendants don't have enough cash money or collateral to meet their bail requirements; therefore, they must employ the services of a bail bondsman. A bail bondsman charges a nonrefundable 15 percent of the total bond amount. The bondsman then posts the full amount of the defendant's bond with the court.

The full responsibility of ensuring that the defendant appears in court now rests upon the bail bondsman. If the defendant doesn't appear for her hearings or trial, the bail bondsman forfeits the full amount of the bond to the court. The same holds true for family members who have posted a property bond for a defendant.

Some locales have an option that allows defendants to post their bail directly with the police. The amount of bail is set by a predetermined bail schedule based upon the severity of the crime.

If a defendant has no ties to the community where he has committed his crimes (no family, no job, no home) or, if for any other reason, the judge thinks the defendant is a flight risk, he may order him held without bail.

A judge may also determine that a defendant poses no risk and may release him on his own recognizance (O.R.). All that's required of the defendant in this instance is that he signs a written promise to appear in court on the each of the dates specified. If he doesn't appear in court on the designated date, the judge will issue a bench warrant for his arrest. A bench warrant is a warrant that's issued by a presiding judge.

A judge might also choose to impose certain restrictions as conditions for a defendant's bond, such as curfews, not having any contact with the victim of the crime, and submitting to alcohol and drug testing. If at any time the defendant doesn't meet the bond conditions established by the judge, the bond may be revoked. When this happens, the defendant is immediately taken into custody and held without bond until his trial. Additional felony charges may also be filed against the defendant if he doesn't appear in court as scheduled.

At the conclusion of the defendant's trial, all bond money paid to the court is returned to the person who posted it if the defendant has met all his court appearance requirements. To release the bond, the judge must file a court order. In some locations, this order is called an entry-releasing bond.

In the case of the federal court system, there's no predetermined bond; each defendant must be brought before a federal magistrate for a bond hearing. Federal bond hearings are held only during daytime business hours, so an offender arrested at night by a federal law enforcement officer is normally held in a jail cell until the following day. If he's arrested on the weekend, which begins on Friday night, he's held in a jail cell until the following Monday. It is an old law enforcement trick-of-the-trade for officers to make a point of arresting someone whom they've had a particularly difficult time with on Friday afternoon. By doing so, they ensure the criminal will have to remain in jail without bail for an entire weekend. At the conclusion of the hearing, then, the defendant is either allowed to go free on bond or is immediately taken to jail.

Appointment of Attorney

During the arraignment, the clerk of the court calls each case on the court docket (the list of cases to be heard on any given day), and, if a defendant isn't using a privately retained attorney or defending herself, an attorney from the rotating sideline pool of lawyers is summoned to the bench. (Attorneys aren't normally appointed at the time of the initial arrest and questioning. If a defendant requests an attorney at that time, officers simply cease their questioning until an attorney has been appointed). The attorney is assigned to the case and to his new client. At this moment, the defendant is introduced to the person who will represent her during her quest for freedom. This may also be the only opportunity she has to speak with her attorney prior to court day.

Due to their extremely excessive caseloads, court-appointed attorneys are sometimes forced to discuss the defendant's case with her for the first time in the hallways of the courthouse, mere moments before the case is to be tried. Obviously, with no real preparation by the attorney, the defendant stands little chance of winning the case.

After the defendant is either appointed an attorney or has retained a private attorney, the judicial process can begin. The defendant's constitutional right to a speedy trial must be observed, so the defense and prosecution must agree upon a date for trial. The accused and his attorney must be allowed ample time to prepare an adequate defense, and the prosecution must be allowed ample time to conduct their investigation, evidence examinations, and analysis.

A trial date isn't set in stone, and each side may request a continuance of the proceedings, if needed. The judge may grant a continuance for many reasons, such as the need of additional investigation time by the defense or the prosecution, illness, conflicting attorney schedules, or newly discovered evidence.

PRETRIAL MOTIONS

Many times, before a trial begins, attorneys for both the prosecution and the defense make several requests to the court. These requests are called pretrial motions, which may be made at any time prior to trial. There are many types of pretrial motions, including:

- **Motion for discovery:** a motion used by both sides (the defense and prosecution) to learn what information and evidence the other side plans to present during trial.

- **Motion for continuance:** a motion that asks for a delay or postponement of an upcoming hearing or trial.

- **Motion to suppress:** a motion normally used by the defense to eliminate a particular piece of evidence or statement.

- **Motion for change of venue:** a motion used to ask for a change in the location of a trial.

- **Motion to dismiss:** a motion normally used by the defense to ask for the dismissal of a court case, usually based upon a total lack of evidence.

A trial judge listens as each attorney presents her reasons for having a particular motion granted. The judge also listens to the opposing attorney list the reasons why the motion should be denied. At the conclusion of the arguments the judge decides whether or not to grant the motion.

With the preliminary hearing and pretrial motions complete, the judge sets a court date for the trial. Continuances are still permitted for just cause. Subpoenas are issued for each witness whose presence is required for both the prosecution and the defense. When all loose ends are tied up and neither of the parties requires additional continuances, a final trial date is set. The defendant and his attorney must decide upon having a jury trial or a trial by the judge.

THE TRIAL BEGINS

On the day of the trial, the courtroom bustles with activity, much like an arena where a stage production is about to take place. The day actually begins in the wee hours of the morning in prison or jail, sometimes several hours away from the courthouse.

The star of the show, the defendant, is normally awakened by corrections officers (unless he was allowed to remain free on bond) around three in the morning and told to dress and get ready for court. He's placed in handcuffs, leg shackles, and waist chains and then loaded into the back of a sheriff's office van for the trip. A sheriff's deputy hands the defendant a brown paper bag containing two boiled eggs, a slice of stale bread, and a single-serving size carton of juice—his breakfast.

Upon arrival at the courthouse, the defendant is escorted by sheriff's deputies to a holding cell that's usually located in the rear, or in the basement, of

A prisoner's view from inside a courthouse holding cell.

the court facility. The holding cells are sometimes filled to standing room only with defendants waiting for their turn in court. The cells may or may not contain a toilet; if they do, it's in plain view of all the other defendants. Sometimes, the defendants must wait for several hours before they're called. Those who are still waiting at noon are normally served a bologna and cheese sandwich and a carton of fruit-flavored juice.

Security for the courts falls under the bailiwick of the local sheriff's office. The sheriff assigns deputies to work metal detectors and to guard prisoners within the courtroom. In some jurisdictions a sheriff assigns a deputy to serve as bailiff.

The tables in the front of a courtroom are reserved for the prosecuting and defense attorneys. The table to the left of the judge is for the prosecution and her assistants; the defense team works from the table to the judge's right. Witnesses in a criminal trial are normally sequestered in a witness room outside the courtroom. This act of seclusion prevents witness contamination and influence of their individual testimony by statements made in the courtroom, or from other people involved in the case. The bailiff or an assistant escorts each witness from the witness room as the clerk of the court or judge calls them to the stand.

Court begins with the bailiff calling the court to order and then announcing the name of the sitting judge. The judge enters from a rear door leading from his chambers (his private office and library area).

When everyone has taken a seat and the court comes to order (everyone is still and quiet), the clerk calls the first case and the judge asks if the attorneys for both the defense and the prosecution are ready to proceed. The lawyers reply with an affirmative response, or possibly a request for another continuance or other motion. At this point a judge rarely grants another continuance.

If the defendant is in custody, a sheriff's deputy escorts him from the holding cell to the defense table. If he's not in custody and has been allowed to remain free on bond, he rises from his seat in the courtroom to take a place at the defense table beside his attorney.

It's not uncommon for jail inmates to be in the courtroom without restraints. Most judges require the removal of all shackles prior to trial. Some courts believe if a jury sees a defendant in handcuffs and leg irons, their decision may be prejudiced, causing them to render an unjust guilty verdict.

Court Security

Deputy sheriffs who are in charge of courtroom security are not always certified police officers. They attend a special course of study in an academy designed for jailers and/or courtroom security persons. The training is not as in-depth or as intense as police officer training. Jailers and courtroom security personnel face different challenges that don't normally involve firearms. These officers also wear specially designed holsters, called security holsters, that require them to perform a certain procedure before their guns can be removed from the holster. Level II holsters are now available and are thought to be more secure than ever. A gun isn't easily removed from these holsters unless someone knows how to do so properly.

Inadequate training and failure to follow proper security procedures could have been a possible factor in the March, 2005, courthouse shootings of Judge Rowland Barnes, his court clerk, and two sheriff's deputies in Atlanta, Georgia.

The defendant, Brian Nichols, was a known violent offender who had been caught possessing two homemade shanks (shank is jail or prison slang for a knife) fashioned from metal hinges, just two days prior to the courtroom

---

murders. Officers should have taken every precaution available to maintain control of such a vicious offender.

It's common procedure throughout the law enforcement community to use two officers when escorting or transporting known violent prisoners, especially those obviously intending to commit bodily harm. In the case of the Atlanta shootings, a single female deputy was assigned to supervise and escort this extremely dangerous prisoner. Nichols easily overpowered the officer, took her weapon, and went on his murderous rampage.

The duties of a courtroom security officer are, at times, no less dangerous than that of a police officer. The sheriff I worked for many years ago was adamant about his assignment of sworn, trained police officers in the courts. He didn't believe in courtroom security training for nonpolice deputy sheriffs. He called the training inadequate and impractical. Most officers thought his decision inane and a waste of police manpower. The events that unfolded in that Atlanta courtroom might have proved my former boss quite correct.

OPENING STATEMENTS
With the court in order and everyone in their places, the judge allows attorneys from both sides to begin their opening statements. These statements are basically their outlines or plans of action for their cases and their expectations

A prosecutor makes his opening statements to a jury.

of the trial's outcome. Opening statements are always made prior to the introduction of any evidence.

The prosecution is allowed to speak first, followed by the attorney for the defense. If the trial is a jury trial, the attorneys speak directly to the jury; in a trial by judge, they address the judge with their statements.

SWEARING IN WITNESSES

The bailiff or an assistant escorts witnesses from the witness room as the clerk of the court calls them to the stand. Each witness must be sworn in by the bailiff, the clerk, or the judge. To be properly sworn in, he must raise his right hand and promise that everything he tells the court is the truth, to the best of his knowledge. The swearing-in process is performed so that, if the witness is not truthful while testifying, he may be prosecuted for perjury. If he's not sworn to tell the truth, no perjury charges may be brought against him.

Police officers are often called to testify in cases involving criminal matters. In each case, the police officer normally has met with the prosecutors well in advance of the trial, has rehearsed his individual testimony, and has knowledge of all questions that will be asked of him. Many times, a mock trial is set up to allow the officer to practice his testimony in front of the prosecution team. The team asks a set of suspected defense questions as well. The entire questioning process is very well rehearsed to prevent mistakes during the actual trial. This rehearsal partially explains the canned tone of voice and the monotonous responses we hear from police officers as they testify on televised criminal cases.

PROSECUTOR'S DIRECT EXAMINATION

At the conclusion of the opening statements, the prosecutor begins to call forth each of her witnesses. The questioning of a witness who's been called on to testify by either the prosecution or defense is called direct examination. One at a time, each of the witnesses recounts his knowledge of the crime. The prosecutor also calls on police officers and expert witnesses to provide testimony.

Police officers answer questions regarding their investigation of the crime. Experts are called upon to testify about their background (education and experience) and the results of any testing they may have performed on individual items of evidence, such as fingerprints and DNA. Medical examiners and coroners may also be called on to testify about their findings during autopsy.

Defense's Cross-Examination

Upon completion of the prosecutor's questioning, the defense is allowed to cross-examine each witness. Cross-examination of a witness occurs when the opposing attorney questions a witness, such as when a defense attorney questions a witness who testified on behalf of the prosecution. During cross-examination, attorneys sometimes attempt to find inconsistencies in a witness's statements by asking tricky or repetitive questions.

Redirect

When cross-examination is complete, the prosecution gets a second attempt to ask her witness additional questions. This second attempt at questioning is called redirect. During the second round of questioning, the prosecutor may try to clarify any questions that may have been brought about by the defense attorney's cross-examination.

Motion to Dismiss

At the conclusion of the prosecution's witness testimony and evidence presentation, cross-examination by the defense, and redirect by the prosecution, the defense normally asks for a motion to dismiss all charges against his client. In nearly all cases, judges refuse to grant this request.

Many judges find this point in the trial—the end of the prosecution's case and the beginning of the defense's case—to be an excellent time to take a break, and the judge may order a recess. If the recess comes at the end of the day, court is adjourned until the following day.

Defendants who are unhappy with the services of their court-appointed attorneys may make a formal request for a change of counsel. Judges rarely grant a change unless the defendant can prove that the attorney has been negligent or ineffective in her duties as counsel, which is a rare occurrence. If the defendant is unhappy and can prove that his attorney provided subpar services, he may ask for a dismissal based upon ineffective assistance of counsel.

DEFENSE'S DIRECT EXAMINATION

After the prosecution has presented their entire case, it's the defense's turn to present theirs. They do so by questioning their own witnesses and presenting their own evidence.

Prosecution's Cross-Examination

Just as the defense had the opportunity to cross-examine the prosecution's witnesses, the prosecution now has the opportunity to question witnesses for the defense.

Redirect

At the conclusion of the prosecution's cross-examination, the defense is allowed to re-question the defense witnesses. They do so to clarify any discrepancies and inconsistencies in their statements that may have been brought about by the prosecutor during her cross-examination. At the conclusion of redirect, the defense attorney must rest his case.

Rebuttal

After the defense rests their case, the prosecutor has one last chance to disprove the case that's been presented by the defense. She does so by attempting to explain away, contradict, or clarify any inconsistent statements. She also may try to discredit evidence that's been presented by the defense. This final effort is called a rebuttal.

DECIDING ON JURY INSTRUCTIONS

Attorneys for both sides meet with the judge to determine which legal rules, called jury instructions, should be provided to the jury for making a decision regarding guilt or innocence. Some standard jury instructions can be found in books and publications that are used as a standard in courts all across the country.

The following is a jury instruction excerpt from the California code. These instructions vary in other locations:

202: DIRECT AND INDIRECT EVIDENCE

Evidence can come in many forms. It can be testimony about what someone saw or heard or smelled. It can be an exhibit admitted into evidence. It can be someone's opinion.

Some evidence proves a fact directly, such as testimony of a witness who saw a jet plane flying across the sky. Some evidence proves a fact

---

indirectly, such as testimony of a witness who saw only the white trail that jet planes often leave. This indirect evidence is sometimes referred to as "circumstantial evidence." In either instance, the witness's testimony is evidence that a jet plane flew across the sky.

As far as the law is concerned, it makes no difference whether evidence is direct or indirect. You may choose to believe or disbelieve either kind. Whether it is direct or indirect, you should give every piece of evidence whatever weight you think it deserves.

204: WILLFUL SUPPRESSION OF EVIDENCE

You may consider whether one party intentionally concealed or destroyed evidence. If you decide that a party did so, you may decide that the evidence would have been unfavorable to that party.

CLOSING ARGUMENTS

Both the prosecution and the defense attorneys present closing arguments to the jury at the conclusion of the trial. Closing arguments afford each side an equal opportunity to summarize all evidence and testimony that's been presented to the jury throughout the course of the entire trial.. This is also each attorney's last chance to attempt to sway the jury into his way of thinking.

Depending upon the complexity of the case, and the amount of evidence presented during a criminal trial, the entire trial can last from any part of one day to several months. In the end, the entire matter is decided by a weighing of the facts. A criminal verdict must be decided only on the evidence that was presented.

The prosecution's case must be proven beyond all reasonable doubt for the jury to return a verdict of guilty. If the slightest doubt exists in the minds of the jury, or judge, about the guilt of the defendant, the defendant must be found innocent.

A civil case verdict is based upon a preponderance of evidence, meaning that more evidence than not must lean toward the plaintiff in order for them to prevail.

INSTRUCTING THE JURY

The judge faces the jury and describes to them the importance of the decision they're about to make. The judge also explains that he's about to give them certain instructions as to how to make that decision. Once the judge is sure that the jury understands the process, he then reads each of the previously agreed-upon instructions to them.

JURY DELIBERATIONS

After receiving their instructions from the judge, the jury is escorted into a private jury room where they begin the process of determining the guilt or innocence of the defendant.

READING OF THE VERDICT

When the jury's reached a verdict, the judge is notified and the bailiff escorts the jury back into the courtroom. The foreman of the jury hands the written verdict to the bailiff, who then presents it to the judge. After reading the verdict the judge orders the defendant to stand and then hands the verdict to the clerk of court to read aloud.

If the jury finds the defendant guilty, the defense attorney normally makes what's known as a posttrial motion for an acquittal or a new trial. These requests are rarely ever granted.

If the verdict is a not guilty verdict, paperwork is completed. The ex-defendant and the judge must sign forms regarding personal property and release of bond money to the proper persons. When this process is completed, the defendant is set free.

SENTENCING

A guilty verdict normally results in the immediate custody of the defendant by corrections officials. The defendant is handcuffed and taken directly to jail to await the next hearing. Her next appearance in court will be for her actual sentencing.

The probation department assigns an officer to the defendant who then begins a thorough background investigation and report. The completed report is called a presentence report. To gather the information for this report, the probation officer assigned to the case generally speaks with family members, friends, neighbors, employers, church members and preachers, doctors,

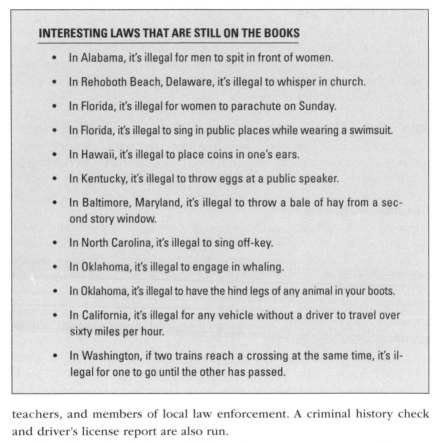

INTERESTING LAWS THAT ARE STILL ON THE BOOKS

- In Alabama, it's illegal for men to spit in front of women.

- In Rehoboth Beach, Delaware, it's illegal to whisper in church.

- In Florida, it's illegal for women to parachute on Sunday.

- In Florida, it's illegal to sing in public places while wearing a swimsuit.

- In Hawaii, it's illegal to place coins in one's ears.

- In Kentucky, it's illegal to throw eggs at a public speaker.

- In Baltimore, Maryland, it's illegal to throw a bale of hay from a second story window.

- In North Carolina, it's illegal to sing off-key.

- In Oklahoma, it's illegal to engage in whaling.

- In Oklahoma, it's illegal to have the hind legs of any animal in your boots.

- In California, it's illegal for any vehicle without a driver to travel over sixty miles per hour.

- In Washington, if two trains reach a crossing at the same time, it's illegal for one to go until the other has passed.

teachers, and members of local law enforcement. A criminal history check and driver's license report are also run.

The information is all compiled into the presentence report and sent to the sentencing judge for review and consideration. The report assists the judge with determining an appropriate sentence. The report is an in-depth look into the defendant's lifestyle and health. Mitigating factors such as mental illness, past criminal record, or outstanding community involvement can influence a judge's decision and may warrant an increased or decreased sentence.

The length of sentence is based upon the defendant's past criminal history, the nature of her current crime, the violence associated with the crime, the defendant's repetitiveness of criminal activity, past probation violations, and past jail and prison records. Sentencing guidelines have been developed to assist the judge in his decision.

The sentencing hearing is a brief affair. The defendant stands as the judge reads the sentence. When the judge is finished pronouncing the sentence, the defendant is no longer a defendant in a criminal trial. He's now an inmate remanded to the custody of the Department of Corrections, and sheriff's deputies will detain him until they personally deliver him to prison. At the prison, he is entered into a reception center or receiving center, where he's processed and begins serving his sentence.

COURTROOM FAUX PAS

Sometimes a prosecutor asks an undercover police officer to wear the same clothing and hairstyle to court as he wore at the time he arrested a particular defendant. This is done to allow the court to see, and the defendant to remember, exactly how things were at the time of the undercover operation. For example, an undercover officer who comes to court wearing a full-dress uniform may look like a different person than the one who bought drugs from the defendant. If the officer wears plain clothes in court, the defendant is more apt to recognize him and remember the exact drug deal.

The intention is to leave as little room for doubt in a criminal trial as possible. It was a procedure that paid off for one officer.

During an undercover operation a veteran narcotics agent arrested a young man for selling marijuana. At the time of the arrest, this officer was dressed in stereotypical attire—jeans and a T-shirt—but he had also donned a long-haired wig as part of his disguise. His real hair was buzz-cut in the normal state trooper style, which, in those days, was not cool among the young. Short hair simply spelled *cop.*

The trooper wore the wig to court when testifying during the suspect's trial. The man remembered the trooper as someone he had sold drugs to, so he pled guilty and was given a suspended sentence. The judge also gave him a stern warning that a repeat violation would earn him some harsh time in the county jail. The young man, of course, said it would never happen again.

Outside the courtroom, the trooper removed his wig and walked to his undercover police sports car where he tossed the hairpiece into the back seat. When he turned around, the suspect he had just finished testifying against was walking by. The officer jokingly asked him if he had any pot for sale.

The newly convicted drug dealer instantly glanced nervously around the parking lot. Suddenly, the officer realized the man didn't recognize him without the wig, even though he still wore the same clothing. The dealer looked from side to side again and said, "Sure, but be careful, man. There are undercover cops everywhere around this place." He pulled an ounce of marijuana from his pants pockets and offered it to the officer. He was, of course, promptly arrested, again. Incidentally, he'd had the pot in his pocket during his trial. This crook deserved the all-time dumb-criminal-of-the-year award. He also deserved the jail sentence that was imposed by a judge who wasn't very lenient the second time around.

CHAPTER 13

PRISONS
AND JAILS

Jails and prisons are complicated places with all the problems of the out-side world, magnified by the pressure every human being feels at the loss of liberty. Writers setting a story inside should start in their own imagina-tion, with the inability to make even the most mundane choices—what to wear, what to eat, how long to stay in the shower—for themselves. And then, make it worse.

—LESLIE BUDEWITZ, AUTHOR OF LAW AND FICTION:
A LAWYER ANSWERS LEGAL QUESTIONS FOR MYSTERY WRITERS

Prisons and jails are crowded. They're bursting at the seams with inmates and there seems to be no solution to the rising rate of incarceration. Each year, the U.S. Department of Justice releases a report detailing the exact number of post-conviction criminal offenders who are currently making their way through the criminal justice system. The 2005 year-end report tells a sad tale.

In the United States, one out of every thirty-two people is either in prison or on probation or parole. Nearly 2.2 million people—a 2.7 percent increase over the year 2004—were serving time in a jail or prison at the end of 2005, and that number is growing with each passing day.

The close of 2005 saw more than four million people on probation and another 784,208 men and women on parole. When these figures are broken down by ethnicity, the numbers are even more alarming. For example, the report shows that one out of every thirteen African-American males between the ages of twenty-five and twenty-nine is currently serving time in an American prison.

There's also an increase in the number of women, many of them single mothers, incarcerated each year. Hand-in-hand with that rising incarceration rate is the growing number of children who are left behind and forced to live with family members, or they're placed in foster care while their mothers and fathers serve their sentences.

Today's prisons and jails sometimes house thousands of inmates, and they offer much more than just a cell, a bed, and three meals. These mega-institutions are like small, self-contained cities capable of making their own furniture, baking their own bread, and raising their own food sources, such as cows, pigs, and vegetables. They manufacture clothing and shoes. Some institutions even train and utilize their prisoners to fight wildfires deep in remote areas of California.

Inmates are required to participate in substance abuse programs if drugs or alcohol contributed to, or was a part of, the commission of their crimes.

PRISONS VS. JAILS

Those who are incarcerated serve their sentences behind the walls of two main types of corrections facilities—prisons and jails. A person convicted of a felony must normally serve one or more years in a state or federal prison, and a person convicted of a misdemeanor is usually sentenced to twelve or fewer months in a county jail. The two types of inmates aren't usually housed together, although there are exceptions to that rule in the case of extreme jail and prison overcrowding. Prisoners who are waiting to be transferred to state prison are held in county jails until a bed becomes available at the prison that's been designated for them by the state.

Separate federal prisons also exist to house criminals who are convicted of federal offenses (crimes against U.S. law), such as drug offenses, treason, and terrorism—these facilities are all prisons (not jails) and house only felons. A sheriff operates most county and city jails; the state government runs state prisons; and the Federal Bureau of Prisons (BOP) supervises federal facilities. Occasionally, in rural areas, several towns and counties join together and operate one multi-jurisdictional jail called a regional jail. The sheriff and chief of police from each of the regions serve as board members for the regional jail. These board members in turn hire and supervise a jail administrator who's responsible for the day-to-day operations of the facility.

An offender who's convicted of a crime normally serves his time in an institution located within the area where the original crime took place. The exception to this rule is when an offender is convicted of a federal crime. Federal inmates may be required to serve their time at any one of the federal prisons located in the United States. Federal Bureau of Prisons officials make every attempt to incarcerate their prisoners within five hundred miles of the inmate's hometown so they may maintain contact and visit with family members.

People who commit federal crimes are sentenced according to mandatory-minimum guidelines. A federal judge must impose a sentence (juries decide a particular sentence, but a judge imposes the sentence) within the range specified by those guidelines, but she may not dole out punishment outside of those limitations without an extremely good reason, such as in the case of an offender's diminished mental capacity, or in the instance where an offender has provided substantial assistance to the government as an informant.

If extenuating conditions exist whereby a federal judge feels a sentence reduction is warranted for a medical reason, the offender may be ordered to serve all or part of his time in a facility that specializes in that condition, such as the Federal Medical Center in Lexington, Kentucky, or the U.S. Medical Center for Federal Prisoners (MCFP) in Springfield, Missouri.

The MCFP specializes in the treatment and care of prisoners who are in need of mental health services and medical and dental treatment. Since there are a limited number of these special federal medical facilities, prisoners who are in need of their services may be transferred several hundred miles away from the cities and towns where their family members reside.

It's interesting to note that all crimes occurring within the city limits of Washington, D.C., may be considered federal crimes since the city isn't geographically located within a state. Offenders who commit crimes within the boundaries of the District may be tried in federal court and sentenced accordingly.

Let's further examine the two types of institutions, county jails and prisons.

COUNTY JAILS

A county jail serves three purposes: to house inmates who have been convicted of minor crimes (misdemeanors); to hold recently convicted felons until a bed becomes available in the state prison where they've been designated to serve their time; and to hold non-convicted criminals who are awaiting trial.

Serving time in a county jail is quite a bit different than serving a sentence in a state prison. Sometimes county jails are more overcrowded than state prisons. County jails are also normally smaller than prisons; therefore, they sometimes offer less in the way of services and programs for inmates.

A sheriff is the highest-ranking official in most county jails. Second in command is the chief deputy followed by a jail administrator, the person who oversees the day-to-day functions and activities of all jail operations. The deputy sheriffs working inside county jails are called corrections officers or corrections deputies. Their duties and training are similar to that of corrections officers in state and federal prisons.

COUNTY JAIL CELLS

A good number of county jails are outdated, understaffed, overpopulated, and underfunded. They feature cells and lockup facilities with poor or nonworking plumbing, inadequate lighting, dark hallways, and many blind corners that are dangerous for both the staff and the inmates. Cells are often infested with rats and roaches, and uncooperative or unruly prisoners are often beaten, pepper-sprayed, and shot with Tasers, beanbags, or stun guns.

County jail cell.

Cells are often not cleaned between the release of one inmate and the reception of another. New arrivals are sometimes forced to sleep on floors littered with feces, urine, vomit, and matted human and rodent hair.

Prisoners don't always have ready access to cleaning supplies. On one occasion I overheard a new prisoner asking a jail officer (a deputy sheriff) for supplies to clean his cell of feces and vomit left behind by a former prisoner. The deputy handed the inmate a washcloth through the bars and gave him the choice of using his one and only washcloth to either wash his body or to clean the floor.

OVERCROWDING ISSUES

Like their larger counterparts, state and federal prisons, county jails are overcrowded. Some jails are filled to two and three times their capacity and simply can't hold even one additional prisoner; therefore, they must request that a neighboring county hold prisoners for them. If a sheriff is asked to house an inmate from another jurisdiction, the sheriff is entitled by law to receive payment from that agency for housing the inmate. The cost to house a prisoner from another jurisdiction in the state of Ohio for the year 2006 was approximately sixty dollars a day.

The overcrowding of jails and prisons has become such an issue that many county sheriffs have learned to be quite creative when it comes to finding bed space for prisoners. Some sheriffs have made the decision to release some low-risk, minor offenders from jail before the completion of their sentences. Sheriff Gene A. Kelly of Ohio looked to an unlikely place for the solution to his overcrowding problem—container ships and oil rigs.

When the sheriff learned that workers on stationary oil rigs located in the Gulf of Mexico slept in compartments fashioned from large, metal shipping containers that had been converted into living quarters, he decided to explore the possibility of converting those containers into portable jail cells. He found the containers to be a perfect solution for jail overcrowding.

Each of the heavy, metal containers is ten feet wide by forty feet long, which allows ample space for inmate sleeping quarters, shower and restroom areas, and a dayroom area for ten inmates. The containers are equipped with heat and air-conditioning, lockable windows and doors, fluorescent lighting, tile floors, sheetrock walls, and bunk beds. The cost of each fully equipped

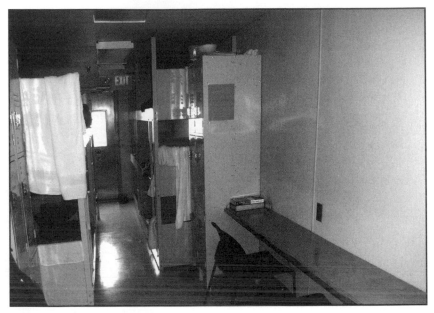

Interior living quarters of a jail pod.

container is just over thirty thousand dollars, a fraction of the cost to build new jail cells.

Sheriff Kelly converted the lower floor of a multilevel parking garage into a jail annex by purchasing and installing seven of the fully equipped shipping containers that he now calls jail pods. He had contractors surround the entire garage area with heavy-duty chain-link fence. The area outside and in between the pods is large enough for a recreation yard equipped with basketball equipment and picnic tables. The entire area is so secure that only one corrections deputy is needed to supervise, and he does so from outside the fence. Should trouble occur on the inside of this mini-compound, other deputies would be summoned to assist.

SERVICES PROVIDED

Most jails have at least one nurse on duty at all times, but many jails are large enough to justify employing an entire medical staff. Some even have fully equipped dental facilities and X-ray equipment. Smaller county jails don't have the budget for a full-time doctor and employ a local doctor on a part-time basis.

County jails offer religious services to inmates, but most don't have full-time chaplains. These facilities often rely on local churches and religious organizations to provide spiritual activities and material. They also rely on civic organizations for other needs, such as Alcoholics Anonymous and Narcotics Anonymous.

SECURITY MEASURES

To prevent illegal activities such as assaults, rape, drug use, gambling, and possible suicide, corrections deputies are required to visit each area of the jail facility several times during their shifts. To ensure that the deputies are making their rounds properly and are checking on each and every inmate within the facility, some jails employ the use of a device they call a pipe.

The pipe is a handheld metal device that's carried by all deputies working inside the jail. The device is approximately eight inches in length and two inches in diameter and contains a small computerized recording mechanism. The tip of the pipe is actually an electronic receiver. Small round transmitters are mounted throughout the jail in areas such as cell doors, dayrooms, recreation areas, the library, medical offices, medical cells, kitchen areas, and shower areas.

When the officers make their rounds, they touch the tip of the receiver portion of the pipe to the transmitters. The pipe then records the time that the officer was in that area. At the end of the officer's shift he inserts the pipe into a master receiver located inside the jail control room. The master receiver then downloads all of the day's data. This information allows jail administration to view the movements of each and every employee.

PRISONS

A defendant who receives a felony conviction in a state court and is sentenced to incarceration must serve his time in a state prison, not jail. Each state operates its own network of prisons, which is comprised of many different institutions, such as juvenile offender facilities and prisons for low, medium, and high-risk (maximum security) adult offenders. There are separate prisons for male and female prisoners.

The U.S. government operates the Federal Bureau of Prisons, which is designed to house inmates who have been convicted of federal crimes. These prisons are located throughout the United States and its territories.

PRISON SYSTEM CHAIN OF COMMAND

The overall day-to-day operations of prison facilities vary greatly from one area to another. These differences can be affected by cultural differences; geographical influences, such as climate and terrain; prison management styles and personalities; and even the mood and attitudes of the corrections staff. For example, a prison facility nestled within a community with deeply religious roots may offer more spiritual programs than facilities in other localities. Harsh winters in the New England states force inmates to remain indoors for many months. Close living conditions and a lack of sunshine and fresh air often cause short tempers to flare up.

In institutions situated in the western states, hot, dry desert weather, with little or no rainfall, can also affect a prisoner's or staff member's temperament.

The warden of a prison greatly influences the atmosphere of the institution he supervises. A warden who excelled in basketball or football in college may encourage a very active sports program at his institution. Another warden may despise sports and offer more support toward academia. A warden's religious beliefs have also been known to play a big part in how he runs his facility. Either way, prisons (state and federal) and jails (as described in the section regarding sheriff's offices) operate much like police agencies and the military, with a rank-and-file system. The warden is the chief officer of the institution, followed by her assistant wardens.

The rest of the prison staff is divided between administrative services and security staff. On the administrative side are counselors, medical personnel, clerical staff, religious services, educational services, recreation services, buildings and grounds maintenance, captains, lieutenants, sergeants, corporals, and officers.

The security staff operates under the supervision of the chief security officer, who normally holds the rank of major. The majors, in turn, supervise the rest of the security staff that includes captains (shift commanders), lieutenants, sergeants, corporals, and line officers. Security staff members are assigned to every location of the prison facility.

FEDERAL VS. STATE PRISONS

The U.S. Department of Justice's Bureau of Justice Statistics reports that nearly 65 percent of federal prisons' population is comprised of low- and medium-security inmates and most of the federal prison system's prisoners—nearly 54 percent—are drug offenders. In the year 2006, only a little more than 14 percent of the federal prison population was incarcerated for weapons offenses; 5.4 percent for robbery; 3.1 percent for homicide, rape, and kidnapping; 2.3 percent for sex crimes; and a scant 0.1 percent of the prison population is serving time for crimes against our national security. The majority of sentences for offenders range between five and ten years in length.

The end of 2005 saw nearly 1.25 million inmates in state prisons throughout the country. An estimated 650,000 were serving time for committing violent crimes, including rape and murder, while just over 250,000 were incarcerated for drug offenses. Another 262,000 were behind bars for property crimes such as larceny.

There's a sharp contrast in the prison population by ethnicity. The male African-American prison population in 2005 was 3,145 inmates per 100,000 African-American males in the United States, while the white prison population was 471 inmates per 100,000 white males in the United States. There were 1,244 Hispanic males per 100,000 male Hispanics in the United States.

State prisoners are forced to serve their time in the jurisdiction where they committed their crimes. Federal prisoners serve their time in federal prisons within five hundred miles of their homes. Since they're sometimes incarcerated too far away for family members to visit, they're given the opportunity to transfer to prisons closer to their homes. Before they can apply for a transfer to another facility they must complete an orientation period, which instructs new prisoners about what they can expect during their incarceration. Some prison orientation periods last for one or two days while others may last for a few months. State prisoners aren't normally given an opportunity to transfer to other prisons.

U.S. Marshals normally transport federal prisoners who have been granted a transfer; however, in some cases prison officials may grant the inmate a "furlough transfer" where he's allowed to check out of prison and catch a bus, plane, or a ride with a family member or friend to the newly designated facility. This procedure is used quite often.

Some inmates are also granted brief furloughs to attend the funerals of family members or to receive hospital care or surgery. Some federal inmates even qualify for a furlough they can use just to go home for a period of up to three days. These furloughs are granted to a prisoner when he's nearing the end of his sentence. The prisoner's time at home is supposed to be used to re-establish family ties and to possibly line up post-incarceration employment.

When furloughs are granted for medical reasons, the costs for the medical procedures must be paid for by the inmate. The same is true for the costs incurred for a furlough transfer—the inmate or his family is required to pay all costs.

To qualify for this short amount of freedom, the inmate must be a model, low custody, nonviolent inmate who poses no risk for escape or harm to others. Of course, there have been instances where inmates have committed murder or failed to report to their new prisons while on furlough.

PRIVATELY RUN PRISONS

Federal and state prisons are operated with tax dollars and are a huge burden on government budgets. To ease the rising cost of prison operation, corrections officials of all levels have begun to utilize privately run facilities. Currently there are nearly twelve thousand federal inmates in such privately run prisons.

There's a stark contrast between state and federally operated prisons and the facilities that are privately run (the prisons for profit). Private institutions are in the business of making money and, like any business, the companies want to turn a profit. To do so, they must cut corners and save money by any means possible. These cuts sometime mean a reduction in staff, food and food quality, and medical care.

Prisoners are sometimes poorly fed and packed into tiny 5' × 8' cells with bunk beds sometimes stacked three high. Three or more prisoners now occupy spaces originally designed to house one.

CORRECTIONS OFFICERS

Corrections officers, or COs, work in prisons and jails. They generally receive less training and equipment to do a job that's equally as important as, and often more dangerous than, the job of a police officer who works the streets. Yet COs are expected to supervise the day-to-day lives of some of the most incorrigible human beings on the face of the earth. Ellen Proffitt, a former state corrections officer, said of her experience:

Working in a maximum security prison is demanding to say the least, especially for female officers working in an all-male facility. There's not a worse feeling in the world than hearing the clang of the steel doors as they lock behind you. That's when the realization hits that you are surrounded and outnumbered by dangerous inmates, two hundred to one. They could take over at any given time. It's frightening if you stop to think about it. I tried not to.

The position of a CO is thankless, dangerous, stressful, and often demeaning; therefore, the job turnover rate among prison security staff is quite high. There are other reasons for the high turnover rate: Some new officers simply can't handle being behind locked steel doors with hundreds of dangerous felons.

New officers sometimes become frightened or claustrophobic after a few hours of being behind the fences and walls and don't even finish their first day on the job. Many prison COs leave their jobs with the corrections departments to become police officers after using the prison system as a sort of stepping stone into the police business.

Some people feel the move from prison guard to police officer is a natural transition; however, many police officers don't feel this way about their prison guard counterparts and don't readily accept them into their fold. Some police officers feel that prison COs are inferior to them. In fact, many feel that the COs are working in a prison because they couldn't get a job with a "real" police department. Those officers feel that many of the COs are just cop wannabes.

These feelings of animosity may be due to the fact that prison COs don't have arrest powers and receive a different type of training that's not as intense or lengthy as police officer training. No how matter unjust or petty the reason, the feelings are there.

On the other side of the coin are the feelings of COs who make a valid point when they speak about the negative attitudes shown toward them by police officers. They feel that their jobs are equally as important, and rightly so. Police officers only have to deal with a violent offender for a few minutes—from the time of arrest until they tuck the crook safely away in a jail cell. Prison staff members must deal with that same offender, without restraints and surrounded by his gang buddies, 24 hours a day, 365 days a year. Each job has its own set of stressors, and each job is equally important. Still, the transition from CO to police officer is often a difficult one.

When a CO resigns or is out sick, his vacancy can create a hazardous situation. Prison officials can't allow any positions to remain vacant. When an officer quits, the administration must immediately hire someone to replace that person. Until the position is filled, staff members from other areas or shifts are called on to handle the job. In many instances this means that someone will have to work a double shift. This also occurs when someone calls in sick. Many prisons have a "draft" system in place to ensure that all positions are filled at all times.

The draft system works from a list of names of all employees on each shift. When an officer calls in sick at the last minute, a supervisor selects the name of the person on the outgoing shift who's next on the draft list. The selected person is required to fill the vacancy that's left by the sick employee from the oncoming shift, meaning that drafted person will have to work for sixteen hours, nonstop. He's also expected to return to work for his regularly scheduled shift the following day.

The draft system fills empty slots with warm bodies; however, the officers who work the draft are unprepared for the long hours and are often quite exhausted before their second eight-hour tour of duty is complete. It's important for security staff to remain alert at all times to prevent potentially dangerous situations from occurring. Unfortunately, exhaustion doesn't allow for a CO to remain as attentive as she could be, and an observant inmate with escape or murder on his mind could easily take advantage of the situation.

In order to keep the prison staffed at full capacity, the hiring process must sometimes be hurried. The incessant need to fill vacant officer positions can cause another type of security risk: hiring people who aren't quite suitable for the job.

Along with the haste of hiring comes an increase in the ratio of less-than-desirable security staff supervising inmates of above-average intelligence. This doesn't make for a good mix. The lesser-qualified officers are sometimes more easily influenced or duped into problem situations by the streetwise and highly educated inmates of today. This same employment problem can be found in almost any business, but when it occurs within a prison system the results can be deadly.

CORRECTIONS OFFICER TRAINING

Prison officials attempt to thwart the many problems they encounter by providing top-of-the-line training with highly skilled instructors, equipment, and training facilities. In some states, newly hired corrections officers attend a training academy where they're required to stay onsite throughout their training period. The length of training depends on the area or state. The state of Virginia, for example, requires their officers to attend a four-week basic certification course followed by a one-week follow-up class that's held after they've been on the job for six months. Every year thereafter they're required to attend a one-week in-service training class where they're updated on all new laws and security techniques.

A prison's staff operates much like a police agency, paramilitary style, so COs must undergo a boot camp-styled training regime. Newly hired COs attend corrections academies where they divide their time between classroom and hands-on training.

During the classroom training portion officers learn about the many cultural backgrounds and lifestyles of inmate populations. They learn how to identify potentially problematic situations; to properly implement crisis intervention and employee conflict management techniques; how to enforce laws and institutional rules and regulations; how to properly supervise prisoners; how to identify drugs and drug use by inmates; how to properly secure a crime scene; and how to handle evidence and other contraband.

Officers receive intensive hands-on training on handcuffing and other restraint device techniques, physical fitness training, military drills, riot squad formations and techniques, use of chemical agents and weapons, defensive tactics, use of batons, and cell searches.

Firearms Training

Like their police officer counterparts, COs are required to be proficient with firearms; however, the firearms training that's taught to COs is geared toward their specific need for weapons. COs are permitted to use deadly force to prevent the escape of inmates, and officers must learn to shoot various weapons from different vantage points in and around the institution. Corrections facilities don't allow firearms inside the institutions with the exception of those with secure gun turrets. These turrets allow COs to stop riots and quell officer-down emergencies. Firearms are normally carried by COs when they're transporting prisoners to and from court and medical appointments, or in gun and observation towers and on patrol of the prison perimeter.

During their firearms training sessions, most COs are taught to use revolvers or semiautomatic pistols, twelve-gauge shotguns, and rifles. They're taught how to disassemble, clean, and reassemble each firearm they're authorized to carry while on duty. The handgun carried by most COs is a .38 caliber revolver. Revolvers are the weapon of choice within most corrections systems because they're less expensive than semiautomatics and COs aren't normally faced with using deadly force on armed subjects; therefore, large numbers of bullets aren't needed.

Many prisons issue twelve-gauge pump-type shotguns similar to those carried by police officers. Automatic shotguns have a tendency to jam whereas pump shotguns don't under normal conditions.

The shotgun chosen for official use by most corrections and police agencies is the Remington 870 Wingmaster. Police officers prefer to use an eighteen-inch barrel on their 870s because most of their shooting situations are at close range. COs prefer a shotgun with a barrel length of eighteen to twenty inches for use during riots situations and a twenty-six-inch barrel for use on manhunts and road gang supervision. The lengthier barrel is much more accurate at longer distances than the short one. A shotgun with a full-length barrel can be fired accurately at distance of forty to sixty yards.

The ammunition used by COs in their shotguns varies. If the guns are used in riot situations, they're loaded with #8 bird shot. In situations where the officers are attempting to stop a fleeing inmate or are using the weapon to stop a prisoner's deadly assault on officers, they'd possibly load the shotgun with #4 buckshot. Shells loaded with buckshot have fewer pellets than those loaded with bird shot, but buckshot pellets are much larger. Bird shot is used in riot situations to quell a potentially dangerous situation. Buckshot is used stop an escaping inmate even if stopping him means killing him.

In addition to firing shotguns at silhouette targets, COs are expected to demonstrate efficiency in skip shooting. Skip shooting is the technique used to fire shotgun shell pellets at the legs of inmates during riot situations. The purpose of this technique is to subdue, not kill.

To perform the skip shooting technique, COs point their shotguns in the direction of the rioting prisoners, but downward at an angle toward the pavement, and then fire. The pellets immediately begin to spread out and, while ricocheting off the pavement, strike several prisoners at once. The technique doesn't require the CO to take the time to aim. When practicing skip shooting at the range, officers use full-size targets.

Some corrections departments conduct their own firearms training, such as the Clark County Sheriff's Office in Ohio. The sheriff's office in that southwestern county maintains a state-of-the-art indoor firing range manufactured by Mancom Manufacturing Incorporated of Canada. The range features self-healing tiles on each side wall, chunk-rubber backstops angled at thirty-seven degrees, electronic target retrieval systems, and elaborate lighting and exhaust systems. The entire range can be operated from within a control booth enclosed with bulletproof glass

The range's lighting system is capable of simulating daytime and night-time firing conditions as well as replicating situations where officers must shoot while strobe and rotating lights are flashing, such as inside nightclubs and in the light of their police vehicle light bars.

Strobe lights tend to give the impression that a stationary object, such as a suspect, is moving from side to side. Practice under these conditions could mean the difference between life and death for a police officer.

The wall tiles in the range can be shot straight-on from close range and the material heals instantly, leaving hardly a trace where the rounds entered. The tile material is so tough it's capable of receiving and stopping rounds of up to .50 caliber military machine gun. This is a unique range system because it features 360-degree target presentation, meaning that officers are able to fire in all directions, like they would have to do in real-life situations. The system is so impressive and advanced that it's used by the FBI Academy, the U.S. Customs and Border Protection Advanced Training Center, and the Drug Enforcement Administration.

The range didn't come cheap, but during President Clinton's administration the government released federal grant money for law enforcement agencies to aid them in the war against drugs. The Clark County Sheriff's Office purchased their indoor range for approximately $320,000, with a good deal of that money coming from the government grant.

Most corrections institutions are surrounded by high fences or walls with towers strategically placed around the perimeter of the prison, providing officers a bird's-eye view of all activities. Officers in the towers are issued rifles due to the possibility of having to stop escaping and rioting inmates from great distances.

While firing ranges like the Mancom ranges are invaluable when it comes to firearms training, they're not equipped to allow COs the opportunity to practice firing from different elevations. Therefore, many corrections academies have built towers on their outdoor ranges to allow officers the opportunity to practice rifle fire.

The types of rifles used by prison staff throughout the country vary. Many of the nation's prisons prefer the AR-15 semiautomatic rifle, the civilian version of the military's M16 rifle manufactured by Colt. The Colt rifle weighs less than eight pounds and fires a .223 caliber round accurately at distances up to five hundred yards—the length of five football fields.

Another popular rifle for use in corrections is the Ruger Mini-14, a three-foot-long, six-pound workhorse of a rifle. The Mini-14 is a little less accurate than the AR-15 but is an extremely reliable rifle mechanically.

Both rifles are capable of holding magazines containing many rounds of ammunition, but most prison policies require that five-round magazines be used.

Officers must practice firing these rifles quite a bit because of the various locations they could be shooting from. It's much more difficult to shoot accurately from an elevated position, such as a tower or catwalk, than on flat ground.

COs practice their shooting skills with all weapons in both day and nighttime conditions. To graduate from the academy, officers must qualify on the firing range with a score of 70 percent.

Upon successful completion of the basic officer's academy, the new COs are outfitted with little more than a can of pepper spray and a set of keys. Then they're immediately assigned to work one of three shifts: day, evening, or graveyard.

THE PRISONER'S JOURNEY

A defendant becomes a prisoner immediately after a judge imposes a prison sentence. He's usually held in the county jail until a cell or bed becomes available in the prison where he's been assigned to serve his sentence. As soon as a bed is available he's transferred from the county jail to prison.

NEW INMATE ARRIVAL

State prisoners are normally delivered to prison by deputy sheriffs from the county where the prisoner was convicted of her crimes; however, most nonviolent federal offenders are allowed to self-surrender to prison. As odd as this sounds, rarely does an offender not show up when and where she's supposed to. In the event that someone doesn't report to federal prison, she's considered an escapee and is immediately placed on the U.S. Marshal's "Wanted" list.

Sometimes, even after they've been found guilty and sentenced, the future federal inmates are allowed to return to their homes to get their affairs in order perhaps take care of a doctor's appointment or undergo surgery prior to reporting to their designated institution. This period could last for as short as a few days or for as long as several months, depending on the reason.

Under normal circumstances deputies deliver state prisoners to a reception center where the new inmate will be processed and receive an orientation to life in prison. U.S. Marshals are responsible for the transporting of federal prisoners.

It's a quite an eye-opening experience for the first-time prisoner when the police transportation van or car rounds the final turn leading to the prison (prisons are often at the end of a long, long road traveled only by those who have business with the prison). The first look at prison offers a view of massive concrete buildings surrounded by miles of high fences topped with looping wire tipped with thousands upon thousands of glimmering razors. If the sun catches those razors just right, and if you're far enough away, they give the appearance of diamonds floating in the air above the fences. If you're standing close to the fence, you can hear the wind causing the razors to vibrate and hum. A really hard wind makes the wobbling razor wire whistle. It's a constant nerve-wracking song that never ends.

As the driver gets closer, his prisoner catches his first glimpse of the rifle-toting officers who man the towers around the perimeter. The officers normally step outside onto their catwalks to see who's driving toward them. The tower officers are the first line of defense against intruders and the last line of defense against escapes and hostage situations. It's their main duty to stop either.

Tower officers never know who may be paying a visit. It could be someone coming to instigate an escape, or it could be a high-profile state official. Either way, they'll call inside to warn the appropriate people. No surprise visitors, friend or foe, ever make it inside a corrections facility.

Peering outside the window of the car, the prisoner is now close enough to see the various groups of inmates outside in the recreation yard. Many are walking laps around the track while others play basketball or soccer. Since weight-lifting has been banned from most institutions, several inmates can be seen bench pressing two pebble- or sand-filled laundry bags that are tied to either end of a mop handle. (Weightlifting and martial arts were banned to prevent prisoners from having a physical advantage over officers during altercations).

Most of the inmates pause to see the new arrival as the deputies turn and park in front of the prison entrance. They're sizing him up, and he knows it. This is where reality normally strikes the prisoner. The prisoner's fear is often evident by nervous chatter and forced laughter, hard swallowing, and sometimes shedding a tear or two. It's not uncommon for a deputy to offer the prisoner a cigarette to calm his nerves. It may be his last chance for a smoke since most of today's prisons are nonsmoking facilities. Tobacco products are now on prison black market lists along with drugs, alcohol, and weapons.

Guns aren't allowed inside prison walls by anyone other than officers inside caged gun turrets, so upon their arrival at the prison the deputies stop outside to lock their weapons in the trunk of their car. With their weapons secure, the deputies get back into their car and drive up to a set of double, fifteen-foot-high drive-through gates called a sally port. There, they're met by a CO who checks and verifies all paperwork regarding the newly arriving inmate. The sally port officer also has the responsibility of checking all vehicles belonging to vendors and maintenance workers.

The sally port is the weakest spot in the prison's outer shell because the gates have to be opened each time a delivery is made. The prison is extremely vulnerable when the gates are open because inmates have a brief opportunity to escape. The proper procedure for the opening of sally port gates is to open only one gate at a time, allow one vehicle to drive inside, close the first gate, search the vehicle and its occupants, and then open the second gate, allowing the vehicle to drive onto the prison grounds. Nonemployee vendors are escorted to their destinations inside the institution by COs.

When the sally port officer is sure that all the paperwork is in order, he radios to a control room, which is usually located in a nearby tower, to have the first gate opened. The deputies drive inside and the first gate is closed behind them, locking them and the vehicle inside the sally port. Inside, COs use mirrors attached to long poles to look beneath the car for secret compartments, items of contraband, and possible explosives. They also look inside the trunk and under the hood.

The prisoner is asked to step outside the car, where deputies remove all restraints. He and his paperwork are turned over to corrections officials. The officials sign a receipt stating that they've received the prisoner and then escort the inmate inside the building. Once the officers have the inmate safely inside the reception center the doors are locked, the outside gate is once again opened, and the deputies are free to leave.

The inmate is taken to a holding cell where he'll remain until he's processed. Processing a new prison inmate can take several hours, in some instances days, due to slowly arriving records or medical clearance. In some cases the prisoner may be problematic or suicidal. In many institutions, processing consists of strip-searching the new arrivals, medical evaluation, psychological evaluation, fingerprinting and photographing for inmate ID cards, and classification for the purpose of determining custody status. Some facilities require delousing, where the inmate is given a small cup of shampoo containing chemicals such as piperonyl butoxide and pyrethrum extract. In those facilities the inmate is ordered to shower and wash his scalp with the special shampoo. Officers watch to make certain the procedure was followed as ordered.

At some point during the reception and orientation process new inmates are issued prison clothing, which normally consists of three white T-shirts, three pairs of white boxer shorts, three pairs of white socks, three institutional shirts, three pairs of institutional pants, and a pair of work boots. Inmates wishing to purchase any additional items of clothing, such as new underwear, may do so through the prison commissary once they leave the reception center and have been assigned to regular housing within the prison. To prevent inmates from blending in with prison staff and leaving the institution undetected, possession of regular street clothing by prisoners isn't permitted.

Many institutions segregate all new inmates until an orientation program has been successfully completed. Orientation teaches inmates prison rules and regulations and the consequences of not adhering to those policies. New inmates are also schooled about life in prison and what to expect during their time behind bars. Each inmate is assigned an ID number that will be used throughout his incarceration. The number prevents future mix-ups between two or more prisoners having the same name. All inmates are required to memorize their prison ID numbers.

All prisoners must work during their incarceration, so department heads sometimes attend orientation programs to explain the various prison job assignments. Some of the jobs available to inmates are carpentry, plumbing, painting, gardening and landscaping, electrical, automobile maintenance, janitorial services, cooking, dishwashing, warehouse labor, shipping and receiving clerk, tool room clerk, timekeeper, record keeper, chapel clerk, librarian, classroom instructor, recreation clerk, and cell block or dormitory orderly. Prisoners are allowed to apply for the job of their choice if there's an opening. Inmates who aren't qualified or don't fit into any these job categories may be assigned to menial chores.

Inmates are classified according to the length of their sentence, security and escape risk potential, educational level, social skills (ability to get along with others), and their medical and psychological well-being. The classification systems vary from state to state, but they're all similar in nature. Some systems prefer to use numerical rankings while others use alphabetical ranking systems.

Level one or "A" custody inmates are at the bottom of the classification system, meaning they pose the least amount of threat to staff members and other inmates. Inmates who are classified at the lower end of the scale may also receive less supervision. At the top of the classification system are level four or "D" custody inmates. Higher-level inmates are possible escape risks and potentially violent. They're never left alone or unescorted. In the federal prison system, nearly 65 percent of the population is comprised of low- and medium-security inmates, and most—54 percent—are nonviolent drug offenders. The majority of sentences for offenders range between five and ten years in length.

Prisons are built with those custody-status levels in mind. The Supermax prisons, such as the U.S. Penitentiary in Marion, Illinois, and the U.S. Penitentiary Administrative Maximum Facility in Florence, Colorado, were designed and built to house the worst of the worst. We'll take a closer look at these prisons on page 306.

With the classification and orientation complete, inmates are assigned to housing units according to their custody status. Prison administrators attempt to keep all similarly classified inmates together. Inmates are also sometimes transferred from reception centers to other institutions that may be more suitable to particular custody statuses. For example, a physically handicapped in-

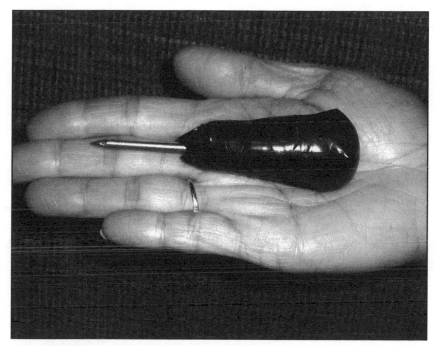

A homemade weapon made from a sharpened nail and electrical tape.

mate may need to be transferred to a facility with areas that are more handi-capped accessible.

LIFE INSIDE

Prison life is tough. Don't let the rumors of Club Fed-type prisons fool you. There are some institutions such as prison camps that are a bit softer on inmates than others, but even in the best of situations, prison life isn't fun.

Most prison populations are controlled by internal gangs, many of which still have strong connections with the outside world. Those gangs are led by inmates called generals or shot callers. The generals have subordinates who deliver their orders to the lowest level of inmates in the gang's chain of command, the soldiers. A prison gang's soldiers do the dirty work. They smuggle in drugs and alcohol and make weapons. They protect the generals and will kill other inmates and prison staff if the generals order them to. They don't question their orders because to do so would mean certain death for the inmate who refuses.

A new inmate must learn the rules of all gangs in order to survive. He may not walk through an area that's been claimed by a gang, and he may not shower in a stall that's reserved by a gang. He must eat at certain tables in the dining hall; he can't use certain sports equipment; he can't speak directly to certain inmates; he must pay for protection; and he must never, ever tell on another inmate. Snitching almost always results in assault or death.

INMATE DISCIPLINE

In addition to unwritten inmate rules, prisoners are required to learn a set of prison rules and regulations. Each inmate must obey these rules during her incarceration. Any violation of these rules can result in disciplinary action and even a loss of good time (time off their sentences for good behavior, called earned good time credit). These institutional rules are divided into categories according to their seriousness.

The Virginia Department of Corrections, for example, lists its offenses in numerical categories. Offenses in the 100 series are the most serious of all offenses followed by the lesser groupings of the 200 series, 300 series, and the 400 series (work-release violations) of offenses.

Offenses in the 100 series, such as escape, rioting, assault, narcotics possession, making sexual advances, and murder, are also considered street crimes, meaning that the offender can be charged and tried with the crime in an outside court of law.

The 200 series contains offenses such as refusing to work and refusing to obey a direct order. Pretending to be sick, hiding, fighting, possessing money of any kind, and lying to a prison employee fall into this category.

The 300 series contains minor offenses, such as failing to clean one's quarters, unexcused absence from school, and unauthorized use of prison tools and equipment.

Some inmates are permitted to work regular jobs outside of the prison walls. This is a rare occurrence and is usually permitted only under a judge's order. Inmates who work outside jobs are normally working to pay outstanding debts such as child support and court fines. The 400 series contains offenses that apply to inmates on such work-release programs. Loss of employment, visiting a private residence, riding in a private vehicle without permission, and establishing a line of credit without permission are all violations of the 400 series of work-release rules.

When staff members—including security personnel, doctors, nurses, librarians, teachers, administrative employees, etc.—find an inmate to be in violation of a prison rule, they fill out a disciplinary form, called a write-up or shot, and submit it to the current officer in charge (OIC). The OIC reviews the form, making sure it contains all pertinent information, such as the correct date, time, location of the offense, and a complete, detailed description of the offense. Missing or incorrect information could result in the charge

The "hole."

getting dismissed at the internal hearing, so when the OIC determines that the form has been properly completed, it's submitted to a hearings officer, who sets a date to hear the case. A copy of the form along with notification of the hearing date is given to the inmate. Depending on the severity of the offense, inmates may be confined to an isolation cell until their hearing.

The inmate may choose to have someone, either another inmate or a staff member, represent her as counsel during the hearing. In most cases, staff members decline to represent an inmate in these proceedings. Inmates aren't allowed to have attorneys represent them during an institutional hearing.

The hearings are informal but allow each side to present evidence and witnesses on their behalf. At the conclusion of the hearing, the hearings officer makes a decision of guilt or innocence. If the finding is one of innocence, the charge is removed from the inmate's record. If the inmate is found to be guilty, the hearings officer must decide on a sentence.

There are specific sentences that can be ordered for each group of offenses. With a guilty verdict stemming from a 100 series offense, an inmate can receive a loss of all or part of his earned good time, or he can be placed in isolation where he's stripped of all privileges and must remain on total lockdown in a cell isolated within a remote area of the prison. A cell such as this is called the "hole." Inmates think of this as the ultimate punishment and try to avoid being placed there. The normal sentence to The Hole is one to fifteen days. Repeat offenders or violent inmates may remain in The Hole indefinitely.

Minor offenses can result in the inmate losing telephone privileges or personal items, such as radios, televisions, or typewriters. Unruly inmates are sometimes restrained in the "chair." The chair is equipped with nylon restraints that hold the inmate securely in place.

The "chair."

An inmate's institutional record is a permanent record and may be viewed by his probation or parole officer once he's released from prison. An unfavorable record may cause the probation officer to watch a former inmate more closely than one who abided by all prison rules and regulations.

No matter the consequences for committing offenses, inmates still attempt to do things against the rules and things that are illegal. To make the commission of these offenses a bit easier, many inmates try to find a staff member who may be willing to help them. They study individual employees, trying to learn their unique personalities and habits. They soon know which employees may be sympathetic to their wants and needs.

Every day, they pick up tiny bits of information until they know which employees they can control and possibly use in some way. Unfortunately, it's most often an employee who brings dangerous contraband inside to the prisoners. Officers have been caught smuggling in items ranging from food items and weapons, and they've even been caught allowing the prisoners to have sex. Some employees have even been caught having sex with inmates.

CELLS AND DORMITORIES

Not all prisons house their inmates in individual cells. Some of the lower-security prisons use a dormitory system where anywhere from a few dozen to more than one hundred inmates sleep in bunk beds inside one large, open room.

Some prison dormitories are equipped with enclosed showers; sinks for shaving; instant hot water dispensers for coffee, soup, and hot chocolate; ice machines; laundry rooms equipped with washers, dryers, irons, and ironing boards; and a room containing microwaves where inmates can get pretty creative with recipes. They make nachos, burritos, spaghetti, meatloaf (with meat stolen from the kitchen), and various chicken dishes (again, with meat stolen from the kitchen). There are also small rooms for watching television as well as a large multipurpose room called a dayroom for playing cards and board games, and for watching special TV programs and movies.

Certain groups of inmates normally take it upon themselves to claim each TV room. For example, a dormitory containing three separate TV rooms may be divided by race with Hispanics in one, African-Americans in another, and whites and other races in the third. It's considered a violation of inmate code for a person of a particular race or group to enter the TV room of another. Fights or death could be the result of such an intrusion. To keep the noise level at a minimum, televisions in most prison TV and dayrooms don't have speakers. Instead, the prison transmits the audio portion via a weak radio signal that can be received through a portable radio and headset. Each inmate must purchase his own radio from the prison commissary.

Nearly all inmates in every prison own a portable personal radio. In fact, these radios are considered status symbols—the better the radio, the wealthier the inmate. The same holds true for tennis shoes. The more expensive the shoes, the higher the prisoner is on the inmate ladder of status. Prisoners have been savagely attacked and even killed over these two items.

Each morning, the inmates are awakened by an announcement or the sound of a ringing bell or buzzer. Inmates must make their bunks properly, and no inmate is allowed to remain in his bed for any reason other than illness. Some jails require inmates to remove their mattresses from their individual cells and place them on the floor of the day room during daytime hours. When all mattresses and inmates are out of their cells, the cell doors are locked until evening. This procedure is done to enable officers to see the inmates at all times other than when they're sleeping. It also prevents the inmates from conducting any

Inside a female inmate's dormitory.

unauthorized and illegal activities inside their dark cells, such as rape and assault. If an inmate becomes ill, he must have a written order from a doctor to be excused from work and school assignments.

JOB ASSIGNMENTS

As noted earlier in the chapter, each inmate is assigned a routine task as a job assignment. The assignments vary in nature and range from picking up trash for a few minutes a day to working as a prison cook.

Prisons and jails maintain their own maintenance workforce made up of inmate labor. The inmates perform all electrical work, carpentry, plumbing, painting, automobile repairs, landscaping, heating and air conditioning repair and installation, and concrete and masonry work. A staff member skilled in each particular trade area supervises the individual inmate crews.

Work crews have even been assigned to build entire facilities in some parts of the country at an enormous saving for the government. Inmates are paid anywhere from $.12 to $1.15 per hour. In certain cases, small monthly bonuses are awarded for exemplary work. An inmate must possess a GED or higher educational level to receive more than the basic wage. Prisoners also must use their salaries to make payments on court fines and fees and other financial responsibilities such as child support. During holiday seasons many inmates donate portions of their wages to charities.

A few prisoners use the remainder of their day to take advantage of educational classes, but the majorities choose to engage in recreational activities of some sort. Inmates who don't have written proof that they completed high school are required, at a minimum, to complete a 240-hour GED program prior to release, and they must participate in classes on parenting, substance-abuse prevention (if their offense involved drugs or alcohol), and résumé preparation.

Local community colleges are paid by the government to supply instructors for a variety of continuing education programs. The inmates that take advantage of the educational programs often earn associate and bachelor degrees in general studies. Prisoners are responsible for the cost of the college coursework.

Computer classes, such as word processing, are offered at many prisons, but inmates aren't allowed Internet access, nor are they allowed to have computer disks in their possession. The disks are checked in and out daily, like library books, from the instructors. If the inmates were allowed control of a disk it would be a simple matter for them to send and receive illegal information to outside sources.

INMATE CURRENCY

Since prisoners aren't allowed to possess cash money, they've devised their own currency. In the days when smoking was allowed in prisons, cigarettes were used as money. Now, most institutions have banned smoking, so prisoners had to come up with a new currency. Today, all prisoners use U.S. postage stamps as money. Each stamp is worth fifty cents, and an entire book of stamps is equal to a ten-dollar bill.

Prisoners need their currency to survive. They operate on an illegal supply and demand system, and they're paid in stamps for the work they do for other inmates. It's against all rules and regulations for inmates to charge other inmates for anything, but they do. Some of the services inmates charge for are cooking, cleaning (cells or dormitory areas), washing and ironing clothes, shining shoes, and stealing food from the kitchen. Inmate clerks working in the prison libraries and chaplain's offices make copies for other prisoners, and inmate barbers cut hair. Some sample prices for illegal inmate services and goods include:

- Washing clothes: four stamps per load
- Shoeshine: two stamps
- Clean cell: one book per week
- Cook meals: four stamps per meal
- Make copies: two stamps per twenty pages (The prison library charges inmates for copies. The money is deducted from their personal accounts.)
- Bottle of wine or liquor: five books
- A piece of dining hall cake: two stamps
- Tattoo: eight to ten books depending on the size
- Marijuana (one joint): five books
- Pair of tennis shoes: ten books
- Knife or shank: ten books
- Oral sex: one book

Some inmates run prison "stores." They buy goods from the prison commissary and resell them, for stamps, to other prisoners who don't have money in their accounts.

Inmates are allowed to receive funds from friends and family, and they're paid for working their prison jobs. The money they receive is placed into an account that they're allowed to draw from by using their ID card, which is similar to a bank ATM or debit card. They're allowed to spend their money in the prison commissary. They can also send money home to their families and can use it to pay court fines and restitution. Their prison ID number must accompany all transactions.

Prison commissaries, where inmates are usually allowed to shop once a week, offer a large selection of goods. Some of the items available for purchase are:

Soft drinks	Sewing supplies
Ice cream	Laundry detergent
Candy	Work shoes
Cookies	Alarm clocks

Cakes	Pencils
Pasta	Canned meats
Tomato sauce	Plastic forks and spoons
Fresh vegetables	Plastic food containers
Tennis shoes	Chips
Tennis balls	Pretzels
Radios	Tortillas
Fruit	Tea
Socks	Coffee
Underwear	Prepaid telephone minutes
Postage stamps	Greeting cards
Stationery	Processed summer sausage

RECREATION

Each prison has a recreation director who oversees the recreational department and arranges programs, sporting events, games, and matches. The recreation supervisor oversees activities such as tennis, golf, basketball, football, soccer, softball, chess, checkers, and backgammon tournaments; picnics; and musical programs. The prisoners play all games on regulation fields and courts with the best of equipment. (It seems odd that so much money is spent on recreation when food and medical care sometimes go lacking.) All players wear uniforms, as do the inmate referees and umpires. Federal prisons used to have swimming pools for the inmate population, but public outcry and civil liability finally forced prison officials to fill them with dirt and concrete.

It's common to see inmates prepping their football or soccer fields by marking the goal and yard lines with lime, while other prisoners lounge around listening to portable radios and tanning in the sun. The regulation-size track encompassing the ball fields is a hub of daily activity. Inmates walk lap after lap, not only for exercise, but also as a means of communicating with one another without being overheard by staff members and corrections officers. The recreation yard is the one place where the prisoners have near-freedom, where the prisoners greatly outnumber the guards, and supervision is at a minimum or nearly nonexistent.

MEALS

Breakfast and lunch are the two busiest times of the day for the prison kitchen staff. These are also two very dangerous times for the prison security staff because these are two times when the largest gathering of inmates is assembled. The evening meals are normally not attended by as many inmates because the meals aren't as good as the other two, so the inmates cook their own food in their dormitories or cells. (In all prisons other than Supermax prisons, where inmates are locked down twenty-four hours a day, the recreation yards are open for all prisoners after the 4:00 P.M. count has cleared. They're normally allowed full access to the entire area—recreation areas, gym, library, music rooms, chapel, arts and crafts, etc.)

Prison kitchens serve special meals for each holiday. These meals are based on the cultural aspect of the holiday and are attended by nearly all inmates. For example, on Cinco de Mayo (Spanish for "fifth of May"), the Mexican holiday celebrating Mexico's defeat of French forces in 1862, federal prisons serve a complete, authentic Mexican meal.

Some federal prisons offer cooking classes. Those facilities serve some of the best meals in the entire prison system. In fact, these institutions are high on the list when it comes to inmates requesting transfers.

There are federal prisons that serve wonderful food. They have complete salad and beverage bars, and the inmates are given a choice of the meat and vegetables they prefer.

PILL CALL

Three times each day, early morning, noon, and 7:30 P.M., the prison medical department holds pill call. This event is the high point of the day for many inmates. It's the time when they receive their much-needed and often-desired medications. Lines outside the medical department begin to form as early as thirty minutes before the doors open.

Inside, nurses insert a single dose of each inmate's medication in a small envelope. When the doors to the medical office are finally opened, the inmates begin to file inside one at a time. They're given their designated envelope along with a small cup of water. They're required to swallow the medication and water while inside the department. A corrections officer is on hand to observe the procedure. After swallowing their medicine, the inmates are required to face the officer, open their mouths, and lift their tongues. Once the officer is satisfied that an inmate has swallowed the pills he's free to return to his designated area.

Today, a great number of prisoners are heavily medicated with drugs such as chlorpromazine (Thorazine), sertraline (Zoloft), trazodone (Desyrel), and alprazolam (Xanax). These drugs are prescribed to calm the prisoners; when they're too tranquil, other drugs are given to perk them up. Ironically, for the vast majority of prisoners, the cycle of using mood- and mind-altering drugs is precisely the reason they're incarcerated in the first place. It's an unending circle.

Some prisons offer excellent medical care and treatment. In these institutions the prisoners are treated with the same care and compassion as are honest citizens on the outside. In fact, some of the medical care given to prisoners has become a subject of recent controversy. Incarcerated individuals have received heart, liver, and kidney transplants, invoking anger among law-abiding persons who themselves are in need of those life-giving organs but can't afford the procedure or locate a donor. Public opinion seems to favor giving those outside prison walls first priority in receiving the donated organs.

VISITORS

Visitation from family and friends is encouraged by prison officials. For rehabilitation purposes it's important for inmates to maintain strong family ties. Regular visits are also good for the temperament of inmates. Inmates who don't receive regular visits are often withdrawn, depressed, and ill-tempered.

Most prisons allow inmates to receive visitors on weekends (some allow weekday visits). Some prisons use open visiting rooms that are much like a high school cafeteria. In these rooms, inmates and visitors are allowed to sit at a table together. Spouses are allowed a brief hug and kiss at the beginning of their visits and another at the end. If time and space allow, some prisons allow prisoners to visit an entire day. Most prisons have a one- or two-hour time limit. Children of all ages are permitted to visit.

In the higher-security facilities inmates may only be allowed to visit for a few minutes. They also may only be allowed to visit while seated in a small booth while their loved one is seated on the opposite side of a small window. They speak to one another via telephone.

Inmates are strip-searched before entering visiting rooms and again when they leave. Visitors are also subject to being searched. If they refuse, they aren't allowed to visit. Former inmates who are still on probation or parole may not visit a prison inmate.

It's not unusual to see inmates sitting alone and crying once they've returned to their cells after a visit. It's hard for them to say goodbye.

THE END OF THE DAY

Prisoners complete the workday around 3:00 P.M. and must be inside their cells or dorms before 4:00 P.M. At prisons all across the country, at precisely 4:00 P.M. all inmates are required to stand beside their beds for an official head count. They can't talk or move during this standing count. Policy requires that two officers from each section of the prison conduct a count in their area. At the commencement of count time, one officer yells, "Count," which is the signal to the inmates that the procedure's begun.

The first officer walks through the designated area (a dorm or cell block) and counts each inmate. When he's finished the second officer walks through, counting. The two officers compare totals and if they agree, the number is called in to the main control office. The tally for the entire prison is called in to a state office where the total for the entire state is verified. In the federal system, the number is verified for the entire country. Anyone violating the count rules (a very serious offense) is taken to The Hole immediately after the completion of the count.

Any discrepancy in the final total requires a second count. If it's determined that an inmate is absent, the entire prison is locked down, the inmates are confined to their cells or dorms, and a search for the missing inmate commences immediately.

After the count is completed, evenings and nights in a prison are times of relaxation for the prisoners. Inmates play sports, cards, watch television, and exercise. Some visit with other inmates recounting the day's activities or reminiscing about life on the outside. Others use the time to call family members from one of the pay phones located with their own dorms (inmates aren't allowed to visit other dorms).

The phone system operates in one of two ways. Prisoners can make a collect call, which normally costs the recipient of the call several dollars per minute (many times the price of calls on the outside). The phone systems in prisons are owned by private companies, and they make a huge profit from each collect call made.

The other way an inmate can place a phone call is through money in his personal account, an account where family members and friends can make deposits. The prison also deposits the inmate's pay into this account. When the inmate places a direct call, funds are automatically deducted from his account on a minute-by-minute basis. Fees for calls made directly are the same as the fees charged on the outside.

Some inmates busy themselves with legitimate activities during the evening hours, such as letter writing, reading, attending church services, choir practice, and playing musical instruments. Evening is also the time when most of the prison's illegal activities occur. It's the time when drugs are sold and used, weapons are made and sold, stabbings occur, homemade wine ("hooch" or "pruno") is made and/or consumed, inmates have sexual encounters, and, in some cases, inmates escape, especially from prison camps where there are no fences or walls. The night ends at 10:00 P.M. when the final count for the evening is held. Inmates aren't required to stand for this count, but they're required to be in their immediate bed area. When 10:00 P.M. count is complete, the lights are turned out for the night.

This day and night cycle of activity is repeated, without change, for the duration of an inmate's incarceration. The only thing that changes is the calendar that most prisoners have hanging on their wall. A favorite saying that's used by prisoners is, "The man can take away everything I've got, but they can't stop my time."

THE LAST DAYS OF CONFINEMENT

Friendships and strong bonds are developed in prison, and when an inmate's release date arrives it's not only a time of joy but a moment of sadness. She wants to leave, but at the same time she hates to leave her close friends behind. Fear is also an emotion felt by many inmates as they prepare to walk outside the prison gates for the first time in many years. They're scared of what the outside world has become since they left it so long ago.

For many, they've never seen a cell phone or a computer. The last car they remember driving had the headlight dimmer switch in the floorboard that was operated with the driver's left foot. Money doesn't look the same, and there was no such thing as a debit card when many prisoners began to serve their sentences.

INTERESTING PRISON FACTS

- Inmates stand in long lines on "chicken day" to receive a rare treat of real meat—bone-in portions of chicken, usually leg quarters.

- Prisoners receive a dessert with each meal.

- Some prisons have a salad bar and a choice of beverages with the evening meal.

- A shank, or shiv, is a knife fashioned from items such as a toothbrush, razor blade, or hard plastic or sharpened metal. The handle is usually wrapped with masking or duct tape stolen from a work crew.

- Hooch, or pruno, is a crude alcoholic beverage made from fermented fruit (inmates can buy fruit from the prison commissary). Sliced bread is placed into the mixture as a substitute for yeast.

- Shorty is a nickname used by inmates for all women.

- Juan and Jody are two universal nicknames used by prisoners for the lovers their wives take on while the husbands are incarcerated.

- Inmates must knock on a table like knocking on a door before standing as a sign of respect to those convicts left seated.

- Prisoners aren't allowed to cut in front of anyone standing in line for anything. It's a sign of disrespect and could result in the death of the line-breaker.

- Prisons offer current movies on weekends for the prisoners.

- The term "big house" is no longer used when referring to a prison.

- Foggy weather is the time when many prisoners choose to escape so they can use the fog as a means of concealment.

- The term "screw" when referring to a guard is no longer used.

- The term "turnkey" is no longer used when referring to a guard.

- The majority of sexual contact between inmates occurs in the shower.

- Inmates toast grilled-cheese sandwiches in their dorms or cells by first placing an uncooked sandwich between two sheets of notebook paper. Then they hold a hot steam iron against the side facing up until the bread begins to brown (the paper traps in moisture and prevents the bread from burning). The sandwich is flipped over and the process is repeated until the cheese begins to melt. Inmates aren't allowed to possess any food products containing yeast; therefore, the bread and cheese to make these sandwiches must be stolen from the prison kitchen.

- Inmates sometimes actually pop popcorn inside the prison's industrial clothes dryers.

- Coffee can be heated inside a jail cell using a nail and a short piece of wire. The inmate wraps one end of the wire around the nail and then places the nail into a cup of coffee. The other end of the wire is inserted into an electrical outlet. The electricity flowing to the nail generates heat that warms the coffee.

They're afraid of coming back, yet many of them know they will because they don't know how to exist in a different world.

COMING BACK

Recidivism is at an all-time high—less than half of all released felons succeed on probation or parole. In many instances, felons return to criminal activity soon after they're released from prison. Police officers know this and focus their attention on the former inmates when they return to their old neighborhoods. It's a distressing sequence that never ends.

The prison population has become an older population due to long mandatory minimum sentences for even nonviolent crimes. The average male inmate is approximately thirty-seven years old. The incarceration rate in the United States is 482 per 100,000 residents. Louisiana, Mississippi, Oklahoma, and Texas lead the country with near-double incarceration rates while Maine, Minnesota, and North Dakota fall well below the national average. Texas and California house nearly one-third of all incarcerated females in the country.

SUPERMAX PRISONS

Supermax prisons are the ultimate in prison security. These prisons were built and designed to house the most dangerous inmates in the country. Inside the Supermax, prisoners aren't allowed to have social contact with humans, other than with guards at count times, shower times, and meal times. There are no work assignments for the general population. Inmate mail in these Supermax prisons is heavily censored, and the prisoners' religious activities are restricted. The inmates spend their entire sentence time at a Supermax prison behind solid steel doors.

The inmates are locked down twenty-three hours a day, at minimum, and are allowed out of their single cells for showering only two or three times per week at the discretion of the guards. When an inmate is allowed to take a shower, his hands and feet are firmly shackled and he's escorted to the shower area by a minimum of two guards. The guards remain with the prisoner for his twenty-minute shower time, and then they return him to his cell. Shaving is normally allowed once per week. The inmates are allowed outside their cells for one hour of recreation per day. Their recreation time is spent inside a small cage much like a dog pen.

Supermax prisons have been under scrutiny since their inception, for many reasons, and their use as a means of punishment has been a hotly debated subject. A prisoner may be sent to one of these prisons as retribution for rule infractions committed at other institutions.

A well-known form of inmate punishment (among the inmates and staff members) is "diesel therapy." Diesel therapy is the transferring of an inmate from one prison facility to another, time after time, day after day, without allowing the inmate to become settled or rested, or to become involved in treatments or activities offered to other inmates. These transfers normally begin in the wee hours of the morning and end sometime late the following evening, at which time the convict must spend the night in a county jail until the travel sequence can begin again. This cycle repeats sometimes for weeks, even months, until the inmate reaches a final destination, usually the dreaded Supermax. It's an expensive form of punishment, but it's used quite often.

PRISON CAMPS

On the other end of the spectrum are prison camps. The camps are usually located just outside the more secure facilities, and the inmates housed in these prisons-without-fences are the supporting workforce for the top-security prison. The camp inmates are low-risk individuals who are nearing the end of their sentences; in federal facilities, that means less than ten years.

Convicts at federal prison camps perform a wide spectrum of nearly free labor, working for as little as twelve cents an hour. In some institutions, the prisoners work as clerks in the medical units, warden's offices, and recreation departments. They teach classes in the schools and preach in the chapels. The inmates even serve as florists, supplying flower arrangements for prison parties, meetings, and for the desks of the employees.

If an inmate's sentence is for less than ten years, and the newly convicted felon is nonviolent, he may be assigned to serve his sentence at one of the federal prison camps located throughout the country. An inmate who's served the majority of his time and has less than ten years remaining on his sentence may also be transferred to a prison camp.

Camp operations differ from camp to camp. The personality of the warden and his staff is often reflected in the mood or ambiance of the camp, and the campers, as the long-timers and the staff call them, react accordingly to the atmosphere. Some facilities are operated by the book, and the residents toe that line. Others are quite relaxed, and the inmates are given nearly free rein to do as they please. Tales of such loosely run camps are passed among inmates, as prison officials move them throughout the country. It soon becomes the goal of prisoners to be transferred to one of these so-called Club Feds.

CHAPTER 14

CON AIR:
COFFEE, TEA, OR HANDCUFF KEY?

It's never been part of my plan to be a guest of the federal prison system. Now I have an entirely new and totally compelling reason why.

—*S.J. Rozan, Edgar Award-Winning Author of In This Rain*

The day-to-day operations of law enforcement are apparent to everyone, but there's one major law enforcement operation the majority of the public doesn't know exists—it's the mass prisoner transit system operated by the Federal Bureau of Prisons and the U.S. Marshals Service.

With today's federal prison population at a record high—just over 190,000 inmates locked away in more than 100 facilities—finding a place to house these men and women is indeed an increasing problem. In addition, getting those prisoners to their destinations and to and from court hearings is a massive undertaking that requires complex planning and the implementation of top security procedures.

The federal prison system is quite a bit different than local prisons and jails. A federal inmate may commit a crime in Massachusetts but be incarcerated, for whatever reason, in another state as far away as California. During his stay in prison, the inmate may have to make several court appearances in the federal courthouse in Boston; therefore, the need to transport the felon comes into play. On any given day of the week, hundreds upon hundreds of inmates are transported to new destinations and to courts throughout the country.

The long-distance transporting is done in unmarked passenger jets flown by the U.S. Marshals Service (this "airline" is unofficially known as Con Air). It's their job to ensure the safe transport of incarcerated men and women. The government jets take off and land at military bases or in remote landing strips inaccessible to the public. These clandestine departures and landings are done under the supervision of a heavily armed collection of officers from police agencies such as the Federal Bureau of Prisons, sheriff's deputies, city police officers, and special agents of the Federal Bureau of Investigation and the U.S. Marshals Service. When these jets land, they're immediately surrounded by dozens of officers armed with high-powered rifles, shotguns, and fully automatic weapons.

PREPARING THE PRISONERS FOR TRANSPORT

A federal inmate begins his journey in the early morning. He's not told of his departure in advance so he can't make plans for escape. The prisoner is awakened around 3:00 A.M. and told to get dressed at once; he's not allowed to shower or eat breakfast. He's ordered to gather up all his belongings, including his mattress and pillow. His scant possessions are placed on the center of a mattress and rolled into a single bundle. In inmate culture, this is known as being "rolled up." His belongings are placed into storage until his return. If the trip is a permanent transfer, his things will be boxed up (an inmate's possessions fit into a single cardboard box) and sent along with him.

He's then taken to a holding cell to await the transportation team, a group of officers specifically assigned to transportation duties. Every morning, the transportation holding cells are filled beyond capacity as inmates from various sections of the prison are brought one by one to await departure. Each inmate is given special transport clothing—a pair of thin, elastic-waist khaki pants, a white T-shirt, a pair of blue canvas slip-on sneakers, and a pair of thin boxer shorts. Officers reach into large boxes of clothing and hand whatever comes out to the prisoners. These items usually aren't the correct size—not even close—and the ill-fitting clothing sometimes gives the prisoners a comical appearance.

The inmates huddle together, like cattle, in a holding cell that's ironically called a bullpen, which is an oversized cell with metal or wooden benches attached to the wall instead of a bed. The transport teams arrive and toss handcuffs, leg irons, and waist chains onto the floor in front of the bullpen. The sound of metal clanging can be heard echoing throughout the silence of the deserted hallways of the prison.

A guard calls out names from a preprinted roster. Each inmate acknowledges his name by approaching the cell door. He holds his hands through a slot in the bars to allow his wrists to be handcuffed. Once the inmate is cuffed, he's brought out, strip-searched, and the shackling is completed by clamping leg irons (oversized handcuffs) to his ankles. A heavy chain is also placed around his waist that's attached to the handcuffs and leg irons. The waist chain reduces movement of the inmate's arms, feet, and hands. All inmates, regardless of their custody status, are restrained in the same manner.

An additional device called a "black box" is locked over the handcuff chain of inmates who pose a high risk for transport security and safety. The black box was, ironically, designed by a former inmate. It totally eliminates hand movement and covers the keyholes on handcuffs. It's secured to the wrist and handcuffs with a separate heavy-duty padlock. The high-risk inmate is kept separate, usually in the front of the plane, from the lower-custody-status inmates for the duration of the trip.

The shackled inmates are lined up single-file along a wall leading to a sally port, (a fenced-in, secure drive-through area for loading and unloading prisoners). Once all the prisoners are properly secured, a head count is taken and the prisoners are loaded into preassigned vans—men and women together.

The hidden airports used by the U.S. Marshals Service can sometimes be several hours away from some prisons, making the journey extremely uncomfortable for all involved. During the trips, transportation officers make stops for coffee, donuts, meals, and bathroom breaks, but the inmates are usually forced to wait in the back of a van that's sometimes quite cold or scorching hot, depending on the season.

AWAITING DEPARTURE

Arriving at the airstrip can be a shocking event for the inmates making this trip for the first time. At this point they still don't know where they're going or why, and to see the vast array of heavily armed officers with machine guns and shotguns can be extremely intimidating.

While waiting for the incoming jets, officers nervously scan the horizon for any unusual activity and people, and their faces reflect the seriousness of the situation. At this moment during transport, the officers are quite vulnerable to a deadly escape attempt.

The wait for the plane also can be unbearable for prisoners who haven't eaten or seen the inside of a restroom for nearly twelve hours. Gradually, more and more vans, buses, and police vehicles line the airfield beside the runway until finally an SUV, driven by a U.S. marshal, rolls onto the runway to alert everyone that the jet's about to land.

Obvious anxiety washes across the faces of the police officers as the big passenger jet ambles down the runway until it rolls slowly to a stop in front of the idling police vehicles. The giant engines continue to snarl as a fuel truck fills the tanks and then moves away. The rear steps lower to the pavement, allowing a team of air marshals (the only officers allowed on the plane) to make their way down the steps amid the wind and roar of the turbines.

The marshals wear light blue golf shirts displaying the U.S. Marshals Service logo, dark blue cargo-style pants, and military-style jump boots. They also wear earplugs to provide protection from the constant roar of the jet engines.

BOARDING AND DEBOARDING THE PLANE

The air marshal in charge of the flight crew meets with the officer in charge on the ground for a moment, and then the process begins of exchanging prisoners already seated on the plane with the new inmates in the vehicles. This procedure is painstakingly carried out, one inmate at a time, until the one hundred and forty or so tattered and filthy plane seats are filled. The prisoners aren't allowed to talk or stand once they're on board, and using the restrooms isn't permitted unless they're directed to do so by a marshal. The inmates can't reach the ceiling air vents so they normally remain in their original positions.

Officers on the plane issue each prisoner a brown paper bag containing food for what could possibly be a sixteen-hour day. Inside the bag are a four-ounce container of water, an apple, and two packages of peanut butter crackers. Sometimes a granola bar is tossed into the mix.

When all is secure and every prisoner's accounted for, the marshals signal to the pilot that they're ready for takeoff. The jet then taxis down the runway to begin the long cross-country trek.

Security is of the utmost importance for the transfer of this many prisoners at once, and rightfully so. Some of the inmates are the nation's worst criminals. Others are merely serving time for petty crimes, but they're all treated in the same manner. All are fully shackled.

For the duration of this journey, the inmates are totally unaware of their location or their destinations. Nearly all the cross-country transferees know they may have an overnight layover in a small, rural county jail before they reach their final destination.

THE TRANSFER CENTER

The jet crisscrosses its way across the nation unloading and loading prisoners at various destinations from California, to Las Vegas, to Salt Lake City, and to a remote airfield in Texas before it finally it touches down on a desolate airstrip outside of Oklahoma City, Oklahoma, the location of the Federal Transfer Center.

The transportation hub for the entire Federal Bureau of Prisons is typically the last stop of the day, and it's where any remaining prisoners will stay until the next plane headed to their final destination arrives. They could leave the next morning or, due to limited flights, they could be confined in the transfer center for months. They won't be told when they're scheduled to leave. That information is considered highly confidential.

Upon arrival in Oklahoma, the jet briefly taxis along a deserted airstrip and parks near the solid, red brick façade of the prison facility. The prisoners stand and exit row by row and then through the front door of the plane, where they walk down an enclosed ramp flanked by U.S. marshals. The walk down the ramp is slow and laborious. The leg chains are short and only allow the prisoners to take a half-step at a time.

After twelve hours of wearing the heavy leg irons, the prisoners' ankles are sore, imprinted with the pattern of the leg irons, and raw. Sometimes their ankles are left bleeding from the constant rubbing of metal against the thin flesh and bone. They wear socks, but the material is nearly paper-thin, and with weak elastic they work their way down during the course of the day, leaving the prisoner's ankles exposed to abuse from the hard steel. The agony caused by the handcuffs and leg irons is unavoidable. For the safety of all involved, inmates must remain safely restrained. Marshals normally do all they can to prevent any discomfort.

Once the prisoners are inside the center, they're ordered to line up, single file, along a brightly lit corridor, where security personnel from the Federal Bureau of Prisons join the marshals to begin the transfer of custody. After a head count, the marshals start the line moving down the hallway. The inmates are still not allowed to speak. The only sounds heard are the clanking of chains on the highly polished tile floor and the occasional groan from a prisoner who's taken too large a step and pulled the leg iron chain tight, which causes the steel cuff to even dig deeper into his already tender ankle flesh.

By now the hallway is filled with nearly one hundred and fifty inmates from all across the country, and several Federal Bureau of Prisons officers are standing ready to quell any situations that may arise. One by one, the prisoners are ordered to step onto a wooden platform where a marshal removes the leg irons. A second officer removes the cuffs and a third pats the inmate down and looks into his mouth and ears for contraband.

The group must stand along the wall until each prisoner's shackles are removed. Then, they're all then led into a bullpen of a much larger capacity than those at local jails or prisons. The room is a rectangular, concrete box with little or no ventilation, no seating, and only one stainless steel toilet. The room could safely hold fifty to one hundred prisoners, but on busy transport day it can be filled with close to two hundred inmates. The prisoners stand elbow-to-elbow, hungry, tired, and desperately needing to use a restroom. The single toilet in the bullpen works on occasion but is still not enough to accommodate the crowd of prisoners (male and female prisoners are kept separate). Here in this room, under some pretty tough conditions, the prisoners must wait for hours as they're processed and assigned to sleeping quarters.

After the processing is complete, the inmates are again strip-searched, a dozen at a time, by both male and female officers (female prisoners are strip-searched only by female officers). The prisoners are issued different ill-fitting clothing, and they're again inspected thoroughly for lice and contraband.

INTERESTING CON AIR FACTS

- Con Air is actually the combined air fleet of the U.S. Marshals Service and the former U.S. Immigration and Naturalization Service, or INS. The INS has recently changed its name and is now called U.S. Immigration and Customs Enforcement, or ICE. The merger of the U.S. Marshals Service and ICE created what's now known as Justice Prisoner and Alien Transportation System (JPATS).

- JPATS transports more than 270,000 prisoners each year.

- JPATS uses a fleet of commercial-type aircraft owned by the U.S. Marshals Service.

- JPATS' air fleet is based in Oklahoma City, Oklahoma.

- The U.S. Marshals Service has been in service for more than two hundred years.

- U.S. marshals are responsible for all federal prisoners until the prisoners are either released or incarcerated.

- The U.S. Marshals Service houses approximately 47,000 prisoners per day.

- U.S. marshals provide daily security for more than two thousand federal judges.

- The Federal Bureau of Prisons has approximately thirty-five thousand employees.

- Inmates often requested transfers to Alcatraz because of the view and the privacy of the one-man cells.

Then, the prisoners are finally divided into groups and led to various sections of the building called pods. Within the pods, the inmates are assigned to individual cells. The prison kitchen is often closed by the time the new prisoners arrive, so they're also given another brown paper bag containing another meager meal—an apple, two packages of peanut butter crackers, and a four-ounce container of water.

It's normally around 8:00 P.M. when the prisoners are finally permitted into their cells and are allowed to rest, shower, and use a working toilet.

The 9:00 P.M. hour causes fervor among the inmates, both male and female, as they rush from the day room to the individual cells along the rear wall of the pod. It's a long-standing tradition for the female inmates in the cells across the narrow courtyard to completely undress and perform as exotic dancers in front of their windows (each female's window lines up directly in front of a male inmate's window). This is the nightly event that makes the Oklahoma City Federal Transfer Center famous among the ranks of federal prisoners, nationwide. When the sun goes down in Oklahoma City, the lights come on, and it's showtime for the frenzied male inmates.

Other than the receiving bullpen, the transfer center is kept spotlessly clean, and the in-house staff is very well trained. They treat the inmates with respect—call them sir and ma'am—and, in doing so, receive respect from their prisoners. There's very little trouble, if any, from the inmates. It's a well-oiled operation that serves pretty good food, except for the initial brown bag meal. Meals served at the transfer center are probably the best that many of the inmates will receive for years to come.

For many of the prisoners, this is the most real meat they'll eat for the duration of their sentences. After leaving the transfer center, they'll more than likely be forced to sustain life on a diet of high carbohydrates and soy products. The transfer center provides a never-ending supply of personal hygiene products such as soap, shampoo, and deodorant. This, too, is something the prisoners won't see after leaving Oklahoma. They're not allowed to take any of these items with them when they leave. Most personal items are purchased by the inmates with money they receive from the outside or from the pay they receive from their prison job assignments.

The inmates' stays at the transfer center are usually short. They can be held there for as little time as an overnight stopover to a period of two or three months, depending on the next flight that's going their way. Each trip also has to coincide with the appropriate ground transportation at the other end of the flight.

On the day of the inmates' scheduled departure, they're awakened once again in the predawn hours and led to the bullpen to begin the next leg of the transport. This leg of the trip can sometimes be made by ground transport if the trip is only for a few hundred miles, or in instances where some of the more remote areas of the country have a lack of airports or runway space.

GROUND TRANSPORTATION

Inmates traveling by U.S. Marshals Service ground transportation make their journey in the back of an unmarked U.S. Marshals Service van. The windows are caged, and a heavy, steel padlock is placed on the outside of the doors. A welded-steel mesh separates the driver's compartment from the inmates in the rear. Male and female inmates are transported together in the back of these vans. The prisoners sometimes get an in-person, up-close look at the entertainers from the previous nighttime window shows.

The marshals drive for up to eight hours at a time, stopping occasionally to drop off and pick up prisoners along the way. The final stop of the day, at the end of their shift, is at a county jail. The jail will hold the remaining prisoners overnight, until they get underway again the next morning. It's here, in the county jail, that many of the federal prisoners get their first taste of a real jail. These felons have been used to the two-person rooms or cubicles, TV rooms, libraries, tennis courts, and freedoms of prison recreation yards, not the twenty-four-hour-a-day lockdown of most overcrowded county jails.

The inmates are booked into the jail as if they'd been arrested. They're fingerprinted, photographed, strip-searched, and—in some cases—deloused again. They're placed into a real jail cell, not a clean cubicle or room as they've been accustomed to in prison. The cells are dark, filthy, and sometimes infested with rats and roaches. The floors and walls are covered in graffiti, fecal matter, blood, and urine, and there's always hair or some unidentifiable substance matted into the dried body excretions and fluids.

A stainless steel toilet and a concrete or steel bed are the only items in the cell, other than the inmates who've already been packed into the concrete enclosure. The door is solid steel with a 6" × 8" thick Plexiglas window to allow jail officers to view the activities of the prisoners. The new, incoming federal prisoners are given a thin army blanket and are forced to sleep on the floor, since the cell's already overcrowded with local inmates.

State inmates regard federal prisoners as "higher ranking." Their status as federal prisoners is easily identifiable by their government-issued, khaki-colored pants and their blue, deck-type shoes. The local inmates, out of respect for their superiors, offer them cigarettes, soft drinks, soups, and hygiene products. The federal prisoners gladly accept these items from their cellmates. The two groups swap legal war stories and comparisons of jails and prisons throughout the night.

At dawn, the transportation process begins again. This procedure is repeated until the prisoners reach their final destinations. If an inmate is going to a court hearing, once the hearing is complete (sometimes after only a few minutes), the inmate must make the long journey back to the prison where she's serving her sentence. The return trip is the same, only in reverse. The entire round trip for a twenty-minute hearing can last up to three or four months and is very expensive, but necessary

CHAPTER 15

THE DEATH
PENALTY

An innocent man is going to be murdered tonight. When my innocence is proven, I hope Americans will realize the injustice of the death penalty as all other civilized countries have.

—ROGER KEITH COLEMAN, EXECUTED IN *1992* FOR THE BRUTAL RAPE AND MURDER OF HIS SISTER-IN-LAW, WANDA FAYE McCOY

The United States has a long history of putting people to death for committing crimes. In the year 2006 alone, fifty-three men (no women) were executed in prison death chambers. Fifty-two of those men met their demise through lethal injection. The fifty-third man was killed via electrocution.

According to the Bureau of Justice Statistics, the majority of those executions (twenty-four) occurred in Texas. The remaining executions were divided among thirteen other states: five in Ohio; four each in North Carolina, Florida, Oklahoma, and Virginia; and one each in South Carolina, Indiana, Alabama, Tennessee, Mississippi, California, Nevada, and Montana.

At the end of 2005, there were 3,254 men and women on death row. Their ages ranged from twenty to ninety. Fifty-two of those prisoners were women.

DEATH WARRANT
Ohio Revised Code Sections 2903.01, 2929.02

The State of Ohio,_____County ss.   COMMON PLEAS COURT

TO THE SHERIFF OF SAID COUNTY:

Whereas, on the_____day of_____A. D. 20_____, as is shown by the record of proceedings of said Court,

_____was sentenced to be executed and said punishment to be inflicted within the walls of the Southern Ohio Correctional Facility,

on the _____day of_____ , in the year of our Lord, two thousand_____

_____, you are hereby commanded that within thirty days from this_____day of_____ , of

the year of our Lord, two thousand_____ , in a private and secure manner, you convey the prisoner, the said_____

_____to the Southern Ohio Correctional Facility at Lucasville, Ohio, where the said prisoner shall be received by the Superintendent, and kept until

the day designated for his execution.

AND THE SUPERINTENDENT OR ASSOCIATE SUPERINTENDENT OF CUSTODY OF SAID SOUTHERN OHIO CORRECTIONAL FACILITY IS HEREBY COMMANDED TO PROCEED AT THE TIME AND PLACE NAMED IN THIS WARRANT, TO CAUSE THE SAID PRISONER TO BE EXECUTED; AND HE SHALL FORTHWITH MAKE RETURN TO THE UNDERSIGNED CLERK OF THE COUNTY, FROM WHENCE THE SAID PRISONER WAS SENTENCED, THE MANNER OF HIS EXECUTION OF THIS WARRANT AND HIS DOINGS THEREON.

Given under my hand and the seal of said Court at_____

Ohio, this _____day of_____A. D. 20_____

_____
Clerk of Courts of Said County.

SUPERINTENDENT'S RETURN

SUPERINTENDENT'S OFFICE, SOUTHERN OHIO CORRECTIONAL FACILITY, AT LUCASVILLE, OHIO

_____A. D. 20_____

To The Clerk Of_____County, Ohio:

On the_____day of_____A. D. 20_____, I received this your warrant, together with the prisoner named herein, whom I kept until

the day designated for his execution; and on the_____day of_____ A. D. 20_____, I caused the said prisoner

_____to be executed.

_____
Superintendent of the Southern Ohio Correctional Facility

LibertyNet Southwestern, Inc. 1-800-621-1900, Re-Order 70453K

State of Ohio Death Warrant.

Upon imposing a death sentence, judges sign an official death warrant ordering the prison's warden to put the prisoner to death. The warrant is read to the inmate by the prison warden just prior to the inmate's execution. At the completion of the execution, the warden signs the warrant confirming the death of the inmate and then delivers the original warrant to the clerk of the court. She then files the death warrant as part of the inmate's permanent record.

DEATH ROW

Death row inmates spend their days alone in a 6' × 9' cell, with the exception of a one-hour recreation period each day and a few minutes to take a shower every other day. Their meals are prepared by prisoners in the institution's kitchen and are delivered to them three times each day.

```
╔══════════════════════════════════╗
║                                  ║
║      D E A T H   W A R R A N T   ║
║                                  ║
║  ──────────────────────────────  ║
║                                  ║
║  ──────────────────────────────  ║
║         CONDEMNED PRISONER       ║
║                                  ║
║  Received _____A.D. 20__  ║
║                                  ║
║  ──────────────────────────────  ║
║                        Sheriff.  ║
║                                  ║
║  Received _____A.D. 20__  ║
║                                  ║
║  ──────────────────────────────  ║
║                  Superintendent. ║
║                                  ║
║        Returned and filed        ║
║                                  ║
║  _____A.D. 20__   ║
║                                  ║
║  ──────────────────────────────  ║
║                 Clerk of Courts. ║
║                                  ║
║                                  ║
║                                  ║
║                                  ║
║                                  ║
║                                  ║
║                                  ║
║                                  ║
║                                  ║
║                                  ║
╚══════════════════════════════════╝
```

Corrections officals must sign the return
portion of the death warrant upon receipt of
the condemned prisoner.

Security is much tighter on death row than in all other areas of the prison. Corrections officers must count the death row inmates at least once an hour to ensure that each of them is present and accounted for.

Prisoners on death row are allowed to receive mail, magazines, books, and newspapers. Some prisons allow death row inmates the luxury of having a small portable TV set inside their cells.

Even though death row prisoners are segregated from other prisoners, they're normally required to wear clothing that's easily distinguishable from all other inmates.

As a prisoner's execution date draws near (approximately two weeks prior to the execution date), he's moved to a cell that's closer to the death chamber, called a death watch cell. Some states, such as Virginia, house their death row prisoners in a different facility altogether than the prison where the execution chamber is located.

A death watch cell is normally larger than the cells on death row (the state of Florida's death watch cells are 12' × 7' × 8½'). Corrections officers must watch prisoners in the death watch cells at all times to prevent suicide attempts. By law, they must be kept alive so they can be officially executed. They must also record each and every move the inmates make during their time on death watch.

On the day of his execution, the condemned prisoner is allowed to request a special meal. His last meal may be prepared in the prison's kitchen or purchased from an outside vendor. Many condemned prisoners choose to have a meal brought in from the outside.

Inmate Arthur Dennis Rutherford, who was executed in Florida on October 18, 2006, enjoyed a last meal of fried catfish, fried green tomatoes, fried eggplant, hush puppies, and sweet tea. Rutherford had been served the same meal in January 2006, just prior to being awarded a stay of execution. His request for a second stay was denied in October.

Prisoners normally spend many years waiting for their execution dates to arrive. In most states, condemned prisoners are afforded every opportunity and every possible appeal to show why they shouldn't be put to death. As a result of the many opportunities for appeal and legal maneuvering, some prisoners have remained on death row for nearly thirty years. The average time spent on death row in Florida is thirteen years.

The costs to try a death penalty case can exceed two million dollars. The costs to try that same inmate without the death penalty would probably be less than $200,000.

Interestingly, some prisoners say they'd rather die than spend their entire lives in prison. They indicate that sitting alone in a 6' × 9' cell every day, wishing and dreaming of being outside, is torture. They compare the years of incarceration to sitting in a tiny closet day in and day out, without the opportunity to eat when you want or take a daily shower. There's no window to see outside, no refrigerator for a snack, and no television to pass the time. The only way to make the day go by is to sit and think and contemplate their reasons for being in prison, with no hope of ever getting out.

WITNESSES TO AN EXECUTION

Most state laws require that a certain number of people be present as witnesses to executions. Normally, the law calls for at least four people from the general population to serve as witnesses. These witnesses are considered official witnesses of record. Some prisons maintain a list of potential witnesses who have requested to volunteer their services, if and when they're needed.

The law also allows for the presence of lawyers, prison staff, police officers, and members of the victim's family. Members of the condemned man's family may also request to be present. Most states have a limit on the total number of witnesses who may be present to observe an execution. North Carolina law restricts that number to sixteen.

IN THE LINE OF DUTY

A WITNESS TO DEATH

Virginia, April 27, 1994. It was just before 11:00 P.M. when I watched convicted serial killer Timothy Spencer walk into the execution chamber at Greensville Correctional Center in Jarratt, Virginia. It was another execution for me, but this time I wasn't on the prison grounds to provide security as a police officer—I was inside the execution building as a witness. I'd been called on, as a police officer, by prison officials to watch Spencer die for killing one of the four women he'd brutally raped and murdered.

DNA testing on evidence samples from Spencer's cases was conducted in Virginia's state forensic laboratory and at two other testing facilities—Cellmark Diagnostics and Lifecodes, Inc. Test results from all three laboratories were conclusive—Spencer was indeed the killer. Spencer (nicknamed the Southside Strangler by the media) was the first person in the United States to be sentenced to death based on DNA evidence.

The case drew so much attention that media all across the country reported the execution. On the night of Spencer's execution, news teams lined the narrow road leading to the prison with their satellite trucks. On-air personalities stood beside their trucks giving live, minute-by-minute progress reports about how Spencer spent his last day. Cameramen scanned the crowd of protesters as they sang songs and prayed.

Spencer's story was hot news. Not only had he killed the young women, but he did so while on work release and living nearly unsupervised in a state-operated halfway house. He'd also almost managed to get away with each of his murders because the police had arrested the wrong man, David Vasquez, for the crimes. In fact, Vasquez served several years in prison for the murders before DNA proved that Spencer was the murderer.

The case of the Southside Strangler was so compelling that best-selling author Patricia Cornwell based her first book, *Postmortem,* on Spencer's killing spree.

Spencer's appellate attorney, Barry Weinstein, fought to save his client's life up until moments before Spencer took the walk from his cell to the execution chamber. The Supreme Court of the United States denied Weinstein's final efforts to spare his client's life at approximately 10:45 p.m.—the precise time when I sat staring at Old Sparky, the state's electric chair. I was thinking that I, as a police detective, had the power to arrest criminals who might one day be placed in the very death chair standing before me. These thoughts of life and death enter the minds of many police officers throughout their careers.

When the door in the back of the execution chamber opened that night, the prison's warden entered first, followed by an assistant warden, a prison doctor, and the prison chaplain. They were followed by two corrections officers. The next person to enter was Spencer. He was dressed in new prison clothes—a light-blue denim shirt and dark-blue denim pants. His prison, deck-style sneakers were light blue-grey. The pant material had been cut away from his lower right leg just below the knee, exposing the flesh. His head was shaved smooth and reflected the white lights from above.

Spencer was surrounded by an execution team, an elite group of corrections officers chosen especially for this assignment. The team had rehearsed its duties many times during the days preceding this event, and it was obvious by their actions that they knew exactly what do and when to do it.

I and several other witnesses looked on as Spencer settled his small-framed body into the wooden seat of Old Sparky. The execution team immediately swarmed around him like bees as they used wide straps to fasten his arms, wrists, legs, and chest to the chair. Then, as quickly as they'd surrounded him, the entire group backed away. One officer stepped forward from the team and placed a metal cap on Spencer's head.

During the pre-execution briefing, an assistant warden explained to those of us who were selected as witnesses that the inside of the cap was filled with a brine-soaked sponge. The solution allows the best possible conditions for the conduction of electricity. The top of the cap is designed to allow for the connection of an electric cable, the first of two cables in a circuit that delivers a thirty-second electric shock of eighteen hundred volts. The amount of electricity used to power a normal household is 220 volts.

Spencer looked confident and unafraid, sort of cocky actually, as his eyes scanned his surroundings. He glanced toward a large, round wall clock that hung above the electric chair. The same officer who had placed the cap on

Spencer stepped forward again, this time to fasten a metal clamp to Spencer's bare right calf. The clamp was attached to the ground wire that completed the electric circuit.

The only thing separating the killer and those of us waiting to see him die was a space of approximately twenty feet and a glass partition that didn't quite reach the ceiling.

The execution chamber where Spencer sat was painted pale gray with snow-white trim and was brightly lit by several rectangular fluorescent fixtures. A telephone with a direct line to the governor of Virginia hung on the wall behind Old Sparky. The warden stood beside the phone. To the warden's right and slightly to the rear of the chamber was a small room where the executioner waited, behind a one-way mirror, for the command to initiate the first of two jolts of electricity. (Two rounds of electricity have been used since an inmate once lived through the single round that used to be delivered. After a few minutes, the executioner was ordered to complete the execution by applying a second burst.) The executioner could see out, but the prison staff, the witnesses, and Spencer couldn't see in. I could imagine the executioner's finger poised above the green button, waiting to end it all.

When I glanced at the mirror I could see the reflection of the back of Spencer's head. I noticed that, in spite of the above-normal warmth of the room and the intensity of the moment, Spencer wasn't sweating. I was. The witness seated to my right was crying softly. The man to my left sat motionless and never took his eyes away from Spencer.

Directly behind the condemned man was the transformer from which the deadly electricity would flow. A small, orange lightbulb on the top of the machine looked almost out of place. The warden had told us that the bulb would begin to glow brightly when the executioner had begun the first cycle. We were also told that the machine would begin to hum a bit.

When the precise time for the execution arrived, the warden read the death warrant to Spencer. The brief reading basically informed the killer that he'd been sentenced to die on this date and that the warden of the facility was charged with causing him to die. Short and sweet.

The warden asked Spencer if he had anything to say—any last words. He muttered, "Yeah, I think I ... ," then stopped talking and looked directly toward us, the witnesses. At the last second, he had elected to remain silent and offered no words of remorse for what he'd done or for the families of his many victims.

He continued to look toward us as officers placed the leather death mask over his face and secured it. I could still see his eyes through tiny slits. His gaze met mine.

The execution team had completed its assignment and, with a nod from the warden, they left the chamber in single file.

The chaplain approached Spencer and placed his hand on Spencer's shoulder. He began to rub Spencer's upper back a little as he quietly recited the Lord's Prayer. Spencer nodded, slightly. The chaplain ended the prayer, and the warden nodded to the person behind the mirror. Spencer sat straight and slowly turned both thumbs upward.

The light on the transformer began to glow, faintly at first then suddenly it was hot orange. Spencer's body lunged tightly against the straps as the first burst of electricity hit him. It appeared as if his upper body had swollen to twice its normal size. When the first jolt was over, his body relaxed slightly. The tension in the witness room had been high, but when the first group of electrical jolts ended, the anxiety dissipated a bit. Audible sighs were heard from our group. Then suddenly the orange light began to glow brightly again. The second and less intense wave of 240 volts hit. That burst lasted for sixty seconds.

He swelled again, but this time fluid gushed from beneath the mask. Small puffs of smoke rose from his exposed calf and from somewhere around his right ear. A sound similar to frying bacon could be heard coming from the chamber, and the odor of burning flesh began to drift into the witness room.

The orange light went out, Spencer's body slumped, and his left arm fell limply to the side of its rest. The prison officials inside the room with Spencer stood still for five long minutes (I later learned that the time was needed to allow the body to cool down enough that the doctor could touch it without being burned).

When the five minutes had passed, the prison doctor walked over to Spencer's body, placed a stethoscope to his chest for a moment, and listened. He then looked up and said, "Warden, this man has expired." It was 11:13 P.M.

A corrections officer, who had been seated near the witnesses during the entire proceeding, stood and closed a row of heavy blue drapes between the witness room and the execution chamber. A prison official then motioned for the witnesses to follow him outside where we were escorted to a waiting prison van, the same van I'd watched leave the institution after many other executions.

We were taken back to our cars and to our lives. Spencer's body was now headed to the morgue for an event that can only be attended by those who are condemned to die: a prescheduled autopsy.

METHODS OF EXECUTION

A handful of states still use the electric chair as a means for executing the condemned. Others use lethal injection to execute prisoners who have been sentenced to death, or they've totally abolished the death penalty as a form of punishment. Idaho and Oklahoma are the only two states where executions by firing squad are still performed, although lethal injection is the primary method used by both states. In 2004, Utah passed a law banning firing squads, although as recently as 1996 the state used the method to execute John Albert Taylor for the rape and strangulation of an eleven-year-old girl.

THE ELECTRIC CHAIR

The electric chair was first used in the United States in the late 1800s and was once a favored means of executing prisoners who had been sentenced to death. However, due to a number of botched executions, its use in several states is merely an option, with many states outlawing it entirely.

Eyewitnesses have reported seeing horrifying side effects of electrocution, such as smoldering flesh and the flood of fluids emitting from body openings, including the eyes. I can personally attest to some of these eyewitness accounts. An execution via electric chair can be quite gruesome.

Only a handful of states still allow the use of the electric chair as an option for execution: Virginia, Florida, Tennessee, Kentucky, South Carolina, Texas, Alabama, Oklahoma, Illinois, and Nebraska.

LETHAL INJECTION

Currently, most states either already use, or plan to use, lethal injection as their primary means of executing condemned prisoners. According to an article in the April 2005 edition of *New Scientist* magazine, lethal injection isn't the painless and humane method of execution it was once thought to be—it's possibly just the lesser of all evils. The death penalty was suggested in the United States in 1972 but wasn't reintroduced until 1976, and the *New Scientist* magazine article refers to study statistics posted in the medical journal *The Lancet* indicating that inmates may have felt pain in forty-three of forty-nine executions by lethal injection and that, in 40 percent of those cases, the prisoners were conscious when they were put to death.

Death by lethal injection is carried out in three stages by the executioner. The first step is the intravenous introduction of sodium thiopental to anaesthetize the inmate. A second chemical, pancuronium bromide, is then introduced into the bloodstream as a muscle relaxant. Finally, the technician injects potassium chloride to stop the heart.

Prisoners receive a dose of approximately three grams of sodium thiopental at the time of execution. This amount is ten times that of the doses administered to a patient during a surgical procedure. If the anesthesia is properly administered, the inmate won't feel pain during the execution. Doctors and nurses are forbidden by ethical guidelines to assist with or participate in executions; therefore, technicians with no formal training in administering anesthetics perform the executions. This technician could very well be a local emergency medical technician, paramedic, or ambulance crew member. In fact, the *New Scientist* article went on to say that technicians in Texas and Virginia (the two have put to death more prisoners than all other states combined) have no training whatsoever. They also introduce the injections remotely via I.V., so they can't possibly monitor the anesthesia.

It's interesting to note that veterinarians in the United States are advised against using muscle relaxants during the euthanasia of animals because the relaxant may hide signs that the anesthesia isn't working. If the anesthesia isn't properly administered, a prisoner may experience asphyxiation, severe burning sensations, massive muscle cramps, and—finally—cardiac arrest. Attorneys for condemned prisoners argue that this type of pain and suffering is a direct violation of the Eighth Amendment of the U.S. Constitution, which prohibits cruel and unusual punishment.

In December of 2006, Angel Nieves Diaz was executed by lethal injection in the state of Florida. Diaz had been sentenced to death by a Florida court for the murder of the manager of a topless bar.

A death that was supposed to be painless and quick took thirty-four minutes and was most likely very painful. Diaz had to be given the death-inducing chemicals twice because the needles that were supposed to be inserted into his veins were instead pushed into surrounding muscle tissue. The Florida medical examiner stated that Diaz had large chemical burns on both arms. Witnesses to the execution said that Diaz was moving, grimacing, and possibly attempting to say something as long as twenty-four minutes after he received the first chemical.

As a result of the botched execution, Florida Governor Jeb Bush immediately issued an order to suspend all executions pending further review. During the same week, a federal judge in California declared that California's method of lethal injection violated the U.S. Constitution's ban on cruel and unusual punishment.

In February 2007, an eleven-member review panel in Florida issued a preliminary report recommending that anyone in the position to administer lethal injections should be required to undergo training and that they monitor the level of the inmate's consciousness during an execution. The panel's final report is due to be delivered on March 1, 2007, to Governor Bush's successor, Governor Charlie Crist.

CHAPTER 16

C.S. . . . I

DON'T THINK SO

The public pays a high price for embracing—without question—the entertaining fantasies about forensic science presented by most television crime dramas and much of crime fiction. That price includes slowed investigations, violent criminals on the loose, innocent people incarcerated, overcrowded jails, clogged court schedules, ineffective homeland security, and many other problems. This is a failure of public policy, not of television and books. Storytelling has its place, but if we don't ask our legislatures to provide real-life support for forensic science, we're living in a costly fool's paradise.

—JAN BURKE, EDGAR AWARD-WINNING AUTHOR OF
BONES, BLOODLINES, AND KIDNAPPED

Fictional TV shows based on criminal investigations have become all the rage in the past several years. The writers of these shows are charged with the responsibility of entertaining their viewing audience, and—based on the shows' extremely high ratings—they seem to be doing quite well with their assignments. Office watercooler chat is another indicator of the popularity of law enforcement reality/fiction shows.

The list of sometimes offensive and inaccurate depictions of how the law enforcement community conducts its day-to-day business grows with each episode of these TV shows. The fallacies not only irritate police officers, scientists, and crime scene technicians, but they wreak havoc in courtrooms all across the country and even into neighboring Canada. These sources of fictional entertainment have created a phenomenon known as the "CSI Effect."

The stars of crime scene investigation shows use forensic testing techniques that would leave Sherlock Holmes in awe. Some techniques used are legitimate, but others couldn't be further from the truth. In some cases, even everyday police procedures are stretched beyond the limits of reality.

The TV-viewing public has learned about DNA, fingerprinting, casting, weapons, firearms testing, blood spatter, entrance and exit wounds, insect evidence, hair, fiber and other trace evidence, tire tracks, Luminol, and alternate light sources. Television has taught its audience about autopsies and time of death, how to use sonar to find a dead body in a bay, how a polygraph works, and how psychics use their uncanny powers to find killers.

We've seen these approaches to crime solving so often that these methods, tools and techniques, and results are what TV viewers expect from the law enforcement community. And they expect nothing less—why, they've seen a famous TV medical examiner slice and dice her way to a cause of death between ads for dog food and shampoo.

As a result of watching television, jurors in criminal trials expect to hear about perfect DNA testing and fingerprint evidence. They expect to hear testimony from supercops and magical crime scene technicians, and they want to hear tales of mystical revelations from a local coroner. Jury members expect a smoking gun in every case. They want slam-dunk evidence.

The reality of the situation is that this isn't reality.

What is reality is that doctors don't leave emergency rooms to poke around someone's house searching for clues. Crime scene technicians don't normally carry weapons. In fact, most of them aren't even sworn police officers, and they have no authority to arrest anyone. Medical examiners don't engage in physical confrontations with armed suspects, and the few cops who do attend autopsies aren't allowed to prod and dig around a dead body looking for bullets or other pieces of evidence. When the real-life professionals go about their daily routines of crime solving, they turn on the lights in every room, unlike their TV counterparts. Real-life law enforcement people don't work in the dark by flashlight!

TV shows and films lead us to believe that there are unlimited funds available for crime solving. Not so. In fact, most forensic laboratories are underfunded, understaffed, and behind schedule in testing the tremendous amount of evidence that's submitted to them each and every day. In fact, many of the facilities where the testing takes place are in poor condition.

Many police labs are equipped with hand-me-down equipment, and often the employees themselves purchase a portion of that equipment. Many police officers buy their own fingerprinting tools, weapons, binoculars, and evidence-collection materials because their departments simply don't have the funds allocated in their budgets for anything that's not absolutely necessary.

Low pay and a lack of proper equipment can make for less-than-desirable working conditions. Many public employees seek employment with private scientific testing companies, leaving the police labs seriously understaffed and causing a backlog of evidence that needs testing. A backlog of cases can be extremely devastating to the court system. Untested evidence means that cases aren't solved, and unsolved cases mean that criminals are still out on the street committing crimes.

In August of 2006, a Jacksonville, Florida, newspaper reported that the crime labs of the Florida Department of Law Enforcement had evidence from approximately one thousand cases on hold, waiting to be examined by forensic scientists. A Maryland newspaper reports that the state police crime lab is understaffed by twelve scientists.

The U.S. Department of Justice reported that, in 2005, the state of Tennessee had one of the most backlogged forensic laboratory systems in the country. The same report indicates that a typical crime lab maintains an average of four hundred backlogged cases per month. The U.S. Department of Justice reported that, at the end of 2002, 351 publicly funded U.S. laboratories had a backlog of more than 500,000 requests for evidence examination.

Television shows us scientists who work almost exclusively on DNA evidence, firearm comparison, and blood and trace evidence. Actually, scientists and other specialists who work in these laboratories spend only a scant amount of their time examining DNA evidence (which, by the way, normally takes a minimum of three days to examine, not the fifteen or twenty minutes suggested on television). The rest of their time is spent examining other evidence, such as tool marks and narcotics, with narcotics being the most frequently examined piece of evidence in nearly all crime labs.

The Los Angeles County Sheriff's Office operates the largest crime lab in the United States, examining more than 500,000 pieces of evidence annually. Their work is about 70 percent narcotics testing. Evidence testing for homicide and rape cases is performed in another, much smaller, downtown facility. There, scientists conduct testing on evidence such as firearms, fingerprints, and DNA evidence.

A backlog in a forensic laboratory slows the entire judicial system. Criminals who are incarcerated while awaiting trial must often remain in jail until the testing of the evidence from their crime scenes is complete. This delay often results in continuances of their trials over and over again. The costs for this wait time can be staggering.

Cops and scientists alike know that, in the world of law enforcement, scientific testing, and evidence collection, the procedures are only as good as the people who perform them. Cops and scientists are human. They make mistakes.

Dr. Dan Krane, one of the world's leading DNA experts, says this about DNA testing and how it's portrayed on television: "You never see a case where the sample is degraded or the lab work is faulty or the test results don't solve the crime. These things happen all the time in the real world."

Dr. Krane's statement is absolutely correct. Many times DNA test results are returned to detectives as being inconclusive due to improper handling of the evidence, or because the sample wasn't large enough to examine properly, if at all.

Thanks to television and the creative minds of writers, courts and police officers are faced with having to overcome the public's perception of how crimes should be solved. It's quickly becoming a difficult uphill battle. Prosecutors are spending almost as much time explaining why little or no evidence will be presented during a trial as they do when they present actual evidence. In fact, *The Toronto Sun* published a story about a detective who spent over two hours on the witness stand, trying to explain to jurors that absolutely no physical evidence was recovered at a particular crime scene.

Actor Robert Blake was arrested in 2002 for the murder of his wife, Bonny Lee Bakley. Blake and his wife had dinner at an Italian restaurant in Studio

City, California, and shortly after dinner Bakley was found dead in the couple's car, which was parked around the corner from the restaurant. Blake later told police he'd returned to the restaurant to retrieve a gun that had apparently fallen out of his pocket during dinner.

Jurors in Robert Blake's murder trial found Blake not guilty because the prosecution didn't present enough TV-type forensic evidence. One juror stated that she just expected much more evidence. Another felt that Blake couldn't have committed the crime because there was no blood spatter found on him.

Blake was later found to be liable for his wife's death by a jury in a civil trial. He was ordered to pay Bakley's children several million dollars in damages. Blake has since filed for bankruptcy.

REAL COPS SPEAK ABOUT TV COPS

Many people who work in the law enforcement field find it difficult, if not impossible, to watch TV shows where their profession is so grossly misstated. The same holds true with written material. Many police officers find it hard to read a book where the action is nonstop and where crime solving techniques are untrue.

Police officers don't talk about their jobs publicly. They're a tightly knit group who pack together like wolves. But if you get a handful of police officers together and ask them about TV cop shows and what they see that's wrong … well, here's what they had to say:

"When officers search a building with their weapons drawn, they don't place their fingers inside the trigger guard. They could trip, accidentally discharge the weapon, and kill their own partners."

—Sergeant Timothy Leedy, Hamilton, Ohio, Police Department

FACT: Cops are taught to hold their weapons pointed downward when searching buildings or pursuing criminals. It's easier to find and stay on target when bringing a weapon upward rather than in a downward movement.

"You never see the officers on television doing any paperwork, which is a huge part of the job."

—Sergeant John Priest, retired, Springfield, Ohio, Police Department

FACT: Most of a police officer's shift is spent observing, patrolling, talking to people, and completing paperwork. Running, shooting, fighting, and car chases aren't the norm.

"To solve crimes within an hour is not reality."

—Crime Prevention Specialist Dave Crawford,
Hamilton, Ohio, Police Department

FACT: It can take days, weeks, even months or years to solve a single case. Most detectives work on many cases simultaneously.

"It's rare that you ever see a cop on television miss a shot during a gun battle, when in reality it's never that cut and dry."

—Lieutenant David Czyzak, Springfield, Ohio, Police Department

FACT: Tunnel vision, adrenaline, and sheer excitement are all factors involved during a gunfight. Normally, many, many rounds of gunfire are exchanged during a shooting situation, and police officers rarely kill the suspect. In fact, most rounds fired don't hit the intended target.

"It drives me crazy when you see a cop on television get into a shootout, and then he immediately goes back to work on the street."

—Lieutenant Jim Hutchins, Springfield, Ohio, Police Department

FACT: Most police departments require that all officers involved in a shooting incident be suspended from normal duty pending an investigation of the incident. The officers are also normally required to receive counseling.

"I think it's so unrealistic when the crime scene investigator also makes the arrest, interrogates the suspect, and solves the case. In a department of any size, that doesn't happen."

—Sergeant Nelson T. Smith, retired, Springfield, Ohio, Police Department

FACT: Crime scene investigators are normally not police officers. They're civilian employees with no arrest powers. Detectives are usually the officers who conduct interrogations.

"I think it's ridiculous when the cop-hero in a movie gets suspended and then goes out and solves the case on his own, proving he was right all along. In the real world, he'd would probably be fired for doing that."

—Officer Mitch Hurst, Springfield, Ohio, Police Department

FACT: When an officer has been suspended from duty, his police powers may also be temporarily suspended. Some departments ask suspended officers to hand in their weapons and badges during a suspension. An officer on suspension who's acting on his own to solve a crime is susceptible to civil liability.

"When police officers get shot or hurt on television, I wish it would be more realistic. They show them running miles and miles after being shot. People need to know that police officers are heroes but aren't invincible."

—Officer Kristy Collins, Hamilton, Ohio, Police Department

FACT: A gunshot wound is traumatic even if it's not life threatening. The psychological impact of being shot is sometimes worse than the gunshot wound itself. Officers who have been severely wounded aren't normally capable of physically pursuing their shooters. Police officers are trained to survive and have been known to subdue and restrain their attackers before succumbing to their wounds.

"On television, you'll sometimes see a defense attorney sitting in on the interrogation of her client, allowing the detectives to berate the client. I've never seen that happen, and I don't expect I ever will."

—Chief of Police Stephen P. Moody, Springfield, Ohio, Police Department

FACT: Most defense attorneys won't allow their clients to speak with police until some sort of agreement has been reached protecting the defendant from further incriminating himself. The attorneys would never stand for verbal abuse or trickery by the police.

"The lead actor shoots three suspects, and then lets the 'lowly' uniformed officers arrive shortly after the fact to clean everything up. I guess a routine shift done with proper police procedures won't sell many books or movies."

—Sergeant Danny Palmer, retired, Springfield, Ohio, Police Department

FACT: Normal, routine police work can be pretty boring. TV producers spice things up a bit to capture the attention of their audiences.

"My favorite is how the star 'hounds' the suspect for several days prior to the arrest. That would never happen!"

—Sergeant Gary Wilson, retired, Springfield, Ohio, Police Department

FACT: Most police investigators don't let a suspect know they're conducting an investigation until that investigation is nearing its end. The element of surprise is an essential part of crime solving.

"I always comment to my wife how silly it is to see the TV police respond to a relatively minor call with lights and sirens."

—Captain Bruce Sigman, Springfield, Ohio, Police Department

FACT: Police officers only use lights and sirens during emergency situations and during traffic stops. They don't normally arrest someone and leave the scene with lights flashing and sirens wailing unless the suspect is injured and they're taking him to the hospital.

"I don't like to see TV detectives physically abuse suspects in an interrogation. The public thinks that's how it's routinely done, and it's not."

—Officer Nick Holt, Springfield, Ohio, Police Department

FACT: Most police departments use video and audio taping during interrogations; therefore, any type of abuse would be caught on camera. Police officers receive extensive training regarding the dos and don'ts of when they can and can't use force on a suspect. Interrogation isn't a time when use of force is permitted, unless the suspect becomes violent.

Other comments from police officers:

"Police officers don't fire warning shots! For goodness' sake, what goes up must come down!"

"Police officers don't receive results from crime labs right away. Sometimes it takes weeks to get answers."

"I really hate to see TV cops spouting off the Miranda warnings as soon as they handcuff someone. It's just not done that way."

"TV cops return to a crime scene over and over again to collect evidence. In real life, you usually get one shot at the scene. If we feel that we need more time, we seal the scene and maintain control of it for as long as necessary. But once we leave, that's it. There's no coming back. Besides, if we did come back, we couldn't use the evidence in court (if it was still there) because we lost our chain of custody when we left."

It takes a special person to become a police officer, and when those hometown heroes see themselves portrayed as violent or abusive, and perhaps even dumb, it can sometimes cause animosity. One comment that surfaced repeatedly during the questioning of police officers for this chapter is best summed up by Crime Prevention Specialist Officer Dave Crawford of the Hamilton, Ohio, Police Department:

> I really dislike it when people call us pigs and talk about us eating donuts. When they do call us pigs, I just smile and think about what those letters actually stand for: Pride, Integrity, and Guts. It takes all those qualities to be a good cop.
>
> Then again, the letters could also stand for Plain, Iced, and Glazed.

EPILOGUE

Not a single day passes by without my thinking of the brave police officers out there who risk their lives so we can be safe. Your families want you to come home tonight, so please be careful, wear your vests, and, in the words of Lewis Grizzard, remember to:

"Shoot low, boys. They might be riding Shetland ponies!"

GLOSSARY OF
TERMS

A&B. Assault and battery.

AKA. Also known as.

AIKIDO. Police defensive tactics techniques developed from this particular style of Japanese martial arts.

ABSCOND. To secretly leave the jurisdiction of a court or to conceal one's self from law enforcement officials.

ACCESSORY. One who aids or assists in the commission of a crime.

AID AND ABET. To voluntarily assist another person in the commission of a crime.

ALTERNATE LIGHT SOURCE. Equipment used to enhance potential items of evidence, either visible or invisible light at varying wavelengths.

AMICUS CURIAE. Latin for "a friend of the court." Someone who isn't a party to court proceedings who supplies information to the court that otherwise may not be readily available.

ARREST. To deprive someone of his liberty, or to seize a person suspected of a crime.

B AND E. Breaking and entering.

BENCH WARRANT. An arrest warrant issued by the court.

BINDLE PAPER. Clean paper folded to contain trace evidence such as hairs or fibers.

BIOHAZARD BAG. A red plastic bag used to contain materials that have been exposed to blood and other body fluids and parts. The container will be clearly marked as *Biohazard Material* in bold lettering.

BIOLOGICAL WEAPON. An agent used to threaten or destroy human life, e.g. anthrax, smallpox, *E. coli*, etc.

BLOOD-BORNE PATHOGEN. An infectious, disease-causing microorganism found in biological fluids.

BLOW. Cocaine.

BOLO. Be on the lookout.

BREAD SLICING. The method of slicing body organs by a medical examiner. The organs are sliced into sections resembling a loaf of bread.

BREAKING AND ENTERING. Any act of physical force in which obstruction to entrance of a building is removed. Simply pushing a door open or raising a window can be considered "breaking." Breaking and entering are two of the elements of burglary.

BULLET. A one-year prison sentence.

BURGLARY. Breaking into any dwelling in the nighttime with the intent to commit a felony.

CI. Confidential informant.

CAPITAL MURDER. A murder that is punishable by death.

CARNAL KNOWLEDGE. Sexual intercourse.

CASE FILE. A collection of documents pertaining to a particular investigation.

CASE IDENTIFIERS. Alphabetic or numeric assignment of characters used to identify a particular case.

CIR. CT. State circuit court.

CHAIN OF CUSTODY. A chronological history of the evidence. This is a list of all persons handling, holding, or having possession of a piece of evidence. The document will contain all pertinent information such as names, dates, victims, suspects, etc.

CHATTEL. Personal property.

CHEMICAL ENHANCEMENT. Use of chemicals to aid in the detection and documentation of evidence (e.g., semen, blood, fingerprints, narcotics) that may be difficult to see with the human eye.

CIVIL. Relating to a person's private rights and remedies.

CLEMENCY. Forgiveness for a criminal act, such as a pardon.

CONSPIRACY. Two or more persons working together to commit an illegal act.

CONTEMPT. A disregard of authority.

CONTRABAND. Anything that is unlawful to possess.

CONTRA PACEM. Latin for "against the peace."

CORPUS DELICTI. Latin for "body of the crime." The proof that a crime has been committed.

CRIMEN FALSI. Latin for "a crime of deceit."

CRIMINAL MISCHIEF. A crime committed against property.

CRIMINALIST. A person who examines and interprets physical evidence.

CRIMINOLOGIST. A person who studies criminal behavior.

CSU. Crime scene unit.

D. District court.

DEADLOCKED. Unable to agree.

DETAINER. An official request filed by a law enforcement agency asking prison officials to hold a prisoner due to pending criminal charges.

DOUBLE JEOPARDY. A second prosecution for the same offense.

DROP A DIME. To snitch on someone.

DROWNING. Water and mucus in the airway of a drowning victim create a foamy mixture as the victim struggles to breathe. The foam is discovered during an autopsy and confirms that a drowning has occurred.

DYING DECLARATION. A statement given by a person who believes he's about to die, concerning the cause or the circumstances surrounding a specific crime or chain of events, usually about his own impending death. A dying declaration is important evidence, but courts no longer accept this type of statement alone as sufficient evidence for a conviction. There must be other supporting evidence.

EDTA. Ethylenediaminetetraacetic acid, an anticoagulant found in purple-topped blood vials.

EN BANC. French for "on the bench." A matter heard by the entire appellate court.

ENTRAPMENT. The act of police officers inducing someone to commit a crime that he normally wouldn't have committed.

ETA. Estimated time of arrival.

EXCLUSIONARY RULE. A rule that prevents a prosecutor from using evidence in court that was seized during an illegal search by police.

EXIGENT CIRCUMSTANCES. Emergency conditions.

FELONY. A crime punishable by either death or confinement in a state correctional facility.

FENCE. A person who receives stolen goods.

FIRST-DEGREE MURDER. Murder by poison, lying in wait, imprisonment, starving, or by any willful, deliberate, and premeditated killing, or in the commission of, or attempt to commit, arson, rape, forcible sodomy, inanimate-object sexual penetra-

tion, robbery, burglary, or abduction. (This definition varies in different states.)

FISHING. The use of a long piece of string or elastic from the waistband of underwear by a prisoner to retrieve an object from an adjoining cell.

FUGITIVE. A person who escapes, flees, or evades arrest or imprisonment.

GSW. Gunshot wound.

HABEAS CORPUS. Latin for "you have the body." A writ that tests the legality of imprisonment or confinement.

HOMICIDE. The killing of any human being by another.

HOT PURSUIT. The action of pursuing or chasing a suspect in a crime. Hot pursuit allows officers to cross jurisdictional boundaries in order to apprehend a suspect; however, the suspect must remain in sight for the chase to be justified as a hot pursuit.

IMPRESSION EVIDENCE. Objects or items that have retained identifying characteristics of another object that's been pressed against them (footprints, tool marks, etc.).

IN CAMERA. Latin for "in a chamber." In private; in a judge's chambers.

INK. Tattoos.

JAILHOUSE LAWYER. An inmate not licensed to practice law who assists other inmates with legal matters, such as appeals.

KNOCK AND ANNOUNCE. A rule of law that requires police to knock on a suspect's door and verbally announce their presence and authority when executing a search warrant.

LATENT PRINT. A print that's not visible to the naked eye, made by contact with a surface by hands or feet transferring human material to that surface.

LEX TALIONIS. Latin for "law of retaliation." The concept of an eye for an eye.

LYING IN WAIT. Hiding for the purpose of committing a crime.

LYNCHING. Any violence by a mob upon the body of any person, resulting in the death of that person.

LZ. A landing zone for helicopters.

MAG. Magistrate.

MAYHEM. An injury involving permanent disfiguration, disablement, and/or dismemberment.

MENS REA. Latin for "guilty mind." Criminal intent.

MIRANDA WARNINGS. Requires that, prior to questioning, anyone who is in police custody must be advised that she has the right to remain silent; anything she says can and will be used against her in a court of law; she can have an attorney present during questioning; and if she cannot afford an attorney one would be appointed for her if she wishes. If police fail to advise the suspect of these warnings, any information obtained from her may not be used in court.

MISDEMEANOR. All crimes not deemed as felonies and punishable by fines and/or incarceration in facilities other than state or federal institutions (county jails, halfway houses, home confinement, etc.).

MODUS OPERANDI. Latin for "the manner of operation." A specific means or method of accomplishing an act.

MURDER. An unlawful homicide. Any murder other than capital murder is deemed to be murder.

MVA. Motor vehicle accident.

NCIC. National Crime Information Center.

NOLO CONTENDERE. Latin for "I do not wish to contend." A plea of not wishing to present a defense in a criminal matter.

PAROLE. Allows a prisoner to serve the remainder of a sentence outside prison walls. He will serve the sentence under the supervision of a parole officer. If the conditions of parole aren't met, the offender will be returned to prison to serve any remaining sentence. Parole isn't a part of a sentence.

PD. Police department.

PERSONAL PROTECTIVE EQUIPMENT. Items such as latex gloves, masks, and eye protection used as a protective barrier against biohazardous materials, disease, and to avoid human contamination of a crime scene.

PETECHIAE. Tiny purple or red spots on the eyes, neck, face, and/or lungs, indicating death by asphyxiation. (Bleeding doesn't have to be present.)

PETECHIAL HEMORRHAGE. Tiny purple or red spots on the eyes or skin caused by small areas of bleeding.

PO. Probation officer.

POV. Privately owned vehicle.

PRESUMPTIVE TEST. A test used to screen for the presence of a specific substance, such as a narcotic. The results of a presumptive test can't be used for evidential confirmation, or as a certification in a court of law. A presumptive test adds to investigators' reasonable suspicions and is considered to be probable cause for the issuance of a search warrant or a warrant of arrest. Certified personnel must complete the final, legal testing in a certified laboratory.

PRO BONO PUBLICO. Latin for "for the public good." Without a fee. An attorney working for free is said to be working pro bono.

PROBABLE CAUSE. Facts that would lead a reasonable person to believe that a person has committed a crime.

PROBATION. A sentence in lieu of imprisonment. A probation officer supervises an offender on probation.

PROJECTILE TRAJECTORY ANALYSIS. The method used for determining the path of travel of a high-speed object such as a bullet or arrow.

PURPLE-TOP VIAL. A vial used for blood samples, which contains EDTA.

RES JUDICATA. Latin for "judged matter." A matter decided on its merits by a court having competent jurisdiction and not subject to litigation again between the same parties.

SEG. Prison segregation unit.

SHAKEDOWN. A search of a prison cell.

SHIV. A homemade knife.

SHU. Special housing unit. A special lock-up facility within a prison that's usually reserved for housing violent offenders.

SLIMERS. Prison inmates who throw urine or fecal matter at people passing by the prisoners' cells. They sometimes pack the offensive substance into toothpaste tubes and squirt it at their intended targets.

SPONTANEOUS UTTERANCE. A statement made immediately after an unusually exciting or horrifying event by an observer or participant in that event.

STOP AND FRISK. A pat down search of a person's outer clothing only. It allows a police officer to search a person for weapons without a warrant.

TRACE EVIDENCE. Evidence in small quantities, such as hair, fibers, gunshot residue, and particles of glass.

TRANSIENT EVIDENCE. Evidence that can be easily lost or destroyed by conditions at a scene if not protected or preserved (evidence exposed to the elements).

VENUE. The place where a trial is held.

VOIR DIRE. French for "to speak the truth." An examination or questioning of potential jurors conducted by the court or attorneys to determine truthfulness and ability to serve for jury duty.

WARRANT. A written order directing someone to do something.

YARD. The outdoor recreation area of a prison.

POLICE
10 CODES

Police 10-codes were originally developed to allow law enforcement officers to converse in secret, preventing the public from understanding their confidential conversations.

Not all departments use the same 10-codes, which makes it difficult for officers from different departments to communicate during times of disaster and mutual aid, such as during the 9-11 and Hurricane Katrina catastrophes. As a result, some police departments in the United States have banned the use of 10-codes. Officers in those departments converse in a universal language—in other words, plain English. Therefore, instead of saying, "10-4," an officer would simply say, "Okay."

Some sample 10-codes include:

10-1: Receiving signals poorly.

10-2: Receiving signals well.

10-3: Stop transmitting.

10-4: Okay/affirmative.

10-5: Relay message.

10-6: Busy.

10-7: Out of service.

10-8: In service.

10-9: Repeat message.

10-10: Fight.

10-11: Talking too fast—repeat message.

10-12: Officials or visitors present—don't transmit sensitive information.

10-13: Advise of weather and road conditions.

10-14: Escort.

10-15: Prisoner in custody.

10-16: Pick up prisoners at____.

10-17: Pick up papers at____.

10-18: Complete present assignment quickly.

10-19: Return to station.

10-20: Location.

10-21: Call by telephone.

10-22: Take no further action.

10-23: Arrived on scene.

10-24: Departing scene.

10-25: Can you contact____?

10-26: Motorist assist at_____.

10-27: Driver's license information.

10-28: Vehicle registration information.

10-29: Check for stolen/wanted.

10-30: Doesn't conform to rules.

10-31: Breathalyzer operator needed.

10-32: Is Breathalyzer available?

10-33: Emergency/officer down.

10-34: Trouble at this station.

10-35: Confidential information.

10-36: Correct time?

10-37: Operator on duty?

10-38: Ambulance needed at_____.

10-39: Your message delivered.

10-40: Advise if officer available.

10-41: On duty.

10-42: Off duty.

10-43: Department vehicle in accident.

10-44: Check for record/wanted.

10-45: Taking a coffee break.

10-46: Mental patient.

10-47: Possibly armed and dangerous.

10-48: NCIC hit—subject is possibly wanted.

10-49: Noninjury accident.

10-50: Traffic accident.

10-51: Tow truck needed at _____.

10-52: Set up roadblock at_____ .

10-53: Discontinue roadblock.

10-54: Estimated time of arrival.

10-60: Traffic stop, location_____.

10-61: Clear of traffic stop.

10-62: Unable to copy; use phone.

10-63: Network directed to_____.

10-64: Network clear.

10-65: Awaiting next assignment.

10-67: All units comply.

10-69: Any traffic for this unit?

10-70: Stopping vehicle; may be danger.

10-71: Officer is clear from 10-70.

10-72: Information incomplete.

10-73: Information not in proper form.

10-77: Negative contact.

10-80: Private vehicle.

10-81: Officer in trouble at_____.

10-82: Trouble at station.

10-83: Bomb threat.

10-84: DOA or dead body.

10-85: Keep vehicle under surveillance.

10-86: Pick up partner.

10-87: Aircraft assignment.

10-88: Advise phone number for call.

10-90: Officer welfare check.

10-91: Talk closer to mike.

10-93: Check my frequency on channel.

10-94: Give me a test count/radio check.

10-97: Report to garage for repairs.

10-98: Last assignment completed.

10-99: Wanted person.

10-200: Police needed at_____.

DRUG QUANTITY
TABLE

Base Offense Level 38	
(1)	30 kg or more of heroin (or the equivalent amount of other Schedule I or II opiates)
	150 kg or more of cocaine (or the equivalent amount of other Schedule I or II stimulants)
	1.5 kg or more of cocaine base (crack cocaine)
	30 kg or more of PCP
	15 kg or more of methamphetamine, or 1.5 kg or more of methamphetamine (actual), or 1.5 kg or more of "ice"
	15 kg or more of amphetamine
	300 g or more of LSD (or the equivalent amount of other Schedule I or II hallucinogens)
	12 kg or more of fentanyl
	3 kg or more of a fentanyl analogue
	30,000 kg or more of marijuana

	6,000 kg or more of hashish
	600 kg or more of hashish oil
	30,000,000 units or more of Schedule I or II depressants
	1,875,000 units or more of flunitrazepam
Base Offense Level 36	
(2)	At least 10 kg but less than 30 kg of heroin (or the equivalent amount of other Schedule I or II opiates)
	At least 50 kg but less than 150 kg of cocaine (or the equivalent amount of other Schedule I or II stimulants)
	At least 500 g but less than 1.5 kg of cocaine base
	At least 10 kg but less than 30 kg of PCP
	At least 5 kg but less than 15 kg of methamphetamine, or at least 500 g but less than 1.5 kg of methamphetamine (actual), or at least 500 g but less than 1.5 kg of "ice"
	At least 5 kg but less than 15 kg of amphetamine
	At least 100 g but less than 300 g of LSD (or the equivalent amount of other Schedule I or II hallucinogens)
	At least 4 kg but less than 12 kg of fentanyl
	At least 1 kg but less than 3 kg of a fentanyl analogue
	At least 10,000 kg but less than 30,000 kg of marijuana
	At least 2,000 kg but less than 6,000 kg of hashish
	At least 200 kg but less than 600 kg of hashish oil
	At least 10,000,000 but less than 30,000,000 units of Schedule I or II depressants
	At least 625,000 but less than 1,875,000 units of flunitrazepam
Base Offense Level 34	
(3)	At least 3 kg but less than 10 kg of heroin (or the equivalent amount of other Schedule I or II opiates)
	At least 15 kg but less than 50 kg of cocaine (or the equivalent amount of other Schedule I or II stimulants);
	At least 150 g but less than 500 g of cocaine base (crack)
	At least 3 kg but less than 10 kg of PCP

	At least 1.5 kg but less than 5 kg of methamphetamine, or at least 150 g but less than 500 g of methamphetamine (actual), or at least 150 g but less than 500 g of "ice"
	At least 1.5 kg but less than 5 kg of amphetamine
	At least 30 g but less than 100 g of LSD (or the equivalent amount of other Schedule I or II hallucinogens)
	At least 1.2 kg but less than 4 kg of fentanyl
	At least 300 g but less than 1 kg of a fentanyl analogue
	At least 3,000 kg but less than 10,000 kg of marijuana;
	At least 600 kg but less than 2,000 kg of hashish
	At least 60 kg but less than 200 kg of hashish oil
	At least 3,000,000 but less than 10,000,000 units of Schedule I or II depressants
	At least 187,500 but less than 625,000 units of flunitrazepam
Base Offense Level 32	
(4)	At least 1 kg but less than 3 kg of heroin (or the equivalent amount of other Schedule I or II opiates)
	At least 5 kg but less than 15 kg of cocaine (or the equivalent amount of other Schedule I or II stimulants)
	At least 50 g but less than 150 g of cocaine base (crack)
	At least 1 kg but less than 3 kg of PCP
	At least 500 g but less than 1.5 kg of methamphetamine, or at least 50 g but less than 150 g of methamphetamine (actual), or at least 50 g but less than 150 g of "ice"
	At least 500 g but less than 1.5 kg of amphetamine
	At least 10 g but less than 30 g of LSD (or the equivalent amount of other Schedule I or II hallucinogens)
	At least 400 g but less than 1.2 kg of fentanyl
	At least 100 g but less than 300 g of a fentanyl analogue
	At least 1,000 kg but less than 3,000 kg of marijuana
	At least 200 kg but less than 600 kg of hashish
	At least 20 kg but less than 60 kg of hashish oil

DRUG QUANTITY TABLE

At least 1,000,000 but less than 3,000,000 units of Schedule I or II depressants	
At least 62,500 but less than 187,500 units of flunitrazepam	

Base Offense Level 30	
(5)	At least 700 g but less than 1 kg of heroin (or the equivalent amount of other Schedule I or II opiates)
	At least 3.5 kg but less than 5 kg of cocaine (or the equivalent amount of other Schedule I or II stimulants)
	At least 35 g but less than 50 g of cocaine base
	At least 700 g but less than 1 kg of PCP
	At least 350 g but less than 500 g of methamphetamine, or at least 35 g but less than 50 g of methamphetamine (actual), or at least 35 g but less than 50 g of "ice"
	At least 350 g but less than 500 g of amphetamine
	At least 7 g but less than 10 g of LSD (or the equivalent amount of other Schedule I or II hallucinogens)
	At least 280 g but less than 400 g of fentanyl
	At least 70 g but less than 100 g of a fentanyl analogue
	At least 700 kg but less than 1,000 kg of marijuana
	At least 140 kg but less than 200 kg of hashish
	At least 14 kg but less than 20 kg of hashish oil
	At least 700,000 but less than 1,000,000 units of Schedule I or II depressants
	At least 43,750 but less than 62,500 units of flunitrazepam

Base Offense Level 28	
(6)	At least 400 g but less than 700 g of heroin (or the equivalent amount of other Schedule I or II opiates)
	At least 2 kg but less than 3.5 kg of cocaine (or the equivalent amount of other Schedule I or II stimulants)
	At least 20 g but less than 35 g of cocaine base (crack)
	At least 400 g but less than 700 g of PCP
	At least 200 g but less than 350 g of methamphetamine, or at least 20 g but less than 35 g of methamphetamine (actual), or at least 20 g but less than 35 g of "ice"

	At least 200 g but less than 350 g of amphetamine
	At least 4 g but less than 7 g of LSD (or the equivalent amount of other Schedule I or II hallucinogens)
	At least 160 g but less than 280 g of fentanyl
	At least 40 g but less than 70 g of a fentanyl analogue
	At least 400 kg but less than 700 kg of marijuana
	At least 80 kg but less than 140 kg of hashish
	At least 8 kg but less than 14 kg of hashish oil
	At least 400,000 but less than 700,000 units of Schedule I or II depressants
	At least 25,000 but less than 43,750 units of flunitrazepam
Base Offense Level 26	
(7)	At least 100 g but less than 400 g of heroin (or the equivalent amount of other Schedule I or II opiates)
	At least 500 g but less than 2 kg of cocaine (or the equivalent amount of other Schedule I or II stimulants)
	At least 5 g but less than 20 g of cocaine base (crack)
	At least 100 g but less than 400 g of PCP, or at least 10 g but less than 40 g of PCP (actual)
	At least 50 g but less than 200 g of methamphetamine, or at least 5 g but less than 20 g of methamphetamine (actual), or at least 5 g but less than 20 g of "ice"
	At least 50 g but less than 200 g of amphetamine
	At least 1 g but less than 4 g of LSD (or the equivalent amount of other Schedule I or II hallucinogens)
	At least 40 g but less than 160 g of fentanyl
	At least 10 g but less than 40 g of a fentanyl analogue
	At least 100 kg but less than 400 kg of marijuana
	At least 20 kg but less than 80 kg of hashish
	At least 2 kg but less than 8 kg of hashish oil
	At least 100,000 but less than 400,000 units of Schedule I or II depressants
	At least 6,250 but less than 25,000 units of flunitrazepam

Base Offense Level 24	
(8)	At least 80 g but less than 100 g of heroin (or the equivalent amount of other Schedule I or II opiates)
	At least 400 g but less than 500 g of cocaine (or the equivalent amount of other Schedule I or II stimulants)
	At least 4 g but less than 5 g of cocaine base (crack)
	At least 80 g but less than 100 g of PCP
	At least 40 g but less than 50 g of methamphetamine, or at least 4 g but less than 5 g of methamphetamine (actual), or at least 4 g but less than 5 g of "ice"
	At least 40 g but less than 50 g of amphetamine
	At least 800 mg but less than 1 g of LSD (or the equivalent amount of other Schedule I or II hallucinogens)
	At least 32 g but less than 40 g of fentanyl
	At least 8 g but less than 10 g of a fentanyl analogue
	At least 80 kg but less than 100 kg of marijuana
	At least 16 kg but less than 20 kg of hashish
	At least 1.6 kg but less than 2 kg of hashish oil
	At least 80,000 but less than 100,000 units of Schedule I or II depressants
	At least 5,000 but less than 6,250 units of flunitrazepam
Base Offense Level 22	
(9)	At least 60 g but less than 80 g of heroin (or the equivalent amount of other Schedule I or II opiates)
	At least 300 g but less than 400 g of cocaine (or the equivalent amount of other Schedule I or II Stimulants);
	At least 3 g but less than 4 g of cocaine base (crack)
	At least 60 g but less than 80 g of PCP
	At least 30 g but less than 40 g of methamphetamine, or at least 3 g but less than 4 g of methamphetamine (actual), or at least 3 g but less than 4 g of "ice"
	At least 30 g but less than 40 g of amphetamine
	At least 600 mg but less than 800 mg of LSD (or the equivalent amount of other Schedule I or II hallucinogens)

	At least 24 g but less than 32 g of fentanyl
	At least 6 g but less than 8 g of a fentanyl analogue
	At least 60 kg but less than 80 kg of marijuana
	At least 12 kg but less than 16 kg of hashish
	At least 1.2 kg but less than 1.6 kg of hashish oil
	At least 60,000 but less than 80,000 units of Schedule I or II depressants
	At least 3,750 but less than 5,000 units of flunitrazepam
Base Offense Level 20	
(10)	At least 40 g but less than 60 g of heroin (or the equivalent amount of other Schedule I or II opiates)
	At least 200 g but less than 300 g of cocaine (or the equivalent amount of other Schedule I or II stimulants)
	At least 2 g but less than 3 g of cocaine base (crack)
	At least 40 g but less than 60 g of PCP
	At least 20 g but less than 30 g of methamphetamine, or at least 2 g but less than 3 g of methamphetamine (actual), or at least 2 g but less than 3 g of "ice"
	At least 20 g but less than 30 g of amphetamine
	At least 400 mg but less than 600 mg of LSD (or the equivalent amount of other Schedule I or II hallucinogens)
	At least 16 g but less than 24 g of fentanyl
	At least 4 g but less than 6 g of a fentanyl analogue
	At least 40 kg but less than 60 kg of marijuana
	At least 8 kg but less than 12 kg of hashish
	At least 800 g but less than 1.2 kg of hashish oil
	At least 40,000 but less than 60,000 units of Schedule I or II depressants or Schedule III substances
	At least 2,500 but less than 3,750 units of flunitrazepam
Base Offense Level 18	
(11)	At least 20 g but less than 40 g of heroin (or the equivalent amount of other Schedule I or II opiates)

	At least 100 g but less than 200 g of cocaine (or the equivalent amount of other Schedule I or II stimulants)
	At least 1 g but less than 2 g of cocaine base (crack)
	At least 20 g but less than 40 g of PCP, or at least 2 g but less than 4 g of PCP (actual)
	At least 10 g but less than 20 g of methamphetamine, or at least 1 g but less than 2 g of methamphetamine (actual), or at least 1 g but less than 2 g of "ice"
	At least 10 g but less than 20 g of amphetamine
	At least 200 mg but less than 400 mg of LSD (or the equivalent amount of other Schedule I or II hallucinogens)
	At least 8 g but less than 16 g of fentanyl
	At least 2 g but less than 4 g of a fentanyl analogue
	At least 20 kg but less than 40 kg of marijuana
	At least 5 kg but less than 8 kg of hashish
	At least 500 g but less than 800 g of hashish oil
	At least 20,000 but less than 40,000 units of Schedule I or II depressants or Schedule III substances
	At least 1,250 but less than 2,500 units of flunitrazepam
Base Offense Level 16	
(12)	At least 10 g but less than 20 g of heroin (or the equivalent amount of other Schedule I or II opiates)
	At least 50 g but less than 100 g of cocaine (or the equivalent amount of other Schedule I or II stimulants)
	At least 500 mg but less than 1 g of cocaine base (crack)
	At least 10 g but less than 20 g of PCP,
	At least 5 g but less than 10 g of methamphetamine, or at least 500 mg but less than 1 g of methamphetamine
	At least 5 g but less than 10 g of amphetamine
	At least 100 mg but less than 200 mg of LSD (or the equivalent amount of other Schedule I or II hallucinogens)
	At least 4 g but less than 8 g of fentanyl

	At least 1 g but less than 2 g of a fentanyl analogue
	At least 10 kg but less than 20 kg of marijuana
	At least 2 kg but less than 5 kg of hashish
	At least 200 g but less than 500 g of hashish oil
	At least 10,000 but less than 20,000 units of Schedule I or II depressants or Schedule III substances
	At least 625 but less than 1,250 units of flunitrazepam
Base Offense Level 14	
(13)	At least 5 g but less than 10 g of heroin (or the equivalent amount of other Schedule I or II opiates)
	At least 25 g but less than 50 g of cocaine (or the equivalent amount of other Schedule I or II stimulants)
	At least 250 mg but less than 500 mg of cocaine base (crack)
	At least 5 g but less than 10 g of PCP
	At least 2.5 g but less than 5 g of methamphetamine, or at least 250 mg but less than 500 mg of methamphetamine
	At least 2.5 g but less than 5 g of amphetamine
	At least 50 mg but less than 100 mg of LSD (or the equivalent amount of other Schedule I or II hallucinogens)
	At least 2 g but less than 4 g of fentanyl
	At least 500 mg but less than 1 g of a fentanyl analogue
	At least 5 kg but less than 10 kg of marijuana
	At least 1 kg but less than 2 kg of hashish
	At least 100 g but less than 200 g of hashish oil
	At least 5,000 but less than 10,000 units of Schedule I or II depressants or Schedule III substances
	At least 312 but less than 625 units of flunitrazepam
Base Offense Level 12	
(14)	Less than 5 g of heroin (or the equivalent amount of other Schedule I or II opiates)
	Less than 25 g of cocaine (or the equivalent amount of other Schedule I or II stimulants)

	Less than 250 mg of cocaine base (crack)
	Less than 5 g of PCP
	Less than 2.5 g of methamphetamine, or less than 250 mg of methamphetamine
	Less than 2.5 g of amphetamine, or less than 250 mg of amphetamine
	Less than 50 mg of LSD (or the equivalent amount of other Schedule I or II hallucinogens)
	Less than 2 g of fentanyl
	Less than 500 mg of a fentanyl analogue
	At least 2.5 kg but less than 5 kg of marijuana
	At least 500 g but less than 1 kg of hashish
	At least 50 g but less than 100 g of hashish oil
	At least 2,500 but less than 5,000 units of Schedule I or II depressants or Schedule III substances
	At least 156 but less than 312 units of flunitrazepam
	40,000 or more units of Schedule IV substances (except flunitrazepam)
	**Base Offense Level 10**
(15)	At least 1 kg but less than 2.5 kg of marijuana
	At least 200 g but less than 500 g of hashish
	At least 20 g but less than 50 g of hashish oil
	At least 1,000 but less than 2,500 units of Schedule I or II depressants or Schedule III substances
	At least 62 but less than 156 units of flunitrazepam
	At least 16,000 but less than 40,000 units of Schedule IV substances (except flunitrazepam)
	**Base Offense Level 8**
(16)	At least 250 g but less than 1 kg of marijuana
	At least 50 g but less than 200 g of hashish
	At least 5 g but less than 20 g of hashish oil
	At least 250 but less than 1,000 units of Schedule I or II depressants or Schedule III substances

	Less than 62 units of flunitrazepam
	At least 4,000 but less than 16,000 units of Schedule IV substances (except flunitrazepam)
	40,000 or more units of Schedule V substances
Base Offense Level 7	
(17)	Less than 250 g of marijuana
	Less than 50 g of hashish
	Less than 5 g of hashish oil
	Less than 250 units of Schedule I or II depressants or Schedule III substances
	Less than 4,000 units of Schedule IV substances (except flunitrazepam)
	Less than 40,000 units of Schedule V substances

FEDERAL SENTENCING TABLE

Criminal History Category (Criminal History Points)

Offense Level	I (0 or 1)	II (2 or 3)	III (4, 5, 6)	IV (7, 8, 9)	V (10, 11, 12)	VI (> 13)
1	0 – 6	0 – 6	0 – 6	0 – 6	0 – 6	0 – 6
2	0 – 6	0 – 6	0 – 6	0 – 6	0 – 6	1 – 7
3	0 – 6	0 – 6	0 – 6	0 – 6	2 – 8	3 – 9
4	0 – 6	0 – 6	0 – 6	2 – 8	4 – 10	6 – 12
5	0 – 6	0 – 6	1 – 7	4 – 10	6 – 12	9 – 15
6	0 – 6	1 – 7	2 – 8	6 – 12	9 – 15	12 – 18
7	0 – 6	2 – 8	4 – 10	8 – 14	12 – 18	15 – 21
8	0 – 6	4 – 10	6 – 12	10 – 16	15 – 21	18 – 24
9	4 – 10	6 – 12	8 – 14	12 – 18	18 – 24	21 – 27
10	6 – 12	8 – 14	10 – 16	15 – 21	21 – 27	24 – 30
11	8 – 14	10 – 16	12 – 18	18 – 24	24 – 30	27 – 33
12	10 – 16	12 – 18	15 – 21	21 – 27	27 – 33	30 – 37
13	12 – 18	15 – 21	18 – 24	24 – 30	30 – 37	33 – 41

14	15 – 21	18 – 24	21 – 27	27 – 33	33 – 41	37 – 46
15	18 – 24	21 – 27	24 – 30	30 – 37	37 – 46	41 – 51
16	21 – 27	24 – 30	27 – 33	33 – 41	41 – 51	46 – 57
17	24 – 30	27 – 33	30 – 37	37 – 46	46 – 57	51 – 63
18	27 – 33	30 – 37	33 – 41	41 – 51	51 – 63	57 – 71
19	30 – 37	33 – 41	37 – 46	46 – 57	57 – 71	63 – 78
20	33 – 41	37 – 46	41 – 51	51 – 63	63 – 78	70 – 87
21	37 – 46	41 – 51	46 – 57	57 – 71	70 – 87	77 – 96
22	41 – 51	46 – 57	51 – 63	63 – 78	77 – 96	84 – 105
23	46 – 57	51 – 63	57 – 71	70 – 87	84 – 105	92 – 115
24	51 – 63	57 – 71	63 – 78	77 – 96	92 – 115	100 – 125
25	57 – 71	63 – 78	70 – 87	84 – 105	100 – 125	110 – 137
26	63 – 78	70 – 87	78 – 97	92 – 115	110 – 137	120 – 150
27	70 – 87	78 – 97	87 – 108	100 – 125	120 – 150	130 – 162
28	78 – 97	87 – 108	97 – 121	110 – 137	130 – 162	140 – 175
29	87 – 108	97 – 121	108 – 135	121 – 151	140 – 175	151 – 188
30	97 – 121	108 – 135	121 – 151	135 – 168	151 – 188	168 – 210
31	108 – 135	121 – 151	135 – 168	151 – 188	168 – 210	188 – 235
32	121 – 151	135 – 168	151 – 188	168 – 210	188 – 235	210 – 262
33	135 – 168	151 – 188	168 – 210	188 – 235	210 – 262	235 – 293
34	151 – 188	168 – 210	188 – 235	210 – 262	235 – 293	262 – 327
35	168 – 210	188 – 235	210 – 262	235 – 293	262 – 327	292 – 365
36	188 – 235	210 – 262	235 – 293	262 – 327	292 – 365	324 – 405
37	210 – 262	235 – 293	262 – 327	292 – 365	324 – 405	360 – life
38	235 – 293	262 – 327	292 – 365	324 – 405	360 – life	360 – life
39	262 – 327	292 – 365	324 – 405	360 – life	360 – life	360 – life
40	292 – 365	324 – 405	360 – life	360 – life	360 – life	360 – life
41	324 – 405	360 – life	360 – life	360 – life	360 – life	360 – life
42	360 – life	360 – life	360 – life	360 – life	360 – life	360 – life
43	life	life	life	life	life	life

*Sentences are in months, e.g., 0–6 months.

INDEX

POLICE PROCEDURE & INVESTIGATION

ABOUT THE AUTHOR

Photograph © Lori Lake

Lee Lofland is a former police detective with nearly two decades of law-enforcement and crime-solving experience. He was in charge of major felony cases, including homicide, narcotics, rape, kidnapping, ritualistic and occult crimes, fraud, and robbery. Lee is a nationally acclaimed expert on police procedure and crime-scene investigation and is a popular conference and workshop speaker. He writes freelance articles for magazines and newspapers across the country and is a consultant for many bestselling authors and television and film writers.

Lee and his wife, Dr. Denene Lofland, live in the Boston area, where he proudly serves on the board of directors for the New England Chapter of Mystery Writers of America.